Imperial Rome AD *284 to 363*

The Edinburgh History of Ancient Rome
General Editor: J. S. Richardson

Early Roman Italy to 290 BC: The Origins of Rome and the Rise of the Republic
Guy Bradley

Rome and the Mediterranean 290 to 146 BC: The Imperial Republic
Nathan Rosenstein

The End of the Roman Republic 146 to 44 BC: Conquest and Crisis
Catherine Steel

Augustan Rome 44 BC to AD 14: The Restoration of the Republic and the Establishment of the Empire
J. S. Richardson

Imperial Rome AD 14 to 192: The First Two Centuries
Jonathan Edmondson

Imperial Rome AD 193 to 284: The Critical Century
Clifford Ando

Imperial Rome AD 284 to 363: The New Empire
Jill Harries

From Rome to Byzantium AD 363 to 565: The Transformation of Ancient Rome
A. D. Lee

Imperial Rome AD 284 to 363
The New Empire

Jill Harries

EDINBURGH
University Press

© Jill Harries, 2012

Edinburgh University Press Ltd
22 George Square, Edinburgh EH8 9LF

www.euppublishing.com

Reprinted 2013

Typeset in Sabon
by Norman Tilley Graphics Ltd, Northampton,
and printed and bound in the United States of America

A CIP record for this book is available from the
British Library

ISBN 978 0 7486 2052 4 (hardback)
ISBN 978 0 7486 2053 1 (paperback)
ISBN 978 0 7486 2921 3 (webready PDF)
ISBN 978 0 7486 5395 9 (epub)
ISBN 978 0 7486 5394 2 (Amazon ebook)

Published with the support of the Edinburgh University
Scholarly Publishing Initiatives Fund.

Contents

Illustrations

All illustrations © J. C. N. Coulston

Series editor's preface

Rome, the city and its empire, stands at the centre of the history of Europe, of the Mediterranean, and of lands which we now call the Middle East. Its influence through the ages which followed its transformation into the Byzantine Empire down to modern times can be seen across the world. This series is designed to present for students and all who are interested in the history of western civilisation the changing shape of the entity that was Rome, through its earliest years, the development and extension of the Republic, the shift into the Augustan Empire, the development of the imperial state which grew from that, and the differing patterns of that state which emerged in east and west in the fourth to sixth centuries. It covers not only the political and military history of that shifting and complex society but also the contributions of the economic and social history of the Roman world to that change and growth and the intellectual contexts of these developments. The team of contributors, all scholars at the forefront of research in archaeology and history in the English-speaking world, present in the eight volumes of the series an accessible and challenging account of Rome across a millennium and a half of its expansion and transformation. Each book stands on its own as a picture of the period it covers and together the series aims to answer the fundamental question: what was Rome, and how did a small city in central Italy become one of the most powerful and significant entities in the history of the world?

John Richardson, General Editor

Author's preface

The accession of Diocletian signalled the beginning of what Gibbon would call the 'new' Roman Empire. Diocletian and his principal successor, Constantine, would rule the Roman world for over half a century and Constantine's sons would build on their legacy. The imperial court and provincial administrations were reorganised, the armies and their commands restructured, and the power of the central government to assess and exploit the economic and manpower resources of the empire enhanced. The period was also one of momentous religious change. With Constantine's adoption of Christianity as the favoured recipient of imperial patronage, the religious landscape would, over time, be radically reshaped.

Romans at the time, however, experienced the 'new empire' in terms of the old. The relative paucity of sources – literary, monumental and epigraphic – for the third century can obscure for us the continuity in problems and policies inherited by Diocletian from his predecessors. As observed in Chapter 1, Diocletian came to power nearly forty years into the eleventh century from Rome's foundation, and like previous emperors was forced to confront the challenges of unstable frontiers, volatile armies and the control and governance of a diverse and far-flung empire. He also drew on earlier emperors' experience for his solutions, as did Constantine, his sons and Julian. Like his predecessors, Diocletian and those who came after had to justify their positions by constructing the appearance of general consent for their rule – hence the increased emphasis on acclamation, public ceremonial demonstrations of support, and a legal discourse which combined self-justification with moral exhortation.

In 284, being accepted as ruler of the Roman world had never been more difficult. From the Severans onwards, emperors proclaimed by armies had to explain to the rest of the population why they, and not some rival general, had a right to rule. Recognition by the other member(s) of the imperial college was one way forward; the members of a united imperial college presided over an 'undivided patrimony' and rulers not recognised by the other members of the college were labelled usurpers, *tyranni*. But membership of the imperial college was, in isolation, an unstable criterion for legitimacy. Recognition by colleagues could be withdrawn and, although the 'glory' and 'victories' of the armies were routinely celebrated on the coinage, emperors knew better than to present themselves solely as a military junta (even if, in fact, that was what they were). Moreover, this limited definition of legitimacy fails to respect local perspectives or to reflect the requirement incumbent on all emperors to conciliate multiple constituencies. In the first two centuries, the endorsement of the senate conferred formal legitimacy and authority; in the third, that convention lapsed but no other agreed process of recognition took its place.

Key to their standing and survival, therefore, would be the emperors' relationship with the divine protectors of the empire. The favour of the emperors' chosen god or gods was demonstrated by emperors' successes in wars and just and harmonious rule in time of peace. Long before Constantine, some emperors had claimed the protection of a single, personal deity. The contrast vividly experienced by Christians between the hostility of Diocletian's government and the active support and patronage afforded them by Constantine is a less reliable indicator of religious change than the underlying shift in the religious culture(s) of the empire towards popular acceptance of a single or most favoured deity, already apparent in the late third century, when Aurelian claimed the endorsement of Sol Invictus, the Unconquered Sun. It was thus inevitable that imperial power struggles would shape religious polemic. The Christian writers Lactantius and Eusebius celebrated Constantine as the chosen of the one true God in terms of the vindication of their faith. In so doing they also contributed to Constantine's political strategy of self-promotion as an emperor whose legitimacy derived from the sponsorship of his favoured deity; inconvenient facts were omitted and those who opposed the 'God-beloved' were vilified as unlawful rulers, *tyranni*.

The word *tyrannus* did not denote an objective status; it was a label, a rhetorical device exploited by victorious emperors and their spokesmen to discredit defeated opponents. Naturally, local rulers who failed to win wider recognition and who were in the end overthrown were dismissed as *tyranni* by the victors. But local rulers, as we shall see, devoted much effort to legitimising their rule in the eyes of those they governed and would not have lasted long but for the support of the local military establishment, concerned for their own security and resentful of the perceived neglect of absent emperors. Repeatedly in the third and fourth centuries, emperors were proclaimed unilaterally by the Gallic army, with little regard for the preferences of their colleagues on the Danube. Those responsible for the security of the Roman empire are more accurately viewed as separate armies, with distinctive local identities and priorities, than a unified 'army'.

The *tyrannus* could also be defined as an oppressor who ruled without due regard for the laws. The accusation of 'tyranny' was therefore levelled against emperors whose position was formally unchallenged, either posthumously or even in their lifetimes, on the grounds that the manner of their rule contravened law. Historians of the 'Great Persecution' vividly portrayed the violence and sadism of the persecuting judges and their imperial masters; such actions, because unlawful, undermined the legitimacy of the persecuting emperors. Conversely, Julian the Apostate's reversing of some laws of Constantine can be read as an attempt to cast a slur on that emperor's legitimacy, without openly challenging his right to rule; Constantine after all, in Julian's personal opinion, was a wastrel who had relied on the wrong god.

Institutional reform, the relationship of the Christian church and the Roman state and the effects of warfare all figure prominently in the history of the 'long third century'. So too do the colossal figures of Diocletian and Constantine, whose changes to the imperial environment were shaped by the institutionalised responsiveness of legislative practice and whose reforming vision was rendered more efficacious by the relative longevity of both. But this book also focuses on aspects of the period which have received less attention. The sons of Constantine, Constantius II (337–61) and Constans (337–50), are overshadowed by their famous father; they should not be. Constantius II has at least the benefit (if such it was) of extensive coverage in the works of the Antiochene soldier-historian Ammianus Marcellinus and the writings of contemporary Christians and later church historians. Constans, however, is largely ignored, even though he ruled almost all of Roman Europe for thirteen years and (as Ammianus, in c. 390, may have anticipated) was the last emperor of the Roman world to visit Britain in person.

The situation of imperial women (aside from the iconic Helena) has also received little coverage. In the sources they are treated as adjuncts to their sons, brothers or husbands, and generally denied a voice in their own right. Yet they were transmitters of the imperial bloodline; many met violent deaths; and Helena, Constantine's mother-in-law Eutropia and his daughter Constantina stand at the beginning of the evolution of a distinctive Rome-based Christianity, which would find fuller expression through the activities of the senatorial followers of Jerome in the 380s and Pelagius a decade later. Rome the city, too, was far from irrelevant, despite its physical distance from the frontiers. Its leading senators corresponded with emperors and married into the imperial family, and its bishops reshaped its identity as one of the leading cities of emergent Christendom.

This book would not have existed but for John Richardson's initiative in setting up the Edinburgh History of Ancient Rome series. The generosity of the University of St Andrews in modifying my contract to give me more space to read, think and write was made possible by Greg Woolf; my grateful thanks to him for that. Tim Barnes, now based 'down the road' at Edinburgh, has been generous with his insights and has allowed me pre-publication access to his latest book on Constantine. I am also grateful to all colleagues, especially in St Andrews, Oxford, Cambridge and Cardiff, who put up with my various musings; Claudia Rapp was a special source of inspiration. The reading programme was latterly much assisted and expedited by my sojourn in Beechwood House, Iffley, Oxford, courtesy of All Souls College. I am grateful too to Jon Coulston for his assistance with the illustrations, to the Barbour Collection at Birmingham for freely granted permission to use the 'Falling Horse-man' coin on the front cover, and to Carol MacDonald and all the staff at Edinburgh University Press for their work in bringing this project to fruition.

Jill Harries

Abbreviations

AJArch.	*American Journal of Archaeology*
AJPhil.	*American Journal of Philology*
Amm. Marc.	Ammianus Marcellinus
Anon. Vales.	Anonymous Valesianus
Anth. Pal.	*Anthologia Palatina*
Apol. contra Ar.	*Apologia contra Arianos*
Aur. Vict. *Caes.*	Aurelius Victor, *De Caesaribus* (*On the Roman emperors*)
BICS	*Bulletin of the Institute of Classical Studies*
CAH	*Cambridge Ancient History*
Chron.	*Chronographia*
Cic.	*Cicero*
Leg.	*De legibus*
Rep.	*De republica*
Tusc.	*Tusculanae disputationes*
CIL	*Corpus Inscriptionum Latinarum*
Cod. Just.	*Codex Justinianus* (529, 2nd edn 534)
Cod. Theod.	*Codex Theodosianus* (438)
Conc.	*Concilium*
Conc. Arel.	*Concilium Arelatense*
Const. Sirm.	*Sirmondian Constitution*
C Phil.	*Classical Philology*
CQ	*Classical Quarterly*
CSEL	*Corpus Scriptorum Ecclesiasticuorum Latinorum*
Dessau, *ILS*	*Inscriptiones Latinae Selectae*, H. Dessau (ed.)
Dig.	Justinian, *Digesta* (533)
DOP	*Dumbarton Oaks Papers*
Epit. de Caes.	*Epitome de Caesaribus*
Eunap. *VS*	Eunapius, *Vitae sophistarum* (*Lives of the Sophists*)

Euseb.	Eusebius of Caesarea,
Mart. Pal.	*De martyribus Palaestinae*
Vit. Const.	*Vita Constantini*
Eutr. *Brev.*	Eutropius, *Breviarium*
FHG	*Fragmenta Historicorum Graecorum*, C. Müller (ed.)
GRBS	*Greek, Roman and Byzantine Studies*
Harv. Theol. Rev.	*Harvard Theological Review*
Hist. Ar.	*Historia Arrianorum*
Hist. eccl.	*Historia ecclesiastica*
Il.	*Iliad*
ILCV	*Inscriptiones Latinae Christianae Veteres*
JECS	*Journal of Early Christian Studies*
JHS	*Journal of Hellenic Studies*
Jones, *LRE*	*The Later Roman Empire: A Social, Economic and Administrative Survey*, A. H. M. Jones
JRA	*Journal of Roman Archaeology*
JRS	*Journal of Roman Studies*
JTS	*Journal of Theological Studies*
Lactant.	Lactantius
De mort. pers.	*De mortibus persecutorum*
Div. inst.	*Divinae institutiones*
Leg. Saec.	*Leges Saeculares*
Lib.	Libanius
Ant.	*Antiochikos*
Or.	*Oratio*
Lib. Pont.	*Liber Pontificalis*
MAMA	*Monumenta Asiae Minoris Antiqua*
Mart. Abit.	*Martyrs of Abitina*
MEFRA	*Mélanges d'archéologie et d'histoire de l'Ecole française de Rome*
MGH	*Monumenta Germaniae Historica*
Not. Dig.[occ.] [or.]	*Notitia dignitatum in partibus occidentis/orientis*
Num. Chron.	*Numismatic Chronicle*
Optat.	Optatus
Or.	*Oratio*
Orat. ad Sanct.	*Oratio ad Sanctos*
Oros.	Orosius
P. Abinn.	*Abinnaeus Papyrus*

Palladius, *Hist. Laus.*	Palladius, *Historia Lausiaca*
Pan. Lat.	*XII Panegyrici Latini*
PBSR	*Papers of the British School at Rome*
P. Cair. Isid.	*The Archive of Aurelius Isidorus in the Egyptian Museum, Cairo and the University of Michigan*, Arthur E. R. Boak and H. C. Youtie (eds)
Pesc. Nig.	*Life of Pescennius Niger*
PLRE I	*Prosopography of the Later Roman Empire*, vol. 1, A. H. M. Jones et al. (eds)
P. Lond.	*London Papyrus*
P.Oxy.	*Oxyrhynchus Papyri*
P. Beatty Pan.	*Papyri from Panopolis in the Chester Beatty Library Dublin*
Quint. *Inst.*	Quintilian, *Institutio oratoria*
RE	*Real-Encylopädie der klassischen Altertum-swissenschaft*, eds A. Pauly. G. Wissowa and W. Kroll
RHDFE	*Revue Historique de Droit Français et Etranger*
RHE	*Revue d'Histoire Ecclesiastique*
RIC	*Roman Imperial Coinage*, H. Mattingly et al., eds
Riccobono, *FIRA*	*Fontes Iuris Romani Anteiustiniani*, ed. S. Riccobono
SHA	Scriptores Historiae Augustae
Sozom.	Sozomen
TTH	Translated Texts for Historians
Zos.	Zosimus
ZPE	*Zeitschrift für Papyrologie und Epigraphik*
ZSS RA	*Zeitschrift der Savigny-Stiftung für Rechtsgeschichte, Römische Abteilung*

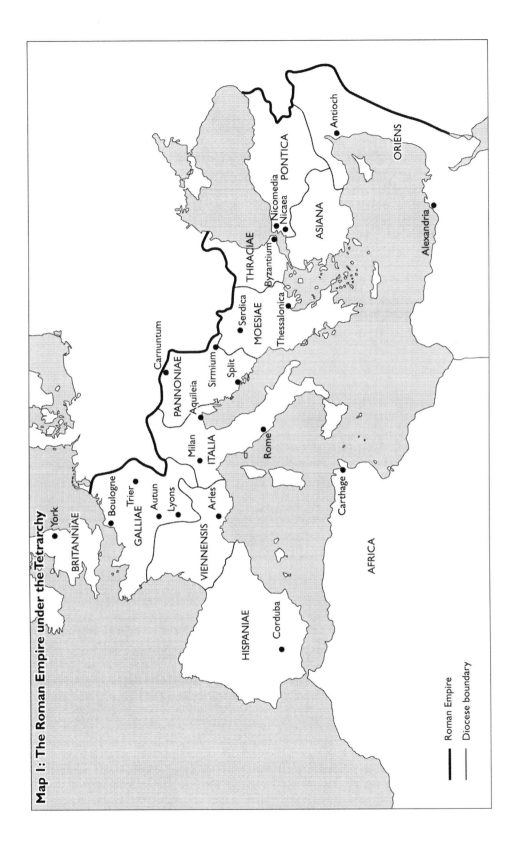

Map I: The Roman Empire under the Tetrarchy

BRITANNIAE
York
Boulogne
Trier
GALLIAE
Autun
Lyons
Arles
VIENNENSIS
HISPANIAE
Corduba
Milan
ITALIA
Rome
AFRICA
Carthage
Aquileia
Carnuntum
PANNONIAE
Sirmium
Split
Serdica
MOESIAE
Thessalonica
THRACIAE
Byzantium
Nicomedia
Nicaea
PONTICA
ASIANA
Antioch
ORIENS
Alexandria

Roman Empire
Diocese boundary

CHAPTER 1

The long third century

In AD 247–8, Rome celebrated the millennium since the foundation of the city, traditionally dated to 753 BC. The emperor, Philip 'the Arabian', celebrated the arrival of the 'new age' (*saeculum novum*) with three days and nights of Secular Games and a special issue of coinage to commemorate the event and look forward to the future. His purpose in reviving a festival of cyclical religious renewal, which dated back to the dawn of Roman history, was to reassure Romans, by drawing hopeful lessons from a thousand years of empire. The emperor therefore honoured the occasion with his personal presence as consul for the year 248, and constructed a new reservoir to help to safeguard the city's water supply. Although pressures on frontier security meant that emperors spent little time at Rome, they continued to respect the symbolic importance of the Eternal City.[1]

By contrast, in 348, the eleven hundredth anniversary of Rome's foundation passed almost unnoticed. As the Rome-based historian Sextus Aurelius Victor observed:

> In my time too, the eleven hundredth anniversary passed by in the consulship of a Philip (Fl. Philippus), but it was celebrated with none of the customary festivities, so drastically has concern for the city of Rome diminished day by day.[2]

1. For narrative see Alan Bowman, Peter Garnsey and Averil Cameron (eds), *Cambridge Ancient History. Vol. 12: The Crisis of Empire, AD 235–337*, 2nd edn, Cambridge: Cambridge University Press, 2005, 36–8, 687: Zos. *New History* 1.18–22; M. H. Dodgeon and S. N. C. Lieu, *The Roman Eastern Frontier and the Persian Wars AD 226–363: A Documentary Study*, London: Routledge 1991, 46–8; David S. Potter, *Prophecy and History in the Crisis of the Roman Empire*, Oxford: Oxford University Press, 1998, 37–41; and Potter, *The Roman Empire at Bay, AD 180–395*, London: Routledge, 2004, 236–41. More imaginatively, see also SHA *Lives of the Three Gordians* 33.1–2. For Philip as, allegedly, a Christian, see Euseb. *Hist eccl.* 6.34 and 39, where he wrongly ascribes Decius' persecution of Christians to his hatred of Philip, whom he overthrew in June 249.
2. Aur. Vict. *Caes.* 28, H. W. Bird (ed. and trans.), *Aurelius Victor: De Caesaribus*, TTH 17, Liverpool: Liverpool University Press, 1994. But base-metal coin issues appear in 347–8 with the motto FEL.TEMP.REPARATIO, which may, tentatively, be associated

The Romans at Rome in 348 had reason to feel neglected. The emperor of the west, Flavius Julius Constans (Augustus, 337–50), youngest son of Rome's first Christian emperor, Constantine, never visited the ancient capital in person.[3] Indeed, after Constantine in 326, there were, in the fourth century, to be only two further imperial visits, those of Constans' elder brother Constantius II in 357 and of Theodosius I in 389. Nor, in 348, were emperors, who were second-generation Christians, likely to go out of their way to favour celebrations originally designed to honour of the traditional tutelary gods of the Roman state.[4]

But the causes of the apparent sidelining of the city of Rome were also longer term and more deeply rooted than Victor acknowledged. The long frontiers of the Roman Empire had, since the late second century AD, required massive military resources and the frequent personal presence of emperors to maintain security. From the 230s onwards, the Rhine and Danube frontiers and the disputed lands between the Roman and Persian empires were under pressures, which would persist into the fourth century and beyond. Emperors, therefore, had little use for a capital geographically remote from the frontiers, where the imperial presence was necessary to inspire and reward the troops – and pre-empt challenges from others. Rome, therefore, was replaced by a set of military capitals,[5] notably Trier on the Moselle, for the Rhine, Sirmium on the Save, for the Danube, Milan, also more convenient for the Rhine and Danube than Rome, and Antioch in Syria, the forward base for campaigns against Persia. Roman emperors also resided in and patronised cities they liked, or with which they had previous associations. Nicomedia was the chief residence for Diocletian, who, on retirement in 305, withdrew to another favoured location, his palace at Split, near Salonae in his native Dalmatia (modern Croatia). Constantine would go further and transform the insignificant garrison town of Byzantium on the Bosphorus, formerly the base of his rival Licinius, into the 'city of

with the anniversary, on which see *RIC* 8, 60, 72 (Alexandria), 82 (Lyon), 103 (Aquileia), 129 (Antioch), 196 (Rome), 221, 235, 239 (Trier), 254 (Siscia).
3. Although he did despatch the Athenian philosopher Prohaeresius from Gaul to Rome, as a demonstration of his concern for culture, and actively intervened in the governance of Rome in the late 340s. See below, p. 192.
4. Zos. *New History*, 2.7.2, following the pagan historian Eunapius, blamed the discontinuance of the Secular Games under Diocletian, an omission not corrected by his successors, for the decline of the Roman Empire.
5. For brief survey, see Fergus Millar, *The Emperor in the Roman World*, London: Duckworth, 1977, 40–53.

Constantine', Constantinople, the future capital of the Eastern, Byzantine Empire. These, not Rome, were the centres for political, administrative and military advancement.

For the senate and senators at Rome the distancing of emperors provided both challenge and opportunity. Military commands and provincial governorships were now largely in the hands of administrators drawn from the wealthy non-senatorial classes and from career soldiers, who had risen through the ranks and who profited from the rise of their fellow generals. Educated non-senators staffed the secretariats and financial posts; the twin peaks of the equestrian career remained the prefectures of the praetorian guard and of Egypt. The power and influence of the Roman senate collectively was limited to Rome and Italy, although senators continued to staff the governorships of a much-reduced Asia and Africa, provinces which were both peaceful and lucrative.

From the first century AD, the senate had provided continuity with the past Roman *res publica* and its institutions, which Augustus had exploited and reworked to create a justification for sole rule by a *princeps*, a 'first citizen'. Late Roman emperors still presented themselves as guardians of the interests of the *res publica*; in addressing the senate at Constantinople, for example, in 355, Constantius II used the form of greeting employed by Roman republican generals to the senate at Rome.[6] But from the mid-third century the senate's nominal right to choose the emperor (or in practice to endorse the choice made by others) had lapsed. Writing in 359, Aurelius Victor, who, as we have seen, complained of the ignoring of Rome by emperors in 348, bemoaned the senate's loss of power and prestige, drawing lessons from the brief reign of Claudius Tacitus in 276: everyone was happy, he asserted, 'because the senate had recovered the right to choose the emperor from the arrogant military'.[7] Victor also believed that the senate should take some of the blame for its failure to assert itself 'through apathy or fear or because of its hatred of civil conflicts'.[8] The senate's failure left a vacuum. Denied the

---

6. Letter of Constantius recommending Themistius, P. Heather and D. Moncur (eds and trans.), *Politics, Philosophy and Empire in the Fourth Century: Select Orations of Themistius*, TTH 36, Liverpool: Liverpool University Press, 2001, 108–14. It should be noted that some editors have questioned the authenticity of the greeting.

7. Aur. Vict., *Caes.* 36 (Bird translation). On the sources for the emperor Tacitus, including Victor, see Ronald Syme, *Emperors and Biography: Studies in the Historia Augusta*, Oxford: Oxford University Press, 1971, 237–47.

8. Aur. Vict. *Caes.* 37.5 (Probus).

legitimacy conferred by senatorial endorsement, emperors turned to a yet higher authority, the gods. Indeed, the gods were perhaps more to be relied on than the fickle armies, whom Aurelian is said to have challenged by invoking the superior authority of Sol Invictus,[9] but it was up to emperors to prove to their subjects beyond doubt, through demonstration of their own success, that God or the gods were on their side.

Despite the sidelining of the local elite in imperial affairs, the city of Rome in the third century did matter, both symbolically, as the ancient capital of empire, and practically. Senators remained wealthy; the province of Africa in particular, where senatorial landholding in the fourth century was extensive, seems to have weathered economic storms better than many. Philip's four successors, Decius (249–51), Trebonianus Gallus (251–3), Valerian (253–60) and his son Gallienus (253–68), all had links with the city through landholding and family, some even claiming descent from the Etruscans;[10] and Aurelian's building of new walls for Rome in the 270s demonstrated continuing imperial concern for the security of the city.[11] Material evidence also suggests that, while population in the surrounding countryside diminished in the course of the third century,[12] numbers in the city itself expanded significantly.[13] While outsiders like the Antiochene soldier-historian Ammianus Marcellinus, writing in Rome in c. 390, stated that nothing of importance ever happened there,[14] from the standpoint of Romans the absence of emperors would allow a freer rein to senatorial self-expression and competition for office and status, and, for Christians, the uninhibited evolution of what would become in the early Middle Ages the religious capital of western Christendom.

9. Anonymous continuator of Dio (now identified as Peter the Patrician) in *FHG* 4, Aurelian 6. For the general point, H. A. Drake, 'Lessons from Diocletian's persecution', in D. V. Twomey and M. Humphries (eds), *The Great Persecution*, Dublin: Four Courts Press, 2009, 49–60.
10. E. Papi, 'A new golden age? The northern *praefectura urbi* from Severus to Diocletian', in Simon Swain and Mark Edwards (eds), *Approaching Late Antiquity: The Transformation from Early to Late Empire*, Oxford: Oxford University Press, 2005, 53–81 at 60–2.
11. Alaric Watson, *Aurelian and the Third Century*, London: Routledge, 1999, 143–52.
12. Papi, 'Golden age', 53–70.
13. For economic background, see also N. Morley, *Metropolis and Hinterland: The City of Rome and the Italian Economy*, Cambridge: Cambridge University Press, 1996.
14. Amm. Marc. 14.6.25.

Rome's 'eleventh century': continuity and change

Aurelius Victor's chronological perspective on Rome's history invites a reassessment of historical assumptions influenced by the modern practice of dividing history into 'periods' for educational purposes.[15] Roman historians writing in the fourth century and later did not recognise a 'third-century crisis'. Ammianus' history took up the story where Tacitus left it in AD 96; the *New History* of Zosimus (c. AD 500), based on the earlier writers Eunapius and Olympiodorus, began with Augustus, as did the various epitomators of imperial history, such as Aurelius Victor (*De Caesaribus*) and Eutropius (*Breviarium*). Specialists in law and legal history had yet another perspective: the compilers of Justinian's Code in 529 and 534, who drew on two collections of rescripts made in the 290s and the Theodosian code of 438, began their authoritative compilation of imperial laws with Hadrian (117–38). Their timescale was dictated by what mattered to them as lawyers, for whom Hadrian, as the codifier of the Praetorian Edict, was a major reformer;[16] any sense of crisis is entirely absent from the steady flow of imperial responses on petitions recorded in the 290s and preserved in the Justinianic Code, which continues unbroken throughout the third century.

Diocletian's accession in 284, the start-date for this volume, would inaugurate over twenty years of dynastic stability, during which radical reforms of administration and finance could take root. After a relatively brief period of confusion (306–13), Constantine emerged, to dominate the record down to his death in 337 and to be succeeded by his three sons, then by his relative Julian. His reign and those of his successors saw the further restructuring of government and the emergence of Christianity as the dominant religion of empire. This prolonged period of apparent stability at the centre stands in sharp contrast to the rapid turnover of emperors that preceded it and is generally regarded as the first phase of 'late antiquity'.[17]

---

15. For many years, for example, Oxford 'modern history' began in 284.
16. Hadrian's codification of the Praetorian Edict was carried out by Salvius Julianus, supervised by Iuventius Celsus (consul II, 129) in the 130s. It became known as the Perpetual Edict (*edictum perpetuum*) and thereafter the emperor was the sole authority for changes to praetorian law (*ius honorarium*).
17. Although Peter Brown's seminal work on *The World of Late Antiquity: From Marcus Aurelius to Muhammed*, London: Thames and Hudson, 1971, begins in the second century, and focuses on the half-millennium after 250. But cf. his aside, apropos the emperor Julian, that 'Late Antiquity is always later than we think' (*Society and the Holy in Late Antiquity*, London: Faber, 1982, 93).

Viewed in the context of Rome's 'eleventh century', however, the significance of 284 is less marked. The century inaugurated in 248 had begun badly, with three decades of turbulence on Rome's borders in both Europe and Asia. Down to the early third century, the eastern frontier had been a profitable source of both revenue and glory for past emperors, such as Trajan (98–117), or Septimius Severus (193–211),[18] but the initiative had lain with Rome. The difference from c. 230 onwards was that Rome was in general on the defensive and obliged to divert resources and imperial attention eastwards, whether or not it was convenient for them to do so. For in the east, a new dynasty, the Sasanians, had arisen in Fars or Persis, and overthrown the previous, ineffectual rulers.[19] The two first kings, Ardashir (224–c. 240) and Shapur I (c.240–72) adopted a more overtly aggressive foreign policy, seeking to revive the glories of ancient Persia and, in pursuit of that goal, reclaiming those parts of the Eastern Roman Empire once part of the domains of Cyrus the Great, Darius and Xerxes. Although Sasanian territorial ambitions were more limited than their rhetoric, they campaigned actively to assert control in the border regions, and in particular the long-disputed client-kingdom of Armenia. Persia destroyed two emperors, Gordian III and Valerian (defeated and captured in 260), and twice took the city of Antioch, capital of Roman Syria, although they were unable to hold onto what they had gained.[20] The rise of the independent kingdom of Palmyra under Odaenathus and later his queen, Zenobia, helped to stabilise the region while also limiting the extent to which Rome could exert direct control.

In northern and central Europe, coalitions of Germanic peoples, notably the Franks on the lower Rhine, the Alamanni[21] on the upper Rhine and Danube, and the Sarmatians, Goths[22] and others on the Danube, exerted continual pressure on the frontiers. The 'Skythai'

18. Trajan's eastern conquests were abandoned by Hadrian immediately on his accession in 117. Septimius Severus, who had seized power in 193, took Ctesiphon in January 198, thereby establishing his credentials as a credible military emperor.
19. R. N. Frye, ''The political history of Iran under the Sasanians', in E. Yarshater (ed.), *Cambridge History of Iran. Vol. 3, part 1: The Seleucid, Parthian and Sasanian Periods*, Cambridge: Cambridge University Press, 2000, 116–80, esp. 116–40.
20. Dodgeon and Lieu, *Roman Eastern Frontier*, 50–6.
21. For the Alamanni coalition, see J. F. Drinkwater, *The Alamanni and Rome, 213–496 (Caracalla to Clovis)*, Oxford: Oxford University Press, 2007, 43–9.
22. For the Gothic sack of Histria on the Danube in 238 and later incursions, see, in brief, Peter Heather and John Matthews, *The Goths in the Fourth Century*, TTH 11, Liverpool: Liverpool University Press, 1991, 1–4.

(a generic description for peoples in the Black Sea regions) broke through the imperial defences to roam at will through Greece, the Aegean and the Black Sea; the Juthungi invaded Italy; an independent 'Gallic Empire' was created under a local ruler, Postumus, in 260; and the Danube area suffered from a series of military revolts.[23] The social disruption caused by the presence of alien raiders is illustrated by a 'canonical letter', written by Gregory the Thaumaturge ('Wonder-Worker'), bishop of Neocaesarea in Pontus, south of the Black Sea, late in the third century. In the letter, the bishop castigates those who plunder or unlawfully retain the property of others to compensate themselves for what the 'barbarians' have taken from them, and excludes from the church community those who have collaborated with the 'barbarians', acted as their guides and attacked the houses of their co-religionists.[24]

But by 284 the crisis had passed and imperial unity had been restored, thanks to the combined efforts of a succession of emperors, who originated from the central European and Danube regions. They were career soldiers and their primary job was the military defence of the empire. Frontier security was re-established by Gallienus;[25] by Claudius II 'Gothicus', who defeated the Goths at Naissus in 269 and from whom Constantine would claim descent;[26] by Aurelian (270–5), in whose reign the Juthungi were crushed, and the 'independent' fiefdoms of the 'Gallic Empire' (260–74) and Palmyra reintegrated into the Roman system;[27] and by Probus (276–82), famed, according to the Historia Augusta, for encouraging peaceful agricultural practices and the cultivation of vineyards.[28]

Emperors dealt with the 'barbarians' as they had always done, through a combination of military aggression, treaties, and

23. On the sack of Athens, see Fergus Millar, 'P. Herennius Dexippus, the Greek world and the third century crisis', *JRS* 59 (1969), 12–29.
24. Gregory the Thaumaturge, *Canonical Letter*, canons 5–9, trans. Heather and Matthews, *The Goths*, 8–10.
25. Although, as *Pan. Lat.* 8 (3).10.1–2, delivered for Constantius I in 297, shows, Gallienus was best remembered, and blamed, for the fragmentation of the Roman Empire in his time. For Gallienus' achievement, see L. de Blois, *The Policy of the Emperor Gallienus*, Leiden: Brill, 1976.
26. Eutr. *Brev.* 9.22; *Pan. Lat.* 5.4.2–3; 6.2.2; SHA *Claudius* 1.1; 1.3; 9.9; 13.2.
27. Watson, *Aurelian*, 57–88 (Palmyra); 89–100 (west). Potter, *Empire at Bay*, 268–75 (on Aurelian). comments that 'no man since the time of Augustus was to accomplish more in less time for the central government than did Aurelian'. See also John F. White, *Restorer of the World: The Roman Emperor Aurelian*, Staplehurst: Spellmount, 2005, which attempts to communicate Aurelian's achievement to a non-specialist readership.
28. Eutr. *Brev.* 7.17. For the 'School of Generals', see Syme, *Emperors*, 208–12.

voluntary or compulsory assimilation through settlements and recruitment into the Roman armies. It was beyond the powers of emperors, however, to address the underlying causes of increased population pressures, especially on the extended river frontiers of the Rhine and the Danube. Migration and its effects were outside the control of any Roman ruler and pressure on the river frontiers continued, until the Rhine defences collapsed early in the fifth century. Sporadic insurgencies on the part of local military rulers[29] in the third and fourth centuries (a phenomenon which would contribute to the fragmentation of the west after 400), were a response, primarily, to the perceived failure of emperors to respond effectively to the defence needs of the frontier regions. Local loyalties and identity played an important part in the behaviour of armies in the third century and in late antiquity, and their behaviour could not be reliably predicted.[30]

The appearance of dynastic stability in the decades after Diocletian's accession was hard-won and, in part, deceptive.[31] Few emperors died in old age and of natural causes; Diocletian, Constantius I and Constantine were the main exceptions to the rule. The circumstances of Diocletian's own accession were not promising. When, on campaign against Persia, the previous emperor, Numerian, was discovered dead of unknown causes, Diocletian, then known as Valerius Diocles, promptly accused the praetorian prefect, Aper, of the murder and ran him through with his sword in front of the whole army.[32] Though accepted by the eastern army, Diocletian had still to deal with his predecessor's brother and co-emperor, Carinus, whom he disposed of at the battle of the river Margus in 285. His direct, public and violent action against Aper, his initial dependence on acclamation by the troops, and his swift follow-up action against his

29. Potter, *Empire at Bay*, 251–7; on Postumus and his successors in Gaul (260–74), see J. F. Drinkwater, *The Gallic Empire: Separation and Continuity in the North-Western Provinces of the Roman Empire*, AD 260–274. Historia Einzelschriften 52, Stuttgart: Steiner, 1987.
30. Cf. the divergent choices of the Gallic and Danubian armies after the murder of Constans in 350, below, p. 223.
31. Successful or partially successful challengers included Carausius in Britain from 286, Constantine I (whose proclamation at York in 306 was initially unauthorised by the Senior Augustus, Galerius), Maxentius at Rome (306–312), Magnentius (Gaul and the west, 350–3), Julian (361–3). The Gallic army was noticeably, if not notoriously, more volatile than its Danubian counterpart.
32. Eutr. *Brev.* 9.20; Aur. Vict. *Caes.* 38–9; SHA *Carinus* 13.1. The date was 20 November 284. See also *P. Beatty Pan.* 2.162; Lactant. *De mort. pers.* 17.1; Zos. *New History*, 1.73.2.

surviving rival were all characteristic of the successful third-century
challenger for empire. But there could also have been little confidence in 285 that Diocletian would not go the way of his military
predecessors, overthrown in his turn by another pretender,
supported by a disaffected and unreliable military.[33]

Extensive new construction of fortifications took place prior to
284.[34] Local people, determined to see to their own security, would
have paid themselves for their new walls with their brick or stone
facing and rubble cores. But fortification was also driven by imperial
initiative. Gallienus erected defence walls for Milan, Verona and
probably Aquileia, and his concern with the Danube resulted in the
fortification of Sardica and other towns. However, the main concentration of Gallienus, Aurelian and Probus was on the European river
frontiers, areas which would also attract the attention of Diocletian
and his colleagues; defence and security policy in those areas is
an unbroken continuum, in which it is often hard to detect the
contribution of individuals. Probus' focus, for example, on urban
fortifications in northern Gaul may have included the building of
the strong points on either side of the Channel, which were aimed
to control piracy and would be under the command of the Count
(*comes*) of the Saxon Shore.[35]

The army, the land and finance

The reforms of emperors in the first part of Rome's eleventh century
provided precedents for their successors after 284. According to later
tradition, which is supported by some coinage and epigraphic
evidence,[36] Gallienus, a perhaps underrated innovator, was the first
to establish a special cavalry force, stationed, in the first instance, at

33. Zos. *New History*, 1 21.3, suggests causes of disaffection may have been relatively
superficial. Philip and Probus are both said to have been killed 'by the soldiers' but no
motive is given (although Probus had allegedly threatened to make soldiers redundant).
34. For general survey and collection of regional bibliographies on archaeological
advances, see John J. Wilkes, 'Provinces and frontiers', in *CAH*² 12, 212–24 and 258–
64; A. D. Lee, *Information and Frontiers: Roman Foreign Relations in Late Antiquity*,
Cambridge: Cambridge University Press, 1993, 53–4 (east), 179–82 (north). For the use
on the eastern frontier of fortified cities, rather than 'forts' or walls, down to the time
of Justinian see B. Isaac, *The Limits of Empire: The Roman Army in the East*, Oxford:
Oxford University Press, 1990, 252–9.
35. S. Johnson, *The Roman Forts of the Saxon Shore*, 2nd edn, London: Elek, 1979;
Andrew Pearson, *The Construction of the Saxon Shore Forts*, Oxford: Archaeopress,
2003.
36. Dessau, *ILS* 569 (of 269), *equites* as a unit; *RIC* 5.1, no 445, Milan (*Fides Equitum*).

Milan and answerable to its own commander. It was thus independent of armies controlled by provincial governors. In addition, Gallienus detached infantry units (*vexillationes*) from the legions, put them under their own commanders and stationed them at strategic points. The creation of this separate cavalry force, backed by the *vexillationes*, can be interpreted as an ad hoc response to crisis, which may have been a temporary measure; northern Italy was under threat from both the 'Gallic Empire' of Postumus from 260 and the resurgent Alamanni, as well as from the Danube regions. Temporary or not, by creating a military force outside the traditional, province-based command structure, Gallienus also provided a blueprint for the mobile striking forces, the *comitatenses*, of the later empire. But the reform also put military power in the hands of independent commanders, who used it to facilitate their own ambitions: Aureolus, who rebelled against Gallienus in 268, Claudius II Gothicus and Aurelian were all commanders of the cavalry. This encapsulated a dilemma with which fourth-century and later emperors were also familiar: the more effective the general, the more suspect he became, as a potential alternative emperor.

The security of empire and emperors depended on contented and well-rewarded soldiers. They could expect regular pay, donatives on special occasions and money, from the military treasury established by Augustus, to buy a plot of land on retirement.[37] Failure to supply these, or the superior attractions of the general with whom they served, prompted army revolts against reigning emperors, which would continue to be a feature of the fourth century. Loyalty, therefore, was not based solely on financial reward; it was also a matter of personal allegiance. At all times, the supply of rewards to soldiers depended on the secure functioning of the economy and the collection of revenue through taxes. Although relatively little precise detail is available for how taxation worked – or failed to work – in the third century,[38] for tax revenue, in money or in kind, to flow smoothly to the centre, a productive economy was a precondition.

Although Romans engaged in trade, both short- and long-distance, and in manufacture, the economy was, still, primarily agricultural, and the two main forms of taxation were taxation of land and its produce, and of individuals (the 'poll tax'). Disruption

37. For the long view, see R. Alston, 'Roman military pay from Caesar to Diocletian', *JRS* 84 (1994), 113–23.
38. For a judicious account of the imperfect state of our knowledge of Roman taxation, see M. Corbier, 'Coinage and taxation: The state's point of view', in *CAH*[2] 12, 327–92.

caused by invasions, the weather or other localised factors would affect the tax take. But how much land had fallen out of cultivation and become 'abandoned land' (*agri deserti*) is debatable. Imperial policy, as set out in fourth-century legal pronouncements issued by emperors,[39] was that cultivators who took over abandoned land and farmed it had a tax holiday for a stated period; this was partly to encourage the would-be farmer, but also would allow time for the land to become productive again, after a period of perhaps prolonged neglect. The laws do not, however, provide evidence for the extent of the problem or the amount of abandoned land affected.

The scale of damage caused to the operation of rural economies in the third century is disputed and land survey evidence shows considerable regional variation. While some areas along with their resident peasant freeholders or tenant farmers suffered, others fared better. Sample surveys in Italy show a marked decline in rural settlement in the third century but Gaul presents a more varied picture, although still with serious localised disruption and changes in patterns of cultivation. The exception to the pattern of some decline in the west is Africa, which was protected from the invaders of mainland Europe; settlement, public building and pottery exports all flourished, as also, perhaps not coincidentally, did the African Christian churches. In the east, the rural economies of both Greece and northern Syria prospered, despite the occasional threat from invaders; Egypt, however, seems to have declined economically, partly due to local factors, such as the functioning or not of the Nile inundations necessary for some villages to survive.[40]

How far revenue streams were disrupted by invasions or other hazards in the third century is therefore uncertain. More obviously problematic was the rapid debasement of the gold and silver coinage in terms of both size and precious metal content, which risked affecting the efficacy as a medium of exchange of the currency in which

39. *Cod. Theod.* 5.14 and 15 for Constantine and after. *Cod. Just.* 11.59 (58). 1 of Constantine to one Capestrinus (undated) refers to an enactment of Aurelian, '*parens noster*', making local councils responsible for bringing back deserted land into cultivation, with a grant of tax exemption for three years. On how survey evidence contradicts assumptions about large-scale failures to cultivate, see C. R. Whittaker, '*Agri deserti*', in M. I. Finley, ed. *Studies in Roman Property*, Cambridge: Cambridge University Press, 1976, 137–65.

40. For a summary by region see R. Duncan Jones, 'Economic change and the transition to late antiquity', in Swain and Edwards, *Approaching Late Antiquity*, 20–52. For growth in economic activity in the countryside in late antiquity, see Jairus Banaji, *Agrarian Change in Late Antiquity: Gold, Labour and Aristocratic Dominance*. Oxford: Oxford University Press, 2001, 6–22.

soldiers were paid. Debasement could have been due to increases in spending and/or a decrease in the availability of precious metals. The gold mines of Dacia would be finally lost in 271 and mines in southern and northwestern Spain seem to have cut back on production during that period, perhaps due to problems of labour supply. Yet Aurelian made a bold attempt to upgrade the gold coinage and link a new silver coin to coppers at a fixed tariff. His attempt to fix rates by fiat faltered, a fate that would also befall Diocletian's analogous attempts to control prices by decree.

Inflation was problematic in terms of both army pay and prices. While annual pay under Caracalla (211–17) was assessed at 600 silver *denarii*, by c. 300, this had risen by up to twenty-fold to 12,000 *denarii*. Yet this had failed to keep pace with prices, which had risen thirty-fold over the course of the century. Two reasons for this are possible. One is that mismatch between supply and demand, forced up prices; this would often be the case, whatever the state of the currency, and would be especially likely to apply on a local and temporary level when large armies collected in cities, swelling the population and driving up the price of commodities. Diocletian's Edict on Maximum Prices, issued in 301,[41] may have been a response to soldiers' resentment at having to pay inflated prices for goods. Secondly, users of coins may have worried about the ever-increasing gulf between the face value of a coin and the value of its precious metal content and therefore required more coins for individual trans-actions. The preference of the imperial government in the fourth century for levying fines expressed in terms of a weight of metal (e.g. ten pounds of gold), which would preserve its value, regardless of the state of the coinage, would support this. However, there are also indications that users were happy with coins if they recognised the emperor's head on the obverse; this provided reassurance that the currency was sound.[42] In response both Diocletian and Constantine worked to stabilise the value of gold and silver currency, the latter with some success, but the value of bronze coins continued to erode.

It is not clear how far emperors attempted to match revenue with expenditure, or, indeed, if there were any reliable mechanisms for so doing. In times of military upheaval and uncertainty, unplanned wars could not be budgeted for, and even planned expeditions had uncertain durations and outcomes. Methods of assessment of

41. See below, pp. 66–9.
42. Potter, *Empire at Bay*, 273–4.

produce of land (*iugum*) and people (*caput, capitatio*) varied in line with local practice, often derived, as in Sicily, from pre-Roman systems inherited by the conquerors. For example, land could be assessed in terms of simple acreage, level of fertility or usage. Similarly, eligibility to pay the poll tax varied between provinces, with varying provisions relating to gender and age. There were also additional indirect taxes, such as percentages levied on the freeing or sale of slaves, or customs dues (*portoria*) levied at a limited number of entry points on the frontiers; Nisibis, for example, was the main conduit for trade with Persia in the third century. Under the early empire, regular censuses collected information on the resources of the empire; these regular assessments, discontinued at some point in the third century, were revived by Diocletian. Revenue could be further affected by imperial grant (*indulgentia*) of total or partial immunity, as happened, for example, for the benefit of the province of Thrace, whose tax arrears were partially reduced by Julian, in order to encourage them to pay over the rest.[43]

Cities, citizens and the laws

The sustaining of the membership and resource bases of city councils (*curiae* or *boulai*), which were responsible for the administration of cities, was a consistent imperial priority.[44] But even in the early second century, as is illustrated by Pliny's letters from Bithynia in c. AD 110–12, councillors, or decurions, were not invariably reliable custodians of city finances. Even in prosperous areas, competitive overspending by city elites could lead to unsustainable deficits and, inevitably, central intervention from the governor or the appointment of a financial trouble-shooter, the *curator civitatis*. The growth of intervention from the centre was a long-term trend, therefore, provoked by cities' own failure to manage for themselves. Consequently, ancient civic freedoms vanished under the pressure from the centre for increased tax revenue; Aphrodisias in Caria, which

43. Julian, *Letter* 27, to the Thracians (Wright Loeb edition numbering).
44. See essays collected by John Rich (ed.), *The City in Late Antiquity*, London: Routledge, 1992. For how cities worked in the Greek east under the early Empire (with emphasis on local factors), S. Dmitriev, *City Government in Hellenistic and Roman Asia Minor*, New York: Oxford University Press, 2004. A. H. M. Jones, *The Greek City from Alexander to Justinian*, Oxford: Oxford University Press, 1940, is a classic; see also his chapter on cities in *LRE*. Late Roman Africa is comprehensively covered by C. Lepelley, *Les Cités de l'Afrique romaine au bas-empire*, 2 vols, Paris: Etudes Augustiniennes, 1979–81.

had celebrated its free status and tax immunities in the second century (and upped its advertisement of these facts in the early third), fell into financial difficulties in the reign of Commodus and had, along with other cities, lost its free status by the mid-third century.[45] Moreover, from the mid-third century onwards, some councils' difficulties were further exacerbated by the increase in demands for services from the central government, a practice which continued into the fourth century.[46] Cities still collected taxes and were responsible for tax records but their revenues were gradually appropriated by the central administration, although the assets from which the revenues were generated remained under local control. This not only generated revenue for the emperor's use but also deprived cities of the chance to divert their resources to support challenges to imperial authority or security.

For many council members, the status of decurion became less attractive, as other opportunities for self-advancement beckoned. The duties carried out by those who served on the councils as magistrates or administrators of *munera* or liturgies[47] were no longer voluntary and therefore conferred less prestige on the councillors as patrons. Their status became hereditary, in the sense that it was expected that sons should replace their fathers, although a process of nomination and perhaps a council vote was required;[48] new councillors still had to be formally approved as suitable. As the better off manipulated the system to avoid the requirements of the rota of duties,[49] shifting the burden to those least capable of bearing it, the poorer members resorted to flight or voluntary bankruptcy,[50] while their wealthier colleagues used influence and connections to move upwards in the social scale into court or army service. Moreover, as

45. Charlotte Roueché, *Aphrodisias in Late Antiquity: The Late Roman and Byzantine Inscriptions*, JRS Monographs 5, London: Society for the Promotion of Roman Studies, 1989, rev. 2004, xxiv.1–4.

46. For Antioch in the third and fourth centuries, see J. H. W. G. Liebeschuetz, *Antioch: City and Imperial Administration in the Later Roman Empire*, Oxford: Clarendon Press, 1972, 119–66.

47. For jurists' explanations of *munera*, see *Dig.* 50.4–5. For the impact of the acquisition of higher offices and ranks (*dignitates*) on willingness to take on liturgies, see Fergus Millar, 'Empire and city, Augustus to Julian: Obligations, excuses and status', *JRS* 73 (1983), 76–96.

48. Regulations for public elections were included in the municipal charters of the first century but do not appear to have operated in the fourth.

49. Governors were supposed to ensure that the rota worked; see *Dig.* 50.4.3.15–16.

50. For examples of decurions in Egypt ceding property to those who nominated them for liturgies, see *POxy* 1405 (200), Rainer Papyrus 20 (250).

cities ceded financial control to the central government, the scope for local euergetism through building and self-laudatory inscriptions became reduced. It may be no coincidence, therefore, that the 'epigraphic habit' also declined during the same period – there was little for the decurion to commemorate. Nonetheless, the status of independent city remained attractive for communities, like Orcistus in Phrygia,[51] which successfully petitioned Constantine for city status in 331, and the legal privileges of decurions as members of the *honestiores*, the social groups deemed worthy of honour and there-fore exemption from the more painful and humiliating aspects of the Roman penal system, such as judicial torture, remained largely intact.[52]

Increased self-assertion by the centre did not make the emperors less dependent on the goodwill of the local elites and the efficient functioning of the *curia*. Therefore, when councils appealed to the emperor for the return of delinquent colleagues, the imperial response was invariably to insist, in general terms, that fugitive councillors be brought back or provided with a replacement.[53] But some councils held back from making such requests, due to fear of reprisals from powerful colleagues; more positively, they could anticipate future assistance from these same colleagues, if their careers prospered. In fact, social mobility posed a dilemma for both councils and emperors, who could lose out if councils became depleted, but whose interest might also be best served if local talent could be pressed into imperial (or later ecclesiastical) service.[54] While lively city politics and bitter personal rivalries are better attested for the second century than the third, there is no reason to assume that city loyalties declined. Popular opinion was still expressed by acclamation, as at Aphrodisias or Perge[55] and inscriptions from Paestum in the 340s show that the assembled people still had a

51. See A. Chastagnol, 'L'Inscription constantinienne d'Orcistus', *MEFRA* 93 (1981), 381–416.
52. See Peter Garnsey, *Social Status and Legal Privilege in the Roman Empire*, Oxford: Oxford University Press, 1970.
53. As reflected in *Dig.* 50.2.1 (Pseudo-Ulpian, *Opinions*).
54. For analysis of the effect of the expansion of Constantinople, see Peter Heather, 'New men for new Constantines? Creating an imperial elite in the eastern Mediter-ranean', in P. Magdalino (ed.), *New Constantines: The Rhythm of Imperial Renewal in Byzantium, 4th–13th Centuries*, Aldershot: Variorum, 1994, 11–33.
55. Charlotte Roueché, 'Acclamations in the later Roman Empire: New evidence from Aphrodisias', *JRS* 74 (1984), 181–99; Roueché, '*Floreat Perge*', in M. M. MacKenzie and Charlotte Roueche (eds), *Images of Authority: Papers presented to Joyce Reynolds*, Cambridge: Cambridge Philological Society, 1989, 218–21.

formal voice in community affairs.[56] What did change in the fourth century, with the coming of Christianity, were the ways in which local euergetism and political competition were expressed.[57]

A legal development with significant consequences for late antiquity had taken place nearly four decades before Philip the Arab's celebration of the Roman millennium. Almost all free people resident in the empire became Roman citizens under Caracalla's *constitutio Antoniniana* of 212, and all were therefore subject to the *ius civile*, the law under which the Roman citizen (*civis*) would live. Although the law was applicable to all, not all citizens were equal under the law. The wealthy and powerful still had privileged access to legal process, and the evolution in the second century of the legal statuses of *honestior* (the 'more honourable' decurion and upwards) and *humilior* (lesser person) allowed the entrenchment of legal privilege based on social status.[58] But, in theory, access to legal remedies was available to all, and so too was the right of appeal to a higher court and ultimately to the emperor himself or his delegate; the result was a significant increase in both the volume of appeals and the regulations attached to how the appeals should be made and administered by the judge concerned (who could feel his own reputation to be at risk).[59]

The ending of 'classical' jurisprudence in the early third century with Ulpian under the Severans and his pupil Modestinus has been held to presage a decline in Roman legal thinking.[60] In fact, the later third century saw the end not of jurisprudence but of the independent jurist, who now became absorbed entirely into the imperial legal bureaucracy. The high quality of the second- and third-century rescripts, assembled into the law-codes of Gregorius and Hermogenian in the 290s and preserved in the Codex Justinianus in 529 and 534, provides no evidence for decline in legal understanding, still less

56. Discussed by Jill Harries, '*Favor populi*: Patronage and public entertainment in late antiquity', in Kathryn Lomas and Tim Cornell (eds), *Bread and Circuses: Euergetism and Municipal Patronage in Roman Italy*, London: Routledge, 2003, 125–41.

57. For reflections on the interaction of religious and social change and its effect on expressions of ambition and public cult, see Peter Brown, *The Making of Late Antiquity*, Cambridge, MA: Harvard University Press, 1978, 27–53: 'the Late Antique city was neither impoverished nor was it devoid of ceremony' (p. 49).

58. Garnsey, *Social Status and Legal Privilege*, passim.

59. See *Cod. Theod.* 11.29–36.

60. As argued by E. Levy, *West Roman Vulgar Law: The Law of Property*, Philadelphia: American Philosophical Society, 1951. The use of such invidious terms as 'post-classical' or 'epi-classical', which assume decline, are avoided in this book, but for the latter see David Johnston, 'Epi-classical law', in *CAH*[2] 12, 200–7.

any break in the juristic tradition or 'vulgarisation' of law. As we shall see below, the legal tradition held good, even when, as under the direction of Constantine, the rhetoric got in the way.

It might be thought that the universal grant of Roman citizenship would result in the suppression of legal diversity. The situation was in reality more complex. Roman judges were content to accommodate local usages by assimilating them to the longstanding Roman concept of custom, written or not, as being itself a valid source of law.[61] Awkward and expensive lawsuits, subject to the exploitation of technicalities by highly paid lawyers, could be avoided by the use of binding arbitration, for which the agreement of both parties was required that they would agree both to the process and the findings of the adjudicator.[62] This bypassed the Roman courts and had the advantage that the dispute would be ended by the judgement. The law's delays and expense could thus be avoided, although arbitrations were often conducted under Roman rules. In Roman legal thought, arbitration provided a convenient means for recognising the decisions of alternative jurisdictions in civil, but not criminal, matters; in the fourth century these would include both Jewish and episcopal courts.[63]

Perhaps the most important single source for the social, economic and administrative history of the fourth and early fifth centuries is the collection of extracts from imperial legal enactments, largely in the form of edicts and letters, from Constantine onwards, which were assembled and edited into a law book (*codex*) on the instructions of Theodosius II at Constantinople between 429 and 437 and formally promulgated in 438. No manuscript of the entire Code survives and the text, as published by Mommsen in 1905, which is still the standard version, represents only a fraction of the lost whole. The textual problems afflicting laws from the reigns of Constantine (with whom the code begins) and his sons are especially acute: inaccurate and/or incomplete transmission of the names of the emperors responsible (all of whose names began with 'Const-'),

61. *Dig.* 1.3. 32 (Salvius Julianus, consul 148). In cases of doubt about what local legal custom was, reference was to be made to previous court decisions (*Dig.* 1.3.37–8).
62. Rules on arbitration agreements and the involvement of the 'praetor' (in fact the provisions of the codified Praetorian Edict) are laid out at *Dig.* 4.8. See also Jill Harries, *Law and Empire in Late Antiquity*, Cambridge: Cambridge University Press, 1999, 175–84.
63. Jill Harries, 'Creating legal space: The settlement of disputes in the Roman Empire', in C. Hezser (ed.), *Rabbinic Law in its Roman and Near Eastern Context*, Tubingen: Mohr Siebeck, 2003, 62–81.

the addressees, and the dates and places of issue (*data*), reception (*accepta*) and public posting (*proposita*) often make certainty impossible.

Much work remains to be done on how these texts should be read,[64] and understanding of the process which generated them is crucial for their use as evidence for late antiquity. As a rule, emperors issued constitutions, loosely also known as 'laws', in response to prompts from others. These could consist of reports (*relationes*) or proposals (*suggestiones*) emanating from officials at court and in the provinces, questions (*consultationes*) from judges uncertain of how to resolve a difficult legal point in a trial, and initiatives from other interest groups, including, from Constantine onwards, Christian bishops. In isolation, each law refers only to the situation which it addresses, although it also provided a guide as to how similar situations should be dealt with. The law cannot, therefore, be used as evidence for the prevalence or seriousness of any given problem. Nor does the repetition of a 'law' mean that previous laws were ineffective; individuals and groups with access to the emperor or friends at court habitually resorted to petitioning or questioning an emperor to check if he still thought the same as he, or a predecessor, had done before. Such approaches might be expected to have an element of self-interest; the petitioner or proposer might already have a fair idea of the answer, and how the response might be used to further the petitioner's own agenda. To further complicate matters, the text of any given 'law' may not necessarily have been framed by the emperor or by his legal draftsmen; if a proposal was simply agreed, the wording of the proposal could have been incorporated into the response.

The emperor was not the only maker of law. Changes in court practice had their own momentum. Much is made, and rightly, of increased judicial severity in late antiquity,[65] the savagery of public punishments, although this was also a feature of the High empire, and in particular the expansion up the social scale of the use of judicial torture to extract evidence. It is likely that this expansion

64. John Matthews, *Laying Down the Law: A Study of the Theodosian Code*, New Haven: Yale University Press, 2000, is the definitive work for now on the Code itself. For its use as historical evidence, see Jill Harries and Ian Wood, *The Theodosian Code: Studies in the Imperial Law of Late Antiquity*, London: Duckworth, 1993, reissued 2010, and Harries, *Law and Empire*, passim.
65. See Ramsay MacMullen, 'Judicial savagery in the Roman Empire', *Chiron* 19 (1986), 147–66.

was driven not by emperors but by the (excessive) zeal of judges to uncover the truth, which over time led them to exceed their authority and reshape the rules. Another, and more benign, court-driven development was Christian canon law, which, when addressing offences also condemned by the state, emphasised penance and reform, rather than retribution.[66]

The religious landscape

The roots of the religion, Christianity, that would dominate the Roman world in the fourth century and thereafter lie in the shared religious cultures and practices of the pre-Christian empire. The third century contains indications of a gradual shift from a polytheistic culture to an increased cultural acceptance of the idea of a single Divinity, which, in the fourth century, would ease the transition to worship of the God of the Christians as the dominant religion.[67] The divinity of emperors was celebrated through the imperial cult, which acted also as a bridge between the emperor and the cities, each reaffirming their goodwill towards the other,[68] as well as, notably, in the language of panegyric, which celebrated the Tetrarchs as divine, as well as imperial, 'presences'.[69] Emperors and citizens alike cultivated personal relationships with the divine. Rites of initiation into a personal cult, which may have offered the hope of 'salvation' thereafter, were common to many mystery cults, as well as Christianity. In addition to these, cities, homes, burial grounds and the countryside were still populated by more intimate deities, guardians of the household and the dead, and by the healing powers of sacred groves and springs.

The marketplace of religions was a crowded one, and open to manipulation and exploitation. The shrines of well-marketed gods

---

66. For the relationship of Christians, the courts and Roman law see Caroline Humfress, *Orthodoxy and the Courts in Late Antiquity*, Oxford: Oxford University Press, 2007.
67. Garth Fowden, *Empire to Commonwealth: Consequences of Monotheism in Late Antiquity*, Princeton. NJ: Princeton University Press, 1993, provides an essential Middle Eastern historical and cultural context. See also articles by the same author in *CAH*[2] 12, 521–72. For relationship of religious 'knowledge' and 'faith', Clifford Ando, *The Matter of the Gods: Religion and the Roman Empire*, Berkeley: University of California Press, 2008.
68. Simon Price, *Rituals and Power: The Roman Imperial Cult in Asia Minor*, Cambridge: Cambridge University Press, 1984.
69. Barbara S. Rodgers, 'Divine insinuation in the *Panegyrici Latini*', *Historia* 35 (1986), 69–104.

benefited from religious tourists, motivated by personal devotion, curiosity or the hope of some practical benefit. Commercial self-interest on the part of the providers of accommodation and materials for sacrifices and ceremonies, or the manufacturers of souvenirs,[70] helped to underpin the promotion of local cult and the overall, non-exclusive ethos of polytheism. But the economic base of traditional cults also made them vulnerable to disruption, when times were bad. As always, the picture varied. In Asia Minor, a series of third-century emperors from the Severans to Aurelian and Claudius Tacitus inaugurated sacred games, linked to their journeys in the eastern provinces. In line with trends elsewhere, the emphasis had shifted from the building of temples to the cheaper, but not necessarily less lucrative, option of sacred activities and ceremonial.[71]

To favour one god (henotheism)[72] was not to follow the Jewish or Christian route of excluding all the rest as idols or demons. However, the effect of imperial concentration on a single, dominant divinity could, in the short term, make his god more equal than others; adherence to the emperor's favourite deity might not be imposed, but careerists among the elite might find it convenient. Emperors from Augustus onwards had also enhanced their status by linking themselves to a favoured divine patron; Augustus, for example, connected his modest dwelling on the Palatine by a ramp to the temple of Apollo.[73] Aurelian's promotion of Sol Invictus, the Unconquered Sun, was thus in line with precedent: he advertised his 'special relationship' with the god on his coinage, built a temple at Rome and endowed Sol with a priesthood (*pontifices dei Solis*) and sacred games.[74] However, while Aurelian did not intend to innovate, his concentration on Sol Invictus, with its associated ideas of

70. The objection of the Ephesian manufacturers of silver statues of Artemis to Paul's preaching of Christianity, as reported at Acts 19.22–40, was based on his threat to their livelihoods.
71. S. Mitchell, *Anatolia: Land, Men and Gods in Asia Minor*, I, Oxford: Oxford University Press, 1993, 221–5.
72. A modern term not recognised in ancient discourse. P. van Nuffelen, 'Pagan monotheism as a religious phenomenon', in S. Mitchell and P. van Nuffelen (eds), *One God: Pagan Monotheism in the Roman Empire*, Cambridge: Cambridge University Press, 2010, 16–33, argues (p. 17) that the term 'pagan monotheism' is a 'useful heuristic tool' for modern students of ancient ritual, tradition and philosophy.
73. P. Zanker, *The Power of Images in the Age of Augustus*, Ann Arbor: University of Michigan Press, 1988, 51–3, 67–9.
74. Watson, *Aurelian*, 188–98. Thereafter the members of the ancient republican pontifical college were known as the *pontifices Vestae*.

light, victory and celestial supremacy, would influence the early religious ideals of Constantine, and with them the nature of imperial Christianity.

More esoteric from a modern standpoint, but also significant for the changing religious climate, was the contribution of (Neo-)Platonic philosophy, which, in the fourth century, would shape both Christian thinking and the ideas of the emperor Julian. While accepting the importance of ritual, as all did,[75] Plotinus drew on the more mystic aspects of Plato, Aristotle and later Pythagorean thinkers and evolved ideas on the journey of the soul, or the divine in man, to union with the perfect One.[76] In so doing he saw no distinction between philosophy and what we would now term theology. Like other intellectuals and professionals, such as doctors and lawyers, philosophers were fiercely competitive among themselves. This competitive culture shaped the terms of debate and the claims made for the leaders of the schools. Plotinus as a 'teacher' was also endowed with status as a 'holy' man, a man with religious power, entitled to pronounce on the validity of religious observances. But 'holiness' required validation, through demonstrations of power, or miracle-working. Plotinus' initial – and very demanding – mysticism thus became adulterated, notably in the works of Iamblichus, by what outsiders would regard as magic.[77] The power of the 'holy' philosopher and his access to knowledge of the divine was demonstrated by his ability in 'working the gods' or 'theurgy'. But such claims did not go unchallenged; the philosopher (or saint) hailed as a miracle-worker by his adherents would be dismissed by opponents as a magician or charlatan.

Cultic diversity and religious competition, the growth of henotheism and the exclusive preoccupation of philosophy with religion

75. John North, 'Pagan ritual and monotheism', in Mitchell and van Nuffelen, *One God*, 34–52, stresses the compatibility of ritual with philosophical advocacy of a single 'divinity'.

76. For surveys on Plotinus in context, see Lloyd P. Gerson (ed.), *The Cambridge Companion to Plotinus*, Cambridge: Cambridge University Press, 1996; and Mark Edwards, *Culture and Philosophy in the Age of Plotinus*, London: Duckworth, 2006. For the thought-world in general and privileged access to the divine, see Robin Lane Fox, *Pagans and Christians*, London: Penguin, 1986, 102–261.

77. For Iamblichus in translation, see Gillian Clark (ed. and trans.), *Iamblichus, On the Pythagorean Life*, TTH Greek ser. 8, Liverpool: Liverpool University Press, 1989; Emma C. Clark, J. M. Dillon and J. P. Herschbell (eds and trans.), *Iamblichus, De Mysteriis*, Atlanta, GA: Society of Biblical Literature, 2003; J. M. Dillon and W. Polleichter (eds and trans.), *Iamblichus of Chalcis, the Letters*, Atlanta, GA: Society of Biblical Literature, 2009.

provide the context for Christianity in the third century. Decius'
initiation of the first empire-wide order to sacrifice and his consequent persecution of Christians heralded a new universalism
in imperial religious policy.[78] Diversity was still acceptable (and
inevitable) but a common level of conformity was required.
Religious groups became in their turn more self-conscious about
their own identity, requiring increased, but not necessarily exclusive,
commitment from their members, and openly professed adherence to
a set of clearly defined beliefs.[79]

Beliefs about the cosmos and associated ritual practices were
thus the subject of intense public debate, in a society which
prized eloquence. To be an effective participant in public life, a
man required mastery of the arts of persuasion in both theory
and practice, a combination of the 'right' language and the ability
to apply it in public debates on policy, in the law courts and in
rhetorical showpieces. In the process, the past and the ancient
classics were reshaped to cater for the needs of the present. Plotinus'
pupil and biographer, Porphyry, wrote not only *Against the
Christians*, to such effect that his work was banned by Constantine,
but also a commentary on a (now) obscure work of rhetoric theory.
Commentaries became a literary fashion, not least the analysis by
Menander of Laodicea of Demosthenes.[80] Christian writing drew on
the commentary form for purposes of biblical exegesis, as well as on
classical conventions and rhetorical theory, because it was through
literary forms familiar to contemporaries that the Christian cause
could be most effectively promoted.

The cult of the followers of Christ was one among many, but
recruitment was assisted by its city-based organisation, headed by
bishops, its lack of social selectivity, strong social identity and
charitable concern for the poor. But, as the churches grew and prospered, fear of worldly temptation was also expressed: in Carthage in
the early 250s, Cyprian complained that Christians had succumbed
to the allure of cosmetics, dyed hair, arrogance, feuding, greed and

78. J. B. Rives, 'The decree of Decius and the religion of empire', *JRS* 89 (1999),
135–54.
79. North, 'Pagan ritual and monotheism'.
80. M. Heath, 'Rhetoric in mid-antiquity', in T. P. Wiseman (ed.), *Classics in Progress:
Essays on Ancient Greece and Rome*, Oxford: Oxford University Press, 2002, 419–39.
Heath's 'mid-antiquity' is the period of Porphyry and Libanius, midway between Homer
and Manuel II Palaeologos (d. 1425).

usury,[81] and a few decades later, Eusebius blamed the laziness and hypocrisy of the bishops for the renewal of persecution under Diocletian.[82] In the first known referral to an emperor of a dispute between Christians, Aurelian was invited to rule on the ownership of a building used by Christians in Antioch which the dissident bishop, Paul of Samosata, refused to surrender. The emperor, presumably having taken advice from courtiers who knew something about Christian organisation, ruled in favour of those endorsed by the verdict of the bishops of Italy and Rome.[83]

Despite the claim advanced by the much-publicised ascetic hermit Antony, among others, that simplicity and truth would always prevail over superficial cleverness with language and the false wisdom of (pagan) philosophers, educated recruits to Christianity brought with them a competitive determination to take on pagan philosophers at their own game. At Caesarea in Palestine, Origen (born c. 185) had rebutted the arguments of detractors of Christianity in his books *Against Celsus*,[84] as well as combining theological and philosophical speculation with biblical scholarship. His most influential intellectual heirs were the priest Pamphilus and Pamphilus' pupil, Eusebius, later bishop of Caesarea. While the last is best known for his *Ecclesiastical History* and *Life of Constantine*, he was also a biblical commentator (on Isaiah and the Psalms) and a controversialist.[85] By the early fourth century, when Lactantius attended lectures at Nicomedia attacking Christians and Eusebius wrote rebutting Sossianus Hierocles' advocacy of the pre-eminence over Christ of the holy man Apollonius of Tyana, the philosophical battle had become intense.[86] While it would be easy to see this

81. Cyprian, *De lapsis*, 5, 6. This says more about the bishop's moral concern than the actual extent of the abuses to which he refers.
82. Euseb. *Hist. eccl.* 8.1.7.
83. Euseb. *Hist. eccl.* 7.29–30. On the wider background to Paul, see Fergus Millar, 'Paul of Samosata, Zenobia and Aurelian: The church, local culture and political allegiances in third-century Syria', *JRS* 61 (1971), 52–83.
84. M. Frede, 'Celsus' attack on the Christians', in Jonathan Barnes and Miriam Griffin (eds), *Philosophia Togata* II, Oxford: Oxford University Press, 1997, 218–40 and, by the same author, 'Origen's response against Celsus', in M. Edwards, M. Goodman and S. Price (eds), *Apologetics in the Roman Empire*, Oxford: Oxford University Press, 1999, 131–56.
85. Accessibly analysed by T. D. Barnes, *Constantine and Eusebius*, Cambridge, MA: Harvard University Press,1981.
86. Lactant. *Div. inst.* 5.2.9 on the lectures. See E. dePalma Digeser, *The Making of a Christian Empire: Lactantius and Rome*, Ithaca, NY: Cornell University Press, 2000, 1–9.

intellectual jousting as endorsing – or, on the Christians' part, seeking to prevent – imperial persecution, at least as important was the longstanding habit of philosophical disputation among rival sects, with its tendency to distort and exaggerate differences of view, to the point where a competitor could be altogether discredited through argument and thus removed from contention.

Both in religious and in other terms, the 'long third century' arguably ended with Julian, the last emperor to seek to restore traditional cults. His failure was not due solely to the brevity of his reign or his early death in Persia; as we shall see, his philosophy was not shared by contemporaries, whether they were Christian or not. His failure therefore also marks how the cultural landscape had changed since the time of Diocletian, not suddenly or dramatically, but by a process of social and cultural evolution, expedited perhaps or even hindered by imperial interventions. For, despite the autocratic powers and visibly demonstrated supremacy of emperors, the process of successful government was carried out through constant communication and interaction between emperor and citizen.

CHAPTER 2

Four lords of the world, AD 284–311

From Diocletian's coup in 284 to Constantine's emergence as sole Augustus after his defeat of Licinius in 325, the Roman Empire was governed by a series of 'colleges' of emperors, who, in theory, co-operated together.[1] In fact, the extent of trust and co-operation between ambitious and assertive colleagues varied. The rule of the first college of four, in its fully fledged form from the promotion of Constantius and Galerius to the rank of Caesar in 293 to Diocletian and Maximian's abdication in 305, was a period of stability and apparent harmony.[2] However, the years that followed saw open competition between rival claimants, which Galerius, the senior Augustus after 306, was unable to control.

All emperors who lacked a dynastic connection with previous rulers and gained power by the sword were open to challenge from new aspirants to the purple. To avoid being represented as usurpers by the propagandists of their enemies, new emperors required more than military success. A narrative, therefore, of the successive experiments in collective rule between 284 and Galerius' death in 311 is not only about the means by which power was achieved and maintained but also about how its seizure was justified in the first place and how new emperors acted to legitimise their rule for the longer term. Among the techniques of legitimation was, as we shall see, the quick creation of victors' history by imperial propagandists. These would include not only official panegyricists but also, for Constantine's benefit, Christian writers. More conventionally,

1. For Diocletian's reign in general, see W. Kuhoff, *Diokletian und die Epoche der Tetrarchie*, Frankfurt: Peter Lang, 2001. R. Rees, *Diocletian and the Tetrarchy*, Edinburgh: Edinburgh University Press, 2004, is a lucid account with collection of sources in English. S. Williams, *Diocletian and the Roman Recovery*, London: Batsford, 1985, is now a little dated but readable. For pertinent observations on the drawbacks of the usual designation of Diocletian's college of four as the 'Tetrarchy', see Bill Leadbetter, *Galerius and the Will of Diocletian*, London: Routledge, 2009, 1–6.
2. Leadbetter, *Galerius*, 73 and n. 187. For *concordia* as dependent on respect for the patronage of the Augustus, ibid., 183–4.

dynasties were created – and rival imperial claimants eliminated – by the use of intermarriage and the summary execution of rivals. While arranged dynastic marriage was not new, imperial women experienced a remarkable degree of brutality both physical and emotional, from the summary executions of Galerius' womenfolk by Licinius in 313 down to the mysterious disappearance of the Augusta Maxima Fausta in 326 and the killing of Constantine's half-sister Eutropia at Rome in 350.[3]

Diocletian and the 'college' of four, 285–305

On 21 July 285, soon after his defeat of the Augustus in post, Carinus, at the Margus[4] and a mere eight months after his proclamation by the eastern army, Diocletian raised a fellow soldier, M. Aurelius Valerius Maximianus, to the rank of Caesar. A year later, probably in the following April, Maximian was promoted to the rank of Augustus.[5] His 'junior' status was affirmed through the divine affiliations adopted by the pair: Diocletian associated himself with Jupiter, the king of the gods, as Iovius, while Maximian adopted the divine identity of Hercules, the son of Jupiter and labourer for the benefit of mankind.[6] Seven years after this, in 293, two further generals were jointly elevated to the rank of Caesar, and each was attached to one of the Augusti.[7] Galerius (C. Galerius Valerius Maximianus) assisted Diocletian in the east and Constantius I, later nicknamed 'Chlorus', 'the Pale' (M. Flavius Valerius Constantius), provided much-needed support to Maximian in the west.

Diocletian moved swiftly to consolidate his position through a combination of black propaganda and the conciliation of former

3. See below, p. 258.
4. Aur. Vict. *Caes.* 39. 11 alleges that Carinus was in fact winning, but was killed by his own men, because he had seduced their wives. Defeated would-be emperors were routinely accused of sexual depravity.
5. Aur. Vict. *Caes.* 39.17; *Epit. De Caes.* 40., Kuhoff, *Diokletian*, 17–35. Bill Leadbetter, '*Patrimonium indivisum*? The empire of Diocletian and Maximian', *Chiron* 28 (1998), 213–28.
6. *Pan. Lat.* 10 (2).13.3; Lactant. *De mort. pers.* 52.3; Kuhoff, *Diokletian*, 40–55; R. Rees, 'The emperors' new names: Diocletian Jovius and Maximian Herculius', in H. Bowden and L. Rawlings (eds), *Herakles and Hercules: Exploring a Graceo-Roman Divinity*, Swansea: University of Wales Press, 2005, 223–40; Leadbetter, *Galerius*, 26–48.
7. For the role of the Caesars as both colleagues and servants, see Leadbetter, *Galerius*, 67–72.

supporters of the previous emperors. His first priority was to discredit the previous Augusti, Carinus and his father Carus. In both Aurelius Victor and Eutropius,[8] the story is told that Carus was killed by lightning, while campaigning in Persia; clearly Carus was no favourite with the gods. Carinus fared no better. Although on the verge of victory at the Margus, he was allegedly killed by his own men.[9] Diocletian was distanced from direct responsibility for the death of Carinus, as he was also from Carinus' brother and fellow Augustus, Numerian, whose mysterious demise was blamed publicly on the praetorian prefect Aper.[10]

Establishing continuity from previous regimes required a different and less obvious mode of operation. Diocletian was quick to enlist the services of prominent senatorial supporters of Carus and Carinus. He shared his first consulship with a senatorial member of Numerian's entourage, L. Caesonius Ovinius Manlius Rufinianus Bassus, whom he later installed as his prefect of the city of Rome.[11] Bassus' successor as prefect was Numerian's former prefect of Egypt, Pomponius Ianuarianus.[12] The most notable new adherent was Ti. Claudius Aurelius Aristobulus, who had been consul with Carinus in early 285; he was continued in his office and went on to be proconsul of Africa in 290–4, and prefect of Rome in 295.[13] The connection of all three favoured notables with the senate and with Rome illustrates Diocletian's concern that the Eternal City should be in safe and experienced hands, while he and his colleagues were occupied elsewhere. Remote though it was from the action on the frontiers, control of Rome remained essential for the perceived legitimacy of emperors.

Where Diocletian differed from precedent was that in 285 he selected a colleague who was not even distantly related to him. Diocletian had no son, either natural or adopted. His swift choice of Maximian as an associate but not as a 'son', while it showed confidence in his loyalty as well as his abilities, may also have been a response to the urgency of the crisis evolving in the west. Gaul was

8. Aur. Vict. *Caes.* 38; Eutr. *Brev.* 9.18.
9. Aur. Vict. *Caes.* 39; Eutr. *Brev.* 9.19; cf. *Epit. de Caes.* 38.7; SHA *Carus* 182; Zos. 1.73.3.
10. Aur. Vict. *Caes.* 39.15; Eutr. *Brev.* 9.20; SHA *Carus*, 7.1; 12.2–13.2.
11. *PLRE I*, L. Caesonius Ovinius Manlius Rufianus Bassus 18, pp. 156–7. For a survey of all the prefects, T. D. Barnes, *The New Empire of Diocletian and Constantine*, Cambridge, MA: Harvard University Press, 1982, 110–22.
12. *PLRE I*, Pomponius Ianuarianus 2, pp. 452–3.
13. *PLRE I*, Ti. Claudius Aurelius Aristobulus, p. 106.

in the grip of an uprising of Bagaudae, led by a would-be emperor, Amandus, whose coinage referred to him as 'Aug(ustus)', and Aelianus;[14] Aurelian had suppressed the last 'Gallic Empire' a little more than a decade before and a repetition of the Gallic secession was unthinkable. In addition, the Channel coasts were threatened by Frankish and Saxon pirates, while the Burgundians, Alamanni and other tribes were massing on the far side of the Rhine. While the choice of Maximian initially appeared to be a good one, as both Bagaudae and the raiders from across the Rhine were soundly defeated in 285, Diocletian's enforced reliance on appointment posed problems for the future.

Maximian's problems did not end with his victories in 285. He had delegated the problem of the pirate fleets to another subordinate, Carausius. After successfully constructing a fleet and neutralising the pirates, Carausius allegedly took some of the recovered plunder for himself, then, fearing the anger of Maximian, resorted to open revolt, winning over two legions and seizing control of Britain and northwestern Gaul.[15] As Carausius may have anticipated, a combination of threats elsewhere and his own control of the Channel crossing allowed his rule to continue undisturbed for several years. This de facto recognition encouraged later historians – and perhaps Carausius' subjects at the time – to believe that he had been left in command as a matter of policy:

> And Carausius was allowed to retain his sovereignty over the island (of Britain), after he had been judged quite competent to command and defend its inhabitants against warlike tribes.[16]

Belief among his subjects in Carausius' legitimacy would have been reinforced after 289 by his coinage slogan celebrating the 'peace' (*pax*) of the 'three' Augusti and featuring conjoined busts of the 'brothers', Diocletian, Maximian and himself.[17] This was never the official view of Diocletian or Maximian, who would have feared that toleration of one pretender would result in more outbreaks elsewhere; the official line taken confidently but erroneously in 289

14. *RIC* 5.2.595; Aur. Vict. *Caes.* 39.17; Eutr. *Brev.* 9.20.3.
15. Aur. Vict. *Caes.* 39.20; Eutr. *Brev.* 9. 21; Kuhoff, *Diokletian*, 65–71; 155–62; Barnes, *New Empire*, 10–11; 57 (Maximian); 60 (Constantius); P. J. Casey, 'Carausius and Allectus: Rulers in Gaul?', *Britannia* 8 (1977), 283–301.
16. Aur. Vict. *Caes.* 39.20. Victor may report the tradition of the now lost *Kaisergeschichte*, or *History of the Caesars*, also used by Eutropius.
17. *RIC* 5.2.550.

by the Gallic panegyricist of Maximian was that Carausius would shortly be annihilated.[18] The two perceptions, that Carausius was a 'usurper', because not recognised by the imperial college, and that he was 'acceptable' (therefore recognised by the others) because 'allowed' to continue, were in fact irreconcilable. The divergence illustrates the confusions that could arise from the dominance, however temporary, of regional warlords who were effectively in command, and whose lack of recognition by the central emperors made no difference to acceptance of their rule as legitimate on the part of those they governed.

Little is known for certain of Carausius' government of Britain and northwest Gaul. Our knowledge is heavily dependent on interpretation of his coinage and the disputed dating of the forts of the Saxon shore, which were probably the creation of Probus, not Carausius. Carausius' issue of a strong silver coinage with a high metal content should have ensured army loyalty and doubtless made him popular with the traders of London and Colchester as well.[19] His control extended as far north as the Tyne and Solway, but he may have concentrated his attention and resources on the southeast of Britain in order to confront the twin threats of the Franks, with whom he successfully negotiated, and Maximian. In the view of Stephen Johnson,[20] the system of forts along the British side of the Saxon shore command was pre-Carausian and designed as protection for harbours and against raids from the sea, not as defended frontier positions, or refuges for the local population. On this interpretation, Carausius' strategy was not to rely on the forts but to pre-empt a landing by Maximian's fleet by defeating him at sea, as he did, in 289. Carausius in fact controlled the Channel down to his loss of his bridgehead into mainland Europe at Boulogne in 293; he also probably minted coins at Rouen.

Maximian's failure in 289 allowed Carausius a further four years of rule and opened the way for the rise of a new general, Constantius, who was married to Maximian's daughter, Theodora,

18. *Pan. Lat.* 10 (2).11–12.
19. On Carausius and his coinage, see N. Shiel, *The Episode of Carausius and Allectus*, Oxford: British Archaeological Reports 40, 1977. On the two British rulers in general, see P. J. Casey, *Carausius and Allectus: The British Usurpers*, London: Batsford, 1994. For briefer narrative, Williams, *Diocletian*, 71–4.
20. S. Johnson, *The Roman Forts of the Saxon Shore*, 2nd edn, London: Elek, 1976, 103–13.

probably also in 289.[21] In 293, Constantius recovered Boulogne[22] and was proclaimed Caesar; within weeks, Carausius was murdered by Allectus, who held out in his turn for a further three years, till the rebellion was finally crushed in 296.[23] The triumphal entry of Constantius into London was celebrated on a gold medallion, preserved in the Beaurains (Arras) collection,[24] which depicted the emperor on horseback receiving the surrender of the suppliant figure of London while below, in the foreground, his ship sailed up the Thames. In celebrating Constantius' victory, a further Gallic panegyricist sought to isolate Allectus, who had been killed in the battle, and his followers, depicting them as 'barbarian' and un-Roman, rather than as the losers in a civil war:[25]

> Almost no Roman died in this victory of the Roman Empire. (4) ... The bodies of these barbarians, or those who lately imitated the barbarian in their mode of dress and flowing red hair, now lay befouled with dust and blood ... And among them lay the brigands' standard-bearer.

Carausius, however, although a Menapian, was in fact in Roman service when he revolted, and his elevation reflected the continuing ability on the part of local leaders on the geographical periphery to exploit the weakness of ties with emperors who were often distant and remote. His and Allectus' *imperium Britanniarum* ('British Empire') had lasted ten years, despite the best efforts of Maximian and Constantius, and had a lasting effect on the wider history of the empire. For Carausius' self-proclamation as Augustus in 286 destabilised the accord established so recently by Diocletian and Maximian, and Maximian's spectacular failure to make any headway against him opened the way for Constantius, formerly governor of Dalmatia under Carus[26] and already successful against the

---

21. For the early career of Constantius I, see T. D. Barnes' full discussion of the evidence, *Constantine: Dynasty, Religion and Power in the Later Roman Empire*, Oxford: Wiley-Blackwell, 2011, ch. 2.
22. *Pan. Lat.* 8 (4).6.1–4.
23. *Pan. Lat.* 8 (4).14–19; Aur. Vict. *Caes.* 39.40–2; Eutr. *Brev.* 9.22; Oros. 7.25.6.
24. See R. Abdy, 'In the pay of the emperor: Coins from the Beaurains (Arras) Treasure', in E. Hartley, J. Hawkes, M. Henig and F. Mee (eds), *Constantine the Great: York's Roman Emperor*, York: York Museums and Galleries Trust, 2006, 52–8.
25. *Pan. Lat.* 8 (4).16, 3–4; C. E. V. Nixon and B. S. Rodgers (eds and trans.), *In Praise of Later Roman Emperors: The Panegyrici Latini. Introduction, Translation and Historical Commentary*, Berkeley: University of California Press, 1994, 137.
26. SHA *Carus* 17.6, supported by Anon. Vales. 1.2.

Alamanni,[27] not only to show his mettle but also to establish his indispensability to the imperial order. Already married to Maximian's daughter, for whom he had abandoned his first wife, Helena, the mother of Constantine, Constantius' claim to the position of Caesar and thus putative successor would have been hard to resist.[28] Diocletian in his turn appointed a younger man, Galerius, and married him to his daughter Valeria.[29]

Moderns give to this gang of four the label 'Tetrarchy',[30] and much was made at the time of the significance of the number 'four', as it reflected the cosmic order of the four elements, the four seasons and so on.[31] How far Diocletian planned in advance, consciously innovated or even was himself the prisoner of events is open to question. The idea of collegiate rule itself was not new. In the first century, Vespasian had ruled with his son Titus as Caesar; Marcus Aurelius and Lucius Verus, later known as the 'deified brothers' (*divi fratres*), were joint Augusti, and for the last four years of his life (176–80), Marcus shared the title with his son and designated heir, Commodus. Septimius Severus in his turn elevated Caracalla to the rank of Augustus after his Parthian victory in 198, thus securing the succession for his new regime. The decades prior to Diocletian had seen the joint rule of Valerian and his son Gallienus down to 260 and the short-lived college of Carus' sons, Carinus and Numerian. The reasons for the formation of the earlier colleges were, as a rule, the need to establish the permanence of an insecure dynasty. In the third century, the ability of joint, and related, rulers to serve personally with more than one army assisted loyalty and (in theory) inhibited rebellion. The sharing of power with a family member had the further attraction of excluding potential rivals from access to

27. *Pan. Lat.* 8 (4).2.1.
28. Barnes, *New Empire*, 125–6. Their six children would include Julius Constantius, father to the Caesar Gallus and the emperor Julian. The sources that date the marriage to 293 to coincide with Constantius' elevation, e.g. Aur. Vict. *Caes.* 39.24–5 and Eutr. *Brev.* 9.22, tend to telescope events. For the family relationships involved, see Bill Leadbetter, 'The illegitimacy of Constantine and the birth of the Tetrarchy', in S. Lieu and D. Montserrat (eds), *Constantine: History, Historiography and Legend*, London: Routledge, 1998, 71–85; Barnes, *Constantine*, ch. 3.
29. Williams, *Diocletian*, 61–70, and Rees, *Dioletian*, 5–8, are useful basic narratives of the formation of the Tetrarchy.
30. For discussion of the terms 'new empire' and 'Tetrarchy', the latter in use from c. 1870 and given wider currency by Otto Seeck in 1897, see Leadbetter, *Galerius*, 2–6.
31. *Pan. Lat.* 8 (4).4.2.

military commands. As Bill Leadbetter put it, 'they kept power in the family by enlarging the family'.[32]

In retrospect, the proclamation of Constantius and Galerius as Caesars in 293 appears the result of consensus, a sensible move to improve the efficiency of government by extending the principle of imperial rule. But the rise of Constantius may not have been welcome to Maximian, simply on dynastic grounds. Already in 289, Maximian's panegyricist had celebrated (with tacit official approval) the presence of the putative heir, Maximian's son Maxentius,[33] yet Constantius' promotion as Caesar placed him (and by extension his son Constantine) in the position of immediate western successor, leaving Maxentius' status in doubt. In the east, the situation was less obviously problematic. Diocletian had no son to complicate the succession and his choice of Caesar, Galerius, though not yet as obviously indispensable as Constantius, was married to Diocletian's daughter and was a tried and tested military man. How far his elevation was Diocletian's enforced response to Maximian's initiative is unknown.[34]

Whatever the private tensions between them, the public face of the four was one of unity and harmony.[35] A tradition recorded by Aurelius Victor recalled their shared training in war under Aurelian and Probus and that they looked up to Diocletian as a 'father', a figure of all-powerful but also benign authority. This shared military experience allowed the fabrication of continuity with past emperors not reflected in dynastic realities. Repeatedly, the relationship of the four is described in familial terms, precisely because they were not related; Diocletian and Maximian were 'brothers in virtue, which is a stronger bond than any tie of blood'.[36] In seeking to compensate for the lack of family ties between the four, the panegyricists protest too much; the college of four was an effective political arrangement but it risked lacking dynastic stability in the longer term, and provided a target for at least one critic to claim that the arrangement, which entailed four separate courts and military establish-

32. Leadbetter, *Galerius*, 6.
33. *Pan. Lat.* 10 (2).14.1.
34. For the view that there was conflict within the four, see I. König, 'Die Berufung des Constantius Chlorus under des Galerius zu Caesaren: Gedanken zur Entstehung des ersten Tetrarchie', *Chiron* 4 (1974), 567–76.
35. R. Rees, 'Images and image: A re-examination of tetrarchic iconography', *Greece and Rome* 40 (1993), 181–200.
36. *Pan. Lat.* 10 (2).9.3.

ments, was expensive and thus an excessive burden on the taxpayer.[37]

Diocletian and the north

How serious a threat did the Germanic peoples pose to the security of the Roman Empire? The threat from the non-Roman peoples on the northern European frontiers was real, in the sense that 'barbarian' incursions, if left unchecked, caused substantial damage and disruption to local economic activity but although locally traumatic, the repeated third-century 'invasions' had not resulted in substantial loss of territory.[38] The main exceptions were Dacia, abandoned by Aurelian in 271, and the Agri Decumates, between the Rhine and Danube sources, an area which was gradually settled by the Alamanni after garrisons were withdrawn by the Gallic emperor, Postumus. In both cases, the Romans had considered further investment in their defence unprofitable. But the constant cycle of campaigns can also be explained in terms of internal priorities. While it is perhaps an overstatement to view the threat from the Germanic peoples merely as an 'artefact',[39] emperors did exploit their restless neighbours for their own ends. Proof of effective military leadership, as shown in repeated 'victories' celebrated in public speeches, coins, milestones and various forms of artwork, and in public processions, advertised to both armies and civilian Romans that the emperors were effective defenders of their security.[40] Victory was also a demonstration of divine favour, a further proof of the victorious general's 'right' to govern.

If some campaigns were the product of imperial trophy-seeking, nonetheless the military threat posed to security and stability in the

37. Lactant. *De mort. pers.* 7.2 argued that the requirements of the four emperors for excessively large armies damaged the economy. However, only the two Augusti, at this stage, had praetorian prefects; see Leadbetter, *Galerius*, 72.

38. For accessible general survey, see M. Kulikowski, 'Constantine and the northern barbarians', in Noel Lenski (ed.), *Cambridge Companion to the Age of Constantine*, Cambridge: Cambridge University Press, 2006, 347–76.

39. J. F. Drinkwater, 'The Germanic threat on the Rhine frontier: A Romano-Gallic artefact?' in R. Mathisen and H. Sivan (eds), *Shifting Frontiers in Late Antiquity*, Aldershot: Variorum, 1996, 20–30.

40. See M. McCormick, *Eternal Victory: Triumphal Renewal in Late Antiquity, Byzantium and the Early Mediaeval West.* Cambridge: Cambridge University Press, 1986; A. D. Lee, *War in Late Antiquity: A Social History*, Oxford: Blackwell, 2007, 37–50.

frontier zones by raids into Roman territory was far greater than it
had been in the first century. The northern 'barbarians' seem to have
learned from their Roman neighbours. Their settlements became
larger, their agriculture more developed and their societies perhaps
more hierarchical, with a greater concentration of wealth, and of
patronage exercised through redistribution of wealth, in the hands of
a powerful few. Both the Alamanni ('all men') and the Franks were
confederacies of previous smaller groupings: according to Gregory
of Tours in the sixth century, following the earlier historian Sulpicius
Alexander, the Frankish groupings were formed from the Bructeri,
Chamavi, Amisavii and Chatti.[41] The Goths too, a confederation of
peoples, whose apparent ethnic unity may have been imposed on
them by Roman misconceptions, created new relationships among
themselves in response to the Roman example.[42] Although in
general unable to defeat Roman armies in direct confrontations,
their increased numbers, improved co-ordination and ability to learn
new military skills from the Romans themselves all supported the
impression that the threat from the northern peoples was real and
required constant containment.

The northern peoples regularly exploited the accession of new
emperors, partly because of the general uncertainty created by a new
ruler, but perhaps also because such treaties as existed tended to be
made between individuals and to require renewal or renegotiation
when one or other party died. After 284, Diocletian and Maximian
faced simultaneous threats on the Rhine, from a combination of
Alamanni, Burgundians, Chaibones and Heruli; on the Danube,
from the Sarmatians; and on the 'Saxon shore' from Franks and
Saxons. All were, in due course, defeated, but at the cost of the
usurpation in 286 of Carausius, the commander against the Franks
and Saxons in Britain. Since the establishing of joint rule, Diocletian,
like Maximian, had been an active campaigner, defeating the Sarmatians on the Danube later in 285. In 288, he assisted Maximian in
Germany, where he won the title Germanicus,[43] but in 289 he was

---

41. Gregory of Tours, *History of the Franks* 2.9. See also *Pan. Lat.* 8 (5).18.3; Zos. *New
History*, 1.71.2; T. D. Barnes, 'The Franci before Diocletian', in G. Bonamente and
F. Paschoud (eds), *Historia Augusta Colloquium Genavense* 2 (1996), 11–18.
42. On Gothic origins, see Peter Heather and John Matthews, *The Goths in the Fourth
Century*, TTH 11, Liverpool: Liverpool University Press, 1991, chs 1 and 2; Michael
Kulikowksi, *Rome's Gothic Wars*, Cambridge: Cambridge University Press, 2007,
34–99.
43. See Dessau, *ILS* 618 of 290, a dedication from Septimius Valentio, governor of
Rhaetia, to Diocletian as 'most far-sighted emperor, leader of the world and master,

again on the Danube[44] and in 290 he returned to Syria, before moving back westwards to confer with Maximian at Milan towards the end of the year. This pattern of long journeys to advertise the imperial concern for all parts of the empire continued after Galerius' elevation as Caesar. Both Galerius in 293–4 and Diocletian himself in 298 made personal visits to Egypt, on each occasion to suppress rebellion. The second emergency was the more serious, as it involved a revolt by a local official, L. Domitius Domitianus, who proclaimed himself Augustus, advertising that fact on his coinage; he was supported by his most prominent aide, Achilleus, whom some sources credit with being the real leader of the revolt.[45]

Galerius and Persia

In 287, Diocletian reached a successful settlement with Persia[46] and established a Roman client king, Tiridates (Trdat) III, on the throne of Armenia; by 290, his success was commemorated with the title Persicus Maximus. It was Galerius, however, the junior Caesar in 293, and far the youngest of the four emperors, who would ultimately achieve the most spectacular military success.

The political geography of the wide swath of disputed lands between the ancient empires of Persia and Rome was complex. The populations spoke a multitude of languages, including Greek, Aramaic, Syriac and Arabic, and trade routes for exotic products extended through the region, connecting the Mediterranean lands to the Silk Road, China and India. Local rulers adopted complex strategies to maintain their positions between the two great powers: in the 260s Palmyra under Odanaethus and, after his assassination in 267, Zenobia sought to carve out an independent kingdom, an attempt quashed by Aurelian in 272. By the time of Constantine a

founder of everlasting peace … unconquered Augustus, *pontifex maximus*, greatest conqueror of Germany, greatest conqueror of Persia'.

44. Aur. Vict. *Caes.* 39; *Consularia Constantinopolitana* s.a. 294, 295, 299; *Pan. Lat.* 8 (5).5.1; 18.5.

45. Williams, *Diocletian*, 79–81. For chronology, see J. D. Thomas, 'The date of the revolt of L. Domitius Domitianus', *ZPE* 22 (1976), 253–79, and by the same author, 'A family dispute from Karanis and the revolt of L. Domitius Domitianus', *ZPE* 24 (1977), 233–40.

46. *Pan. Lat.* 10 (2) 7.5 (Persia voluntarily submits to Diocletian); 10 (2).9.2 (Diocletian displays the booty from Persia to Maximian); 10(2) 10.6 ('submission' of the Great King, Bahram II, with rich gifts, including 'very beautiful' wild animals, and offers of hospitality).

newly powerful Arab kingdom had probably begun to emerge under the leadership of the shadowy Imru' al-Qays, whose funerary inscription, dated to 328, was discovered at Namara, about 120 km southeast of Damascus.[47] In the fourth century, they made themselves felt as a military presence in Roman campaigns in the east, and a bishop of the Arabs attended the Council of Nicaea in 325.

In the far south, on the African side of the Red Sea, the empire of Aksum (modern Ethiopia) mattered to Rome because of its position on the trade route to India. Its ruler's conversion to Christianity in the reign of Constantine or his successor perhaps reflects an eagerness to strengthen cultural ties with Rome, in the hope of keeping the Persians at bay.[48] To the north, the frontier kingdom of Armenia continued to be a source of diplomatic (and occasionally military) confrontation, as both the Sasanians and the Romans sought control, through appointment and support of puppet rulers. As in Aksum, a statement of religious affiliation on the part of the king could be used to reinforce political allegiance. Thus the long-lived Tiridates III lived in exile under Roman protection after his expulsion by Shapur I from Armenia in 252 until his restoration by Diocletian. Converting to Christianity early in the fourth century, in 325 Tiridates cemented his alliance with his co-religionist Constantine; one consequence was that Greater Armenia was represented by its bishop at the Council of Nicaea. A similar strategy, which combined religious with political choices, may also have been taken by the rulers of Iberia, to the east of the Black Sea, who adopted Christianity perhaps in conjunction with a formal political alliance and thereby encouraged the furthering of Roman influence, at the expense of Persia, in the Transcaucasian regions.[49]

Roman military confrontation with Persia should therefore be viewed in the context of the strategies of the smaller regional players, caught between the two empires and seeking to enhance their own security and prosperity. Considerations of prestige in the eyes of their allies as well as subjects mattered for both empires, as

47. Jan Retsö, *The Arabs in Antiquity: Their History from the Assyrians to the Ummayads*, London: Routledge, 2002, 467–85; I. Shahid, 'Byzantium and the Arabs during the reign of Constantine: The Namara inscription, an Arabic *Monumentum Ancyranum*', *Byzantinische Forschungen* 26 (2000), 73–124.
48. See also Stuart Munro-Hay, *Aksum: An African Civilisation of Late Antiquity*, Edinburgh: Edinburgh University Press, 1991, 189–91, for alignment of Aksum gold coinage with Roman standards.
49. Rufinus, *Hist. eccl.* 10.11; for mention of a political alliance see Socrates, *Hist. eccl.* 1.20.11; Sozom. *Hist. eccl.* 2.7.12.

they manoeuvred for advantage. Roman policy was influenced by two figures from the past. One was Alexander the Great, whose exploits many an emperor sought to emulate; Constantine recalled how in youth he had visited Babylon, where Alexander died.[50] The second, less auspicious, precedent was that of Valerian, ignominiously defeated and captured in 260. Legend had it that, when that emperor finally died of old age in Persian custody, his skin was flayed off and carefully preserved, an insult the Romans neither forgot nor forgave.[51] For their part, the Persian kings too, despite their rhetoric about restoring the ancient glories of Cyrus and Darius, seem to have been primarily interested in countering perceived threats from Rome by pre-emptive strikes where possible, thus achieving prestigious victories to enhance their position at home.[52]

It was thus in the hope of reviving the glories of Shapur I that Narses launched his unexpected invasion of the Roman Empire in 296. After a holding action in 297, which prevented the Persians from advancing further but was seen at the time as a defeat,[53] Galerius returned in force the following year, and launched a surprise attack on the Persian army. The family of Narses was captured and his forces crushed. The result of negotiations conducted for the Romans by one Sicorius Probus was a treaty which established Roman dominance along the whole length of the frontier. The provisions of the treaty were preserved by a sixth-century writer:[54]

> that in the eastern region the Romans shall have Intelene, along with Sophene and Arzanene, along with Cordyene and Zabicene; that the river Tigris should be the boundary between each state; that the fortress Zintha, which lies on the borders of Media, should mark the edge of Armenia; that the king of Iberia should pay to the Romans

50. *Orat. ad Sanct*, 16.4, drawing the lesson from Babylon and Memphis that all earthly empires pass.
51. Cf. the vengeful recollection of Valerian ascribed to Galerius in 298 by the sixth-century writer Petrus Patricius, frag. 13, *FHG* 4, 188–8, trans. J. M. Lieu, in M. H. Dodgeon and S. N. C. Lieu, *The Roman Eastern Frontier and the Persian Wars AD 226–363: A Documentary History*, London: Routledge, 1991, 131–2.
52. For mutual suspicion, see A. D. Lee, *Information and Frontiers: Roman Foreign Relations in Late Antiquity*, Cambridge: Cambridge University Press, 1993, 21–5; R. C. Blockley, *East Roman Foreign Policy: Formation and Conduct from Diocletian to Anastasius*. ARCA 30, Leeds: Francis Cairns, 1992, 102.
53. Julian, *Or.* 1.18a–b; Aur. Vict. *Caes.* 39.34; Festus, *Breviarium* 25; Eutr. *Brev.* 9.24. For an account of Galerius' tactics in 297–8, see Leadbetter, *Galerius*, 89–96.
54. Petrus Patricius frag.14, trans. Lieu, 133.

the insignia of his kingdom; and that the city of Nisibis, which is on the Tigris, should be the place for transactions.

The settlement represented a total victory for Roman war aims and its subversion became the main goal for subsequent Persian military policy. The ceding of the five satrapies in the 'eastern region' gave Rome a position of dominance in the regions of the upper Tigris and Transcaucasia. The recognition of the Tigris frontier gave Rome influence in regions beyond the river; and Roman control of Nisibis allowed greater control not only of trade but also of the far less visible traffic in spies.[55] Nisibis was also a potent symbol of imperial one-upmanship, as demonstrated by the scenes of distress on its return to Persia in the aftermath of Julian's death in 363.[56] The settlement following the victory, which confirmed Galerius' conquests as part of the Roman Empire, stabilised that uneasy frontier for the next thirty years.

Building to last

The ambition of all powerful Romans was to leave some lasting memorial behind them. The most durable expression of imperial power and patronage was the shaping of the physical profile of cities through buildings and monuments. Augustus' famous dictum that he found Rome built of brick and left it clothed in marble shaped the aspirations of his more fortunate or effective successors – those, that is, who reigned long enough to put large-scale building projects into effect. But when a new owner took over the buildings of a disgraced predecessor, one demonstration of supremacy was to nullify even that form of memorial; as we shall see, this would be the fate of Maxentius' buildings at Rome. Building, therefore, was a part of the power game among men who sought not only to rule themselves but also to control the record thereafter.

The 'greatness' of emperors was mirrored in the size and splendour of their monumental structures: in the world of Diocletian and Constantine, there was no place for understatement. The significance, both actual and symbolic, of buildings, pictures and sculptures was expounded by those who dealt in words, whether orally in speeches or in other forms of literary production.

55. On spies and 'informal channels' for information, Lee, *Information and Frontiers*, 161–82.
56. Amm. Marc. 25.7–9.

Conversely, the perceived public actions of an emperor, in public procession or audience chamber, addressing the troops or distributing largess to the people, were commemorated and their meaning elaborated through their representations in coinage, in stone and in other monumental forms. Imperial statues, for example, were set up all over the Roman Empire and it was expected that respect should be accorded to them, equivalent to that due to the emperor in person. To damage an imperial statue deliberately was treasonable, as the statue, in a sense, represented the person and presence of the emperor himself.

Though far from the action on the frontiers, the city of Rome remained a focus of attention for the Tetrarchs, as it would also be for Constantine. A year before Diocletian's accession, in the reign of Carinus, a great fire at Rome had destroyed much of the Forum and surrounding areas. This disaster was also an opportunity for the new emperors, who responded by remodelling the Forum along traditional lines, rebuilding the senate house or *curia*, and constructing a new Rostra at the eastern end, adorned by five ceremonial pillars.[57] After his return from Africa in 298, Maximian went further, buying up land in the residential areas of the Viminal and Quirinal on which to erect a large bathing complex, to be named after his 'brother' Diocletian. To this end, the aqueducts were cleaned out and renewed,[58] and the Aqua Marcia, which fed the cistern for the baths, was renamed the Aqua Iovia, to remind the Romans of their benefactor in perpetuity. The baths themselves were a huge structure, comprising not only the bathing complex (hot, tepid and cold pools) but also areas for sport (the palaestra) and recreation. Rooms, the purpose of which can only be guessed at, may have provided space for public lectures and a library; the mischievous late fourth-century author of the Historia Augusta suggested that Rome's main book collection had been moved from the Library of Trajan to the Baths of Diocletian.[59] It was ironic that, despite his public generosity, Diocletian was not personally at ease in Rome; allegedly, he cut short

57. F. Coarelli, 'L'edilizia pubblica a Roma in età tetrarchica', in W. V. Harris (ed.), *The Transformations of Urbs Roma in Late Antiquity*, JRA Supp. 33, 1999, 23–33; John Curran, *Pagan City and Christian Capital: Rome in the Fourth Century*, Oxford: Oxford University Press, 2000, 43–6. For a list of the tetrarchic structures, *Chron.* 354 = *MGH* 1, 148; besides the senate house are listed the Forum of Caesar, the Basilica Iulia, Theatre of Pompey, two porticoes, three nymphaea, two temples, the New Arch (Arcus Novus) and the Baths of Diocletian.
58. Dessau, *ILS* 626 = *CIL* 6.773.
59. SHA *Probus* 2. This is more likely to have been a late fourth-century in-joke.

his visit in 303, because he could not put up with the 'free speech' (*libertas*) traditionally granted the Roman plebs.[60]

With the exception of Maxentius, emperors now spent little time at Rome. Cities more often graced with their personal presence were the capitals close to the frontiers. In many of these, the emperors erected palaces, which varied in design but all contained features more often found in camps, such as fortress-type outer walls. While the plan of the Milan complex is lost, the plans of the palaces at Trier, the capital for the Rhine, Split, the retirement home of Diocletian, and Gamzigrad (Romuliana) on the Danube, the favoured city of Galerius along with Thessalonica,[61] are recoverable. They show the characteristic imperial concern for creating a visual impression and maintaining a sense of hierarchy; visitors and petitioners would pass through a maze of outer rooms before being admitted to the emperor's personal, yet public, space.[62] Like Augustus and Hadrian before them, Diocletian and Galerius both planned their own fates after death with the construction of mausolea: Diocletian's was an ornate octagonal structure with red granite and porphyry columns, carved friezes and a dome.[63]

The Arch of Galerius at Thessalonica provides a useful comparison with that of Constantine, dedicated in 315 at Rome, three years after his defeat of Maxentius, who had ruled as emperor at Rome from October 306. Both monuments were erected with an awareness of spatial context, that of Constantine close to the Colosseum and echoing the design of the Arch of Severus, Galerius' arch erected in c. 300 to commemorate his victory over the Persians, as part of his palace and mausoleum complex. Both also drew on a standard repertoire of triumphal imagery: battle scenes, sacrifice, entering conquered cities, and addressing the victorious troops (*adlocutio*). Galerius' sculptors supplied, in crowded detail, a narrative of the Caesar's achievements in Persia, with depictions of the Romans in battle, the cavalry charging with Galerius at its head, the fallen being trampled, the Persians in flight across the Tigris. Galerius in person

60. Lactant. *De mort. pers.* 17.1–2.
61. On Galerius' buildings at Romuliana, see D. Srejovic and C. Vasic, 'Emperor Galerius' buildings in Romuliana', *Antiquité Tardive* 2 (1994), 123–41.
62. Rees, *Diocletian* 47; plans, 183–4; John J. Wilkes, *Diocletian's Palace, Split: Residence of a Retired Roman Emperor*, Sheffield: Department of Ancient History and Classical Archaeology, 1986; E. Wightman, *Roman Trier and the Treveri*, London: Hart-Davis, 1970; D. Srejovic (ed.), *The Age of Tetrarchs*, Belgrade: Serbian Academy of Sciences and Arts, 1995.
63. On Diocletian's mausoleum at Split, see Wilkes, *Diocletian's Palace*, 46–52.

is seen having captured the Persian king's wives, including the queen, then in hand-to-hand combat with a Persian general, perhaps Narses himself (with the latter at a clear disadvantage). In victory, the emperor receives the submission of the Persian captives and their cities. The celebration of the individual victor is carefully modulated to include the Tetrarchy as a whole; Diocletian and Galerius sacrifice together and the four are pictured enthroned above a globe, receiving the submission of the provinces of Syria (for Persia) and Britain (for Carausius).[64] Moreover, the narrative and the more symbolic and abstract messages are intended to cohere: Galerius' victory, an expression of military might, was also proof of his imperial virtues – clemency, harmony, courage and piety – and the favour of the gods.[65]

The disputed succession, 305–11

On 1 May 305, Diocletian abdicated at Nicomedia. Simultaneously, but more reluctantly, Maximian stepped down at Milan. Both withdrew to their private residences, Diocletian to his fortified palace at Split near Salona in his native Dalmatia to 'grow cabbages',[66] and Maximian to Lucania. The reasons behind Diocletian's unprecedented action were, and are, debated. Most authors cite a combination of old age (Diocletian was about sixty years old) and illness, but Lactantius also provides a lengthy indictment of the pressure exerted by the arch-persecutor of Christians, Galerius.[67] Whatever the power plays behind the scenes, it was agreed that Diocletian's health had deteriorated. After celebrating his twenty years of rule (*vicennalia*) at Rome in 303, Diocletian had set out for Nicomedia but fell ill on the journey in 304 and nearly died. Although partially recovered by early 305, his narrow escape and the arguments of Galerius could have convinced him of the need to

64. On the globe symbolism, S. MacCormack, *Art and Ceremony in Late Antiquity*, Berkeley: University of California Press, 1981, 127–9.
65. For full description of the arch and photographs, see M. S. Pond Rothman, 'The thematic organisation of the panel reliefs on the Arch of Galerius', *AJArch.* 81 (1997), 427–54; also Kuhoff, *Diokletian*, 598–627.
66. *Epit. de Caes.* 39.5. On Diocletian's palace at modern Split in Croatia, see Wilkes, *Diocletian's Palace*.
67. Lactant. *De mort. pers.* 18. For doubts as to the reliability of Lactantius, see J. Rougé, 'L'abdication de Dioclétien et la proclamation des Césars: degré de fiabilité du récit de Lactance', in M. Christol (ed.), *Institutions, société et vie politique dans l'empire romain au IVe siècle ap. J.-C.*, Collection de l' Ecole Française de Rome 159, Rome: Ecole Française de Rome, 1989, 76–89; Leadbetter, *Galerius*, 118–55 (on the abdication narrative and Galerius' alleged role in the 'Great Persecution').

ensure a smooth transition of power. To this end, an assembly of the army was convened, to legitimise the public declaration of the succession, which would see the elevation of Galerius and Constantius as the two new Augusti and the nomination of two new Caesars:[68]

> An assembly of the soldiers was summoned, at which the old man addressed the soldiers in tears: he was not a well man (he said), he sought rest after his labours and he now handed over the imperial rule to men in better health than he, and appointed other Caesars to succeed them.

But, according to Lactantius, who may have been an eyewitness, a shock was in store. When all expected the young Constantine, who was present, to be named as Caesar to his father Constantius, now Augustus, Diocletian instead announced the appointment as Caesars of Galerius' longstanding friend Severus, an experienced soldier who had served in Pannonia, and his nephew, Maximinus, known as Daia or Daza. 'All', observed Lactantius, 'were struck dumb by amazement.'[69]

As an enthusiast for the future Christian Constantine, Lactantius might be expected to overdo the expectations for his future. Yet he may also be right. If the army was indeed shocked that Constantine, the son and heir of the new Augustus – and perhaps also Maxentius, son of the former Augustus and son-in-law of Galerius himself – had been passed over for cronies of Galerius, it was because Roman soldiers expected that sons should inherit *imperium* (rulership of the empire) from their fathers, when such sons were available. The precedent set by Diocletian was in line with the succession practices of the Antonine emperors in the second century and acted as a reminder that appointments were also acceptable. But Trajan, Hadrian and Antoninus Pius had had no sons of their own – unlike Maximian, the father of Maxentius, and Constantius I, the father of Constantine. The situation was not improved by the fact that Galerius' appointments were made without advance publicity, which could have justified his choice and dispelled any impression that the new men owed their promotion to their personal connections with him. The reaction of Constantine to Galerius' coup was swift: hotly pursued by Galerius' agents (we are told), he fled across Europe to

68. Lactant. *De mort. pers.* 19.3.
69. Lactant. *De mort. pers.* 19.4. For a distinctive interpretation of these events, see Leadbetter, *Galerius*, 114–55.

join his sick father, riding the horses of the *cursus publicus* (public post) so hard that they fell dead.[70] Soon after his arrival, Constantius I Augustus died and, on 25 July 306, Constantine was proclaimed as his successor by the army of Britain at York.[71]

Constantine had no intention of going the way of previous British 'usurpers'. When Galerius elevated the Caesar Severus to the rank of Augustus, in succession to Constantius, he offered the title of Caesar to Constantine, who accepted it. The situation was unstable and both played for time. Then, in October 306, the other forgotten heir, Maximian's son Maxentius, whose pretensions were supported by his marriage to Galerius' daughter Valeria Maximilla, was proclaimed Augustus by the senate and a perhaps disaffected praetorian guard at Rome,[72] supported by the people.[73] Maxentius' appeal was not only his imperial father but also his willingness to support the Romans in their resistance to proposals from Galerius to remove tax exemptions from Rome and the neighbouring regions of Italy. He further enhanced his dynastic credentials by recalling from retirement and reinstating his old father, Maximian. His initial ambition was to be recognised by his father-in-law, perhaps by his replacing Maximinus Daza or the Augustus Severus. For Galerius and Severus, however, this unilateral expansion of the imperial college was unacceptable and they turned to armed force to suppress the dissidents. Briefly, Italy became the scene of civil war. Severus besieged Rome unsuccessfully early in 307 and was later defeated, captured and, after an interval of imprisonment, executed. In the same year, Galerius arrived in Italy with reinforcements too late and was forced to withdraw.[74] His loss of control of 'his' college was now plain to see.

Throughout this period of turbulence, Constantine remained largely aloof, emphasising on his coinage his friendly relations with other emperors, including Maxentius, and his connection with his popular father.[75] Correctly anticipating that Galerius and Severus

---

70. Lactant. *De mort. pers.* 24.2–8; Aur. Vict. *Caes.* 40.2. Also Euseb. *Vit. Const.* 1.19–21, where Constantine's flight is compared to that of Moses in Egypt.
71. For projection of dynasty of Constantius I, see Averil Cameron, 'Constantius and Constantine: An exercise in publicity', in Hartley et al., *Constantine the Great*, 18–30.
72. Aur. Vict. *Caes.* 39.47.
73. Leadbetter, *Galerius*, 178–81. Maxentius was still married to Valeria Maximilla, daughter of Galerius, and had a son by her. Galerius' opposition to Maxentius was therefore contrary to the dynastic interest of his grandson.
74. Lactant. *De mort. pers.* 27; Leadbetter, *Galerius*, 188–9, 192–7.
75. As outlined by R. R. R. Smith, 'The public image of Licinius I: Portrait sculpture and imperial ideology in the early fourth century', *JRS* 87 (1997), 170–202, at 185.

would be unable to impose themselves by force on the west, Constantine accepted Maximian's offer of marriage with his daughter, Fausta, which was celebrated in 307,[76] but took no part in the campaigns in Italy. Soon after, in 308, Maximian quarrelled with his undutiful son, whom, at one point, he publicly stripped of his purple robe, and took refuge with his new son-in-law. In the meantime, as he viewed the dynastic chaos, for which he was partly responsible, Galerius sought to regain the moral high ground and convened a meeting of the three survivors of Diocletian's college at Carnuntum on the Danube in November 308. The three agreed that Galerius' friend Valerius Licinianus Licinius, a man 'energetic in war',[77] should replace the dead Severus as Augustus and that Maximian should again retire.[78] However, the three lacked both the authority and the military force to impose their will and Licinius was obliged to wait his turn in Pannonia. Freed from any fear of consequences, both Constantine and, in the east, Maximinus Daza declared themselves Augusti, making a total of six emperors. In 310, the field was a little thinned by the demise of Maximian, who had re-emerged from retirement, only to turn against Constantine; he was forced to surrender at Marseille and take his own life.[79] This left Constantine and Maxentius in their respective spheres as the sole warlords in the Western Empire.

In 311, Galerius died, probably of cancer: the disgusting description of his symptoms provided by Lactantius is designed to drive home the point that this dreadful fate is ordained by God for those, like the first sufferer, Herod, who engage in persecution of Christians.[80] Galerius' failure to construct or maintain a united

76. *Pan. Lat.* 7 (6).1.5; 6.2; 14.4–6. Fausta is depicted as a child offering a helmet to a young Constantine as a betrothal gift. For Constantine's image in the Latin Panegyrics after 306, and continued emphasis on the popular Constantius, see Barbara S. Rodgers, 'The metamorphosis of Constantine', *CQ* 39 (1989), 233–46.
77. Eutr. *Brev.* 10.4.1 'in bello strenuus'. For his public, Galerius-style image, fat-faced and 'expressing the joyfulness of the victorious commander', see Smith, 'Public image', 187–94.
78. T. D. Barnes, *Constantine and Eusebius*, Cambridge, MA: Harvard University Press, 1981, 32; Barnes, *New Empire*, 6.
79. It is at this point that *Pan. Lat.* 6 (7).21–2, delivered in the summer of 310, connects Constantius I with Claudius Gothicus and connects Constantine with Apollo, thus severing his links with the Herculian dynasty. For Constantine's serene, bright-eyed and non-tetrarchic image, see Smith, 'Public image', 185–7, 194–201. For Constans and Constantius II as *abnepos* and *pronepos* (great-grandson) of Claudius Gothicus, see Dessau, *ILS* 723 (Noricum) and 730 (Braga, Spain). The inscriptions also reinstate Maximian in the dynasty as 'grandfather' to both (through Fausta).
80. Lactant. *De mort. pers.* 33.

college of emperors was due to some factors beyond his control, such as the self-assertion of the natural heirs of previous rulers, Constantine and Maxentius. However, he also made mistakes of his own. He proved unable to replicate the model of the imperial college created and sustained by Diocletian. Diocletian's college of four had evolved over a period of nine years, and each member earned his place within it. It was also in the self-interest of all four to be loyal to the rest. They were therefore able not only to work together but also to sustain an appearance of unity, which discouraged rivals. Galerius, however, had neither the time nor the diplomatic subtlety of a Diocletian. By sidelining Constantine and his son-in-law Maxentius at the outset, he undermined his own credibility. His recognition of Constantine as Caesar might have retrieved that error, but for the further uprising of Maxentius and Maximian, who together created an alternative focus for imperial authority in the west. With Constantine neutral and Maximian and his son out of control, Galerius was forced to resort to military means to reassert his authority, with disastrous effects. Without even the appearance of unity among the Caesars and Augusti, it was no longer possible for Galerius as Senior Augustus to claim the moral leadership of the imperial college of a united empire. The rule of the Roman world, east and west, would, once again, be decided by force of arms.

Figure 1 Curia Iulia, Forum Romanum, Rome, Italy

Figure 2 Diocletianic Rostra, Forum Romanum, Rome, Italy

Figure 3 Basilica Iulia, Forum Romanum, Rome, Italy

Figure 4 Victories relief, Decennalia Base, Forum Romanum, Rome, Italy

Figure 5 Sacrifice with gods, Decennalia Base, Forum Romanum, Rome, Italy

Figure 6 Central block, Baths of Diocletian, Rome, Italy

Figure 7 *Frigidarium* interior, Baths of Diocletian, Rome, Italy

CHAPTER 3

The empire renewed

Unable to anticipate the duration of his reign, Diocletian did not plan in advance a systematic programme of reform. Rather than acting in accordance with some grand design, Diocletian took a series of decisions, over a period of twenty years, which reshaped the provincial governance and tax and revenue systems of the Roman Empire. Taken separately, his reforms can be argued to be a series of adjustments to the existing order, which were in line with the policies of previous emperors but which over time allowed Diocletian to stamp his own personality on the emerging new order. As his position strengthened, he became more assertive in his quest for solutions to longstanding problems, notably those associated with the debasement of coinage and inflation, yet where he was most radical, he was probably least successful.

Provincial organisation

Diocletian inherited a provincial structure largely unchanged since the Severans. This consisted of some small provinces, such as Cyprus or Sicily, which were secure in the heartland of the empire and easily managed, but there were also larger provincial units, some of which, such as the two British provinces or Egypt, were the scenes of local uprisings. Like previous emperors, Diocletian sought to head off potential threats to his personal security but he also saw the potential for improving efficiency by operating through smaller provincial units. Larger provinces were therefore divided, on an ad hoc basis, into smaller entities, each with its own provincial governor, usually called a *praeses* – but in Italy a *corrector*, later a *consularis* – and administrative capital. The process of division would result over time in the doubling of the number of provinces from forty-five to over one hundred.[1] For Lactantius, this was part of Diocletian's programme to terrorise the empire:

1. Much of the evidence for the new provinces comes from the Verona List, usually dated to c. 314, although some put parts of it are later. For the Latin text, see O. Seeck

And so as to fill everywhere with terror, the provinces too were cut up into fragments, many governors and even more bureaucratic burdens were loaded onto individual regions, even cities, and in addition many finance officers (*rationales*) and masters (of the imperial estates?) and deputies (*vicarii*) of the prefects.[2]

Doubtless one effect of Diocletian's changes would have been to raise the profile of the central government, especially in the new administrative centres, created by the subdivision of larger areas. The advent of governors with their armed retinues may have frightened some but Diocletian's motives were more mundane: the promotion of efficiency in the collection of tax revenues and the more effective imposition of control from the centre over local affairs, which, as Pliny had found in the early second century, were often mismanaged.[3] Governors of smaller districts were also far less likely to acquire imperial ambitions of their own, especially as their role was increasingly confined to civil matters, in particular jurisdiction. Diocletian's provincial organisation had the effect of removing what little remained of the special statuses of Italy and Egypt as provinces. However, the past was acknowledged in official titulature. The governor of Egypt was the distinctively named *praefectus Augustalis*, the Italian 'provinces' were supervised by governors known as *correctores*, not *praesides*, and new, smaller provinces of Africa and Asia each continued to be governed by proconsuls, as they had been since the time of Augustus.

There was no centrally created blueprint for the provincial structure of the Roman Empire. Boundary changes and the creation of new units were carried out as required, often as a result of an imperial visit. Reasons for changes are not always known, and the changes themselves are often only attested in inscriptions, papyri and

(ed.), *Notitia Dignitatum* 1876, repr. Frankfurt: Minerva Press,1962, 247–53; T. D. Barnes, *The New Empire of Diocletian and Constantine*, Cambridge, MA: Harvard University Press, , 1982, 201–8, 209–25, providing the original and a comprehensible Latin version; translation of List at R. Rees, *Diocletian and the Tetrarchy*, Edinburgh: Edinburgh University Press, 2004, 171. On the Verona List (or Laterculus Veronensis) see A. H. M. Jones, 'The date and value of the Verona List', *JRS* 44 (1954), 21–9, although modified on matters of detail by later work.
2. Lactant. *De mort pers.* 7.4: 'Et ut omnia terrore complerentur, provinciae quoque in frusta concisae, multi praesides et multa officia singulis regionibus et paene iam civitatibus incubare, item rationales multi et magistri et vicarii praefectorum.'
3. Pliny, *Letters* 10, is a dossier of letters between Trajan and Pliny, most of which concern Pliny's governorship of Bithynia in c. 110–12.

imperial constitutions addressed to governors. The restructuring of Egypt, for example, seems to have been a direct consequence of the revolt of Domitius Domitianus; the separate provinces of the Thebaid and Libya (Superior and Inferior) were created in 298 and there were further short-term tinkerings with the provincial structure.[4] The dismantling of the large and proverbially rich province of Asia may have taken place in stages, with Caria and the (Aegean) Islands being the first to acquire separate administrations. In Maximian's domain, North Africa, (Valeria) Byzacena and Tripolitania were split from the senatorial province of Africa Proconsularis before 305, and the ancient provinces of Mauretania and Numidia were divided in two in 303. How far the members of the Tetrarchy other than Diocletian took initiatives of their own in provincial reorganisation is uncertain. As the conqueror of Allectus, Constantius I may have driven the creation of two new provinces in Britain, Maxima Caesariensis and Flavia Caesariensis, in 296; as with the later changes in Egypt these can be read as a response to previous instability and the need to tighten supervision. Constantius may therefore also have been instrumental in the radical restructuring of the Gallic provinces: according to the Verona List, an administrator's list of the provinces of the Roman Empire tentatively dated to the early fourth century, the former Gallia Comata or Tres Galliae was split into eight, including two Belgicae, Germaniae and Lugdunenses (also Sequania and the Alpes Graiae et Poeninae); Aquitania became three (Aquitania I and II and Novem Populi); and Narbonensis four (Narbonensis I and II, Viennensis and the Alpes Maritimae).[5]

The proliferation of governors and their administrations threatened to fragment the collection of taxation. To strengthen local organisation on a regional basis, as well as to help to channel and perhaps filter the flow of documentation to the centre, Diocletian created clusters of provinces, known as dioceses, which were each placed under the supervision of a deputy to the praetorian prefect, the *vicarius*.[6] There were twelve dioceses in all: Britain, Gaul (Galliae), Viennensis (southern and eastern Gaul), Spain (Hispaniae), Italy and Africa; Pannonia, Moesia and Thrace, all in the central

4. For details, R. S. Bagnall, *Egypt in Late Antiquity*, Princeton, NJ: Princeton University Press, 1993, 63–4.
5. For a complete survey of provincial changes see John J. Wilkes, 'Provincial reorganisation', in *CAH*[2] 12, 212–64. For Verona List, see above, note 1.
6. For fiscal role of the *vicarius*, see M. Hendy, *Studies in the Byzantine Monetary Economy, AD 300–1450*, Cambridge: Cambridge University Press, 1985, 371–95.

European and Danubian regions; and Asiana, Pontica and Oriens in the east. While the changes in provincial boundaries were piecemeal, the creation of dioceses must have resulted, exceptionally, from a single initiative, although there was, of course, scope for later modification; Italy, for example, although one diocese, had two *vicarii*, one for the north and the other with some role in connection with Rome, as well as southern Italy, which had to be negotiated with the urban prefecture.[7] There was also a progressive restructuring of mints for the production of coinage; the overall number increased from eight, including Alexandria, to fourteen, but two of the three mints used by Carausius were closed down.[8] The likely date for the creation of an empire-wide system of dioceses and *vicarii* is 297. However, a *vicarius* of the *urbs Roma*, Septimius Valentio, is attested earlier (293–6),[9] perhaps evidence of experimentation with the role of 'deputies', prior to a wider reform.

In the new, smaller provinces, the main functions of the governor were non-military, a completion of the third-century trend towards the formal separation of civil from military offices. The governor was in charge of jurisdiction in the province, but could also be appealed from to higher authority, and he was responsible to the *vicarii* for the supervision of tax collection.[10] As the *iudex* (judge), the governor heard criminal cases and civil disputes involving sums above a certain figure (lesser cases were delegated to city jurisdictions). Caracalla's grant of near-universal Roman citizenship in 212 opened access to the courts for almost all the inhabitants of the Roman Empire, new citizens as well as old. This would have entailed some immediate increase in workload, which may have expanded further, as the new citizens became more confident in the exercise of their rights. The rapid expansion of governors' courts led to a corresponding increase in the number of referrals and appeals of cases to the emperor and his judicial deputy, the praetorian prefect. The extensive rescript literature from Diocletian's reign shows that governors, though powerful, were also vulnerable. Petitioners

7. See A. Giardina, 'La formazione dell'Italia provinciale', in A. Schiavone, ed., *Storia di Roma. Vol. III.1: L'eta tardoantica: crisi e transformazione*, Turin: Giulio Einardi, 1993, 51–68.
8. For locations of mints, see Hendy, *Studies*, 378–80.
9. Dessau, *ILS* 619. *Vicarii* are then attested for 298 (Aurelius Agricolanus, *Acts of Marcellus* 3), and Aemilius Rusticianus (*POxy.* 1469; *PLRE*, p. 787).
10. On the role of the governor in the Diocletianic rescripts, see Simon Corcoran, *The Empire of the Tetrarchs: Imperial Pronouncements and Government*, AD 284–324, 2nd edn, Oxford: Oxford University Press, 2002, 234–53.

circumvented the governor's court to approach the emperor directly, hoping for a favourable response.[11] In the course of this legal correspondence, an unfavourable decision might be attributed by the litigant (perhaps correctly) to bribery and corruption;[12] and governors were susceptible to pressures from locals more powerful than they, which they would be exhorted to resist.[13]

Vicarii were answerable to the praetorian prefects. Although military involvement on the part of a prefect was still acceptable (as was the case with Maximian's praetorian prefect, Asclepiodotus, serving with Constantius I in Britain in 296), the career of the jurist Hermogenian, who was Diocletian's chief legal adviser in 294–5, and praetorian prefect in 298, was more typical of things to come.[14] The praetorian prefects, who combined judicial functions with over-all responsibility for the assessment of taxes, functioned as a college in their own right and issued enactments in common. The extent to which praetorian prefects were tied to individual members of the imperial college is uncertain. After much debate, it is now agreed that Diocletian and Maximian had one praetorian prefect each, but their Caesars did not.[15] Likewise, although three prefects are known for Maxentius' period of rule, Constantine and Licinius had one prefect each between 315 and 317. However, there may have been as many as five operating in the 330s, of whom only four, at most, can be accounted for as being attached to the Caesars.[16] After 337, the praetorian prefects' responsibilities, and the number required, came to be defined by the regions, consisting of clusters of dioceses, that they supervised; Constans' probable creation of the separate

11. Corcoran, *Empire*, 236; W. Turpin, 'Imperial subscriptions and the administration of justice', *JRS* 81 (1991), 101–18, at 114–18.
12. *Cod. Just.* 7.64.7.
13. *Cod. Just.* 2.13.1, citing Claudius Gothicus.
14. Corcoran, *Empire*, 87–9.
15. T. D. Barnes, 'Emperors, panegyrics, prefects, provinces and palaces (284–317)', *JRA* 9 (1996), 532–58, rejects his previous view in *The New Empire of Diocletian and Constantine*, Cambridge, MA: Harvard University Press, 1982, that Diocletian's Caesars also had praetorian prefects. See A. Chastagnol, 'Un nouveau préfet de Dioclétien', *ZPE* 79 (1989), 165–8, on a dedication to Constantius Caesar by Asclepiodotus and Hermogenianus, Praeff. (the two f's showing that the college consisted of two, not four). See also Corcoran, *Empire*, 87–9, 268–70; Bill Leadbetter, *Galerius and the Will of Diocletian*, London: Routledge, 2009, 71–2.
16. *L'Année Epigraphique* 1981, 878 (for 328); 1925, 72 and 1985, 823 (for 335). On provincial administration in general, see Elio Lo Cascio, 'The new state of Diocletian and Constantine: From the Tetrarchy to the reunification of the empire', in *CAH*² 12, 170–81.

prefecture of Illyricum in 345, when he already had prefects in post in Italy/Africa and Gaul (including Britain and Spain), shows that the regional model was now established. By the late fourth century, the empire was split into the prefectures of the Gauls (still including Britain and Spain), Italy and Africa, Illyricum, and the east.

The armies

In the decades preceding 284, military commands had evolved independently and were exercised in areas requiring military attention, irrespective of provincial boundaries. How far Diocletian and his colleagues, all of whom were active campaigners, made use of local regional commanders, *duces*, is doubtful. Most evidence for *duces* is later than Diocletian, although the creation of their spheres of operation may nevertheless be his doing. One *dux*, Firminianus, was active in the newly created province of Scythia on the Danube in 311,[17] and there are also *duces* attested for the period in Illyricum, Egypt and Africa. The *Notitia Dignitatum*, a list of military and civilian officials and their remits, dating mainly from the late fourth or early fifth century, listed *duces* in a number of areas to which attention was paid by Diocletian, Galerius and Constantius: these included Armenia, Syria, Pannonia and Britain, but certainty as to the date of the creation of these posts – and thus the extent of Diocletian's reorganisation of *duces* and their commands – is impossible.[18] Co-operation on the ground between *duces* and the governors of the areas in which they operated would have been essential and it is likely that only under Constantine was the formal separation of civil from military commands completed.[19]

More contentious, and of far greater relevance to the ability of the Roman Empire to maintain the security of its borders, was the alleged divergence of policy between Diocletian and Constantine over the manning of the frontiers. The pagan historian Zosimus (early sixth century), following Eunapius (late fourth century), credited Diocletian with a programme of strengthening the frontiers with fortifications and large garrisons, maintaining that Constantine subsequently reversed the policy and drained frontiers of their defenders in order to billet them on peaceful cities, with no need of

17. Dessau, *ILS* 4103.
18. *Not. Dign.* [or.] 33; 38; [occ.] 32; 34; 35; 37; 40.
19. J. C. Mann, '*Duces* and *comites* in the fourth century', in D. E. Johnston (ed.), *The Saxon Shore*, London: Council for British Archaeology, 1977, 11–15.

their services. This, the historian claimed, drained the unlucky host cities of their population, made the soldiers effete, and planted the seeds of the fall of the Roman Empire.[20]

Such claims owe more to the polemical agenda of anti-Christian sources than fact. No such drastic shift of policy can be detected in material and epigraphic evidence. The Gallic panegyricist celebrated the restoration of walls, camps and forts on the northern frontiers[21] and archaeology shows that new forts were constructed in the late third and early fourth centuries, although their ascription to emperors is uncertain.[22] Against Persia, a different strategy was employed, which took account of the topography of the desert frontier. The Strata Diocletiana was a road which ran from north-eastern Arabia and the area of Damascus in Syria to the Euphrates via the route centre at Palmyra, which was also the base of the Legio I Illyricorum. The road was lined with forts and strong points at twenty-mile intervals, allowing rapid transit of forces to areas under threat; the forts also afforded protection to garrisons who could hold out under attack and thus slow any hostile advance.[23] On the Euphrates, Diocletian fortified Circesium, 'when he was organising the inner lines of defence along the frontiers' to prevent the overrunning of Syria by the Persians;[24] this was garrisoned by the IV Parthica. The late sixth-century Byzantine chronicler John Malalas also described Diocletian's frontier strategy in terms of the fortified camps and the essential role of the mobile reserve behind the lines:[25]

> On the frontiers of Egypt to the Persian borders, the same Diocletian built camps, settling frontier troops in them: he chose generals and stationed one in each province behind the camps with large numbers of men as a mobile reserve.

20. Zos. *New History* 2.34.1. It is his (and Eunapius') habit to ascribe military defeats and the disintegration of the western Roman Empire in the fifth century to mistakes made by Christian emperors.
21. *Pan. Lat.* 9 (5).18.4. For tetrarchic restoration of towns see Dessau, *ILS* 620, translated Rees, *Diocletian*, 147, commemorating the restoration of the town gates at Grenoble, renamed the 'Jovian' and 'Herculian' gates.
22. For ascription of many forts to Tetrarchs, see H. von Petrikovitz, 'Fortifications in the north-western Roman Empire from the third century to the fifth century', *JRS* 61 (1971), 178–218; S. Johnson, *Late Roman Fortifications*, London: Batsford, 1983.
23. B. Isaac, *The Limits of Empire: The Roman Army in the East*, Oxford: Oxford University Press, 1992, 162–6.
24. Amm. Marc. 23.5.2 (of Julian's Persian expedition).
25. *Chron.* 308.17 = trans. Rees, *Diocletian*, 128.

While Malalas is important for his emphasis on Diocletian's interest in a central striking force, which contradicts Zosimus' over-simplified version, his account may underestimate the importance of legions in forward positions in the Eastern Empire. In addition to the legions stationed at Palmyra and Circesium, there were also legions at Danaba (III Gallica), Oresa (IV Scythica) and Sura (XVI Flavia).[26]

Diocletian and his colleagues also retained substantial military forces under their personal command and mobile field armies. Inscriptional and papyrological evidence, and a martyr-act, refer to the *comitatus* or military 'companions' attached to emperors. Martianus, '*optio* (staff officer) of the *comites* of the emperor', is attested in Egypt in 295[27] and Christians allegedly served as soldiers 'in the sacred (i.e. imperial) *comitatus* [escort of 'companions']'[28] of all four Tetrarchs. Valerius Tertius,[29] member of the praetorian guard at Rome, whose career included eleven years with the *lanciarii* (lightly armed spearmen), was probably also associated with the *comitatus*; Valerius Thiumpus was 'recruited into the sacred *comitatus* as a *lanciarius*' before serving as *protector*, a member of the emperor's personal staff, and later prefect of the second Herculian Legion.[30] In the 350s, the historian Ammianus would serve as *protector domesticus*, with access not only to emperors but also to generals, such as Ursicinus, to whom he was seconded for a while. The Diocletianic *comitatus* thus probably consisted of several disparate elements: the elite palatine legions, the Ioviani and Herculiani, the *protectores*, various cavalry units and the *scholae*, or bodyguards, who were sometimes recruited from non-Roman peoples.

How many individual soldiers were on the payroll cannot be determined with any certainty. Even if a paper total could be established, this would not necessarily reflect the reality on the ground.

26. Brian Campbell, 'The army II: The military reforms of Diocletian and Constantine', in *CAH*[2] 12, 120–30; Isaac, *Limits*, 161–71.
27. *P.Oxy.* 1.43, recto col ii, lines 17, 24, 27.
28. *Acts of Maximilian* 2.9, accessible in H. Musurillo, *Acts of the Christian Martyrs: Introduction, Texts and Translations*, Oxford: Clarendon Press, 1972. Maximilian had passed the height test (5′10″) imposed on prospective recruits for admission to the army but, as a Christian, refused to serve. There are signs of two recruitment processes at work in this text, suggesting either a conflation of two accounts or imperfect understanding of the process on the part of the author.
29. Dessau, *ILS* 2045.
30. Dessau, *ILS* 2781.

A number of statistics, of varying reliability, suggest a substantial increase over the Severan period. In the course of the third century, the number of legions increased from thirty-three under the Severans to sixty-seven or more, although they contained fewer men. The concentrations of troops reflected the same military priorities, with some twenty-eight legions in the east and strong forces on the Danube (seventeen) and the Rhine (perhaps ten). There were also some eight legions in North Africa, a new area of concern, which, in a significant departure from precedent, was personally visited by Maximian in 298. Various tendentious or late sources offer figures of varying degrees of unreliability; none can be trusted, even as a replication of official records.[31] The figures, while unhelpful as an accurate guide, have one thing in common: all support a substantial paper increase in the military establishment.

While it has been persuasively argued that the system was not excessively burdensome, because the legions contained fewer men,[32] the case for an increase in the burden of supporting the military establishment can be supported by evidence that military effectiveness was undermined by potential manpower shortages. Diocletian would split up single legions and station them in a number of areas, thus spreading the pain but also exposing smaller detachments to greater risk. For example, the third Legio Diocletiana had four bases in Egypt, including three in the Thebaid. Clearly if a legion deployed to several sites was substantially below the expected c. 5,800 to start with, a detachment might find it hard to carry out its mission effectively.[33] How far these changes had an impact on ease of recruitment is uncertain. An early law of Constantine[34] to a governor in southern Italy complains, probably in response to information passed to him, that the sons of veterans, who were routinely required to follow their fathers' professions, had made themselves unfit for military service by cutting off their fingers; the delinquents were to be punished by being forced to forfeit the privileges of exemption granted to soldiers and veterans, and instead carry out the obligations of town councillors.

From Augustus onwards, army service conferred on serving soldiers and veterans social and legal privileges. But like other

31. See below, p. 211.
32. R. Duncan Jones, *Structure and Scale in the Roman Economy*, Cambridge: Cambridge University Press, 1990, 105–17.
33. Campbell, 'Military reforms', 124; Jones, *LRE*, 681, 1440–1, 1478.
34. *Cod. Theod.* 7.22.1 (313) may refer back to legislation by the Tetrarchy.

sections of society, some soldiers found that privileges could be challenged and eroded in the courts. A rescript from the emperors in ?292 addressed to the governor Sallustianus[35] reveals the fragility of defences from abuse, which relied on (theoretical) legal privilege: the emperors were obliged to reiterate what the governor should have known already, that the social status of serving soldiers, as well as those honourably discharged, precluded the use of judicial torture on them for the extraction of evidence. This, wrote the emperors, should apply to their sons as well. The rescript then continues with general remarks on the advisability of avoiding the use of torture where at all possible and being careful about ascertaining the status of witnesses before torture was used. While the story behind the rescript is unknown, the situation can be inferred; some provincial judge cared more about extracting evidence than safeguarding legal rights, and even supposedly privileged soldiers were not immune from judicial malpractice.

Taxation and finance

Looking after the interests of the expanded army was an imperial priority, which connects together reforms of taxation, the coinage and prices. The balance of taxation revenue with expenditure was obviously desirable but very hard to achieve in practice. Emperors therefore resorted to 'indictions', formal assessments of the tax revenue required in a given period, and duly displayed on public notices. Diocletian's innovation seems to have been to put the indictions on a regular footing, although a stable system involving fifteen-year cycles was not established before 312. The two main forms of taxation were the land tax, or *iugatio*, and the *capitatio*, or poll tax, a tax on 'heads' (*capita*).[36] Information about tax liabilities was widely disseminated in public places. The edict issued by the prefect of Egypt, Aurelius Optatus, in 297 publicised the schedule and ordered it to be posted, along with the emperor's own pronouncement on the matter, 'in every village and locality'. Optatus' language combines the practical necessities of tax administration with moralising on the emperors' generosity in removing unfairness from the system, while keeping taxes low. Taxpayers therefore (he

35. *Cod. Just.* 9.41.8.
36. A. H. M. Jones, '*Capitatio* and *iugatio*', *JRS* 47 (1957), 88–94. For Diocletian and taxation in general, see Jones, *LRE*, 62–6.

wrote) should pay up 'with enthusiasm' and not wait to be forced by the tax collector:[37]

> From the divine edict which has been published and the schedule attached to it (copies of which I have prefaced for public display with this edict of mine), everyone can know the levy on each *aroura* [unit of assessment expressed in terms of land] according to the quality of the land and the levy on each of the peasants and the upper and lower age limits for liability. And so, since in this matter too the provincials have been treated very generously, let them take care to pay their tax contributions according to the imperial statutes with all speed and in no way to wait for the collector to force them (etc.).

The census was carried out progressively; Syria and Arabia were under assessment before 293, and declarations of land were collected in Egypt from 298.[38] The unit of assessment was the *iugum* (plural *iuga*, not to be confused with *iugera*, a measurement of acreage). *Iugum*-equivalents varied from province to province; this was consistent with traditional Roman taxation practice, which conformed to local systems and usage as far as possible. Any attempt to understand the system as an empire-wide unity was probably doomed to failure; each assessment, therefore, by province and diocese, would operate by its own rules. The tenacity of local measures can be illustrated from a collection of 'laws' (*nomoi*) dating probably from the 470s, originally in Greek but rendered into Syriac, then translated into Latin under the title of *Leges Saeculares*. One paragraph explained how Diocletian's measures of tax assessment worked in Syria:[39]

> 100 *perticae* equal one *plethron*. The *iugum* (*iougon*) was defined as a measure (of assessment) in the days of king (*regis*) Diocletian and put into law: five *iugera*, which make up ten *plethra* of vineyard, equal one *iugum*, and 20 *iugera* of arable land which make 40 *plethra* give one *iugum* of *annona*, 220 *perticae* of old olive trees give one *iugum* of *annona* and 450 *perticae* in mountainous areas equal one *iugum*.

The tax assessor in Syria was thus required to juggle *perticae*, *plethra* and *iugera*, as well as take account of nature of cultivation, age of

37. P. Cair. Isid. 1, trans. Rees, *Diocletian*, 158.
38. A. H. M. Jones, 'Census records of the later Roman Empire', *JRS* 43 (1953), 49–64.
39. *Leg. Saec.* 121 in Riccobono, *FIRA* 2, 795–6. No emperor is named after Leo ('rex fidelis', 118), who died in 491, and it is assumed that the collection dates from soon after his reign.

trees and type of terrain in order to calculate the *iugum* equivalent. Elsewhere systems were less complicated: Italy and Africa, for example, seem to have taken into account acreage alone. But in Egypt, the taxman dealt not in *iuga* but in the traditional *aroura*, applying the measure to arable land, vineyards and olive trees.

Personal eligibility for the 'poll tax' (*capitatio*) also varied in terms of both age and gender. In Egypt only males from perhaps age 12 upwards were liable but elsewhere women were also included, either as a whole 'head' (Syria, Illyricum) or half a 'head' (Pontica, Asiana). Animals were also assessed as fractions of *capita*. Initially the *capitatio* seems to have been levied on country-dwellers only but Diocletian's successors attempted, with little success, to extend it to town populations as well; the Augustus Severus' policy after 305, of trying to register the plebs in Rome, may have been one reason for his downfall.[40] While the land tax was collected in kind, the *capitatio* was to be paid in coin, and the decurions were ultimately responsible for the collection of both:

> Those who organise or collect or contribute the tax in kind (*annona*) and those who raise revenue by the poll tax, sustain the responsibility of a personal *munus* (curial obligation).[41]

Further costs were incurred by local populations – and considerable agitation was caused among local officials[42] – when a special event took place, such as the imperial visit of Diocletian to Panopolis in the lower Thebaid province in Egypt in September 298. Papyri from Panopolis reveal the problems faced by administrators in the collection of supplies and ships, which were exacerbated by the non-co-operation of various key personnel. The harassed local administrator (*strategos*) was required to appoint 'overseers of vegetables' and to designate a local bakery 'near the theatre' as the headquarters for bread distribution to the soldiers. He sent (he said) repeated instructions for the collection of supplies for 'the most noble

40. Lactant. *De mort. pers.* 23.2 (Nicomedia); 26.2 (Severus at Rome). At *Cod. Theod.* 13.10.2, Maximin Daza remits urban poll tax in Asiana; this was included in error by the compilers as a law of Constantine.
41. *Dig.* 50.4.18.8, Arcadius Charisius (jurist contemporary with Diocletian and Constantine), *On Civil Munera*: 'Qui annonam vel suscipiat vel exigat vel erogat, et exactores pecuniae pro capitibus personalis muneris sollicitudinem sustinent.'
42. P. Beatty Panop. 1. 53–9, 167–79, 184–7, 213–16, 221–4, 249–51, 264–71, 332–7, 353–64, 365–8, 369–73 and 400–1, trans. Rees, *Diocletian*, 148–53, are twelve letters from the *strategos* (local administrator) of Panopolis, all dating from September 298, although not all are concerned with the imperial visit.

soldiers' and complained bitterly about the outright disobedience of the accountant requested to supervise expenditure on the ships (the accountant claimed that 'the city ought not to be troubled by this'). Further problems arose with the *strategos*' attempts to enlist four town councillors as additional supervisors of the treasury estates; it emerged that the governor of the Thebaid, Athenodorus, had already ruled that decurions were exempt from treasury service and the *strategos* was forced to request that four other men be chosen instead. Multiple failures on the part of this or a later *strategos* became so serious as to merit a fine two years later in 300. The collection of the fine was enforced in spectacular fashion by confining the ten local tax collectors, who were also complicit, to prison, pending payment.[43]

The impression created by the correspondence is of an administrative system which was so seriously dysfunctional that it could hardly operate at all. Corruption appears omnipresent. Letters from the procurator of the lower Thebaid, Aurelius Isidore, reveal alleged flaws in earlier census declarations: arrears in paying over taxes in wine over the last two indictions were now to be made up.[44] In another letter, a few days later, Isidore publicly castigated corrupt behaviour in the collection of the *annona militaris*, which allowed substitution of cash for payment in kind; in addition, the collectors (allegedly) used over-weighted scales to extort more than was due.[45]

The vigour with which petitioners expressed themselves suggests that they had some confidence that officials accused of corruption might be held to account. From the 340s we have the Abbinnaeus archive, a collection of documents relating to the career of a local commander in Egypt, whose duties included supervision of tax collection (in conjunction with the civil official) and local jurisdiction. Abinnaeus was ordered to supply soldiers to assist with collection, on pain of being denounced for having 'impeded the collection of the imperial revenues'.[46] On another occasion, new rules on the *annona* and confusion over their implementation prompted a letter from the military accountant Agathos, who was

43. P. Beatty Panop. 2. 61–4, 68–71, dating from 8–9 February 300, trans. Rees, *Diocletian*, 153.
44. P. Beatty Panop. 2.145–52, 13 February 300.
45. P. Beatty Panop. 2. 229–44. For a sustained argument that the extent of corruption in late antiquity did indeed paralyse the system, see Ramsay MacMullen, *Corruption and the Decline of Rome*, New Haven: Yale University Press, 1988.
46. P. Abinn. 3.18–20. P. Abinn. 11 is a demand for a military escort for Felicissimus.

unable to attend himself because of being detained by his superior for non-payment of 'gratuities':[47]

> At the request of the *actuarii* [bean-counters, stock-checkers] of the Upper Thebaid ... the *dux* ordered all the *annona* quotas for the year to be locked up in camp; and he ordered that after the wheat had been locked up, an official should be sent and should assist in inspecting the wheat and barley not accepted.

Although tax collectors were often the oppressors, they were also themselves at risk; one Plutammon worried that he had been endangered because he had been mistakenly given horses rather than the monetary equivalent, and on another occasion bitterly complained that his grandson had been attacked by 'thirty' thugs from Hermopolis.[48] And a grain collector, Demetrius, was assaulted by one Athenodorus, a drunken soldier under Abinnaeus' command who 'offered me no small violence and not only to me but he goes out continually drunk into the fields and makes the village his prey'.[49]

Though Isidore's and, later, Abbinnaeus' correspondence, and the Panopolis archive in general, reveals inefficiency, systemic malfunction and corrupt behaviour by taxpayers (who failed to declare vineyards) and tax collectors, they do not prove that the system as a whole was a failure. The evidence is anecdotal and based on a series of individual cases; they are unreliable guides as to the scale of any given problem. Officials were afraid of incurring blame and thus sought also to avoid taking responsibility; it was the object of the letter-writers to exculpate themselves by casting the blame for failings on the incompetence, bloody-mindedness and alleged corruption of others, but their narratives alone do not establish the guilt of those they accused. 'Corruption' is itself a loaded term. Activities designated on cultural or moral grounds as 'corrupt' may still make perfect economic sense. Corruption may also be defined by social assumptions about what is and is not acceptable behaviour; for example, a present may be designated as a gift' or as a 'bribe', depending on the context. Moreover, some of the officials' difficulties were due not to corrupt or contumacious behaviour but to Roman citizens' understanding of their rights and their confidence in asserting them. The decurions who refused to act for the treasury

47. *P. Abinn.* 26, 16–24.
48. *P. Abinn.* 13; 15, 13–15.
49. *P. Abinn.* 28, 8–15.

knew they were exempt and supported their claim with proper documentation; official attempts at subversion of the rights of individuals could be counteracted by adroit exploitation of the law. And there is a bias in the nature of the evidence itself. The letters and petitions are often a response when something has gone wrong; they do not record the occasions when the system worked as it should.[50]

Coinage and prices

The debasement of the coinage in which army pay was issued was a longstanding problem. Romans evaluated their coinage in terms of numbers of coins struck to the pound. Under the early empire, silver *denarii* were struck at 85 to the pound; by the early third century, the figure had risen to 226–7. Not surprisingly, prices had also soared, and continued to do so into the fourth century. The prices for wheat quoted in Diocletian's Edict on Maximum Prices were in the region of seventy times greater than those quoted in the second century AD; some thirty years later, wheat was quoted at sixty-three times its price in the edict,[51] although we cannot assess the impact of local factors. The situation was less desperate than might appear; much taxation was paid in kind and Romans could get by using the traditional methods of exchange of the barter economy. For emperors, however, as paymasters of the soldiers, whose loyalties depended on their monetary rewards and a reasonable standard of living, stability in coinage and prices was important.

Diocletian therefore focused first on gold, and in c. 286, gold coinage was standardised at sixty to the pound. Some eight years later, silver coins were to be struck at 96 to the pound, meaning that this new silver coin would be tariffed at 62.5 *denarii*. Then, at some point before 1 September 301, Diocletian issued the so-called Currency Revaluation Decree, which partially survives.[52] There was

50. For how the system worked despite or because of 'corrupt' practices, Christopher M. Kelly, *Ruling the Later Roman Empire*, Cambridge, MA: Belknap Press, 2004, 138–85.
51. R. Duncan Jones, *Money and Government in the Roman Empire*, Cambridge: Cambridge University Press, 1994, 223–8 (denarius); Duncan Jones, *The Economy of the Roman Empire*, 2nd edn, Cambridge: Cambridge University Press, 1982, 366–9.
52. For the Aphrodisias fragmentary text, see K. T. Erim, J. Reynolds and M. H. Crawford, 'Diocletian's currency reform: A new inscription', *JRS* 61 (1971), 171–7; C. Roueché, *Aphrodisias in Late Antiquity: The Late Roman and Byzantine Inscriptions*, *JRS* Monographs 5, London: Society for the Promotion of Roman Studies, 1989, rev. 2004, 254–65; also Corcoran, *Empire*, 177–8, 214–15.

no physical change made in the coinage but a wider gulf was created between the face value of the silver coins and their precious metal content. This was done by fixing the value of the coin at 100 *denarii*, not the lower figure extracted from the number struck per pound of silver. Other valuations were also quoted, as Diocletian sought to stabilise the coinage, by creating a fixed relationship between gold, silver and bronze coins in terms of their *denarius* equivalents. From 1 September 301, new debts to (and incurred by) the imperial treasury were to be paid 'in the same coin' but with an increased face value, which was greater than the value of the bullion silver it contained; debts incurred before that date were to be paid in the coins at the old face value.[53]

The purpose of the currency decree was to establish a fixed tariff of the values of the new coins by imperial fiat, using the *denarius* as a unit of value. The *denarius* was no longer a coin in circulation but served as a tariff expressed as a currency, which could be conceptualised as a fixed unit of value for accounting purposes; the same was also true of the (ancient) Greek equivalent, the drachma (at four to the *denarius*), tetradrachm (one *denarius*) and talent (1500 *denarii*). The accounts of Theophanes, a 'wealthy gentleman of Hermopolis' in Egypt, and his journey from his home to Antioch in c. 320, when Licinius was Augustus in the east, are expressed in drachmas, even though his daily outgoings in cash would have been in the currency in use, probably the Licinian *nummus*.[54] The difficulty for Diocletian was that any revaluation of an individual coin in relation to its actual precious metal content might prove inflationary, if the users of real coins preferred to focus on precious metal content rather than face value. A likely consequence was that prices were adjusted upwards in real terms as the values of small, cheap coins depreciated.

The Edict on Maximum Prices, issued in November 301, was Diocletian's most comprehensive attempt to cap the prices charged for goods and services. Although the text survives in slightly over forty separate epigraphic versions, its known dissemination is restricted to five provinces: Egypt, Achaea, Crete, Cyrenaica (Ptolemais) and Caria and Phrygia combined. Accidents of survival mean that we cannot be sure that other governors did not oblige

---

53. Hendy, *Studies*, 278–80, 449.
54. For Theophanes' accounts and currencies, see John Matthews, *The Journey of Theophanes: Travel, Business and Daily Life in the Roman East*, New Haven: Yale University Press, 2006, 96–7.

by setting up inscriptions of their own; the fact that Lactantius at Nicomedia also knew (and disapproved) of the edict shows that generalisation is risky.[55] However, the lack of any western text suggests that dissemination of the edict in epigraphic form was confined to (some of) the eastern provinces. The trouble and expense of posting up a long edict in epigraphic form signalled the importance of the measure, even to those who could not read it. The symbolism was all-important. In Achaea, the thoughtful governor provided a Greek translation of the prices, but the preface remained in Latin; elsewhere the entire inscription was in Latin, the language, still, of administration, even in the Greek east. In addition, some versions were rendered impractical by their positioning. At Aphrodisias, much of the edict, set up on the walls of the local basilica, was too high up to read and for many its usefulness, at least as an inscription, would have been more symbolic than real. On the other hand, the very existence of a tariff in epigraphic form provided some guarantee against forgery; it was much harder to alter a stone carving than figures on a papyrus.[56]

The preface to the Edict on Maximum Prices, issued in the name of all four emperors, is one of the fullest attempts extant on the part of emperors to formulate their self-image in words in the context of reforming legislation. The opening paragraph after the titles (5) celebrates the emperors' restoration of peace, tranquillity and calm after stress and conflict, a peace won by divine favour, which must be fortified with the defences of justice. By contrast (6–7), greed and avarice had raged unchecked in the Roman Empire; the 'untamed fury' of wicked and extravagant people had created a 'religion of greed'. Faced with this outbreak of unbridled materialism, the emperors had hesitated, hoping that the greedy people might reform themselves through the laws of nature (8), but their hope had been

55. Lactant. *De mort. pers.* 7.6–7; for the Aezani text, inscribed on the wall of the local market (Macellum), see J. Reynolds and M. H. Crawford, 'The publication of the prices edict: A new inscription from Aezani', *JRS* 65 (1975), 160–3, and by the same authors, 'The Aezani copy of the prices edict', *ZPE* 26 (1977), 125–51, and 34 (1979), 163–210. For the Aphrodisias copy, see Roueché, *Aphrodisias*, 265–318.

56. For the process of discovery and the importance of autopsy in determining how inscriptions on monuments worked, see M. H. Crawford, 'Discovery, autopsy and progress: Diocletian's jigsaw puzzles', in T. P. Wiseman (ed.), *Classics in Progress: Essays on Ancient Greece and Rome*, Oxford: British Academy and Oxford University Press, 2002, 144–63. Another defence against forgery was multiple copies from a controlled official source, on which cf. *Gesta Senatus* 5 (438) on the promulgation and copying of the Theodosian Code.

vain.[57] Now, therefore, the emperors had decided to act – and could not be accused of acting in haste (10). Everyone of any human feeling (the emperors said) would recoil from the exploitation of even good harvests by the speculators and the abuse of high interest rates for loans when harvests were bad (11–12).

But there was a specific reason for the reform, which was that soldiers had been especially disadvantaged by the extortionate practices of the greedy:

> So who does not know that audacity, ambushing the public well-being, comes to the mind of the profiteer – wherever the common safety of all demands our armies be directed, not only through villages and towns, but through their entire journey – the audacity to extort a price for goods, not fourfold or eightfold but such that human speech cannot find words for the price and the act. Who does not know that sometimes a soldier is deprived of his donative and salary in the transaction of a single exchange, and that the whole world's entire tax contributions for the maintenance of armies is spent on the hateful profits of thieves, so that by their own hand our troops seem to transfer the hopes of their military career and their past efforts to universal profiteers, and those who ravage the state seize more day by day than they know how to hold? (Edict on Maximum Prices 14, trans. Rees)

It was the soldier on the move, then, that Diocletian was most concerned to help. However, as was often the case with imperial enactments, the scope of a law could be wider than the problem which prompted it. Diocletian's setting of maximum prices would not apply only to soldiers, and some of the items listed, such as shoes worn by patrician senators and equestrians (*Prices Edict* 9.7–9), are unlikely to have concerned soldiers in service. But for the reform to work, there must be penalties for infringement – as 'it is unusual for a policy improving the human condition to be embraced of its own accord', while salutary terror was known to have the desired effect (18). Diocletian stipulated that capital punishment – which entailed penalties ranging from death or exile to loss of property and civil rights – should be inflicted on those who set extortionate prices, those who colluded by paying them and those who withdrew goods from the market, thus causing unnecessary shortages (18–19).

The list of maximum prices follows. They relate to a list of about

---

57. For imperial concern with greed as a motive, see *Cod. Just.* 9.9.23; 10.42.6; Corcoran, *Empire* 209.

1,500 items, ranging from the rates for grains and beans per army
modius (measure) to wages supplied for various forms of service.
Diocletian had been careful to stress that the tariff referred to the
highest rate possible; he hoped that, in areas of surplus, the market
might drive prices down. Can we assume that Diocletian's tariffs,
which may have been based on official records,[58] bore a reasonable
relationship to reality? As the aim was to restrict prices, the tariff in
the edict probably undercut the rates set in the open market. There
was no acknowledgement of regional variation, or that prices might
vary between town and country, and some of the rates quoted, such
as the daily or piece rate of 25 *denarii*, may be over-schematic. Nor
was there acknowledgement of the problems faced by a retailer
of goods who saw his profit margins wiped out by the wholesaler's
adherence to the maximum allowed.[59] Nonetheless, the comparison
of rates applicable to different occupations is instructive. Skilled
tradesmen, such as carpenters, cabinet makers or stonemasons, at
50 *denarii* could expect twice the daily wage (plus maintenance)
of a farm labourer at 25 *denarii*, but their takings were dwarfed by
those of the figure painter at 150 *denarii*. At the other end of the
scale, shepherds (who were often associated with banditry) received
20 *denarii* per day, the same sum as was paid to a vet for a single
operation on the head of a horse. If a soldier's sons required an
education, they could be taught arithmetic or shorthand at the relatively cheap rate of 75 *denarii* per month, but over three times as
much would be asked of the ambitious father wishing to have his
son trained up in rhetoric (monthly rate, 250 *denarii*). And, as ever,
going to law was expensive. An advocate or jurist (legal consultant)
could charge a fee of up to 250 *denarii* for initiating a case but four
times as much for pleading it: that 1,000 *denarii* was the equivalent
of four months' wages even of the teacher of rhetoric (and more than
a year's work by the less favoured educators). At the top end of the
scale were items beyond the range of all but the most wealthy and
powerful: a man with 150,000 *denarii* to spare could invest in a
grade A lion for the arena or one pound of double-dyed purple
silk, the latter a risky investment on other grounds, as ownership of
purple cloth could be construed as treasonable.[60]

Lactantius' verdict, predictably, was that the Edict on Maximum

58. Corcoran, *Empire*, 219–21.
59. See Duncan Jones, *Economy*, 366–9.
60. Amm. Marc. 16.8.8; *Cod. Just.* 4.40.1; *Cod. Theod.* 10.20.18; 10.21.3. See *Prices
Edict* 32.1a (lion) and 24.1a (purple silk).

Prices was a failure.[61] He argued that, having caused shortages through his own excesses, Diocletian caused many people to be killed because of infringements over low-value items, and the shortages became even worse because goods were withdrawn from sale. In the end the law was abandoned. But, given his bias, the value of Lactantius' analysis is questionable. The limited geographical occurrence of the inscription suggests that governors outside the favoured five provinces thought it not worth their while to give the law permanent form, but this alone is not proof of failure. The content of the prices edict suggests that it was intended to apply in the west as well: the section on sea freight charges shows prices for transport within the western Mediterranean between Africa, Rome, Sicily, Sardinia, Spain and Gaul.[62] Lack of any epigraphic trace of the edict may indicate indifference, or official reluctance to invest in a large inscription that might quickly become out of date: the Aphrodisias version, for example, shows that revisions were very quickly made to the transport section.

Ancient emperors were not economists in any modern sense. Diocletian's moralistic diagnosis of the problem as 'greed' is rhetoric but it also reflects, at least in part, how he saw inflation as the product of moral failure. However, his actions suggest that he did also have some appreciation of the need to regulate supplies to match demand. As Simon Corcoran has argued, the edict may have been prompted by the charging of inflated prices at Antioch, a city often obliged to play host to influxes of soldiers on campaigns against Persia, and where Diocletian was resident in the summer of 301.[63] Significant shifts in population numbers, such as those regularly experienced in a front-line city such as Antioch, would inevitably affect the balance between supply and demand, and thus the prices charged for goods and services.[64] What Diocletian saw as avarice on the part of local traders was in fact the market at work. The fact that Diocletian, while denouncing the greed of speculators, also authorised the building of grain stores for the city shows that he

61. Lactant. *De mort. pers.*7.6–7.
62. Corcoran, *Empire* 223–5.
63. *Cod. Just.* 3.28.25 (July 301). Diocletian travelled to Alexandria later in the year and the edict may have been issued en route. However, its complexity, and the fact that Diocletian's administration was largely based at Antioch, suggest that the text is a product of his experience of that city.
64. In the fifth century, this was well understood, in relation to Julian, by Socrates, *Hist. eccl.* 3. 17, who blames rising prices on the influx of soldiers recruited for Julian's Persian campaign.

shared the wider awareness in the ancient world of the impact of seasonal shortages on the price of food.

Diocletian's attempt to 'fix' prices by imperial fiat is paralleled by similarly unsuccessful reforms attempted by the emperor Julian at Antioch in 362–3.[65] In his own, self-satirical[66] address to the city, the *Misopogon* ('Beard-Hater'), Julian complained of the greed of the rich.[67] He had learned from acclamations in the theatre that prices were high, even though goods were plentiful, and, the next day, had summoned those responsible, leaving it to them to solve the problem. Only when, after three months, they had failed to do so did Julian intervene:[68]

> And when I saw that the outcry of the people was true and that the marketplace was in dire straits, not because of a shortage but because of the greed of the well-heeled, I fixed a fair price for each item and made it public to all.

Finding also that prices of grain were being driven up by a real shortage due to local crop failure, Julian intervened and imported fresh, cheap supplies from neighbouring cities and from Egypt – only to see them bought up by the speculators and resold in the countryside at a higher price. Avoiding the imperial gaze, by staying clear of the city, worked for the Julianic speculators – and similar entrepreneurial tampering with the market may have helped to subvert the reforms of Diocletian also.

Law and morality

The relative peace enjoyed by the Roman Empire, as advertised in the Edict on Maximum Prices, created space for moral and legal reform in the Augustan tradition. Under Diocletian, the first attempt since Hadrian was made to impose a system on legal texts and provide reference works, which could act as sources of information on what the law was. Diocletian's, or his officials', project was to collect and codify imperial rescripts, which mostly related to civil rather than criminal law, and which had been issued in response to problems raised by individual cases. The collections began

65. Corcoran, *Empire*, 215–19.
66. As argued by Maud W. Gleason, 'Festive satire: Julian's *Misopogon* and the New Year at Antioch', *JRS* 76 (1986), 106–19.
67. Julian, *Misopogon*, 368C–369A.
68. Julian, *Misopogon*, 369A.

with Hadrian and the Hadrianic precedent is instructive on other grounds, although it may also be misleading. In c. 130, Hadrian had ordered legal experts to recast the Praetor's Edict, an important source of civil law, in permanent form.[69] Thereafter, the edict was no longer revised by the praetors on an annual basis, as had been the case (at least in theory) hitherto. Instead the emperor, his councillors and authoritative legal interpreters would build on and modify the law as covered in the edict. Hadrian's aim was thus not only to simplify the law, by providing a single authoritative text for reference purposes. It was also to formalise imperial control of praetorian law for the future.

This last aim of Hadrian, to impose control on law for the future, appears not to apply to the Diocletianic project and there is no direct extant evidence that Diocletian took an active role in the compilation. Two officials gave their names to the 'law-codes' as they emerged in the 290s. The first, Gregorius, collected rescripts from the time of Hadrian down to 291; the second, Hermogenian, known to have been the author of rescripts himself in his capacity as master of petitions (*libelli*), updated the collection down to 295, producing a further edition in 298.[70] The 'official' nature of the codification is debatable.[71] Certainly, the 'Codex of Gregorius and Hermogenian' carried authority, not least because it conferred general application on a series of imperial decisions made initially in response to individual cases. The codes would have served as a work of reference for governors in their judicial capacity, as well as for hard-pressed imperial bureaucrats, although how far it eased officials' workload or precluded continued reference of difficult or embarrassing cases to the emperors cannot be known. But Diocletian, unlike Theodosius and Justinian, saw no need to attach his name to the project; the Codex Gregorianus and the Codex Hermogenianus, though useful, were not designed as an overt demonstration of imperial prestige. Indeed, compared with the Theodosian Code, issued in 438, and the

69. The law of the Praetor's Edict, or *ius honorarium* (the praetorship being an *honos*, or magistracy), is distinguished from the civil or citizens' law (*ius civile*) on historical grounds. In practice the overlap between them was extensive.
70. The standard account of this in English is Corcoran, *Empire*, 25–42; on Hermogenian, ibid., 75–83. See also Serena Connolly, *Lives Behind the Laws: The World of the Codex Hermogenianus*, Bloomington: Indiana University Press, 2010.
71. On problems with the public/private dichotomy suggested by the word 'official', see Jill Harries, 'Roman law codes and the Roman legal tradition', in J. W. Cairns and P. du Plessis (eds), *Beyond Dogmatics: Law and Society in the Roman World*, Edinburgh: Edinburgh University Press, 2007, 85–104, esp. 86–92.

Code of Justinian, the Diocletianic project has a slightly casual air. No known measures were taken to provide updates or revisions in the future, or to protect the texts from unauthorised interpolations. Naturally, in the fourth century, lawyers who found it useful to collect rescripts from official noticeboards occasionally provided 'revised versions' of the two codes, and a few additional private rescripts survived due to this, through such collections as the Vatican Fragments or the *Collatio* (Comparison) of Mosaic and Roman Law.[72]

Diocletian and his colleagues saw the making of law as something more than merely a series of restatements or minor modifications of regulation. Its purpose was also to serve as an educator in virtue, an idea present from Plato onwards, and present too in the prefatory documents to the Theodosian Code, which described the end-product as a 'teacher of life' (*magisterium vitae*).[73] As we have seen with the preamble to the prices edict, the emperors' rhetoric created two communities: the virtuous, led and personified by the wise, restrained and kindly emperors, stern only to evildoers, and, on the other side, the wicked, greedy and unscrupulous, happy to sacrifice the general good for their private gain – and thus unworthy to be members of that community. The aim of legislative propaganda was not, therefore, merely to project the image of the good emperor. It was also to explain to the Romans the proper character of the *res publica* of which they were all part, a state subject to good emperors, who were themselves, as members of the Jovian and Herculian houses, connected to the traditional gods.

To this end, the Roman state, as envisaged by Diocletian, was contrasted with those barbarians and outsiders who would undermine its laws and values. Regulation, even of a relatively minor matter, became a showcase for imperial ideology. This can be illustrated by the edict issued in 295 outlawing incestuous marriages. The content is a reiteration of the traditional policies on the unlawfulness of marriages between close kin, and the forbidden relationships are specified (5); the consequences for such unions were that the children were illegitimate, but there was to be a period of amnesty, till the end of the year. From the start, the rhetoric invokes

---

72. The restriction of the Theodosian Code's contents, from Constantine onwards, to laws of general application (mostly edicts or letters) means that most private rescripts from the fourth century have not survived.
73. *Cod. Theod.* 1.1.5 (429).

traditional morality, the ancient laws and the gods, all of which are required for the proper functioning of society:[74]

> Since to our god-fearing and pious minds, those measures, which have been established chastely and religiously by Roman statutes, seem to be most especially worthy of veneration and deserving of preservation by everlasting religious observance, those acts, which have been committed by some individuals wickedly and incestuously, we believe should not be overlooked by us ... For thus there can be no doubt that the immortal gods too will continue, as they have always been, favourable to the Roman name, and pleased with our service, if our gaze perceives all under our rule conducting their lives in accordance with duty to the gods, religion, peace and chastity in all things.

The edict then proceeds to castigate incest as un-Roman, alien to the Roman usages on marriage as sanctioned by Roman religion and the '*disciplina* of the ancient law [*iuris veteris*]';[75] the culprits' 'promiscuous' rush to illicit coupling in the manner of herd and wild animals, driven by 'detestable passion' (*execrandae libidinis*), overwhelms them regardless of modesty (*pudor*) and right conduct in relation to both men and gods (*pietas*); forsaking Roman usage, as sanctified by antiquity, they have signed up to the monstrous rites of the *ius barbaricum* ('laws of the barbarians', with specific reference, perhaps, to Persia). By contrast, the emperors are merciful, allowing time for the delinquents to sort out their lives and avoid the penalties of the law.[76]

In the ideology of Diocletian and his colleagues, wise and enlightened legal provision and the Roman morality approved by the emperors and sanctioned by the gods and by antiquity were essential

---

74. *Collatio of Mosaic and Roman Law* 6.4 = Riccobono, *FIRA* II, 2nd edn, 558–60; *Cod. Just.* 5.4.17 (shorter extract): 'Quoniam piis religiosisque mentibus nostris ea, quae Romanis legibus caste sancteque sunt constituta, venerabilia maxime videntur atque aeterna religione servanda, dissimulare ea, quae a quibusdam in praeteritum nefarie incesteque commissa sunt, non opportere credimus ... Ita enim et ipsos immortales deos Romano nomini, ut semper fuerunt, faventes atque placatos futuros esse non dubium est, si cunctos sub imperio nostro agentes piam religiosamque et quietam et castam in omnibus mere colere perspeximus vitam.' The *Collatio* is a comparison of Roman law, as set out in imperial legal pronouncements and juristic texts, with the 'law of Moses', as set out in the Ten Commandments. In its present (incomplete) form, it dates from the late fourth century, but may be a revision of an earlier work.
75. For reiteration of references to the 'ancient ordinances' of Roman law (*iura*) or statutes (*leges*), see *Edict on incest*, 3, 4 and 6.
76. Cf. *Collatio* 6.5, Diocletian and Maximian to Flavianus in 291, letting off a pair who married incestuously in ignorance – provided they divorce at once.

to the well-being of the Roman *res publica*. Incest was a special case because of its religious connotations: although the incest edict refers to the lesser infringement of the law, marrying within the forbidden degrees of relationship, *incestum* was also the word applied to sexual activity which incurred religious pollution, such as to the crime of the Vestal Virgin who broke her vow of virginity and thus potentially brought disaster on the whole community.[77] The emperors believed that law, with its moral content backed by religious sanction, helped to safeguard the community; to disobey the law was to flout the authority not only of the emperors but also of the gods, as upholders of *pietas*; outside the community governed by ancient law and morality and protected by the gods was the world of beasts and barbarians. For those who did not share the emperors' religious assumptions, the dangers were clear. Failure to honour ancient religions would not only incur the wrath of the offended gods; it would also undermine the whole value-system on which the new empire of Diocletian was founded.

77. For a brief account of *incestum* with more bibliographical references, see Jill Harries, *Law and Crime in the Roman World*, Cambridge: Cambridge University Press, 2007, 90–5.

Figure 8 Arch of Galerius, Thessalonike, Greece

Figure 9 Enthroned Tetrarchs, Arch of Galerius, Thessalonike, Greece

Figure 10 *Adlocutio* frieze, Arch of Galerius, Thessalonike, Greece

Figure 11 Sacrifice frieze, Arch of Galerius, Thessalonike, Greece

Figure 12 Camp of Diocletian, Palmyra, Syria

Figure 13 Diocletianic wall, Palmyra, Syria

Figure 14 Baths of Diocletian porch, Palmyra, Syria

Figure 15 Market building, Aezani, Turkey

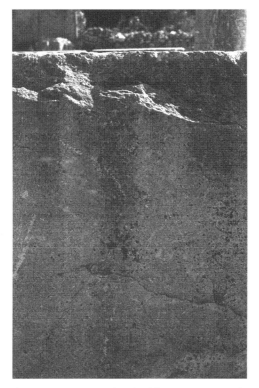

Figure 16 Price edict inscription, market building, Aezani, Turkey

CHAPTER 4

The return of the old gods

The 'Great Persecution' of 303 to 313 bulks large in the self-presentation of early Christianity. Eusebius conveys passionate sympathy with the fates of people, some of whom were personally known to him, and Lactantius' perspective was influenced by the prolonged ordeal of his teacher, Donatus.[1] But, writing or revising their work under Constantine,[2] and with the benefit of hindsight, the Christian authors shaped a providential narrative, in which the persecutions were the prelude to vindication.[3] The motives of Diocletian and Galerius, on the other hand, can be inferred from the chance survival of the rescript against the Manichaeans and the content of the legal sanctions against Christians issued from 303 onwards,[4] but the voices of the philosophical opponents of Christianity are largely silent. The attacks on Christians of Celsus in the second century, of Porphyry, in the late third (possibly early fourth) century[5] and of Sossianus Hierocles in the early 300s[6] survive only in fragments or in the works of the Christians who rebutted them.[7]

1. Lactant. *De mort. pers.* 16.3; 35.2. Individual martyr-acts also survive but some, composed by Donatists in Africa, had a polemical purpose.
2. For the date of Lactantius, *De mort. pers.* (between 313 and 315), and his relatively mild treatment of Maxentius, see T. D. Barnes, 'Lactantius and Constantine', *JRS* 63 (1973), 29–46. Eusebius' *Historia ecclesiastica* went through several revisions, the last probably in 325.
3. Eusebius' earlier perspective, that the persecutions were a punishment for Christian failings, survives at *Hist. eccl.* 7.1.
4. *Collatio of Mosaic and Roman Law*, 15.3.
5. For the destruction of Porphyry's writings and their condemnation as 'infamous' under Constantine, see Socrates, *Hist. eccl.* 1.9. For their date in early 300s and Porphyry's integrity as a scholar, see T. D. Barnes, 'Scholarship or propaganda? Porphyry, *Against the Christians*, and its historical setting', *BICS* 39 (1994), 53–65.
6. See T. D. Barnes, 'Sossianus Hierocles and the antecedents of the Great Persecution', *Harvard Studies in Classical Philology* 80 (1976), 239–52.
7. See Andrew Louth, 'Philosophical objections to Christianity on the eve of the Great Persecution', in D. V. Twomey and M. Humphries (eds), *The Great Persecution*, Dublin: Four Courts Press, 2009, 33–48 (on Porphyry, 38–45).

Imperial legitimacy was also at issue in the persecution narratives. Cicero, whose influence on Lactantius' *Divine institutes* was profound, had argued that it was possible for governments (such as the Thirty Tyrants in Athens) to act unlawfully and in contravention of natural justice, a quality innate in men and derived from the gods.[8] Resistance to such governments was justifiable as a last resort, because, by acting against natural justice, the rulers had forfeited the right to rule. Lactantius did not go that far, even expressing disapproval of the angry Christian who, in February 303, tore down a copy of the persecuting edict.[9] Still, in the Christian authors, the figure of the persecuting emperor or judge is presented as the stereotypical *tyrannus*, violent, cruel and prone to outbursts of ungovernable rage (*furor*).[10] Although the measures taken against Christianity were lawful in the sense that they were passed by emperors, whose positions in 303 were unchallenged, they, and those who implemented their instructions, acted in violation of natural justice. Such was the message conveyed by Christian accounts of the content of the edicts and the violent behaviour of those who implemented them.

Emperors and gods

For Diocletian and his colleagues, the Christians were not a pressing problem; after his accession in 284, nearly nineteen years were to pass before formal action was taken in the first of four decrees against Christian religious practices, on 24 February 303.[11] The emperors' religious agenda was, at least to start with, a positive one, the promotion of the ancient gods, under whose patronage Rome and the empire had prospered. The identification of Diocletian with Jupiter and of Maximian with Hercules was part of a general attempt at religious revival, as the Gallic panegyrist of 291 appreciated:

8. As argued in Cic. *Leg.* 1. See Jill Harries, *Cicero and the Jurists*, London: Duckworth, 2006, 185–229, for other references and implications. For Lactantius and Cicero, see A. Bowen and P. Garnsey (eds and trans.) *Lactantius, Divine Institutes*, TTH 40, Liverpool: Liverpool University Press, 2003, 20–36.
9. Lactant. *De mort. pers.* 13.2: 'non recte magno tamen animo' ('wrongly, but with a noble spirit').
10. For the literary construction of the persecuting judge, see Jill Harries, 'Constructing the judge: Judicial accountability and the culture of criticism in late antiquity', in Richard Miles (ed.), *Constructing Identities in Late Antiquity*, London: Routledge, 1999, 214–33, esp. 225–31.
11. Although Christians, such as the recusant solider Marcellus, who refused duties such as military service were liable to punishment on those grounds prior to 303.

How great is your piety towards the gods, whom you honour with altars, statues, temples, donations, with your own names and images as well, and have made more sacred by the example of your veneration! (3) Now men truly understand what the power (*potestas*) of the gods is, since you honour them at such expense![12]

Panegyric creatively blurred the boundaries between the human and divine, setting the gods or the godlike in human history, alongside the emperors, and raising emperors to the level of gods.[13] In an earlier speech, probably delivered at Trier, the orator celebrated the birthday of the city of Rome (21 April) and waxed eloquent on the topic of Hercules. The hero, claimed the orator, was all but the real founder of Rome, an historical fact (he said) attested by the great altar of Hercules at Rome.[14] The descent of the Spartan kings from Heracles (and thus ultimately from Jupiter) is also accepted as fact, although the speaker's point is that the two emperors, unlike the Spartan kings, ruled together in harmony;[15] a similarly unfavourable comparison is made with the feuds of Rome's (other) joint founders, Romulus and Remus.[16] Imperial actions mirrored the achievements of their gods: Diocletian accepts the help of Maximian, as Jupiter did that of Hercules in the battle against the Giants, also a popular theme on the coinage;[17] later Diocletian is seen subduing Persia, 'in the manner of his Jupiter'.[18] Though not divine themselves, emperors took on such attributes of divinity as the ability to see and know all, standing on the apex of the world and surveying it with their all-seeing gaze.[19] Maximian is called a 'god manifest' whose presence (*praesentia*) brings benefits, even when he is physically absent.[20]

In the coinage of Diocletian and Maximian, however, the

---

12. *Pan. Lat.* 11 (3).6.2–3, eds and trans. C. E. V. Nixon and B. S. Rodgers, *In Praise of Later Roman Emperors: The Panegyrici Latini. Introduction, Translation and Historical Commentary*, Berkeley: University of California Press, 1994. The restoration of the ancient cults was also noted and approved of by Aur. Vict. *Caes.* 39.45.
13. See Barbara S. Rodgers, 'Divine insinuation in the *Panegyrici Latini*', *Historia* 35 (1986), 69–104.
14. *Pan. Lat.* 10 (2).1.3.
15. *Pan. Lat.* 10 (2).9.4–5; 10.10. 1–11.
16. *Pan. Lat.* 10 (2).13.1–2.
17. *Pan. Lat.* 10 (2).3.3–4; on coins, Jupiter is often entitled 'Fulgurator', wielder of the thunderbolt, and on some issues is shown in action, striking down the Titans with thunderbolts, e.g. *RIC* 5.2, p. 234, 144, 145 (AD 293–4).
18. *Pan. Lat.* 10 (2).7.5.
19. *Pan. Lat.* 10 (2).3.34.
20. *Pan. Lat.* 10 (2).2.1.

emperors, although associated with the gods and sometimes wearing their insignia, are not depicted as gods themselves. Jupiter and Hercules feature prominently on the coins of both emperors, the former as *Conservator* ('Preserver'), *Propagator*, *Tutator* ('Guardian'), *Ultor* ('Avenger') and *Victor*, while Hercules shares some of the epithets and is associated with *Virtus* ('Virtue' or 'Courage'); Maximian himself is also represented as Hercules, with the club and the lionskin.[21] Both are represented as making sacrifice to their gods for victory. A silver coin from Siscia shows the two Augusti and the two Caesars sacrificing at an altar in front of a camp with a door and eight towers, to give thanks for victory over the Sarmatians;[22] and the Arch of Galerius in Thessalonica in northern Greece shows Diocletian and Galerius sacrificing to Hercules in commemoration of Galerius' Persian victory. Emperors, therefore, are clearly distinct from the gods. Some designs even aim to convey a quasi-republican impression. Abstracts such as *Concordia* ('Harmony', of the emperors and the soldiers), *Pax*, *Providentia*, *Salus* ('Safety'), *Securitas*, *Victoria* and *Virtus* feature, as also does the 'Genius of the Roman People' (*Genius Populi Romani*), complete with cornucopia and other emblems of prosperity. This reinforces the ethos present in the legal pronouncements of the emperors; the style of their rule reflected a return to the simplicity and virtue of earlier times.

Did the panegyricists go further than their predecessors in fusing the human and the divine in their presentation of emperors, contributing to the creation of what would become the Byzantine theocracy? The Eutropius/Aurelius Victor tradition suggested that Diocletian introduced a more overtly autocratic, 'Persian style' of rule. Victor observed that Diocletian took to wearing jewels on his sandals and a gold-embroidered robe, and was the first since Caligula and Domitian to allow himself to be called 'Lord' (*Dominus*) in public and to be worshipped (*adorari*) as a god.[23] In fact, Diocletian's innovations were a continuation of a long-term development. Aurelian, Probus and Carus had received salutations on their coins as *deus et dominus*, 'god and lord', and the adjective 'sacred' was already routinely applied to the emperor, his family, his

21. A. S. Robertson (ed.), *Roman Imperial Coins in the Hunter Coin Cabinet*, Oxford: Oxford University Press, 1982, vol. 5, p. 23, 40.
22. *RIC* 6, p. 459, 34a. Also commemorated by the mint at Nicomedia (*RIC* 6, p. 556, 22b).
23. Aur. Vict, *Caes.* 39.2–4; Eutr. *Brev.* 9.26.

laws, palace and government – and would continue to be applied to Christian emperors. As emperors had been objects of cultic worship since the time of Augustus and had every reason in the third century to reinforce their personal security by enhancing their sacred character, court ceremonial had inevitably become more formal over time and the persona of the emperor more overtly autocratic and remote.

Ritual and ceremonial assisted communication, both with crowds and with individuals. Emperors were both autocrats and comrades. The public image of the imperial persona as set apart from ordinary mortals coexisted with an ethos of soldierly 'comradeship', which was expressed in the designations of officials as *comites*, companions (or 'Counts'), and the emperor's army as *comitatus*. This assisted the effective functioning of government and in particular of the emperor's ruling council, the consistory (*consistorium*), allowing advisers to have the confidence to speak frankly. Powerful and favoured individuals were granted privileged access to the imperial presence, where they were permitted to kiss the imperial purple. The ceremony, known as *adoratio*, while permitting the subject to offer homage, also enabled the emperor to reassure the adviser that he was still in favour. By the mid-fourth century, *adoratio* was understood to be a means of reciprocal communication between emperor and subject. Ammianus, who criticised Diocletian (though not by name) for introducing foreign ceremonial 'in the manner of monarchy',[24] recounted the favourable reception accorded by Constantius II to a somewhat hesitant generalissimo, Ursicinus; by contrast, Julian refused permission to one Thalassius to 'adore and be present among the honorati' but relented later.[25]

The identification of deviance

The old doctrine, that the empire's safety depended on right religion, acquired a more powerfully negative character in Diocletian's later years. Adherence to 'right' religion also entailed the identification and obliteration of 'wrong' religion. It is a measure of the changed

24. Amm. Marc. 15.5.8, 'regio more'.
25. Amm. Marc. 22.9.16; see also 21.9.8 (Julian reproves Lucillianus for taking advantage of his favour); *Pan. Lat.* 11.11.3 comments that only men of rank have access to *adoratio*; *Cod. Theod.* 6.24.4 refers to 'those considered worthy to touch our purple'. On this, see John Matthews, *The Roman Empire of Ammianus*, London: Duckworth, 1989, 244–7.

religious climate of the later third century that, while the Persian deity Mithras, the god especially favoured by soldiers, was acceptable,[26] being already established and adapted to his new context, the followers of another Persian, the prophet Mani, were not. The terminology used in the early fourth century to outlaw 'wrong' religion (or *superstitio*) helped to define the ways in which that religion was 'wrong', and drove a wedge between deviant 'superstition' on the one hand and, on the other, mainstream *religio*, the right beliefs, which safeguarded emperors and community,[27] and which consisted of the worship of the old gods and adherence to received religious wisdom. The rescript to Julianus, proconsul of Africa, against the Manichaeans dated probably to 302 presents the new, foreign and corrupting doctrines of Mani as a threat to the contented and peaceful condition of the Roman state.[28] As Mani styled himself an 'apostle' of Jesus Christ, and claimed that his teachings were a fulfilment of the Christian gospels, his followers may initially have attracted official attention as 'Christians'. However, the focus of the rescript against them on their 'Persian' origin and alleged political affiliations differentiated them from Christians within the empire.

The sharp distinction drawn by Diocletian between right and wrong belief reflects an intolerance of dissent, which foreshadows the Christian rhetoric against heretics to come. The 'immortal gods', wrote the emperors, had so ordained it that what is good and true had been long determined and established 'by the counsel of many, good, worthy and most learned men'; to contradict this received religious wisdom was contrary to natural right. It was a most serious charge, that anyone should undermine 'what is once decided upon and set out by the men of old'. It was therefore the emperors' 'very earnest endeavour' (*ingens nobis studium est*) to 'punish the obstinate persistence (*pertinaciam*) of the depraved mind (*pravae mentis*) of very wicked men'. The fear was that the Manichaeans

26. See Manfred Clauss, *The Roman Cult of Mithras: The God and his Mysteries*, trans. Richard Gordon, Edinburgh: Edinburgh University Press, 2000.
27. This anticipates the language used in the outlawing of heresy, on which see Caroline Humfress, *Orthodoxy and the Courts in Late Antiquity*, Oxford: Oxford University Press, 2007, ch. 8. On the fate of the Manichaeans in the Roman Empire, see collection of articles by Samuel N. C. Lieu, *Manichaeism in the Roman Empire and the Near East*, Leiden: Brill, 1994.
28. *Collatio* 15.3.1–8, at Ricccobono, *FIRA* II, 580–1. See also Simon Corcoran, *The Empire of the Tetrarchs: Imperial Pronouncements and Government*, AD 284–324, Oxford: Oxford University Press, 2000, 135–6.

would corrupt the Romans through their subversion of the traditional religious order. Through their possible introduction of 'the harsh laws of the Persians', they would act as a form of Persian fifth column, infecting 'with their deadly poisons the modest and peaceful Roman race – and our whole world'. Their practices were therefore to be classified as *maleficia*, evil magic,[29] and Julianus was ordered to burn their books and subject the Manichaeans themselves to capital punishment. If, however, aristocratic people were converted, their property was to be confiscated and they were to be banished to the mines. Bringing the Manichaeans within the criminal law was thus a two-stage process: their religion was classified as criminal 'magic', therefore their religion was itself a criminal activity.

As we have seen, Diocletian and his colleagues required conformity to his new moral and religious order from *all* his subjects. Those, like the followers of Mani, who were seen to challenge imperial authority did so at their peril. Roman religion is often characterised as dependent on ritual or cultic observance, rather than belief, but it was not always possible in practice to separate the two. For the Romans under the empire, the distinction may even have been immaterial; action and intention, although not identical, were interdependent. In 251, as reported to the bishop Cyprian, the edict against Christians of Valerian and Gallienus commanded that 'those who do not observe Roman religion, should acknowledge Roman rites';[30] later, a new proconsul upbraided Cyprian for having lived for a long time 'with a sacrilegious disposition',[31] adding that the bishop had gathered together 'wicked men' in a 'conspiracy' and acted as 'an enemy of the Roman gods and sacred religion'. While the disposition (*mens*) could only be proved by action (or lack of it), proven actions also established the nature of the *mens*, which motivated the actions in the first place; the forming of a 'conspiracy' implied premeditated sedition, the corruption of others and even treason.

From the standpoint of Diocletian and Galerius, the principal

---

29. The letter to Julianus was preserved in the Gregorian and Hermogenian Codes, book 7, section 'de maleficis et Manichaeis' ('magicians and Manichaeans').
30. *Acta Cypriani* 1.1: 'qui Romanam religionem non colunt, debere Romanas caerimonias recognoscere.' Text and translation are accessible in H. Musurillo, *Acts of the Christian Martyrs: Introduction, Texts and Translations*, Oxford: Clarendon Press, 1972.
31. *Acta Cypriani* 4.1: 'Diu sacrilega mente vixisti.'

architects of the measures against 'wrong religion', the Christians were a deviant religious group, who vaunted their defiance.[32] A clutch of martyr-acts describing events in the late 290s (though the texts are later) show public rejection of military service by a recruit, Maximilian, in 295; a serving soldier, Marcellus, who throws off his military belt in full view of the governor (c. 298); and a veteran of twenty-seven years, Julianus, who refuses obedience to the edict issued early in 304, ordering all to sacrifice.[33] According to a story found in both Christian and non-Christian sources, an attempt by Diocletian to take the omens at a public sacrifice was disrupted by a number of Christians, who surreptitiously made the sign of the Cross, thus rendering the entrails of the sacrifices unreadable.[34] For Christians like Lactantius, this was a demonstration of God's power over the 'demons'; Diocletian, however, overcome by rage (*furor*), a reaction typical of 'tyrants', ordered all soldiers to sacrifice or be discharged from the army.

The edicts against the Christians are presented by Lactantius as an unwelcome and unprovoked initiative, emanating from the promptings of Galerius, who was emboldened to take action against the Christians by his victory in Persia in 298.[35] The general legislative practice of emperors, however, which extended to edicts, was to act in response to situations brought to their attention. One source of complaints against Christians could have been Sossianus Hierocles, the anti-Christian courtier and pamphleteer, who was later to be an active persecutor of Christians in Egypt; a second spur to action was an anti-Christian oracle issued at Apollo's shrine at Didyma in 302.[36] For Diocletian and his colleagues, Christians' reported refusal to conform to the new world order resembled a challenge to their authority and to the foundations of their newly restored Roman

32. For the perspective of the authorities, see M. Humphries, 'The mind of the persecutors: 'By the gracious favour of the gods'', in Twomey and Humphries, *The Great Persecution*, 11–32. The authorities would not, of course, have seen themselves as persecutors.
33. Musurillo. *Acts of the Christian Martyrs*, 244–9 (Maximilian), 250–9 (Marcellus), 260–5 (Julianus). For the martyrdoms of Typasius, a veteran who refused to re-enlist, and Fabius, a *vexillifer* who refused to carry his standard in procession, see G. E. M. de Ste Croix, in the collection of his work by M. Whitby and J. Streeter (eds), *Christian Persecution, Martyrdom and Orthodoxy*, Oxford: Oxford University Press, 2006, 75–6.
34. Lactant. *De mort. pers* 10.1–5.
35. Bill Leadbetter, *Galerius and the Will of Diocletian*, London: Routledge, 2009, 126–34. See also P. S. Davies, 'The origins and purpose of the persecution of 303', *JTS* 40 (1989), 66–94, arguing against the importance of Galerius.
36. Euseb. *Vit. Const.* 2.50.

community (*res publica*). Thus their legislation against deviant cult and belief was not simply aimed at suppressing dissent through legal sanctions, public trials, torture and executions, the stuff of which Christian accounts of 'persecution' are made. By prohibiting meetings, destroying meeting-places and the sacred writings, and imposing legal disabilities on adherents, Diocletian and Galerius hoped to excise from the Roman community a group whose beliefs and practices were incompatible with the re-established ancient Roman religious order. For their part, Christians could not devote their literary efforts solely to celebration of the constancy of their martyrs, important though their example was for the survivors. Their challenge was also to counter the old gods of Rome on their own ideological terrain.

Laws against Christian observance, 303–13

Four edicts were issued against Christian practices in 303–4, beginning on 24 February 303, the day after the Terminalia festival.[37] The Terminalia itself had been marked by a display of state terror; the church at Nicomedia, which was visible from the imperial palace, was subjected to a dawn raid by soldiers and accountants, who burned the sacred books, grabbed what plunder they could and then razed the building to the ground.[38] The raid was immediately followed by the first edict, ordering the destruction of churches, the burning of the Scriptures, and the legal degradation of men in positions of honour and Christian members of the imperial administration.[39] Lactantius reflects a more elite perspective, focusing on the provisions which deprived Christians of legal rights and were especially damaging to members of the curial class and upwards (*honestiores*), who were not normally liable to judicial torture:

> The day after (the Terminalia), an edict was posted by which warning was given that men of that religion should be deprived of all official rank and status, that they should be made liable to torture, whatever their order in society or rank, that any legal action brought against them should be valid in court, while they themselves were not permitted to bring suit for outrage, adultery or theft, in short they were to be deprived of their freedom and right to speak.

37. For discussion of the four, see G. E. M. de Ste Croix, 'Aspects of the Great Persecution', *Harvard Theological Review* 47 (1954), 75–113 = Whitby and Streeter (eds), *Christian Persecution*, 35–68.
38. Lactant. *De mort. pers.* 12. 2–5.
39. Euseb. *Hist. eccl.* 8.2.4; Lactant. *De mort. pers.* 13.1.

Soon after, the palace itself was set on fire, but those responsible were never found.[40] Lactantius blamed it on Galerius, but suspicion also fell upon the Christians. Disturbances in Syria and Melitene seem to have exacerbated imperial doubts as to their loyalty and prompted the second edict:[41]

> Not long after, as people in the country called Melitene (eastern Cappadocia) and others throughout Syria tried to take over the government unlawfully, an imperial edict ordered that the heads of the churches everywhere should be thrown into prison and chained … A huge crowd were thrown into prison everywhere and prisons long designed for murderers and grave-robbers were filled with bishops, priests and deacons, readers and exorcists, so that there was no longer room left in them for condemned criminals.

From the imperial perspective, the second edict was a logical extension of the first. The destruction of the churches and sacred books deprived Christians of their meeting-places and the texts on which their religion was based. However, Christian assemblies were not tied to sacred places and, so long as their leaders remained at large, meetings could continue. The arrest of the clergy should therefore have denied Christians the ability to celebrate their rites at all.

While Eusebius may have exaggerated the effect on prison accommodation, it may well have been the scale of the operation required which, in the end, defeated the authorities. Prisons were designed as holding sites for people awaiting trial or execution, not (in theory) as places of long-term incarceration. The third edict, therefore, signalled a relaxation of policy – to a point. The emperors now allowed the clergy to leave prison, provided that they offered sacrifice; failure to do so would result in torture. Finally, the fourth edict, issued early in 304, ordered that all in the Roman Empire should sacrifice.[42] This last was a reversion to the Decian policy in 250 of conciliating divine favour through universal sacrifice, established through individual certification. However, in 250, the 'Decian persecution' had been triggered by Christians' refusal to sacrifice or be certified; in 303–4, this order of events was reversed.

All four edicts would have been forwarded from the praetorian prefects to the governors, who would issue further regulations

---

40. See also Euseb. *Hist. eccl.* 8.6.6; 'Constantine', *Orat. ad Sanct.* 25. A second fire two weeks later was reported by Lactantius (*De mort. pers.* 14.6), but not Eusebius.
41. Euseb. *Hist. eccl.* 8.6.8–9.
42. Euseb. *Hist. eccl.* 8.6.10.

in their own name. Thus in Africa, the edict which commanded sacrifice is referred to by a local author not as 'imperial' but as 'proconsular.'[43] The edicts were reinforced by further communications, such as letters enjoining sacrifices by whole communities issued in 304/5.[44] A year later, the Caesar Maximinus Daza sent more letters insisting that the census lists should be used to check that all had sacrificed;[45] this was reinforced by instructions to city curators and other local officials to enforce the order to sacrifice. Naturally, resolute Christians refused to do so, and paid the price.

From February 303 to Galerius' Edict of Toleration issued on his deathbed in 311, Christians all over the empire could have stood in fear of arrest, interrogation under torture and painful forms of execution. In practice, the intensity of enforcement depended on local initiatives, or lack of them. While Christians in Constantius' domain (where there were relatively few of them) seem to have suffered merely the loss of a few churches, governors in the areas controlled by Maximian down to 305 (which included Africa), Galerius and, after 305, Maximinus Daza responded to the edicts with varying degrees of enthusiasm; especially active were Urbanus, governor of Palestine from 304,[46] and Sossianus Hierocles, governor in Egypt from 307,[47] and already author of a tract attacking Christianity. Most martyrs received public trials before the governor, at which the martyr 'bore witness' under interrogation, held out under extreme tortures and was then killed by wild beasts or fire, standard forms of execution inflicted on members of the lower classes. But some deaths, as recorded, were due to lynch law: the Christian population of a small town in Phrygia, men, women and children alike, were imprisoned in their church by rampaging soldiers and burned alive.[48]

Martyr-acts from Africa, based on court records but luridly glossed by Christian hagiography, show that some officials, at least,

43. Optatus, *Against the Donatists*, Appendix 2.4; trans. and ed. Mark Edwards, *Optatus Against the Donatists*, TTH 27, Liverpool: Liverpool University Press, 1997. For the argument, which provoked dissent at the time, that the edict commanding sacrifice was not enforced in the west, see de Ste Croix, 'Aspects of the Great Persecution', in Whitby and Streeter, *Christian Persecution*, 46–56.
44. Euseb. *Mart. Pal.* 3.1.
45. Euseb. *Mart. Pal.* 4.8; 8.1; 8.5.
46. Euseb. *Mart. Pal.* 3.1ff.
47. Euseb. *Mart. Pal.* 5.3; *Lactant. De mort pers.* 16.4; on Hierocles in Bithynia, Lactant. *Div. inst.* 5.2.3; T. D. Barnes, *Constantine and Eusebius*, Cambridge, MA: Harvard University Press, 1981, 22, 164–7.
48. Euseb. *Hist. eccl.* 8.11.1; Lactant. *Div. inst.* 5.11.

were scrupulous in adhering to the letter of the edicts they were obliged to enforce. Roman law lacked the language to ban a belief. Instead, the law banned the practices associated with Christianity, appreciating that, for Christians, their practices were central to their faith. Celebration of the Eucharist was, for Christians, all-important and in the African town of Abitina, a group of Christians were arrested for contravening the edict by holding meetings in various houses, arraigned in the forum of their local town and then transported to Carthage to be tried before the proconsul, Anullinus.[49] While the narrative, which was compiled in its present form early in the fifth century,[50] is clogged with standard rhetorical references to Anullinus' intemperate behaviour, the interrogations, as recorded, are focused on alleged infringements of the edict's prohibitions of meetings and the storage of sacred books, not on the question of whether or not the accused were Christians. Those who replied to questions with the affirmation that 'I am a Christian' were quickly called to order: 'I am not asking whether you are Christian but whether you hold assemblies or whether you have any scriptures.'[51]

Christians were in fact faced with a conflict of laws. The martyrs of Abitina admitted that they convened or attended 'meetings' to observe the Eucharist, which was enjoined on them by their Law, a Law explicitly set up against that of the state.[52] Repeatedly, Anullinus insisted that the Christians had disobeyed or 'made light of' the orders of the emperors. Despite the rhetorical emphasis on his anger, the questioning suggests a magistrate still vainly hoping to bring the Christians to see the error of their ways:[53]

> Annullinus: Were assemblies held in your house against the order of the emperor?
> Emeritus (presbyter): We did hold the Lord's Supper in my home.
> Annullinus: Why did you permit them to enter?

49. For translation, see M. Tilley (ed. and trans.), *Donatist Martyr Stories: The Church in Conflict in Roman North Africa*, TTH 24, Liverpool: Liverpool University Press, 1996. For Anullinus, see *PLRE*, C. Annius Anullinus 3, p. 79. The record is consistent in portraying him as a brutal interrogator who pushed the boundaries of legality; the details of the exchanges with the martyrs suggests that he was, to a point, the victim of 'persecutor' stereotyping.

50. See A. Dearn, 'The Abitinian martyrs and the outbreak of the Donatist schism', *Journal of Ecclesiastical History* 55 (2004), 1–18, for date in aftermath of the anti-Donatist Council of Carthage in 411. The interrogation material is, however, earlier and probably authentic.

51. *Mart. Abit.* 13 and 15.

52. *Mart. Abit.* 11 and 12.

53. *Mart. Abit.* 12 (trans. M. Tilley, adapted).

Emeritus: Because they are my brothers and sisters and I could not prevent them from doing so.
Annullinus: You should have prevented them.
Emeritus: I could not, because we cannot go without the Lord's Supper.

Predictably, the martyrs are returned to prison and in due course are executed, not for being Christian but for disobedience to the edict. In due course, they would become heroes to the Donatist schismatic movement, as examples of those who did not 'hand over' sacred books or renounce their faith under pressure. Despite the lurid rhetoric, the court record is almost certainly authentic, as both sides would resort to the official written record to prove their claims to be the 'true' church.[54]

Financial motives also played a part in attacks on Christian organisations, as buildings belonging to Christians were attacked and their property seized. At Cirta in Africa in May 303, the local *curator civitatis*, Felix, was quick to enforce the first edict on the confiscation of Christians' assets and the destruction of the scriptures. His records, as read out later in hearings on the Donatists (who prided themselves on their refusal to help the authorities), catalogued the assets seized from the Christian community at Cirta:[55]

two gold chalices, six silver chalices, six silver urns, a silver cooking-pot, seven silver lamps, two wafer-holders, seven short bronze candlesticks with their own lights, eleven bronze lamps with their own chains, 82 women's tunics, 38 capes, 16 men's tunics, 13 pairs of men's shoes, 47 pairs of women's shoes, 19 peasant clasps (or capes).

Felix's investigations uncovered further undeclared items in other rooms, despite the Christians' attempts at concealment, all of which were formally recorded. The same process was extended to hunting down copies of the Scriptures. Several houses were visited, including those of a tailor and a grammarian. On each occasion, a recorded assurance was given that all had been surrendered. The language of the record is formal and dispassionate but the threat of sanctions against the obstructive and disobedient is plain: when two clerics

54. The Abitinia martyrs are represented as being denied food by the intervention of the deacon Caecilian, whose consecration at Carthage sparked the schism.
55. Optatus, *Against the Donatists*, Appendix (*Acta Zenophili*) 1. 3, trans. Edwards, 154.

deny that they know where their colleagues live – or even what their names are – they are taken into custody. Thus the dramatic scenes evoked by Eusebius and others of heroic resistance to tyrannical governors on the judicial tribunal and in the arena should be set alongside an experience of state power that was less dramatic but no less deadly, the relentless oppression exercised by the local bureau-crat with his scribes, official records and, where required, military backup.

After 305, imperial disunity created more pressing concerns than the suppression of religious dissidence. Maxentius, who had no reason to love his colleagues, was the first to lift the measures against the Christians in his area of control, Africa, Rome and Italy, perhaps hoping to gain political advantage.[56] In 311, Galerius' Edict of Toleration, issued also in the names of his colleagues in the imperial college, Constantine and Licinius, lifted the legal sanctions, and allowed Christians to worship as they chose, provided that they also offered prayers for the safety of the emperor and empire.[57] Galerius' change of tack was represented as a deathbed repentance, but the wording of the edict is less than conciliatory. While the Christians were to be reabsorbed into the religious community as people whose cultic observance would be compatible with the welfare and security of the empire at large, the opening sentence is an affirmation that Galerius has not abandoned the Diocletianic religious agenda:

> Among those other arrangements which we always set in train for the benefit and advantage of the *res publica*, we had previously wished to put everything on a right footing in accordance with the ancient laws [*iuxta leges veteres*] and the public discipline of the Romans, and to have taken thought that the Christians too, who had abandoned the religion of their parents, should return to a good understanding [*ad bonas mentes redirent*].

Galerius' view of the Christians was, still, that they had exchanged observance of 'those principles established by men of old' (*illa veterum instituta*) for a religion based on self-will, making up their 'laws' (*leges*) as they saw fit. This, Galerius argued, was not proper worship either of the old gods or even of the Christians' god. The return to a good *mens*, which would presumably entail the abandoning of unauthorised innovations, would therefore also help

56. Euseb. *Hist. eccl.* 8.14.1 records this but maintains (with hindsight) that Maxentius' favour to the Christians was hypocritical.
57. Latin text at Lactant. *De mort. pers.* 34.1–5; Leadbetter, *Galerius*, 224–5.

Christians to be better adherents of their own religion. So now, in accordance with habitual imperial clemency and indulgence, Galerius would restore freedom of meetings and worship:

> Wherefore, in accordance with this indulgence of ours, they will be obliged to pray to their god for our safety and for that of the *res publica* and for themselves, so that on all sides the *res publica* will be preserved in safety and they may live free from fear in their own habitations.

In 312, Maximinus Daza briefly renewed the persecutions, in consultation with the cities of his domains. Exploiting the intricacies of the interactions between rulers and ruled, which allowed policy to be created with the appearance of consensus,[58] Maximinus, according to Eusebius, refused to promulgate Galerius' edict directly, allegedly issuing verbal instructions only to the praetorian prefect, Sabinus.[59] Sabinus' letter to the provincial governors, translated by Eusebius, grudgingly ordered that Christians should no longer be molested, even though they had failed to respond to the emperors' call to follow 'the holy and correct course of life'; the new policy was to be communicated to curators and other official enforcers but no mention was made of freedom of assembly or the right to build churches conceded by Galerius. Through his echoing of Galerius' negative rhetoric, Maximinus paved the way for a renewal of sanctions against Christians.

City leaders, aware of Maximinus' religious views, now sought to win favours from him by 'petitioning' against the offending religion. Having forbidden Christians to meet in graveyards, Maximinus then 'agreed' to renew legal sanctions against the Christians, in response (it was claimed) to petitions from Nicomedia, Antioch and other cities.[60] This is verified by the existence of two inscriptions, found at Colbasa in Pisidia and Arycanda in eastern Lycia, which record fragments of the Latin text of Maximinus' rescript to the cities against the Christians.[61] Eusebius preserved Maximinus's instructions in full in his Greek translation from a bronze tablet, posted on a column

---

58. S. Mitchell, 'Maximinus and the Christians in AD 312: A new Latin inscription', *JRS* 78 (1988), 105–24. See also Corcoran, *Empire*, 149–51.

59. Euseb. *Hist. eccl.* 9.1.1; letter reproduced at 9.1.4–5.

60. Euseb. *Hist. eccl.* 9.2.1–2.

61. Mitchell, 'Maximinus', 108 (Colbasa text); *CIL* III.12132 (Arycanda). The latter also contains part of a petition in Greek against the Christians from the province of Lycia and Pamphylia addressed to Maximinus.

in Tyre.[62] At great length, Maximinus' proclamation associates the prosperity of the cities with their adherence to right religion and the 'immortal gods'. Harvests, peace, good weather and the absence of storms or earthquakes (calamities which in the past were caused by Christians) were now a sign of divine favour.[63]

Possibly this celebration of prosperity relates to a grand tour by Maximinus of centres of traditional cult worship. Certainly the focus of the ensuing clamp-down was on Christians in major provincial or imperial capitals: Peter, bishop of Alexandria, was beheaded in November 311 and Lucian of Antioch was tried by the emperor in person and executed at Nicomedia in January 312. Elsewhere, cities were urged to expel Christians from their centres and territories. Nor were Maximinus' measures only negative. He sought to restructure the established cults with a new organisation of provincial high priests, whose job it was to revitalise traditional worship:[64]

> Agreeing to their requests, he adopted a new custom and appointed high priests, one for each city, recruiting them from the leading men, who were to offer daily sacrifices to all the gods; relying on the services of the established priests they were also to ensure that Christians should not engage in any building works, nor should they hold meetings in public or in private; they could arrest Christians on their own authority and force them to sacrifice or hand them over to the governors for judgement.

Although this experiment was cut short by the victory of Licinius over Maximinus at Hadrianople in 313 and the suicide of the latter at Tarsus, Maximinus' measures anticipated ideas that would be developed in due course by the emperor Julian.

Christian propaganda made the most of the martyrs' witness for their faith, but how seriously did the emperors take the perceived threat from the Christians? The complexity of the apparatus of enforcement activated by successive edicts and letters suggests that the measures were intended to render the cult unviable. Although it was predictable that some governors would react with more enthusiasm than others, the impact of the laws against Christians, where applied, should not be underestimated. As we have seen, some governors were motivated by ideological dislike of Christianity, while others would see advantage to themselves in following the

62. Euseb. *Hist. eccl.* 9.7.14.
63. Euseb. *Hist. eccl.* 9.7.3–4.
64. Lactant. *De mort. pers.* 36.4–5.

official line. Further down the administrative hierarchy, *curatores* like Felix of Cirta would anticipate promotion (and perhaps a share of the spoils) from their zeal in plundering the churches. The 'spontaneous' petitions from Lycia and Pamphylia and the eastern cities to Maximinus, already revealed as anti-Christian, illustrate the willingness of cities to implement and even anticipate imperial instructions. Although the edicts against the Christians failed to turn adherents from their faith, as an exercise in the enforcement of correct belief, to be achieved through the marginalisation and suppression of a dissenting group, they were a foretaste of techniques to be imitated by Christian emperors in the years to come.

Lactantius, *Divine institutes*

Lactantius' celebration of the deaths of the persecutors, written in 313–15 with the benefit of hindsight, has overshadowed the more substantial philosophical contribution of his earlier work, the *Divine institutes*, written in 303 or soon after. Although dedicated, by the addition of last-minute modifications, to Constantine, the *Divine institutes* is in fact a response to the persecuting ideology of Diocletian and Galerius, and those philosophers and governors, such as Sossianus Hierocles, who backed them up[65] and whose arguments Lactantius had heard for himself at Nicomedia. The divine order favoured by Diocletian was specifically targeted. For Lactantius, Diocletian's favoured Jupiter was not a god but a man, and, worse, a usurper, who had overthrown his father, Saturn. During the Saturnian Age, only one god had been worshipped;[66] by contrast, Jupiter 'exercised an impious tyranny of violence and armies',[67] substituting worship of himself for that of the 'true god'. The slur on Diocletian is inescapable – even the Titans, commemorated, as we have seen, on Diocletian's coinage, are brought in as an example of Jovian genocide.[68]

Readers of an *Institutes* would have expected a book offering basic guidance on legal principles,[69] and questions of law and lawfulness were central to his work. Law and how to live well were closely linked in ancient thought: law was expected to educate the citizen

65. Lactant. *Div. inst.* 5.2–3.
66. Lactant. *Div. inst.* 5.5.3.
67. Lactant. *Div. inst.* 5.6.6.
68. Lactant. *Div. inst.* 6.6.7.
69. Bowen and Garnsey, *Lactantius, Divine Institutes*, 13–14.

in right and wrong actions (partly through establishing the inconvenient or unpleasant consequences of the latter). Therefore to
associate law with moral philosophy was a legitimate undertaking.
Moreover, as we have seen, some martyr accounts made Christian
obedience to their Law, which meant contravening that of the state,
a central part of their witness. It was thus also possible, within the
context of an *Institutes*, to advance theological propositions, such
as Lactantius' distinctive solution for the problem of the existence
of evil in a world governed by an omnipotent God: that it was
necessary for evil and wickedness to exist, so that virtue could be
tested.[70]

Lactantius, himself a convert to Christianity, addressed an elite
audience largely unconvinced by the merits of Scripture. His strategy
therefore was to use pagan authors to discredit pagan views of the
world (or, by judicious selection, support that of Lactantius). Thus
he made a conscious decision, against the precedent set by Cyprian
of Carthage and others, to use traditionally respected Roman
authors, such as Cicero, Vergil, Horace, Ovid and Seneca, to support
his case. In addition, he resorted, perhaps surprisingly, to authorities
credited by pagans as possessing divine inspiration; these included
Apollo,[71] Hermes Trismegistus, whose writings combined Egyptian
and Greek religion with philosophy (as well as treating magic and
astrology), and the Sibylline Oracles.

In his first two books, Lactantius argued for the idea put forward
by Euhemerus in the third century BC that the gods were really men
who had earned promotion to godhead (in the view of Lactantius,
undeservedly). By rooting Christian monotheism in an earlier,
Saturnian Golden Age, where true justice prevailed, Lactantius
invited monotheists in general to accept that they had more in
common with Christianity than with the decayed and corrupted
gods of Roman polytheism. Use of this argument suggests that
Lactantius may have envisaged some kind of monotheistic coalition
of Christians with sympathetic non-Christians, which he could
deploy against imperial polytheism, arguing, as did many Christian
apologists, that the legends about the immoral behaviour of the
Olympian gods, Jupiter not least, discredited their worship. But

70. Lactant. *Div. inst.* 3.29.16.
71. Lactant. *Div. inst.* 1.7. This, despite the unhelpful intervention of Apollo at Didyma
in 302. After 325, the god's oracles would be explicitly attacked and discredited by
Constantine. On oracles as the expression of community opinion, see Peter Brown, *The
Making of Late Antiquity*, Cambridge, MA: Harvard University Press, 1978, 37–8.

the form and purpose of the *Institutes* was primarily didactic. Knowledge was not virtue but must precede virtue,[72] without which there could be no immortality, and it was Lactantius' job to instruct his elite audience in that true knowledge, trusting that one effect of this would be the end of Christian persecution.

But Cicero dominates the main discussion, and it is partly thanks to Ciceronian citations in Lactantius that sections of the former's *De republica* have survived. It is even possible to read the *Institutes* as an extended refutation of Cicero's religious and philosophical thought, although Cicero is also frequently quoted as an authority for Lactantius' own views. Cicero's treatises on gods and men shape Lactantius' structure: his *De natura deorum* explored different philosophical understandings of the divine and underlies the first two books; the *De republica* and *De legibus* influence the fifth on justice and the state; and the *De officiis* (*On duties*) is central to the discussion in book 6 of the obligations of the good citizen.

Christians had long been the target for attacks by philosophers. Lactantius' aim was to separate philosophy, as traditionally prac- tised by Porphyry or Celsus, from true wisdom. All, said Lactantius, who claim to 'pursue wisdom' were by definition not wise, as they had failed to catch up with what they sought. This even applied to his hero, Cicero: 'if philosophy is the teacher of life, why did you see yourself as blind, dim and dull?'[73] Inevitably the relationship with Cicero was not straightforward. Lactantius diverged from him on the meaning of virtue, which he saw in more private terms; while Cicero explored the virtues of the public man in terms of service to the community, Lactantius emphasised man's duty to God and his 'neighbours', meaning the poor. For Lactantius, the virtuous man was under constant attack from temptation. Virtue, which for Cicero and the Stoics was the guarantee of happiness, was, in Lactantius' world, only sustained by struggle. Nor, then, could virtue be its own reward; the real reward for the good was immortality.

Running through the *Divine institutes* is the insistence, based on Cicero's reading of natural law, that the persecutions were not, in the true sense, lawful. Although Cicero did not, of course, have access to the divinely inspired 'true' wisdom advocated by Lactantius, he, like the Christian philosopher, believed in a justice that existed

---

72. Lactant. *Div. inst.* 6.5.1.
73. *Div. inst.* 3.14.16; but at 3.15.9, he is back with Cicero (*Tusc.* 2.11–12) cited in support of Lactantius' view of the uselessness of all philosophers.

independently of human laws, which could be unjust; 'true law is right reason, in accord with nature, universally distributed, consistent, perpetual'.[74] Lactantius, however, argued that only the Christian, with his knowledge of God, could understand the 'true' justice:

> The gap between justice and expediency is well illustrated by the people of Rome, who got themselves control of the whole world by using Fetiales to declare wars and by using forms of law to cover their wrongdoings and to seize and take other people's property. (5) These Romans think they are just if they do nothing against their own laws, but that can be put down to fear ... (6) Does obedience to human institutions make them just, when human beings themselves have been quite capable of error or injustice, like the authors of the Twelve Tables? ... (7) Civil law, which varies everywhere according to custom, is quite different from true justice, which is uniform and simple, being God's provision for us all.[75]

Further distance from Cicero and traditional ideas of *aequitas* ('justice', 'equity' or 'fairness') is created by Lactantius' contention that true 'duty' (*officium*, echoing Cicero's title) is redistribution of wealth through charitable feeding of the poor (thus 'equalising' resources) while not seeking to take any credit for it. Glory, therefore, also a Ciceronian motive for good citizenship, provided it is consistent with virtue, is rejected; justice is about behaving humanely, affording a funeral to the unburied and 'providing for others through humanity what we provide for our families through affection'.[76]

The author of the *Divine institutes* would live to celebrate the destruction of the persecutors and become the tutor to Crispus, the son of the victorious Christian, Constantine. But the *Divine institutes*, despite later and minor modification, remains a document of the period before Christianity won imperial acceptance and protection. As a convert himself, Lactantius saw his mission as being in part to explain the values of the one true belief to a public of classically educated unbelievers. He also took from an earlier classical past a belief in the desirability of religious toleration. But, though he engaged with Cicero, he did not address the issue so central to

74. Cic. *Rep.* 3.33, described by Lactantius as 'the sacred and heavenly law described in almost godlike terms', is quoted verbatim at *Div. inst.* 6.8.7–9. Cicero, according to Lactantius, gets it right unawares, due to 'some spiritual instinct'.
75. Lactant. *Div. inst.* 6.9.4–7, trans. Bowen and Garnsey.
76. Lactant. *Div. inst.* 6.12.29–31.

Cicero's thought, the role of civic and public virtue, or how a Roman citizen would fulfil his public duty in a Christian empire.

Aftermath

The 'Great Persecution' was not an aberrant or isolated event. Imperial policy was increasingly concerned with 'right religion' and the enforcement, if necessary, of man's duty towards the gods (or god). Diocletian and his colleagues embedded their revival of traditional polytheism in a context which drew on antiquity, in particular ancient law and morality, to legitimise their restoration, or rather 'conservation', of the Roman order. Universal observance was expected, be it of laws against incest – a religious crime as well as a form of unlawful wedlock – or sacrifice to the gods. The foreign and the new were suspect and dangerous. Much of this would shape the legislative programme of Christian emperors against religious deviants, defined by them as heretics, pagans and, on occasion, Jews. While measures against sacrifices concentrated on redefining what was meant by unlawful sacrifices, enactments against heresy, like those of Diocletian against Christians, targeted meeting-places, assets, and the legal rights and career prospects of those identified as members of heretical sects.

While the number of those who died may be less than the rhetoric suggests, the impact of the 'Great Persecution', when combined with the advent of Constantine in 312, was out of all proportion to its actual severity. Those who suffered and died, as martyrs, or lived, but as confessors, provided role models for future Christians, who were not faced with the same threat but who nonetheless aspired to perfection as Christians. In Africa, those who had allegedly compromised by handing over sacred writings, the *traditores*, found themselves under attack by the rigorist Donatist faction; a lasting schism was the result. Over time, the graves of those who died in the Great Persecution or earlier purges became the focus of devotion as the saints took on the character of local patrons and protectors. As the memory of the actual experience of persecution receded, the narratives of their sufferings became increasingly lurid; 'courtroom dramas' had (and have) their own appeal[77] and the greater the trial, it was urged, the greater the victory.

---

77. Lucy Grig, *Making Martyrs in Late Antiquity*, London: Duckworth, 2004, 59–78; and Harries, 'Constructing the judge'.

As laws against Christians receded into history, what mattered were not the facts of the 'Great Persecution' but the story that Christians told each other about it, one of the triumph of devout individuals over adversity and oppression. In reality, the picture was less clear cut. The effects of the sanctions against Christians were partial and sporadic. Many lapsed and quietly returned later, when all was safe. Those who kept their heads down or who were not affected, whom we may call the 'middle Christians', had no part in the legend of the persecutions as a form of heroic age. Yet it was they, not the high-profile role models or their purist followers, who formed the bedrock for the evolution of Christianity in the fourth century.

Figure 17 Mausoleum of Diocletian, Split, Croatia

Figure 18 Peristyle court, Villa of Diocletian, Split, Croatia

Figure 19 Temple of Jupiter, Villa of Diocletian, Split, Croatia

Figure 20 West gate, Villa of Galerius, Gamzigrad, Serbia

Figure 21 Apsidal *aula*, Villa of Galerius, Gamzigrad, Serbia

Figure 22 Labyrinth mosaic, Villa of Galerius, Gamzigrad, Serbia

Figure 23 Mausoleum of Galerius, Thessalonike, Greece

Figure 24 Octagonal hall, Palace of Galerius, Thessalonike, Greece

CHAPTER 5

The victory of Constantine, AD 311–37

In October 312, Constantine defeated his rival Maxentius at the battle of the Milvian Bridge. By force of arms he had become Augustus of the Western Empire, while Licinius established himself in the east, destroying his rival, Maximinus Daza, in 313 and ruthlessly exterminating his entire family.[1] Although Licinius was married to Constantine's half-sister, Constantia, the marriage tie did not guarantee harmony. In 316–17, there was an outbreak of hostilities, assisted by plotters from within Constantine's family, but the outcome was indecisive. In 324–5, however, on the pretext that Licinius was persecuting Christians, Constantine again went on the offensive. After Licinius' defeat and death, Constantine became the sole Augustus of the Roman world, and remained so, unchallenged, till his death in 337. In such unstable times, this was an extraordinary achievement, reinforced by Constantine's formidable skills as a propagandist. Although 'oppositional narratives' were not entirely obliterated from the historical record,[2] Constantine's worldview would dominate to the virtual exclusion of all others. Even the most dangerous of crises to threaten the regime from within, the events surrounding the execution of his son Crispus in 326 and the disappearance or death, from unknown causes, of his wife, Fausta, were buried in official secrecy.

Constantine's success was also assisted by the advertisement of divine support – and indeed love – that was put about by his grateful Christian adherents, notably by Lactantius, and, later in the reign, by Eusebius of Caesarea, in his revised *Ecclesiastical History* and, more important, his *Life of Constantine*, written soon after the emperor's death.[3] The core concern of both was with the vindication

---

1. Lactant. *De mort. pers.* 50–1.
2. See Garth Fowden, 'The last days of Constantine: Oppositional versions and their influence', *JRS* 84 (1994), 146–70.
3. For a brief but trenchant survey of Eusebius' shortcomings, see Richard Burgess, *Studies in Eusebian and Post-Eusebian Chronology*, Historia Einzelschriften 135,

of the power and rightness of Christianity as the true religion. However, the effect of what they wrote was to make them complicit in Constantine's self-interested version of events, which systematically denigrated opponents and omitted inconvenient facts. Thus, while Christians exploited Constantine in support of their version of providential history, Constantine in turn used the services of grateful Christians to confirm the acceptability his rule in the eyes of the Deity.

Constantine and Maxentius

On his deathbed, Galerius had entrusted his wife and son to the guardianship of his friend Licinius,[4] thus signalling his lack of confidence in his nephew, Maximinus. Fearing that Licinius, designated as Augustus for the west, would instead replace him in the east, Maximinus hastened to assert his control over the whole Eastern Roman Empire as far as the Bosphorus and Hellespont, winning immediate popularity by a blanket remission of taxes.[5] A temporary settlement was patched up, while both searched for allies. Licinius struck a bargain with Constantine to share the empire as joint Augusti, accepting the promise of Constantine's half-sister, Constantia, in marriage. Maximinus, in his turn, allied with Maxentius.[6]

Maxentius, based at Rome and therefore a Roman emperor in the true (if narrow) sense, took positive steps to identify himself with the interests of his new subjects and with the status and history of the ancient capital.[7] He designated himself briefly on his coinage by Augustus' title, *princeps*,[8] and advertised his allegiance to Mars the Unconquered and his twin sons, the founders of Rome, Romulus and Remus.[9] Like all emperors but one down to 383 (the exception

Stuttgart: Franz Steiner, 1999, 66–74. Eusebius 'remodelled history to vindicate what he saw as the truth' (p. 71).

4. Lactant. *De mort. pers.* 35.4.

5. Riccobono, *FIRA* 1.93; T. D. Barnes, *Constantine and Eusebius*, Cambridge, MA: Harvard University Press, 1981, 40.

6. Lactant. *De mort. pers.* 43.

7. On Maxentius as emperor, see E. Groag in the first edition of the *RE* (Pauly-Wissova), 14, 2417–84; also, in less depth, M. Culhed, *Conservator urbis suae: Studies in the Politics and Propaganda of the Emperor Maxentius*, Stockholm: Svenska Institutet, 1994.

8. C. E. King, 'The Maxentian mints', *Num. Chron.* 19 (1959), 47–78; Groag, 'Maxentius,' 2442; Culhed, *Maxentius*, 39–41; 46–9. See also Dessau, *ILS* 674, *restitutor publicae libertatis* (restorer of public freedom).

9. Dessau, *ILS* 8935, 'to Mars the unconquered father and the founders of their eternal

was Constans), Maxentius used the title of *pontifex maximus*, emphasising his connection with the ancient sacral past, when the *pontifices* were guardians of religious law. Although not Christian himself, he avoided persecution of Christians. Later stories about bishops at Rome in his time make him out to be a persecutor, reflecting the line taken by Constantinian propaganda.[10] In fact Christians at Rome in the first decade of the century engaged in violent feuding among themselves over the question of how to handle readmission of those who had lapsed from the faith; Maxentius, in the interests of public order, exiled the rigorist bishop Marcellus in 309 and then, in 310, both his quarrelsome successors, Eusebius and Heraclius.[11]

Maxentius further exploited his association with the ancient capital by embarking on a lavish building programme. Between them, he and his father Maximian imprinted the legacy of their rule on the urban landscape.[12] Maximian had already erected a large bathing complex, to be named after this 'brother' Diocletian; the structure included not only the bathing suite (hot, tepid and cold pools) but also areas for sport and recreation. Other rooms may have provided space for public lectures and a library.[13] To keep the water flowing, aqueducts were refurbished, and the Aqua Marcia was renamed the Aqua Jovia. Both Maximian and his son remodelled the Roman Forum, the heart of the city's ancient (and republican) identity. Early in his reign, the senate house, burned down in a fire shortly before, was rebuilt and a new Rostra constructed. Maxentius continued the work with the erection of a massive basilica at the southeastern end of the Forum. Although

city etc.'. *Pan. Lat.* 12 (9).18 refers to Maxentius as the 'fake Romulus', although C. E. V. Nixon and B. S. Rodgers (eds and trans.), *In Praise of Later Roman Emperors: The Panegyrici Latini. Introduction, Translation and Historical Commentary*, Berkeley: University of California Press, 1994, 321, questions the identification.
10. *Liber Pontificalis* 31. For Maxentius' toleration of Christianity, see Euseb. *Hist eccl.* 8.14.1; Optatus of Milevis, 1.18. For his religious policy in general, D. de Decker, 'La politique religieuse de Maxence', *Byzantion* 38 (1968), 472–562.
11. As recorded by their successor, Damasus (bishop of Rome, 367–384), whose election was also attended by violent disturbances, suppressed by the (pagan) prefect of the city, Vettius Agorius Praetextatus. On Marcellus, see A. Ferrua, *Epigrapmmata Damasiana*, Rome: Pontificio Istituto di archeologia cristiana, 1942, *Epig.* 18, pp. 129–33; *Epig.* 18 (1), pp. 133–4; and *Epig.* 40, p. 181.
12. For details of buildings, see F. Coarelli, 'L'edilizia pubblica a Roma in età tetrachica', in W. V. Harris (ed.), *The Transformations of Urbs Roma in Late Antiquity*, JRA Suppl. 33, 1999, 23–33; also Culhed, *Maxentius*, 49–60.
13. SHA *Probus* 2.

only the north side survives, its impressive dimensions can be ascertained. The floor space measured 100 by 65 metres,[14] with a central nave and an apse at the western end, perhaps containing a colossal enthroned statue of Maxentius (later replaced by Constantine). This vast space was not just for show. Its proximity to the headquarters of the urban prefecture and the probable supervision of the work by the urban prefect Attius Insteius Tertullus suggest that the basilica was the main location for the prefect's court, dealing with legal and administrative business. Maxentius also revived the religious affiliations of the site, by restoring the adjacent Hadrianic temple of Venus and Rome, destroyed by fire in 306.

But problems piled up. A challenge to Maxentius' authority in Africa in 308–9, mounted by the acting prefect, Domitius Alexander, was suppressed with difficulty.[15] At Rome, Maxentius' financial difficulties alienated the support of the urban plebs and worried the senate, who would be expected to contribute. From 311, he could expect attack from either Licinius to the northeast, or Constantine from his base in Gaul. In 312, Constantine invaded northern Italy, taking Turin, Milan, Verona after much resistance, and Aquileia.[16] The anonymous panegyricist who recalled these events in the presence of Constantine at Trier in 313 made much of the emperor's personal bravery in battle against the 'ferocity' of Maxentius' commanders.[17] Slightly inconsistently, the orator also asserted that the invader was welcomed with near-universal jubilation; embassies, he said, arrived from all directions and supplies for the army were willingly forthcoming – even though the outcome of the conflict was still unknown. Whatever the real state of popular feeling, Constantine had now secured his line of communications and could march on Rome.

Constantine's defeat of Maxentius and the death of the latter at the battle of the Milvian Bridge outside Rome on 28 October 312 were a political and, in the long-term, a religious turning point.[18] The victory rapidly became the stuff of legend. Christian celebrants of the event maintained that Constantine's victory against the

14. For comparison, Rome's largest basilica, built by Trajan, the Basilica Ulpia, measured 170 metres by nearly 60.
15. Zos. *New History* 2.12 and 14.
16. *Pan. Lat.* 12 (9).5.4–11.1.
17. *Pan. Lat.* 12 (9).8.1 (of Pompeianus at Verona).
18. For non-Christian celebrations of the victory, see *Pan. Lat.* 12 (9) of 313 and 4 (10), delivered by Nazarius at Rome in 321.

odds had been due to the help of his tutelary deity, the God of the Christians, whose adherents he was soon to favour with restoration of their rights and grants of land, buildings and other endowments. Lactantius was the first to record Constantine's experience but he wrote as a Christian propagandist and polemicist: his closeness to events in terms of time of writing and his access to privileged information as the tutor of Constantine's son do not in themselves establish the truth of his account.[19] According to Lactantius,[20] Constantine was advised in his sleep to mark 'the heavenly sign of God' (caeleste signum dei) on the shields of his soldiers and then give battle. He marked the shields with the chi-rho symbol and was duly victorious. In Eusebius' later, more elaborate version in the Life of Constantine,[21] a vision of the 'sign of salvation', in the form of a cross, not a chi-rho, is displayed for all to see in the sky with the motto, 'by this conquer', and Constantine's standard, the vaguely cruciform labarum, in fact an idiosyncratic Celtic device likely to appeal to Constantine's Gallic army, is read as a further expression of Christian symbolism. Other adherents were less specific as to the source of Constantine's divine auxiliaries: in 321, a non-Christian panegyricist at Rome declared that Constantine had been assisted by a supernatural army, sporting flashing shields (but no shield device).[22]

All this fits with the standard ancient discourse on, and experience of, the divine. Lactantius' chi-rho was not unambiguously Christian[23] and both visions and dreams were accepted means of communication between the favoured human and the gods.[24] It suited the Christians, and doubtless Constantine himself, to depict the conflict as being one between a man of piety, favoured by the God of the Christians, and a pagan degenerate, Maxentius, obsessed with Jupiter and the Sibylline Books, which he is alleged to have

19. For rationalising of Constantine's vision/dream as a solar halo, see T. D. Barnes, *Constantine: Dynasty, Religion and Power in the Later Roman Empire*, Oxford: Wiley-Blackwell, 2011, 74–80.

20. Lactant. *De mort. pers.* 44.5.

21. Euseb. *Hist. eccl.* 9.9.2–8 has no vision. For the vision, imparted by Constantine to the bishop much later, but connected to an earlier campaign, not the battle at the Milvian Bridge, see Euseb. *Vit. Const.* 1.28–32.

22. *Pan. Lat.* 4 (10).14, delivered at Rome, in Constantine's absence.

23. On the chi-rho, R. Grigg, 'Constantine the Great and the cult without images', *Viator* 8 (1977), 1–32 (at 17–18).

24. As discussed by Ramsay MacMullen, 'Constantine and the miraculous', *GRBS* 9 (1968), 81–96.

consulted on the eve of the battle.[25] But, as we have seen, emperors habitually aligned themselves with patron deities, as Aurelian had done with Sol Invictus. Aside from the association of Diocletian and Maximian respectively with Jupiter and Hercules, Constantine himself had, by 310, acquired a well-publicised (and non-Herculian) connection with Apollo, whom he 'saw' in a vision presenting him with the laurels of victory in 310;[26] the panegyrist on this occasion had expressed the hope that Apollo's sacred springs at Autun would receive material benefits in return for the god's aid.

Constantine and Licinius

Lactantius' drawbacks as a reporter of religious affiliation are more clearly demonstrated in his coverage of the non-Christian Licinius, whose victory over Maximinus Daza at Hadrianople on 30 April 313 is also ascribed, by implication, to the divine favour of the Christians' God.[27] At Milan in February 313, Constantine had honoured his bargain with Licinius, who had duly married Constantia.[28] After agreeing with Constantine a law, known, inaccurately, as the 'Edict of Milan', which reiterated Galerius' permission to all to practise their religions freely and restored to Christians their properties and civil rights,[29] Licinius then departed for the east to deal with Maximinus. On the night before the battle, Maximinus allegedly vowed to Jupiter that, once victorious, he would exterminate all Christians. Licinius, however, was visited in a dream by an angel of God, who taught him a prayer. He awoke and dictated the prayer, copies of which were distributed throughout the army, who then recited it three times, before advancing on the enemy. Licinius was duly victorious and Maximinus fled, having exchanged his imperial purple for the rags of a slave, to die shortly afterwards at Tarsus. Lactantius' technique in linking the victorious Licinius by implication with Christianity is masterly. Licinius, unlike Constantine,[30] is never explicitly associated with Christ and the deity of the

25. Zos. *New History* 2.16.1.
26. *Pan. Lat.* 6. (7).21.3–4.
27. Lactant. *De mort.pers.* 46.1–11.
28. Lactant. *De mort. pers.* 45.1; Aur. Vict. *Caes.* 41.2.
29. For Latin and Greek versions, see Lactant. *De mort. pers.* 48 and Euseb. *Hist. eccl.* 10.5.2–14. The text is in fact not an edict but a letter and was issued by Licinius, in the names of both emperors, to governors in his jurisdiction (see Barnes, *Constantine*, 93–7).
30. Contrast Lactant. *De mort pers.* 44.5 on Constantine, 'he marked Christ on their shields' (*Christum in scutis notat*).

prayer is not specified. Yet Lactantius has already established that it is the Christian God who brings victory; therefore, it is implied, the angel is a sign of God's favour to Licinius. Moreover, the impression is reinforced by Licinius' actions on reaching Nicomedia, where he posts up the law granting freedom and support to the Christians agreed with Constantine at Milan.[31] Only at this point does Lactantius supply the whole text, thus establishing Licinius as not only a 'Christian' victor but the author of a law favouring Christians. Licinius is thus cast with Constantine as the restorer of the persecuted church 'after ten years and approximately four months'.[32]

Lactantius' celebration of the deaths of the persecutors is dated to the aftermath of the victories of Constantine and Licinius, before the breakdown of the relationship between the two in 316.[33] The grounds for dispute were, apparently, the succession. Both emperors now had sons, as Constantia had recently given birth to Licinianus, while Constantine's teenage son Crispus by his first wife Minervina[34] would soon by joined by Fausta's (or a concubine's) first-born, Constantine II.[35] After abortive negotiations on the creation of new Caesars,[36] Constantine advanced into the territory controlled by Licinius and defeated him at Cibalae on the road to Sirmium and again near Hadrianople. Licinius retreated on his eastern heartlands and stalemate ensued. A peace was patched up at Sardica in March 317, which recognised the appointment of three Caesars: Crispus, the baby Constantine and the toddler Licinianus. It also shifted the boundaries of Constantine's territory eastwards as far as Thrace and Moesia.

31. Lactantius uses the Nicomedia text, which is in the form of a letter, 'posted at Nicomedia, 13 June 313', because it was the one he himself saw, but the positioning in the *De mort. pers.* after Licinius' victory is for polemic effect. Cf. *De mort. pers.* 35.1 for the posting of Galerius' Edict of Toleration at Nicomedia, 30 April 311.
32. *De mort pers.* 48.13.
33. T. D. Barnes, 'Lactantius and Constantine', *JRS* 63 (1973), 29–46, for chronology of these years. On Licinius and Constantine, see also Noel Lenski, 'The reign of Constantine' in Noel Lenski (ed.), *The Cambridge Companion to the Age of Constantine*, Cambridge: Cambridge University Press, 2006, 72–5.
34. For the suggestion, which has no evidential support, that Minervina was related to Diocletian, see Barnes, *Constantine*, 48–9.
35. There are problems with the dates of the births of Constantine II and the next son, Constantius II, very soon after (see entry in *PLRE* on Constantine II). If, hypothetically, Constantine was the son of an unknown mother, not Fausta, this would have implications for the position of the still childless Fausta in 316, whose future could be threatened by the mother of Constantine's second son; and for the relations of her sons, Constantius II and Constans, to Constantine II thereafter (see below, Chapter 8, 189).
36. Barnes, *Constantine and Eusebius*, 66–8; *Constantine*, 100–3.

The settlement marked two significant breaks with the principles on which Diocletian had worked in his formation of his imperial college. First, and in line with how Galerius too had operated, the Augusti now had territories with defined boundaries, which they were expected to observe; no longer did they exploit the flexibility of collegiate rule, as Diocletian had done, which enabled a Caesar or an Augustus to be deployed at will to the areas under greatest threat. Secondly, the criterion for inclusion was no longer military ability and experience but membership of an imperial house. While a child could have his own court and represent the imperial 'presence', it was no longer expected of the young Caesars, except perhaps Crispus, that they should take the field in their own right.[37] Consequently, the college could now dispense with the advertisement of harmony and unity which had been so prominent in the propaganda of the Tetrarchy. In 321 at Rome, the orator Nazarius spoke in praise of Constantine but ignored Licinius and his son altogether. That year was also the first in which the two Augusti refused to recognise the consuls appointed by the other.

Given the absence of trust between the two, further war was inevitable. Constantine concentrated on establishing himself in central Europe and, in 323, allegedly violated Licinius' territory while campaigning against the Sarmatians on the Danube. An additional grievance, on Constantine's part, was that Licinius had persecuted Christians within his domain: if true, this could reflect Licinius' perhaps understandable fears that eastern Christians could act as a fifth column for his rival. Certainly, Constantine's preparations had been extensive. Using two fleets and a large land army, he defeated Licinius by land, at Hadrianople, and by sea. Licinius fled to Byzantium, then, after losing command of the sea to Crispus, to Chalcedon. On 18 September 324, Constantine won his decisive victory at Chrysopolis, outside Chalcedon. Licinius fled again to Nicomedia, where his wife Constantia and the bishop Eusebius of Nicomedia acted as intermediaries to broker terms. Licinius was sent into internal exile at Thessalonica, with a promise of safe conduct. A year later, both he and probably his 8-year-old son too were dead; the killing was believed to have been at the instigation of Constantine 'in violation of his oath'.[38]

37. Cf. *Pan. Lat.* 4 (10).3.4–4.5, delivered by Nazarius at Rome, noting Crispus' success as a general and the potential of the 5-year-old Constantine II (neither is named).
38. Eutr. *Brev.* 10.6.3. But see Barnes, *Constantine and Eusebius*, 214, for the

Techniques of legitimation

After 324, down to the death of Julian in 363, the Roman Empire was ruled by descendants of Constantius I. Successive emperors benefited for some forty years from the appearance of family solidarity and dynastic continuity. That image did not reflect the reality of distrust and insecurity which undermined the relationships between them, especially the dealings between Constantius II (337–61) and his two Caesars, Gallus, executed in 354 for suspected treason, and Julian. Of the four emperors who reigned as Augusti after Constantine, only one, Constantius II, died of natural causes, carried off by illness at the age of 44. Constantine II was killed in Italy in 340; ten years later, Constantine's youngest son, Constans, was murdered by the regional emperor Magnentius in Gaul; and Julian died on campaign in Persia. Membership of an established dynasty did not, therefore, guarantee imperial security. However, no successor of Constantine was required to counter the accusation of 'usurpation', the seizure of power unlawfully by force of arms; even Julian, who revolted against Constantius II, was believed to have been recognised by the latter on his deathbed, before the issue could be decided in battle. By contrast, Diocletian, who supplanted the dynasty of Carus, and Constantine, who prevailed in a series of wars against rival claimants, had to argue successfully from the outset for their own, superior, claim of right to rule.

As we have seen, the term *tyrannus* was a label, not an objective status. 'Usurper' is a modern term for an emperor held to be, in some sense, not legitimate. However, in using it ourselves, we run the risk of accepting the values inherent in ancient exercises in propaganda. *Tyrannus* was not a term of fact, still less of analysis. And, as we have seen, an emperor's status could be altered by events. Licinius, for example, was elevated by the Senior Augustus Galerius in 308, recognised as joint ruler by Constantine, and praised for his actions by Lactantius, who died before Licinius' fall.[39] Yet his acts were annulled by Constantine after 324[40] and he was castigated by

suggestion that Licinius was, or was suspected of being, involved with a further conspiracy against Constantine in 325.

39. Lactant. *De mort. pers.* 43.1–2; 44.10–12; 45–7; 46.3; 49.

40. *Cod. Theod.* 15.14.1. However, because all laws were issued in the names of the whole college, some Licinian enactments did survive; see Simon Corcoran, 'Hidden from history: The legislation of Licinius', in Jill Harries and Ian Wood (eds), *The Theodosian Code: Studies in the Imperial Law of Late Antiquity*, London: Duckworth, 1993, reissued 2010, 97–119.

Eusebius, writing after 325, as both a usurper and a persecutor of Christians.[41]

Therefore, rather than seeking to offer a fixed or precise definition of the term, we should consider 'usurpation' as a matter of perspective, and of outcomes. An emperor who failed became labelled as a '*tyrannus*'; as Mark Humphries put it, 'the term *tyrannus* designated emperors who had been defeated in civil war and whose regimes were retrospectively condemned as illegal'.[42] To ensure that a rival would be remembered (if at all) only as a *tyrannus*, surviving members of the fallen dynasty were destroyed, predecessors and rivals were vilified, and, where possible, their memory was obliterated with the destruction of their statues and images and the erasure of their names from inscriptions. Yet, paradoxically and with less fanfare, continuity was also maintained with previous 'usurping' regimes, through marriage alliances[43] and the conciliation of powerful supporters. All this had a profound impact on the record, both literary and material.

The avoidance of direct responsibility for a rival's death was a technique used regularly in the propaganda of Constantine, as it had also been by Diocletian: Maximian took his own life (albeit under duress), after repeated plots against his son-in-law; Maxentius drowned in the Tiber, after falling off his defective bridge of boats, designed as a trap for Constantine;[44] the exact reasons for Licinius' death were shrouded in obscurity, although Constantine did not escape blame for it. There was clearly a convention that legitimate emperors should not be personally associated with the killing of rivals. However, it was also important that there should be no doubt about the ending of a regime; Constantine paraded the severed head of Maxentius at Rome, before despatching the grisly relic to Africa.

Sexual promiscuity with other men's wives was also characteristic of the stereotypical *tyrannus*. Like Carinus before them, Maximinus

---

41. Euseb. *Hist. eccl.* 10.8–9 (revised in the light of later events); *Vit. Const.* 1.49–59 and 2.1–22.

42. M. Humphries, 'From usurper to emperor? The politics of legitimation in the age of Constantine', *Journal of Late Antiquity*, 1 (2008), 82–100, at 85. Humphries also cites the fourth-century author of the Historia Augusta (*Pesc. Nig.* 1.1-2), that 'usurpers' were 'made *tyranni*' by the victories of other men'.

43. The marriage of the later Valentinian I with Justina, widow of the failed local ruler Magnentius (350–3), may fall into this category.

44. As alleged by Zos. *New History* 2.15.

Daza and Maxentius are depicted as lustful and promiscuous despots from whom no good-looking woman was safe.[45] In 321 at Rome, Nazarius, the panegyricist of Constantine, concisely reflected the 'official' view of Maxentius: he was murderous and lustful, and he had purloined inheritances.[46] The tradition followed by Eutropius and Victor also condemned Maxentius for cruelty to the Roman aristocracy and atrocities in Africa, following his suppression of the revolt there.[47] Christian writers echoed the propaganda of the Christian conqueror, and were happy to elaborate the details. Maxentius had an alleged predilection for senators' wives; in Eusebius' account, the Christian wife of a senator chose death before dishonour to her chastity in the literary manner of Lucretia.[48] Maxentius was also accused of indulging in magic and sorcery, he oppressed the people of Rome, and, after initially conciliating Christians, turned to persecuting them. In the east, Maximinus's alleged excesses also did not stop at sexual abuse; women who rejected his advances were drowned; the rights of free-born women seduced by Maximinus were violated through their forced marriages with slaves; and Maximinus's barbarian acolytes imitated his behaviour and lorded over the terrified Romans.[49] This is not simply the rhetoric of defamation as an end in itself. The conduct ascribed to Maximinus and Maxentius contravened not only sexual but also social and legal norms. By their unlawful behaviour, they were 'proved' also to have been unlawful rulers.[50]

An alternative to vilification was oblivion as the 'usurper's' name was erased from inscriptions and his images obliterated in the process known as *damnatio memoriae*. Such was the posthumous fate

---

45. Lactant. *De mort. pers.* 38–40 (Maximin); Euseb. *Hist. eccl.* 8.14.1–2; 12–16; *Pan. Lat.* 4 (10).34.

46. *Pan. Lat.* 4 (10).8.3.

47. See Aur. Vict. *Caes.* 40, 17–19; *Epit. Caes.* 40.2; Zos. *New History* 2.12.1–3; 14, 2–4.

48. Euseb. *Hist. eccl.* 8.14.17; *Vit. Const* 1.34. Sexual abuse as a feature of tyranny was a commonplace in the classical sources, e.g. Periander of Corinth (necrophilia and the attempted creation of eunuchs from freeborn youths); Hipparchus of Athens, killed by Harmodius and Aristogeiton after his failure to seduce the former; Sextus Tarquinius, rapist of Lucretia and thus responsible for the expulsion of the kings from Rome.

49. Lactant. *De mort. pers.* 38.

50. Cf. also Lactantius' allegation (*De mort. pers.* 22.5) that Galerius ignored the law not only in the cruelty of his persecution of the Christians but also in general: 'having set aside the laws, arbitrary control of everything was assumed (by the emperor) and granted to the judges' (*licentia rerum omnium solutis legibus adsumpta et iudicibus data*).

of Maximian's statues in Gaul, a measure which had an unintended effect, noted by Lactantius:[51]

> At the same time, the statues of the old man Maximian were being torn down at the order of Constantine and images, wherever he had been portrayed, were being dragged away. And because both old men (Diocletian and Maximian) were usually depicted together, so the images of both were simultaneously cast aside.[52]

Constantine's intention was to distance himself still further from Maxentius, who had now taken up his father's cause, but he may have had few objections to the collateral damage caused to the memory of Diocletian either.[53] *Damnatio memoriae* was used again against Maxentius and Licinius in their former territories, as the defaced milestones testify.[54] At Rome on the Arch of Constantine, the emperor's victory over the '*tyrannus*' and all his 'faction' was celebrated, alongside Constantine's *decennalia* (tenth anniversary celebrations); the date, 315, established his rule retrospectively as running continuously from 306, treating the period of Maxentius' government as if it had never existed.

Maxentius and his father had, however, left more enduring monuments of their rule. Sooner than tear down the buildings of his defeated rival, Constantine simply annexed Maxentius' structures as his own.[55] Nor did he stop there. Maxentius had promoted an imperial ideology which drew on the symbols of Rome's ancient history, associating the emperor and his buildings with the republican heart of the city and its ancient heroes and gods. With characteristic ruthlessness, Constantine appropriated for himself Maxentius' former ally, the Roman senate, obliging it publicly to ratify both his own position and his version of recent events.[56]

---

51. Lactant. *De mort. pers.* 42.1–2.
52. But Eutr. *Brev.* 9.28, supported by Aur. Vict. *Caes.* 39. 48, saw Diocletian's peaceful and voluntary retirement as his crowning achievement: 'he experienced therefore what no-one else has since the creation of man, namely that although he had died as a private citizen, he was nevertheless enrolled among the gods', although Lactant. *De mort. pers.* 42.2–3 has Diocletian committing suicide in despair.
53. Cf. *Pan. Lat.* 4 (10).12.2 for the assertion that Maxentius responded in kind with attacks on images of Constantine in his domain.
54. Humphries, 'Usurpers to emperors', 98–9.
55. John Curran, *Pagan City and Christian Capital: Rome in the Fourth Century*, Oxford: Oxford University Press, 2000, 79–90.
56. For black propaganda against Maxentius, see *Pan. Lat.* 12 (9).4.4; Anon. Vales. 4.12; Aur. Vict. *Caes.* 40.24; Euseb. *Vit. Const.* 1.39.

Although triumphalism in civil war could be frowned on,[57] the Arch
of Constantine, dedicated in 315, on the 'tenth anniversary' of
Constantine's accession in 306, records in detail the overthrow
of Maxentius, with a series of depictions of key events in 312 – the
departure of Constantine's army from Milan, the siege of Verona,
the battle of the Milvian Bridge, Constantine's triumphant arrival
(*adventus*) in Rome,[58] and the victorious emperor addressing the
Roman people in the Forum from the Rostra. The message, however,
was that this was not civil war. If Constantine had reigned for ten
years, from 306, then Maxentius had not reigned at all. The episodes
recorded, therefore, were not stages in an internecine conflict but
the liberation of Italy and the heart of empire from tyranny. The
inscription, too, celebrated Constantine as the champion of the
res publica:

> To the emperor Caesar Flavius Constantine, Greatest, Pious Fortu-
> nate Augustus, because at the prompting of god and in the greatness
> of his mind, with his army he took vengeance with just arms on
> behalf of the res publica at one stroke on both the usurper and all his
> clique, the senate and people of Rome have dedicated this arch made
> glorious by his victories.

The new ruler's legitimacy was thus doubly affirmed, both by the
senate and by the reference to divine support.

The arch contained other messages too. Conventional depictions
of barbarian prisoners and figures of Victory bearing trophies were
a reminder of Constantine's victories in Gaul and on the Rhine. But
the arch also made extensive use of sculptures and other archi-
tectural features from older buildings. One possible explanation for
this recycling of old material was a lack of local artisans with the
requisite skills: sidelined from the centres of power, Rome could
offer little employment to sculptors or builders.[59] An alternative view

57. For example, by Amm. Marc., 16.10.1–2 of Constantius II in 357, *ex sanguine
Romano triumphaturus* ('intending to triumph through the shedding of Roman blood').
But for emperors' lack of concern, as shown by the frequency of celebrations of victories
in civil wars, see M. McCormick, *Eternal Victory: Triumphal Rulership in Late
Antiquity, Byzantium and the Early Mediaeval West*, Cambridge: Cambridge University
Press, 1986, 80–3, contradicted by Jas Elsner, 'Perspectives in art' in Lenski, *Age of
Constantine*, 259. For the public parading of Maxentius' head, Zos. *New History* 2.17.1;
Pan. Lat. 12 (9).18.3; 19.1; 4 (10).31.5.
58. S. MacCormack, *Art and Ceremony in Late Antiquity*, Berkeley: University of
California Press, 1981, 36–8.
59. F. Coarelli, *Rome and Environs: An Archaeological Guide*, Berkeley: University of
California Press, 2007, 161.

is that, by this use of *spolia* (recycled artwork plundered from earlier monuments), which was not in itself unprecedented, Constantine sought to lay claim to continuity with past emperors.[60] Like his predecessors', Constantine's celebration of his personal achievements was also an affirmation of the victorious nature of emperorship, as it had always been (and, by implication, always would be). Thus scenes of hunting and sacrifice featuring Hadrian were reused, but with Constantine's portrait replacing that of Hadrian in the hunts and those of Constantius I Chlorus or Licinius in the sacrifices. Marcus Aurelius' wars against the Marcomanni and the Quadi also appear, implying continuity with Constantine's victories over other barbarians.

Senatorial co-operation was also required to dispose of the memory of Maxentius' achievement as builder. His structures were not destroyed, but simply rededicated, by the senate, for the services of 'Flavius' (Constantine).[61] The emperor then made improvements to Maxentius' buildings on his own account.[62] Moreover, within days of his victory in 312, Constantine had asserted territorial control of significant sites. The praetorian guard, who had also been suspect in the eyes of the Tetrarchs,[63] were now fully disbanded and the *equites singulares* (elite cavalry), who had stood by Maxentius to the last, were left without a base, as their camp on the Caelian Hill was totally destroyed.[64] On the site of the camp – and close to both Fausta's Roman residence and the 'Sessorian' palace on the Esquiline, now refurbished for the use of the emperor's mother, Helena[65] – was built the earliest of Constantine's Christian structures, the 'basilica Constantiniana', dedicated on 9 November 318.[66]

60. Jas Elsner, *Imperial Rome and Christian Triumph*, Oxford: Oxford University Press, 1998, 81–2; P. Pierce, 'The Arch of Constantine: Propaganda and ideology in late Roman art', *Art History* 12 (1989), 387–418.
61. Aur. Vict. *Caes.* 40.26.
62. Curran, *Pagan City*, 79–90.
63. Lactant. *De mort. pers.* 26.3; Aur. Vict. *Caes.* 39.47.
64. See Coarelii, *Rome and Environs*, 224–5, for plan of the *castra* (camp) of *equites singulares* and the *Domus Faustae* (Fausta's residence).
65. Part of the Sessorian palace was redesigned as a church; later, a larger church on the site became S. Cruce in Gerusalemne (see *ILCV* 1775 for first mention of Jerusalem in dedication by Valentinian III, c. 425). For Helena at Rome till 326, see E. D. Hunt, *Holy Land Pilgrimage in the Later Roman Empire, AD 312–460*, Oxford: Oxford University Press, 1982, 31–3; J. W. Drijvers, *Helena Augusta: The Mother of Constantine the Great and the Legend of her Finding of the True Cross*, Leiden: Brill, 1992, 31–4.
66. *Liber Pontificalis, vita Sylvestri*, 1.172, trans. Raymond Davis, *The Book of Pontiffs (Liber Pontificalis)*, TTH 5, Liverpool: Liverpool University Press, 1989, rev. edn 2010.

This would later be known as the church of St John Lateran, the seat of the bishops of Rome.

Constantine is also associated with a number of other Christian sites: the Basilica Apostolorum on the Via Appia appears to be Constantinian, as also does another basilica on the Via Labicana, which has no association with any known martyr but occupies ground previously used as a necropolis by the *equites singulares*.[67] These new endowments represented more than patronage of a favoured cult; they were a statement of Constantine's confidence in divine support for his rule. Thus the Lateran palace, now identified as the *Domus Faustae* (Fausta's residence), and therefore originally a part of Maximian's family holdings, retains murals perhaps depicting members of the imperial house; but in 313, Constantine used his wife's palace as a convenient venue for a council of bishops.[68] The *Liber Pontificalis* also ascribed to Constantine a basilica for St Laurence, later a favourite saintly patron of the Roman Christian aristocracy;[69] this received endowments of estates in the Eastern Empire, suggesting a later date for its foundation. But most spectacular of all was the cross-shaped basilica of St Peter on the Vatican hill, which was built to accommodate the existing shrine of the martyr. Prominently displayed were inscriptions celebrating the power and piety of the founder and a great gold cross, dedicated by Constantine and his mother, Helena Augusta.[70]

Constantine made no radical attempt to change the religious geography of the Eternal City, and it may never have occurred to him to do so. The choice of sites for basilicas associated with him can be explained by the availability of imperial landholdings, such as the Laurentum estate, owned by the empress Helena, revenues from which supported the basilica by the Via Labicana,[71] or by his determination to obliterate all traces of his defeated opponents. A further element, which is impossible to assess, is the extent to which his actions as a builder of churches, and their locations, were a response

---

67. Curran, *Pagan City*, 97–9 (Via Appia); 99–102 (Via Labicana).

68. On the *Domus Faustae* and the Lateran Palace, see V. Santa Maria Scrinari, *Il Laterano Imperiale I: Dalla aedes Laterani alla Domus Faustae*, Vatican City: Pontificio Istituto di Archaeological Cristiana, 1991, 136–61.

69. *Lib. Pont.* 1.181. For Laurence and the Roman aristocracy by the late fourth century, see Prudentius, *Peristephanon* 2.

70. Curran, *Pagan City*, 109–15, with full bibliography at 109, n.197. Helena's title is important for the date, as Helena became Augusta in her mid-seventies in 324, and died in the late 320s.

71. *Lib. Pont.* 1.183.

to promptings from the Roman clergy themselves. Christian shrines were already located on the outskirts of the city, in suburban cemeteries, connected to the catacombs and the graves of the martyrs, and had long been the centres for worship. There was therefore no reason why Christians themselves, at this stage, should seek to interfere with sites associated with Roman traditional religion or history in the centre.[72]

Constantinople and Rome

In 330, Constantine dedicated a new city, called after himself. Although ancient observers speculated that Constantine aimed to found a 'New Rome', Constantinople was primarily designed to be a demonstration of the greatness of its founder in perpetuity and a showcase for all that was best in the Roman world. Constantine had considered Sardica ('My Rome is Sardica'),[73] Ilium (Troy) and other cities, before fixing on Byzantium, an ancient Greek colony on the Bosporus, formerly the imperial residence of Licinius, whose memory would now suffer the same fate as had befallen that of Maxentius at Rome. Constantine's first ritual act in 324/5 was to pace the circuit of new walls, which would enclose an area four times the size of the old settlement and shield it from attack by land from the west. The new city, a far larger one than Byzantium had been, was designed around a main street, leading east to west, the Mese, which was bisected by the Cardo Maximus, running north to south. At the crossroads enclosed by a four-arch structure (Tetrapylon) was a milestone (Milion), from which all distances from the new city would be measured, as they were from Rome.[74]

Constantine remodelled the heart of the old city, with a renovated Augusteion, named in honour of his mother, Helena Augusta, a basilica, incorporating a library and a law court, and, to the south, the baths of Zeuxippos and the Hippodrome, which was joined in turn to the imperial palace further south through the royal box, from which emperors would watch the races. This impressive statement of imperial power and prestige was completed with two temples

72. Michelle Salzman, 'The Christianization of sacred time and sacred space', in Harris (ed.), *Transformations*, 123–34.
73. Anon. continuator of Dio (= Peter the Patrician), *FHG* 4, 199, Constantine 15. For Ilium (Troy), see Sozom. *Hist. eccl.* 2.3; Zos. *New History*, 2.30.
74. See S. Basset, *The Urban Image of Late Antique Constantinople*, Cambridge: Cambridge University Press, 2004, 22–36.

to traditional but innocuous deities, Rhea/Cybele and Fortune. To the north was an open space where the army carried out military exercises and could be assembled to be addressed by the emperor; this was the Strategeion.

Further to the west, but still east of the Milestone, was the Forum of Constantine, which was bisected by the Mese. Its design marked a conspicuous departure from what would be expected at Rome: the Forum was circular, not rectangular, and partly surrounded by colonnades. At its centre was a porphyry column, on the top of which stood a conspicuous and colossal statue of Constantine. From his lofty eminence, the emperor's statue looked down on a new senate house on the north side of the forum, the meeting-place for Constantine's new senators, who would hold the rank of *clari*, 'distinguished', which differentiated them from their counterparts at Rome, the *clarissimi*, 'very distinguished'. The intention, that the new senate would be honoured but purely advisory, is reflected in the placement of its building in relation to imperial statue and forum. The streets, adorned with colonnades in the manner of Hellenistic cities,[75] the baths and the Hippodrome were decorated with ancient and prestigious objects imported from all over the Roman world: the Serpent Column at Delphi, which commemorated the Greek defeat of Persia in 479 BC, was there.[76] While this collecting activity would have been criticised by some as despoliation,[77] for others the opportunity to showcase their treasures more than counteracted the inconvenience of their removal. Constantine even hoped to erect an obelisk, brought from Egypt, but in the event the monument was redirected to Rome in the reign of his son, Constantius II.

Much interest has been expressed in the religious identity of Constantinople as a 'Christian city' (or not).[78] Those who favour the religious neutrality of the city have pointed out that pagan philosophers seem to have been content to act, although perhaps in a limited capacity, as treasure-hunters on the emperor's behalf and that Constantine appeared welcoming to non-Christians: the

75. M. M. Mango, 'The porticoed street at Constantinople', in N. Necipoglu (ed.), *Byzantine Constantinople: Monuments, Topography and Everyday Life*, Leiden: Brill, 2001, 29–51.

76. Basset, *Urban Image*, 50–78.

77. Cf. Jerome, Chronicle, s.a. 334 *Constantinopolis dedicatur paene omnium urbium nuditate* ('Constantinople is dedicated, having stripped bare almost every city').

78. Barnes, *Constantine*, 126–31, has no doubt that (a) old Byzantium was entirely razed to the ground and obliterated, and (b) Constantinople was unambiguously a 'Christian city'.

philosopher Sopatros, who left his peaceful retreat in Apamea in hopes of preferment, Nikagoras of Athens, who took a state-sponsored trip to Egypt, and the panegyricist-historian Praxagoras, also of Athens, who wrote a history in praise of Constantine, all had great hopes of favours from the new emperor of the east, regardless of his known adherence to the Christians' God.[79]

Moreover, Constantine felt no need to impose an explicit religious identity on his new foundation; had he wished to do so, he could have called it Christopolis (or something similar). Constantine's thinking on his new city is best understood with reference to his building at Rome. Constantinople was designed with the topography and history of ancient Rome in mind not because this was the 'New Rome' but because Rome provided the model of what a capital city should be. There was therefore a Capitol, where the Mese forked, with roads leading to the northwest and southwest, and an honoured place was given to the statue of the wolf suckling the twins Romulus and Remus, and to the Palladium, a statue of Pallas Athena which had allegedly been brought by Aeneas to Italy, and thus to Rome, after the sack of Troy. And as at Rome, new churches, most notably the Church of Holy Peace, were founded, but they were away from the centre, in areas where land was perhaps more easily acquired.

The new city was incidental to Constantine's main political aim in the years after 324: to consolidate his political position. In the Eastern Empire, Constantine's well-known generosity had a motive: to conciliate powerful groups who had served Licinius for over thirteen years. He therefore advertised his 'clemency', made a tour of the imperial capitals at Nicomedia and Antioch, and, as he had done at Rome after Maxentius' fall, appointed a prominent supporter of the old regime to the consulship.[80] He had also to find men of experience to serve in his government, and membership of a new city senate, with the prospect of privileged access to the emperor, provided an attractive incentive for local careerists to try their luck in the capital. However, it would be left to later emperors to develop

79. See S. Bassett, 'The antiquities in the hippodrome at Constantinople', *DOP* 45 (1991), 87–96. Against this, see Barnes, *Constantine*, appendix E, 192–4, which argues that this should be seen in the context of the continuance of imperial patronage of intellectuals; for Praxagoras of Athens' *History* of Constantine as summarised by Photius, see ibid., appendix F, 194–7.
80. Julius Julianus, *PLRE I*, 478–9.

the potential of the site as a fixed imperial capital and an alternative to Rome as a centre of both actual and symbolic power.

After 326, when he celebrated twenty years of rule (his *vicennalia*) at Rome, Constantine was not to return to the west. Hostile sources maintained that he created his new capital because he had quarrelled with pagan senatorial Rome in 326, a year which also saw the execution and *damnatio memoriae* of the emperor's son, Crispus, and the death or disappearance of his wife Fausta.[81] But Constantine's concentration on the Eastern Empire from 325 to his death in 337 should not be assumed to derive from hostility to Rome or to the Roman senatorial order. He spent generously on building in the capital, as had the Tetrarchs and Maxentius before him,[82] and, as we shall see, legislated extensively in response to senatorial concerns, especially, but not exclusively, in the first part of his reign prior to 324. The new 'distinguished' (*clari*) senators at Constantinople posed no threat, at least initially, to the dignity of the 'very distinguished' (*clarissimi*) members of the senate at Rome; it was only in the reign of Constantius II that the potential of Constantinople as an alternative capital began to be realised.

Yet the Roman senators may have had their doubts. Their numerical exclusivity was undermined both by the privileged access to the emperor enjoyed by Constantine's new eastern senators, and by the possibility that their numbers would expand through recruitment to the eastern praetorship, the office which provided the gateway to senatorial membership. Moreover, the emperor extended Roman senatorial rank, the clarissimate, to members of the imperial administration who had no connection with the city of Rome. His intention was that the award of senatorial rank would contribute to the honour and status of both administrators and senators. However, the conferment of 'senatorial rank' on prominent courtiers could not in itself integrate a senate based at Rome with an imperial court, based elsewhere. Once Constantine was settled permanently in the east, the court at Constantinople or Antioch and the senate at Rome would evolve a separate political and social dynamic.

81. Zos. *New History*, 2.29–31. Zosimus/Eunapius also ascribe Constantine's conversion to Christianity to the aftermath of the deaths of Fausta and Crispus.

82. Constantine's building programme aimed to counteract those of his predecessors, asserting his control over the capital; this then would be more a power play than a sign of favour. See below, p. 150, for his legislation before 324 as responding to and favouring the Roman senatorial elite.

Figure 25 Maxentius pedestal inscription, Via Sacra, Rome, Italy

Figure 26 Circus of Maxentius, E. du Pérac 1577, Via Appia, Rome, Italy

Figure 27 Starting gates, Circus of Maxentius, Via Appia, Rome, Italy

Figure 28 Mausoleum of Romulus, Via Appia, Rome, Italy

Figure 29 Milvian Bridge, Rome, Italy

Figure 30 Aula Palatina, Trier, Germany

Figure 31 Constantinian cathedral exterior, Trier, Germany

Figure 32 Statue of Constantine I, Campidoglio, Rome, Italy

Figure 33 Colossal head of Constantine I, Basilica Nova, Rome, Italy

Figure 34 Basilica Nova, Rome, Italy

Figure 35 Arch of Constantine, Rome, Italy

Figure 36 Victory pedestal, Arch of Constantine, Rome, Italy

Figure 37 Milvian Bridge battle frieze, Arch of Constantine, Rome, Italy

Figure 38 *Adventus* frieze, Arch of Constantine, Rome, Italy

Figure 39 *Adlocutio* frieze, Arch of Constantine, Rome, Italy

Figure 40 *Congiarium* frieze, Arch of Constantine, Rome, Italy

Figure 41 Sol *tondo*, Arch of Constantine, Rome, Italy

Figure 42 Dedicatory inscription, Arch of Constantine, Rome, Italy

CHAPTER 6

Towards the sunrise: Constantine Augustus

> Having the power of this God as ally, beginning from the shores of Ocean, I have raised up the whole world, step by step, with sure hopes of salvation.[1]

Constantine's assertion, that his career had consisted of a steady advance, west to east and under divine guidance, was contained in a letter to Shapur II of Persia written at some point after 325.[2] The implication, that the advance was not yet ended, expresses Constantine's unique brand of religious imperialism. From his proclamation in Britain in July 306 he had won mastery of the whole west in October 312 and finally achieved control of the Roman east after the defeat and death of Licinius in 325. As emperors had done before him, he ascribed his continuous success to the favour of his patron deity, while an alleged persecution of his co-religionists by his rivals for empire became a justification for military aggression. After using Licinius' treatment of Christians as a pretext for intervention,[3] the pattern was repeated in 337, when Constantine prepared to embark on a campaign against Persia, moving still further 'towards the sunrise'. Ancient authors were divided as to who initially was the aggressor, with several ascribing the first move to the Persians. Eusebius, however, testifies that Constantine had expressed concern for the fate of the Christian communities in the Persian Empire,[4] and the neutral historian Ammianus reported that 'it was not Julian

---

1. Cited by Euseb. *Vit. Const.* 4.9 in his Greek translation of the original Latin text.
2. For discussion of the authenticity of the letter, see T. D. Barnes, 'Constantine and the Christians of Persia', *JRS* 75 (1985), 126–36; on Constantine's projected Iranian campaign in 337, see Garth Fowden, 'The last days of Constantine: Oppositional versions and their influence', *JRS* 84 (1994), 146–70; and Fowden, *Empire to Commonwealth: Consequences of Monotheism in Late Antiquity*, Princeton, NJ: Princeton University Press, 1993, 93–7. For a sceptical view of the letter, see A. D. Lee, *Information and Frontiers: Roman Foreign Relations in Late Antiquity*, Cambridge: Cambridge University Press, 1993, 37.
3. Euseb. *Vit. Const.* 1.51; 56–9; 2.1–3.
4. Euseb. *Vit. Const.* 4.56.

but Constantine who kindled the fires of Parthia'.[5] Twice, then, Constantine used his religion to justify an expansionist war.

Constantine's exploitation of Christianity in the service of his imperial agenda is not a comment on the sincerity or otherwise of his Christian beliefs. Like other emperors, his actions were intended to accord with the will of the divinity. It is therefore misleading to make a distinction between Constantine the emperor and Constantine the Christian. He was content to be both – but on his own terms, which, as the first emperor to take the god of the Christians as his patron, were his to define. Nevertheless, for the sake of convenience, Constantine's role as an emperor in a general sense can be separated from those policies which were prompted by his religion, such as his dealings with bishops, councils and heresies or his laws which related specifically to Christianity. This chapter, therefore, will discuss Constantine the emperor.

'He enacted many laws, some good and equitable but most of them superfluous and a few severe.'[6] Constantine is often seen as an initiator of change, the creator over time of a new, centralised, administrative, military and religious order. This is not, however, how it would have appeared at the time. While extracts from the laws of Constantine, recorded along with those of later emperors down to 437, in the Theodosian Code provide essential evidence for Constantine's legislative programme, they also illustrate the fact that Roman imperial government tended to function re-actively, rather than through constant production of governmental 'initiatives'. Therefore, in the Theodosian Code we do not find – nor should we expect to find – enactments detailing radical new policies or sweeping departures from precedent. Much of what appears with hindsight to be a coherent programme of reform was in fact an accumulation of responses to problems as they arose. But a reactive mode of legislating should not be confused with passivity or with lack of central direction. As we have seen with Maximinus' persecution of the Christians, the relationship between report or proposal from 'below' and the imperial 'response' was a complex one. Constantine had no blueprint for administrative reform, but his 'solutions' to questions as they arose derived from his personal philosophy of government and allowed for a process of cumulative

5. Amm. Marc. 25.4.23.
6. Eutr. *Brev.* 41.8 (H. W. Bird trans.).

change, which, over time, had radical consequences for the conduct of imperial business.

Gold and the economy

Constantine's starting-point was the legacy of Diocletian. In 309, while still based in Gaul, he reduced the weight of Diocletian's *aureus* from about 6 grams to 4.5 grams, striking 72 to a pound of gold. Learning perhaps from the failure of Diocletian's currency revaluation in 301, he avoided diluting the gold content of the coin, thus keeping its face and real values in line. After 324, when Constantine had gained control of the precious metal resources of central Europe, the numbers of gold coins issued appears to have increased, especially towards the end of his reign.[7] Mass production of this gold coinage, known from military slang as the *solidus*, enabled the creation of a 'gold standard', partially displacing other metals and denominations. Years later, an anonymous petitioner to Valentinian I and Valens in c. 369 responded, in his own eccentric fashion, to Constantine's coinage reform:[8]

> In the time of Constantine, extravagant expenditure caused the use of gold in place of bronze, which had formerly been highly valued in everyday business transactions. The initial cause of this greedy behaviour is believed to have derived from the following. For when gold and silver and a huge quantity of precious stones stored up in the temples from ancient times flooded the open market,[9] it inflamed a general desire for spending and acquisition.[10]

The consequence, according to the Anonymous, was that gold displaced bronze, the rich became more oppressive and the poor resorted to crime, banditry and support of usurpers. Like the

7. G. Depeyrot, 'Economy and society', in Noel Lenski (ed.), *Cambridge Companion to the Age of Constantine*, Cambridge: Cambridge University Press, 2006, 237–9.
8. *De rebus bellicis* 2.1–2. For text of *De rebus bellicis*, translation and interpretative essays, see M. W. C.Hassall and R. I. Ireland, *De Rebus Bellicis*, Oxford: British Archaeological Reports Int. Ser. 63, 1979. The text is perhaps best known for the Anonymous' illustrated military inventions.
9. For an exhortation to the sons of Constantine to melt down pagan temple gold for coinage, see Firmicus Maternus, *On the error of pagan religions*, 28.6.
10. 'Constantini temporibus profuse largitio aurum pro aere quod antea magni pretii habebatur, vilibus commerciis assignavit; sed huius avaritiae origo hinc creditur emannasse. Cum enim antiquitus aurum argentumque et lapidum pretiosiorum magna vis in templis reposita ad publicum pervenisset, cunctorum dandi habendique cupiditates accendit.'

Tetrarchs in the preamble to the prices edict, the Anonymous saw economics in moral terms and his solution for these various ills was as moral as his diagnosis: the emperors should control extortionate provincial governors and tax collectors. He added that expenditure on the army should be reduced, and the value of the *solidus* protected by confining all the workers in the imperial mints to one island. Whatever may be thought of this analysis, the Anonymous testifies to Constantine's reputation as a man interested in the getting and spending of precious metal.

Generous and ambitious, Constantine in the early part of his reign had need of gold. In c. 314 he imposed a sales tax in gold and silver, the *chrysargyron*, on the sellers of wares in cities, including prostitutes (who were already liable to local levies).[11] Some interest groups were quick to assert that the tax did not apply to them; by 320, Constantine had proclaimed their exemption to a public meeting of soldiers and veterans,[12] and the privilege had been extended to shipmasters (*navicularii*) by 326.[13] While many exemptions were based on traditional practice, their granting also allowed emperors to demonstrate their generosity in public; the consequent narrowing of the tax base was a less welcome outcome. But precious metal revenues could also be raised from the traditional 'offerings' made to emperors on their accession and on subsequent significant anniversaries, the 'crown gold' (*aurum coronarium*) levied on cities and city councillors and the 'gold offering' (*aurum oblaticium*) contributed by the senate. Senators were also required to pay a land tax in gold.

Agricultural productivity, and the keeping of land under productive cultivation, was important to emperors because it underpinned the successful delivery of taxes. However, the extent of imperial concern for *agri deserti*, uncultivated land, is unclear, as also is the extent of the problem. After his conquest of the east, Constantine declared that veterans were to be settled on *agri deserti*, they would be exempt from taxation in perpetuity and would have their start-up

---

11. Zos. *New History* 2. 38.2–4. The chapter summarises Constantine's taxation and administrative reforms, without reference to chronology.
12. *Cod. Theod.* 7.20.2. The extract is taken from the minutes of a meeting between Constantine and the veterans, who express their wishes through a series of acclamations. See Serena Connolly, 'Constantine answers the veterans', in Scott McGill, Cristiana Sogno and Edward Watts (eds), *From the Tetrarchs to the Theodosians: Late Roman History and Culture, 284–450* CE, Cambridge: Cambridge University Press, 2010, 93–114.
13. *Cod. Theod.* 13.5.5.

costs as farmers covered;[14] a much smaller sum would be made available for would-be business entrepreneurs and all concerned were advised to take advantage of the offers. Constantine's aim here, clearly, was to reward soldiers about to be discharged in the aftermath of the civil war with Licinius without disrupting existing landholding patterns; the tax exemption shows that this measure was not concerned with revenue.[15] Moreover, the bulk of legislation on *agri deserti* contained in the Theodosian Code (5.14 and 15) applies to imperial or emphyteutic land, the latter the term for land leased over the long term and often passed down through the generations. The legal pronouncements on *agri deserti* respond to problems raised with the emperor qua landowner and are not evidence for wider trends. Archaeology and land surveys show too that, while some parts of the empire were adversely affected by military instability or other local factors (for which redress could be sought, and sometimes granted), others prospered.[16] The issue of 'deserted land' should not, therefore, be seen as a Constantinian priority.

It may have been Constantine, rather than Diocletian, who perceived the implications of the regular tax indictions for tenancy agreements. The farming of large estates by tenant farmers was, of course, not new. The state's concern was with the taxation to be levied on the land and who was responsible for it. Tenants, *coloni*, were registered by the landlord in the municipal tax office and thus acquired a fiscal identity. The cultivation of land by tenants was always a mixed blessing for both them and the owners. Short-term contracts resulted in over-exploitation of land by farmers who had no incentive to conserve its productivity; this lessened the value of the land as an asset and its attractiveness to future tenants. And, in situations where there was more land available than tenants to farm it, landlords competed for tenants, offering incentives for mobility. Behind the legislation which survives from a later period and which enforced the return of fugitive *coloni* to their place of origin is a competition among landowners to acquire workers; this, and not kindness of heart, explains the willingness of some owners to harbour runaway *coloni*, despite the legal sanctions imposed.

14. *Cod. Theod.* 7.20.3.
15. Although *Cod. Theod.* 7.20.4, a few months later in 325, defines tax exemptions due to veterans; perhaps Constantine had second thoughts.
16. See C. R. Whittaker, '*Agri deserti*', in M. I. Finley (ed.), *Studies in Roman Property*, Cambridge: Cambridge University Press, 1976, 137–65.

To preserve stability and the accuracy of the tax records, emperors legislated to limit the mobility of at least some *coloni*, by creating a tie between them and the land, and refusing permission to engage in other activities or undertake other obligations.[17] One consequence was an inevitable limiting of the freedom of men who were technically free citizens but whose freedom was now in practice restricted. In 332, Constantine issued an edict to his provincials which stated that:

> Those *coloni* themselves who plan flight, should be bound with iron chains in the manner of slaves, so that they should be compelled to carry out the duties (*officia*) which befit free men, under the penalty of servitude.[18]

The unfortunate objects of the legislation were tenants who were found – or might be found in the future – to be obligated to estates other than those on which they were discovered to be resident. Tax penalties were imposed on the landlords who had harboured them and the fugitives were compelled to return and be physically bound, in the manner of slaves. This terminology was clearly unsatisfactory; the tenants were not legally slaves at all, as later laws would acknowledge.[19] Constantine's creation of a paradox, the bound ('slave') carrying out the obligations of the free, is an instance of the rhetorical concern with effect at the expense of strict accuracy which, as we shall see, characterised some of his legislation. But it was also, inadvertently, an admission of a willingness on the part of emperor and lawmakers to use the law to undermine the civil rights of the free citizen.

Administrative changes

A further legacy from the Tetrarchy was Diocletian's reshaping of administration, in the shape of praetorian prefects, attached to emperors, with immense responsibilities military, judicial and

---

17. *Cod. Just.* 11.68.1–2, 325 and post-335.
18. *Cod. Theod.* 5.17.1.1. On the 'colonate' (a perhaps misleading modern term) and issues arising from the surviving legal evidence, see A. J. B. Sirks, 'Reconsidering the Roman colonate', *ZSS RA* 110 (1993), 331–69; C. Grey, 'Contextualising *colonatus*: The *origo* of the late Roman Empire', *JRS* 97 (2007), 155–75, arguing that legislation on *coloni* responds to different situations inconsistently; challenged on some points by A. J. B. Sirks, 'The colonate in Justinian's Reign', *JRS* 98 (2008), 120–43.
19. *Cod. Just.* 11.52.1 (393).

financial.[20] They were at the apex of a pyramid consisting, first, of their deputies, the *vicarii*, under whose authority were over hundred provincial governors (*iudices*). Constantine left this hierarchy of three levels unchanged and used it as a model on which to create further multi-layered structures. Probably soon after 312, he appointed a new official, the master of the offices (*magister officiorum*), to whom would answer the heads of the three traditional secretariats, the offices (*scrinia*) of the records (*memoria*), correspondence (*epistulae*) and petitions (*libelli*). Initially, the master held the relatively modest rank of *tribunus*, but, by 346, he had risen to the rank of *comes* ('companion', or 'count').[21] The evolution of the powers of the master over the next few decades were probably mostly due to bureaucratic empire-building, helped by the fact that their oversight of the secretariats allowed access to many areas of policy. The first two named *magistri* are known from responses in the Theodosian Code to questions raised about religion and taxation. In 320, one Heraclianus is referred to as having been in correspondence with the prefect of Rome over the significance of a lightning-strike on an amphitheatre;[22] and in 323, Proculeianus referred to Constantine the problem of how slaves taken in pledge for the payment of overdue taxes should be disposed of.[23] Already, therefore, the masters of the offices were asserting their authority in widely different areas of government.

Bureaucratic turf wars with the praetorian prefecture were also to be expected. Supervision of the *cursus publicus* and arms factories (*fabricae*) were shared responsibilities, but perhaps more alarming for the prefecture was Constantine's revival of the (unofficial) spy service, originally called the *frumentarii*, but now relabelled the *agentes in rebus*.[24] Before their abolition by Diocletian, the job of the *frumentarii* had been to convey messages between provincial governors and the centre. Constantine's new *agentes* continued to

20. On late Roman government, see Christopher M. Kelly, 'Emperors, government and bureaucracy', in *CAH*[2] 13, 138–83; Kelly, *Ruling the Later Roman Empire*, Cambridge, MA: Belknap Press, 2004; Kelly, 'Bureaucracy and government' in Lenski, *Age of Constantine*, 183–204. Jones, *LRE*, chs 11–13 and 16, are also still fundamental.
21. *Cod. Theod.* 12.1.38.
22. *Cod. Theod.* 16.10.1.
23. *Cod. Theod.* 11.9.1.
24. The first two *agentes in rebus* listed in *PLRE* are Gaudentius 1, p. 385, and Syncletius 1, p. 871, who were letter carriers between Constantine and Athanasius of Alexandria. Fl. Palladius 16, p. 661, is mentioned by Athanasius as a *curiosus*, also late in the reign.

convey messages and by the 350s had acquired the related duty of inspecting the warrants of those entitled to use the public post.[25] More significantly, they were expected to gather information on how the provinces were being administered, and then report to the master of the offices – hence their later designation as 'snoopers' (*curiosi*). As governors answered ultimately to the praetorian prefects, not the master, the aim was clearly to provide a supplementary check on the governors' behaviour, potentially undermining the authority of the prefectures. There is some evidence too that the agents exceeded their authority; complaints of unlawful imprisonment were made against them and the emperor was obliged to remind them of their obligations to obey the law.

Further departments of state evolved out of the former sprawling remit of the prefecture. Towards the end of the reign, the military commanders (*duces*) of various field armies were brought under the overall control of two chief generals, the masters of horse (*magister equitum*) and of foot (*magister peditum*). Any formal say in military activities was thus removed from the prefecture;[26] even the imperial bodyguard and household troops (*scholae palatinae*) now answered also to the *magister officiorum*. By dividing the supreme command, excessive concentration of military power in the hands of an individual who could threaten the emperor's position was (in theory) avoided.[27]

In the area of finance, at some point before the mid-fourth century, the administration of the central treasury was upgraded, with the appointment of two *comites* ('counts').[28] Responsibility for this is more likely to rest with the underrated reformer Constantius II than with his father. The first counts of the *largitiones* ('largesses', handouts) known both served under Constantius in the 340s.[29] By

25. *Cod. Theod.* 6.29.1 (355) and 2 (357).

26. Zos. *New History* 2, 38 complained that the separation of the role of commander from that of paymaster undermined military discipline.

27. The merging of the two chief generals into the office of *magister militum* ('master of the soldiers') later in the fourth century revived the threat posed by generals to weak emperors, especially in the west; examples are Merobaudes, Arbogast, Stilicho, Aëtius and Ricimer.

28. The most detailed analysis of the counts of finance, but mostly applying to a later period, is by R. Delmaire, *Largesses sacrées et res privata: l'aerarium imperiale et son administration du IVe au Vie siècle*, Paris: Ecole Française de Rome, 1989; on Constantine, see pp. 30–8.

29. *PLRE I* Nemesianus 1, p. 621, was a relatively lowly *vir perfectissimus* (*Cod. Theod.* 11.7.5, of May 345), who earlier had perhaps had charge of the *res privata* (*Cod. Theod.* 12.1.30, to Nemesianus *comes*, office unspecified).

c. 350, Constantius' count of the *largitiones* was a senior administrator, Domitianus, who as praetorian prefect would clash disas-
trously with the Caesar Gallus in 353–4, and had previously been in
charge of the *largitiones*. Their responsibilities covered the administration of indirect taxes, such as customs dues, along with coinage,
mints and mines, and quarries and textile factories. It is characteristic of late Roman official language that the focus is on the dis-
tributive aspect of the count's job, not his role as tax collector.
The other chief finance officer, the *comes rei privatae*, assisted by
a *rationalis* (finance officer), inherited the responsibilities of the
secretariat *a rationibus* which had previously administered the
imperial estates, using their revenues for the upkeep of the imperial
household; again, holders of this or an equivalent office are not
attested before the 340s. This left the praetorian prefects still in
charge of the assessment, collection and distribution of direct
taxation in money and in kind, through the governors and their
subordinates. Relations between governors and imperial procurators
had been difficult under the early empire; in the fourth century,
there were doubtless similar tensions between agents of the *res
privata*, who reported to the *comes*, and governors answerable to the
prefecture.

The secretarial remit of the master of the offices was partially
restricted by the upgrading of the department of the *notarii*
(civil service clerks and stenographers), under their new chief, the
primicerius; the shorthand recording of official *acta* and minutes
appears routine but was nonetheless crucial for administrative
decision-making. The *notarii* were also responsible for the issue of
codicils of office, which allowed scope for some surreptitious trading
in honorary offices, but they did not control the appointments
themselves. More intimate and therefore less accountable were the
officers of the bedchamber, under the *praepositus*, prefect, of the
'imperial bedchamber' (*sacri cubiculi*); their access to the emperors
on terms of intimacy allowed for the exercise of an influence
which outsiders would find hard to assess or counter. Despite these
limitations, the master's office evolved to provide a powerful
counterweight to the prefecture in civil matters. The praetorian
prefects now became the highest courts of justice, short of the
emperor himself, but they shared their ex officio membership of
the consistory – and thus access to the emperor's ear – with the other
senior managers of the empire, the master of the offices, the two
counts of finance, and the chief generals. The result may have been

a greater formalisation of consistory membership, although some flexibility was still maintained.

The authorship of the emperor's laws, later the responsibility of the imperial quaestor, remains in doubt. Officially, emperors were themselves the authors of their own public pronouncements, and earlier emperors had prided themselves on their rhetorical skills. Spokesmen who delivered imperial addresses to the senate, and who were known as *quaestores candidati*, were the forerunners of the fourth-century quaestors (*sacri palatii*, 'of the sacred palace') who retained the role of 'mouth of the king' as well as that of legal adviser well into the sixth century.[30] The pagan historian Zosimus,[31] perhaps following an earlier source or what was believed in Constantinople in his own day, ascribed to Constantine the reinvention of the quaestor as 'the man appointed to communicate the emperor's decisions', but his statement is not backed by any other contemporary evidence. The first individual described as 'quaestor of the sacred palace' was Flavius Taurus, dispatched on an embassy to Armenia as imperial spokesman in 354.[32] The first known to have intervened in a consistory meeting on a legal matter was Eupraxius, the quaestor to Valentinian I, who, in 370, corrected the emperor on the judicial torture of senators under the treason law.[33] Given the total absence of attested Constantinian quaestors, Constantine's legislation was probably drafted by the senior master of the secretariats, the *magister memoriae*, who may occasionally have deputised for the quaestor later in the fourth century, and the *magistri epistularum*, who incorporated imperial decisions into letters to governors and other relevant recipients. However, Constantine was also known for having authorial aspirations on his own account, and the possibility that he drafted some of his laws for himself cannot be entirely discounted.

Through a revamped system of rewards and honours, the loyalty of the most powerful administrators was ever more focused on the person of the emperor. Ancient sources agreed that Constantine was remarkable for his generosity, although the hostile Zosimus,

30. *Anth. Pal.* 16.48.
31. Zos. *New History* 5.32.6. Zosimus' statement may reflect a wider tendency to ascribe to Constantine reforms that should be ascribed to his sons or other emperors.
32. Amm. Marc. 14.11.14.
33. Amm. Marc. 20. 1.25. Jill Harries, 'The Roman imperial quaestor from Constantine to Theodosius II', *JRS* 78 (1988), 148–72, building on Tony Honoré, 'The making of the Theodosian Code', *ZSS RA* 104 (1986), 133–222.

predictably, dismissed his open-handedness as extravagance.[34] But, just as *adoratio* served to communicate reassurance as well as subjection, so the terms in which Constantine framed his honours were calculated to fashion a relationship of 'companionship' between emperor and favoured subject. The gift of the emperor's friendship was an act of patronage, as it had been in the early empire, when the emperor's administrators were also his 'friends' (*amici*). Eusebius acutely connected Constantine's penchant for handing out money and goods with his creation of a new system of honours:[35]

> Some were appointed *comites* (companions) of the first order, some of the second, others of the third. Similarly, many thousand more shared honour as *clarissimi*, or with a wide range of other titles; for in order to promote more persons, the Emperor contrived different distinctions.

The immediate inspiration for Constantine's denomination of favoured individuals may have been the now accepted term for the emperor's central striking force, the *comitatus*. It was also characteristic of Constantine's method that he sought to expand military terminology into the civil sphere: administrative service, for example, was itself called *militia* (from Latin *miles*, 'soldier').

The careers of two early *comites* show how the conferment of the title could help to formalise reconciliation between the victorious emperor and prominent supporters of a defeated rival. Both at Rome in the years after 312 and in the east after 325, Constantine conciliated and promoted supporters of the vanquished, thus enhancing the efficiency of government, by ensuring continuity of personnel, and his own reputation for clemency. Vettius Cossinius Rufinus served Maxentius as *corrector* (governor) of Campania, and returned under Constantine as prefect of the city of Rome in 315–16, with the title of '*comes* to both the Augusti'.[36] C. Ceionius Rufius Volusianus, founder of a powerful fourth-century senatorial dynasty, was born in the late 240s and was already over 60 in 312. He had served Maxentius as praetorian prefect in Africa, where he suppressed the revolt of Domitius Alexander in 309, was prefect

34. Zos. *New History* 2.38.1.
35. Euseb. *Vit. Const.* 4.1.2, trans. Averil Cameron and Stuart Hall (eds and trans.), *Eusebius, Life of Constantine*, Oxford: Oxford University Press, 1999.
36. *ILS* 1217, *PLRE I*, Vettius Cossinius Rufinus 15, p. 777.

of the city of Rome in 310, and reached the consulship in 311.[37]
Volusianus was then rewarded for his co-operation with a second
prefecture of the city (313–15) and a second consulship in 314. His
career inscription at Rome[38] has two features of interest; one is
that his offices under Maxentius are omitted (they are known from
literary and chronographic sources); the second is that he was
awarded the title of *comes* 'to the unconquered ever-Augustus,
Constantine' (*comes domini nostri Constantini invicti et perpetui
semper Augusti*). Along with public rewards for loyalty to the new
order came a parallel insistence on denial of the past. But the past
still mattered. In a further expression of continuity, Constantine
reinstated Aradius Rufinus, Volusianus' co-consul in 211, as prefect
of the city. Aradius, though favoured by Maxentius, had been
demoted at the last minute and replaced by C. Annius Anullinus,
already implicated, as we have seen, in the enforcement of laws
against Christians in Africa; Anullinus' prompt demotion would
have confirmed Constantine's religious allegiance to the Romans at
Rome.[39]

Public and criminal legislation

All imperial legislation could be described as moral, in the sense that
it was presented as beneficial to the community and to virtuous
people within it. Like Diocletian, Constantine believed that good
laws, well implemented, also pleased 'the divine power'. As part of
his propaganda offensive in the east after Licinius' fall, Constantine,
now at Nicomedia, exhorted his new subjects to come forward,
whatever their rank, and denounce official abuses to him personally,
promising that he would personally 'avenge' himself on them and
reward the informers:

> Thus may the highest divinity [*summa divinitas*] always be
> favourable towards me and preserve me in safety as I wish, while the
> state too is most happy and prosperous [*felicissima et florente re
> publica*].[40]

37. Aur. Vict. *Caes.* 41,18; Zos. *New History*, 2.14.2. *PLRE I*, C. Ceionius Rufius
Volusianus 4, pp. 976–8.
38. *ILS* 1213.
39. Aradius Rufinus 10, *PLRE I*, p. 775, served Maxentius as his prefect of the city
down to 27 October 312. He was back in post a month later.
40. *Cod. Theod.* 9.1.4.

This concern for the accountability of officials dated back to earlier in his reign, when Constantine ruled that men of senatorial rank guilty of such abuses of power as the abduction of a maiden or invasion of the boundaries of another should face criminal charges in the province where the offence happened (where the accused was less likely to fix the outcome).[41] Later the tone became harsher, when he insisted that governors acting as trial judges be available to litigants freely and ordered savage punishments for those rapacious officials who tried to fix the system for money:[42]

> Now at once the grasping hands of the officials shall cease, they shall cease, I say; for if after being warned they have not ceased, let them be cut off with swords. The judge's curtain, let it not be for sale, entry shall not be bought, nor the private council room be shamed by bribes, nor the very sight of the governor have its price.[43]

In the same enactment, he offered the provincials further opportunity to demonstrate their opinion of their rulers; both acclamations and demonstrations against governors were to be formally recorded and forwarded to the emperor.[44] The language was designed to intimidate, imposing on delinquent officials, their associates and the public at large the powerful image of an avenging emperor. How far such sanctions worked in practice is harder to assess. The violence of the rhetoric suggests that Constantine believed that the projection of power through words could have a real effect. More important, his reiterated concern with official malpractice and accountability to the population in general reflects a fourth-century legislative culture which cloaked the reality of autocracy in the rhetoric of making the agents of the ruler subject to the judgement of the ruled.

Constantine's language was most extreme when directed against wrongdoers, whether officials or offenders against the community in

41. *Cod. Theod.* 9.1.1, given at Sardica in December 316, received at Corduba March 317, to the *comes* of Spain. The questions relating to *praescriptio fori*, the choice of where a trial took place, were much contested, because of the interests involved. Other examples are the right of clergy to be tried by their peers, and of soldiers involved in lawsuits to be heard by military courts.
42. *Cod. Theod.* 1.16.7, 1 November 331.
43. 'Cessent iam nunc rapaces officialium manus, cessent, inquam; nam nisi moniti cessaverint, gladiis praecidentur. Non sit venale iudicis velum, non ingressus redempti, non infame licitationibus secretarium, non visio ipsa praesidis cum pretio.'
44. *Cod. Theod.* 1.16.6.1. The Theodosian compilers were empowered to split up constitutions and place fragments of text under different relevant headings; different rules made in a single constitution may therefore crop up under a variety of headings.

other ways. In the area of criminal law, Constantine was not, as a rule, a radical innovator in terms of content. But the distinctively lurid rhetoric appears from the limited evidence to be a feature of his legislation, especially later, although the record may be distorted if relevant western texts failed to survive, unlike texts stored at Constantinople. This posed no problems for his relationship with the 'highest divinity', as even non-imperial Christians might react to wickedness in the same way: the denunciations by Lactantius of the wickedness of the persecutors were no less ferocious.[45]

The emperor's suggested solutions for problems in the criminal law were not always workable. In 317, a question arose as to the punishment of people guilty of 'violence' during a dispute over ownership of an estate; Constantine ruled that whoever was responsible for a homicide should be punished, whether it was the possessor or the one seeking possession, thus ignoring the problem of determining who initiated the violence, or the traditional rights of possessors who killed in self-defence.[46] Moreover, further complexities could be introduced when an action for violence was combined with a suit over ownership; by making the penalty for the (criminal) action for violence, which was taken first, dependent on the outcome of the (civil) ownership suit, Constantine created further potential for confusion and delay.[47]

In 319, perhaps in response to questions on several criminal cases raised by his judges, Constantine attempted to summarise his policy on criminal law. A series of texts, probably part of the same enactment, was sent to the *vicarius* of Africa in 319; these re-enacted the 'penalty of the sack' for parricides, established a range of penalties for counterfeiting, dependent on the status of the culprit, and ordered that writers of defamatory writings be punished, even if their allegations turned out to be true.[48] Whatever the question

---

45. On the brutality of Constantine's rhetoric, see Y. Rivière, 'Constantin, le crime et le christianisme: contribution à l'étude des lois et des moeurs de l'antiquité tardive', *Antiquité Tardive* 10 (2002), 327–61.

46. *Cod. Theod.* 9.10.1. Although book 9 contains what fifth-century lawyers categorised as criminal law, the question of violence in the context of disputed possession was also covered by praetorian law and the use of the praetor's interdict *de vi armata* ('on armed violence'; cf. Cicero, *Pro Caecina*, of 69 BC). Constantine admits that violence may be an attribute of a crime as well as a crime in its own right.

47. *Cod. Theod.* 9.10.3; Jill Harries, 'Violence, victims and the legal tradition' in Hal Drake (ed.), *Violence in Late Antiquity: Perceptions and Practices*, Aldershot: Variorum, 2006, 85–102.

48. *Cod. Theod.* 9.15.1 (parricide); 9.21.1 (counterfeiting); 9.34.1 (defamatory writing).

which triggered this comprehensive response, Constantine saw it as his chance to provide a general statement of his views on 'public crimes', thus (he might vainly hope) pre-empting further questions.

An edict issued in 326 illustrates Constantine's traditionalism in his approach to both criminality and the safeguarding of the family unit as part of Roman society. A law against *raptus*, abduction marriage, was issued, addressed 'to the people'.[49] The abductor is defined as a man who (or whose family) has made no marriage agreement with the parents of the girl. The runaway bride, if abducted against her will, would, despite her innocence, be penalised with loss of inheritance rights, if she did not shout out for rescue loudly enough; if she left willingly – in other words, eloped – she would suffer the same capital penalty (meaning death, exile and/or loss of property and civil rights) as the abductor. The full authority of the legal tradition is invoked to nullify the value of the bride's consent: even if she had agreed, wrote the legislator, her opinion had no legal value because of the frivolity and fickleness of her gender and judgement ascribed to her by the ancient laws.[50] The penalties were correspondingly severe: not only would the consenting couple be executed, but conniving parents also could be punished as accessories. Most vividly – and in line with literary stereotyping – the nurse who, bribed by the suitor, corrupted her charge would 'have her throat closed by the swallowing of molten lead'.

Despite the rhetoric, the content of the law was not new. Like much of Constantine's 'moral' legislation, it was a projection of the imperial legislator as a guardian of public probity and of his priorities as, in this case, an enforcer, not a reformer, of existing law. Forcible abduction of girls (and young boys) was outlawed under the Augustan Lex Julia on public violence, and similar prohibitions had been re-enacted by Diocletian.[51] Augustus' aim would have been to supplement the authority of the heads of families, the *patres familias*, rather than replace them with state sanctions; before

49. *Cod. Theod.* 9.24.1. On what follows, see J. Evans Grubbs, 'Abduction marriage in antiquity: A law of Constantine (*CTh* ix.24.1) and its social context', *JRS* 79 (1989), 59–83. See also Grubbs, *Law and Family in Late Antiquity: Emperor Constantine's Marriage Legislation*, Oxford: Oxford University Press, 1995, 183–93.
50. Cf. *Cod. Theod.* 9.1.3 ruling that women were not allowed to act as prosecutors in criminal cases, except in suits of *iniuria* (outrage, a lesser crime), although it was conceded that they could act as useful witnesses. Had he read Gaius, *Institutes*, he would have known that his views on the *imbecillitas* of women were out of date.
51. For Diocletian's rescript on abduction and unlawful imprisonment see *Cod. Just.* 5.1.1 + 9.12.3, of 293.

Augustus, the offence could have been followed up by the family through the traditionally accepted exercise of private justice, and this may well have remained the case. Although the legal position was that 'bride theft' was illegal, it was in fact a traditional mode of contracting a marriage alliance in parts of the Mediterranean and, provided that all concerned went along with it, would have continued. The snag was the power of an unrelated person to bring a prosecution. The third-century jurist Marcian, writing in textbook mode,[52] explained that the punishment for abduction was 'the extreme penalty' and added that, if the father condoned the 'injury done to him', prosecution by a third party was permitted, as is also implied, but not stated, in Constantine's text. Despite this, elopements doubtless continued, with subsequent reconciliations. As always with the criminal law, which required action to be taken first by an individual accuser, the law would apply only if it was invoked.

There is no evidence that Constantine did anything to mitigate the harshness of the penal system as a whole.[53] Crucifixion remained in use for slaves who informed against their masters,[54] and an author on astrology, writing in Constantine's final decade, predicted, for those born under certain star signs, the traditional canon of punishments: crucifixion, burning alive and exposure to the wild beasts in the arena.[55] Whatever the implications of Constantine's Christianity in other respects, in the area of penal policy, as in the other traditional spheres of policy and activity discussed above, he worked within the frameworks and assumptions established by his imperial predecessors.

Property, marriage and family

Threats to amputate the hands of bribed officials are hardly consistent with modern notions of a compassionate Christianity. Yet there is no sense in the Christian sources that the more violent aspects of Constantine's rule troubled his Christian supporters. Rather, Christian bishops boasted of their new access to the emperor. Given that emperors issued laws in response to representations made to them, it would follow that Christians were in a position to

52. Marcian, *Institutes* 14, at *Dig.* 48.6.5.2.
53. On the increased harshness of penal policy in late antiquity, see Ramsay MacMullen, 'Judicial savagery in the Roman Empire', *Chiron* 16 (1986), 147–66.
54. *Cod. Theod.* 9.5.1.1.
55. Firmicus Maternus, Mathesis, 8.7; 8.25; Jill Harries, *Law and Empire in Late Antiquity* Cambridge: Cambridge University Press, 1999, 138–9.

influence Constantine's legislative activity. But, while some reforms, as we shall see, were influenced by Christian thinking or were directly relevant to Christian concerns, the character of much of the emperor's legislation was consistent with that of his predecessors in its adherence to the Roman legal tradition, and was addressed to a traditional recipient, the Roman senate. It is not possible to guarantee that recipients recorded in the imperial law-codes were always those whose reports or suggestions had prompted the law; multiple copies were often required so that all concerned should know what to do. But many of Constantine's early laws are addressed to Rome and the prefect of the city, and deal with matters of property and succession that had long preoccupied Roman senators and would continue to do so. As a group, therefore, they show Constantine as an emperor determined to act responsively to the Roman senate and its concerns.

Constantine's legislative instinct was for simplicity. One batch of laws reformed rules on the transmission of property between parents and children. Widower fathers, for example, whose children were still in his *patria potestas* ('father-power', which meant they had no legal right to own or control property independently), had the right of usufruct of the property of the deceased wife but no right of alienation; if a child was emancipated from father-power, he was to receive his share of the maternal assets, less one-third.[56] Another set of enactments reinforced and simplified the rights of a mother to inherit from her dead children, even allowing her to sue a dead child's executors if she had been unreasonably excluded from the will.[57] Constantine's rulings on these matters were not in themselves radical innovations, but they did formally confirm and provide legal backing for longstanding expectations of how succession should work in elite families, making it harder for those disadvantaged by the conventions to appeal against them. How far the solutions offered in the laws were those suggested by the senators or prefect themselves cannot be determined. However, a constitution which survives almost in its entirety in the *Fragmenta Vaticana* shows Constantine legislating on the formalising of gifts, in response to what he had 'learned' of legal disputes on the subject.[58] His solution

56. *Cod. Theod.* 8.18.2, of 319.
57. *Cod. Just.* 6.556.3, of 315; *Cod. Theod.* 5.1.1 + *Cod. Theod.* 11.35.1 + *Cod. Theod.* 2.6.3, of 317–19; *Cod. Theod.* 2.19.2, of 321.
58. *Fragmenta Vaticana* 249: 'Multas saepe natas ex donatione causas cognovimus' ('We have become aware that many legal cases often arise from (problems with) gifts').

was to tighten up procedures: gifts must be made in the presence of many witnesses (*scientibus plurimis*) and the whole transaction must be entered in the public records before a *iudex* (judge, governor) or a substitute, so that future challenges could be ruled out. The provision that the donation should be recorded publicly before a state official and preserved in writing in the archives was consistent with evolving bureaucratic practice throughout the empire; validation by witnesses had long been customary practice.[59]

Constantine's legislation on property and succession was thus in line with legal convention, but could it also have been influenced by Christianity? In 320, Constantine repealed the penalties for celibacy established by Augustus in the Lex Papia Poppaea, which restricted the rights of the unmarried and childless to benefit from wills.[60] Nearly two decades later, and in the eastern part of the empire, Eusebius included the reform among several which illustrated Constantine's Christian character as legislator.[61] According to Eusebius, perhaps echoing the preamble of the law itself, Constantine had abolished the injustice of the 'ancient law' against celibates, which punished them as if they had done wrong; both those unable to have children and those who chose 'philosophy' over marriage (which would include pagan philosophers) had suffered unfairly. But while the contents of the law may have appealed to Christian celibates or Christian ideals of celibacy and asceticism, Christians are unlikely to have been the main movers of the law as a whole. It was the senate, not Christians as yet, who were most concerned with questions of inheritance.

The removal of testamentary restrictions on the unmarried and childless was part of a wider policy, the aim of which was to simplify the wording of wills, along with apparently unrelated regulations on debt. As there was a long tradition of leniency in juristic writing where matters of wording in wills (as opposed to intention) were concerned, this is again consistent with past practice: reassurances offered elsewhere in the same law, on how to manage the institution of heirs[62] and their entrance on the estate,[63] should be read as a reassertion of accepted legal practice, perhaps in response to

---

59. On Constantine's civil legislation, see the accessible account by Caroline Humfress, 'Civil law and social life' in Lenski, *Age of Constantine*, 205–25.
60. *Cod. Theod.* 8.16.1, 'To the people'.
61. Euseb. *Vit. Const.* 4.26.
62. *Cod. Just.* 6.23.5 and 6.37.21.
63. *Cod. Just.* 6.9.9.

attempts by lawyers to question the 'small print' in documents left by unwary testators. Thus not only Christian interest but also the lack of real innovation elsewhere may explain the emphasis of the sources on the celibacy provision.

The scope of the reform was also more limited than Eusebius implied. The drafter of the law celebrated the release of celibates from 'the looming terrors of the laws' but he was also careful to observe the conventions of legal jargon: using the Roman legal device of *fictio*, which allows treatment of some person or thing or situation 'as if' it were something different, Constantine's spokesman declared that the beneficiaries 'are to live in such a way as if [*ita vivant ac si*] they were sustained by the tie of matrimony ... Nor moreover, is anyone to be held to be childless [*nec vero quisquam orbus habeatur*].'[64] In other words, Constantine abolished not the penalties of the law but the categories of person to whom the penalties applied; for the purposes of this law, every adult now had the status of being married with children. The conservatism of the legislator is reinforced with an immediate reminder that a further legally disadvantaged category, husbands and wives, were still not entitled to inherit by will from each other,[65] a rule not to be repealed for a further ninety years.[66]

As Judy Evans Grubbs has convincingly argued, Constantine's laws on marriage in general show no explicitly Christian influence; rather, they reflected the social values within which Christianity was itself evolving. His general policy was to uphold the importance of promises made during the contracting of a marriage, while making unilateral divorce virtually impossible. In 319, he was prompted to provide guidance on the financial consequences of the breaking off of a betrothal and ordered that, whatever the reason, the party responsible must forfeit gifts already made and hand over gifts received;[67] no inquiry was to be made on the causes of the rupture.[68] Although betrothal was not normally recognised as part of a formal contract in classical law, Constantine's reform may reflect

64. On the so-called *fictio legis Corneliae* (an assumed situation based on the Cornelian law), which validated the will of a Roman citizen captive 'as if' he had not been captured, see W. W. Buckland, *Textbook of Roman Law*, ed. Peter Stein, 3rd edn, Cambridge: Cambridge University Press, 1966, 68 and 289.
65. *Cod. Theod.* 8.16.1.2.
66. *Cod. Theod.* 8.17.2–4, of 410–13.
67. *Cod. Theod.* 3.5.2, first part only at *Cod. Just.* 5.3.15.
68. *Cod. Theod.* 3.5.3 (330) provides clarification on a point of detail, that prenuptial gifts are valid at the time of divorce, despite their non-registration in the public records.

changed social assumptions about the contractual basis of betrothal.[69]

On divorce, Constantine severely restricted the grounds on which a contested divorce could take place. The legislation did not affect divorce by mutual agreement, but was nonetheless a clear departure from the classical rules. These were that either party could end a marriage by sending a *repudium*, notice of divorce, and were based on the belief that marriage was based on the 'intention to marry' of both parties, and therefore either had the right to dissolve it. A convention that the *repudium* should be validated by seven witnesses was reinforced by Augustus' law on adulteries (18 BC), which insisted that a husband divorce his wife before prosecuting her and the alleged lover; the witnesses could prove that he had done so and was not therefore liable to prosecution in his turn as a *leno* (procurer). Although in classical law, no blame was attached to either party in the divorce process itself, the financial consequences with regard to the dowry were dependent on the culpability of the parties; a wronged husband could retain the dowry and in any event was entitled to a share for the upkeep of the children of the marriage.[70]

In 331, Constantine ruled that a unilateral divorce could be valid only if the other party were guilty of a serious criminal offence.[71] A wife must prove that her husband was a murderer (*homicida*), poisoner (*medicamentarius*) or violator of tombs (*sepulcrorum dissolutor*), while a husband was required to demonstrate that his wife was an adulteress (*moecha*), poisoner or procuress (*conciliatrix*). The terminology is untechnical (*moecha*, for example, is the Greek-derived word for adulteress or fornicator, used in preference to the Latin *adultera*), and the practical application of the regulation is not addressed in the surviving text. As legal proof of criminality was a condition of the divorce, the complaining party would be required either to 'prove' the case before divorce, or to bring a prosecution after the divorce (as was already the requirement for adultery), with the attendant risk that failure of the case would retrospectively invalidate the divorce itself. The penalties for the erring wife were in line with those convicted of a criminal offence: if

69. On betrothal and its consequences in general, Grubbs, *Law and Family*, 140–83.
70. Jane Gardner,. *Women in Roman Law and Society*, London: Routledge, 1986, 84–91; Susan Treggiari, *Roman Marriage: Iusti conuiges from the Time of Cicero to the Time of Ulpian*, Oxford: Oxford University Press, 1991, 435–82.
71. *Cod. Theod.* 3.16.1.

she sent an unjustified *repudium*, she would forfeit the whole dowry and be deported to an island. The husband, however, merely forfeited the dowry and could not remarry; if he did, the first wife was (bizarrely) empowered by the law to raid his house and seize control of the second wife's dowry as well.

Constantine's law may have been welcomed by men worried about what some saw as the irresponsible appetite of some women for multiple divorces on frivolous grounds.[72] However, it may also have come to be seen as eccentric as well as unworkable. The recipient, Fl. Ablabius, the praetorian prefect of the east in the 330s, was a prominent Christian who may not only have received but also influenced the content of laws addressed to him. These may have included another ill-judged initiative, that the testimony of a bishop in a trial could be accepted without corroboration from other witnesses, a violation of fundamental procedural principles which was reversed within a year.[73] Constantine's divorce law was repealed by the emperor Julian, an act which triggered, it was later alleged,[74] a flood of divorces initiated by women. The law was also excluded from the Justinianic Code.[75]

The imperial legislator accepted the more humane aspects of the legal tradition. When imprisoned awaiting charge, people were not to be confined in heavy chains, in the darkness of the 'inner prison', but were to have access to daylight, their trials were to be held as soon as possible and the guards had a duty of care for the inmates;[76] one change, of limited benefit to those affected, was the new stipulation that the branding of convicts sent to the arena or the mines was to be on the arm or leg, not the face, which was made 'in the image of heavenly beauty'.[77] A more significant shift was the emperor's agreement in 326 that third party accusations in cases of adultery should no longer be permitted, on the grounds that such vexatious accusations merely destroyed good marriages.[78] On

---

72. Grubbs, *Law and Family*, 230–1.
73. *Constitutio Sirmondiana* 1, 5 May 333, repealed or contradicted by *Cod. Just* 4.20.9, of 334, which lists successive imperial decisions on witnesses and corroboration; the 'Sirmondian Constitutions' may be a Merovingian forgery.
74. Ambrosiaster, *Quaestiones Veteris et Novi Testamenti*, 115.12. This anonymous author wrote in the 380s and was not keen on women's rights.
75. For other evidence that Constantine's law was never reinstated in full, see Grubbs, *Law and Family*, 232–7; the liberality of the legislation varied but incidences of imperial intervention seem to have increased.
76. *Cod. Theod.* 9.3.1.
77. *Cod. Theod.* 9.40.5, of 316.
78. *Cod. Theod.* 9.7.2.

interrogation under torture, he upheld the longstanding principle that accusers in treason cases would be liable to torture if they failed to provide strong evidence to corroborate their allegations.[79] However the fact that decurions were now made liable for torture in cases of forgery[80] was illustrative of the gradual spread of the use of judicial torture up the social scale, a development perhaps driven more by the judges' need to ascertain the truth than by imperial initiative.

At no time does Constantine the legislator appear to be a radical constitutional or legal innovator. Where he institutes change, as in the divorce law, the causes can be found in wider shifts in social mores. Generous to those he favoured, occasionally erratic, Constantine nonetheless maintained a sense of direction, reshaping administrative structures to suit his needs. Harsh and ruthless to enemies, stern in his condemnation of wrongdoers, Constantine was also the master politician, responsive to those, like soldiers and the Roman senate, whom it was in his interest to concilate. Was this also how he would conduct himself towards the Christians?

79. *Cod. Theod.* 9.5.1, cf. *Dig.* 48.18.1.1.
80. *Cod. Theod.* 9.19.1.

CHAPTER 7

Constructing the Christian emperor

Constantine the soldier, the politician, the giver of laws, the administrative reformer, the favoured friend of the divine power, interpreted the imperial office in a manner that his predecessors would easily have recognised. In one particular, they could even have envied him his success. Unlike Diocletian and his associates, Constantine succeeded, for thirteen years, in ruling the empire alone. Although his young sons were promoted to be Caesars, to project the imperial presence over the whole empire, from Trier to Sirmium to Antioch, they were in no sense his equals. As he and his Christian admirers, especially Eusebius, contemplated his career, one conclusion was inescapable. The place of the first Christian emperor in the order of things required explanation.

Contemporary representations of Constantine drew on the political, the literary and the philosophical or theological (ancients saw philosophy as addressing questions about the cosmos). Not all of Constantine's admirers were Christian. The traditional styles of the panegyrics addressed to him at Autun in 310 and by Nazarius at Rome in 321[1] accorded with what was expected of a public performance and were deemed by their authors to reflect the culture of the ruling power; and pagan philosophers featured prominently at court. While actively exercising patronage of the Christians' God from 312 onwards, Constantine exploited a public language which tapped into a wider monotheistic discourse,[2] by contrast with the traditional-style polytheism favoured by Diocletian's regime. This was consistent with emperors' previous friendly relationships with the divine patrons they saw also as 'companions'.[3] Ideas of light associated

---

1. *Pan. Lat.* 10 (4).
2. Lactantius' careful cultivation of a monotheistic, rather than exclusively Christian, theology in the *Divine institutes* would have helped.
3. See A. D. Nock, 'The emperor's divine *comes*', *JRS* 37 (1947), 102–16, on usage on coins and elsewhere and discussion of subordination or equality of gods/men labelled as *comes*. For the wider evolution of 'friends of God' (Christian and non-Christian), see

with Aurelian's promotion of Sol Invictus and Constantine's early connection with Apollo translated easily into Christian ideology. Like previous emperors, Constantine also assessed divine favour in terms of the worldly success it conferred. By these criteria, the conqueror of Maxentius and Licinius was shown not only to have chosen an effective patron but to have governed in line with what the 'highest divinity' demanded. It was also his imperial duty to sustain the relationship, by ensuring or imposing harmony, both on the church and on the empire as a whole.

At a party with bishops, Constantine described himself as the 'bishop' or 'overseer' (*episkopos*) of those 'outside the church'.[4] This did not preclude his active intervention in church disputes, as evidenced in his attendance at the Council of Nicaea in 325 and his exhortations to the disputants over what became known as the Arian controversy, to resolve their differences (or face the consequences). The safeguarding of right religion had always been the duty of emperors. As *pontifex maximus*[5] – a title retained even by Christian emperors (except Constans) down to its repudiation by Gratian in the early 380s – he was expected to provide guidance on religious questions, such as the meanings of omens. In the Eastern Empire, after 325, he inherited the mantle not only of previous emperors but also of the Hellenistic kings, who had patronised temples and adjudicated in disputes over property and the suitability of individuals to act as priests.[6] Baptised only on his deathbed, he maintained an imperial role as an external benefactor, combined with benign non-involvement with the day-to-day concerns of the church as an institution. Where he did intervene, his instinct was to seek consensus and avoid extremes. But his stance towards the competitors with Christianity in general was far from neutral. As we shall see, while Constantine refused to endorse forcible conversions of non-Christians, his rhetoric on the subject of the 'errors' of the pagans was unambiguous.

Over a period of quarter of a century, Constantine evolved his

Peter Brown, *The Making of Late Antiquity*, Cambridge, MA: Harvard University Press, 1978, 56–80.

4. Euseb. *Vit. Const.* 4.24, made in the context of a dinner-party with bishops. On Eusebius' development of Constantine as 'bishop', see Claudia Rapp, ' Imperial ideology in the making: Eusebius of Caesarea on Constantine as "bishop"', *JTS* 49 (1998), 685–95.

5. On emperors as *pontifex maximus*, see Fergus Millar, *The Emperor in the Roman World*, London: Duckworth, 1977, 359–61.

6. Millar, *Emperor*, 447–56.

role as a Christian emperor, through public pronouncements, laws and even sermons;[7] his so-called *Oration to the Saints* may well be authentic. But his image was also the creation of others, notably of Lactantius, and of Eusebius, the final version of whose *Ecclesiastical History* concludes with Constantine's accession and the benefits to some Christians arising from it, and who would spend his last years constructing his celebration of the *pius princeps* in the *Vita Constantini*. Despite appearances, both writers were primarily concerned with showing the workings of divine providence through history. Through the victorious Christian Constantine, the power of the Christians' God was revealed.[8] From Constantine's standpoint, this was consistent with his aims, a further demonstration of his potency as the favourite of the divine. And, for a man who twice annexed the territories of other emperors by military force, and who also killed his father-in-law (Maximian) and his brothers-in-law (Maxentius, brother to Fausta, and Licinius, married to Constantine's sister), as well as, in 326, his son and, probably, his wife, opinion formers who would denigrate and dismiss his rivals as *tyranni*, while asserting that his seizures of power were divinely sanctioned, provided much-needed assistance in securing legitimacy for his rule. Nor was such support provided only by Christians; the non-Christian Athenian writer Praxagoras was quick to write a history of Constantine's successive victories to celebrate his accession to the Eastern Empire in 325.[9]

It has been said of Constantine that 'he could for a time be all things to all men'.[10] Certainly, Constantine was content to live with the ambiguities (as we would see them) in religious and indeed in ceremonial discourse. As Augustus, among others, had done, he made creative use of existing discourses on power to achieve his ends;[11] for example, the traditional, and indeed recycled, motifs on the Arch of Constantine, erected after his defeat of Maxentius to commemorate his victories, reflect not a compromise over the use

7. Euseb. *Vit. Const.* 4.29–33.
8. For Constantine as the 'chosen one', see Euseb. *Vit. Const.* 1.24.
9. T. D. Barnes, *Constantine: Dynasty, Religion and Power in the Later Roman Empire*, Oxford: Wiley-Blackwell, 2011, appendix F, 195–7.
10. Averil Cameron, 'Constantinus Christianus', *JRS* 73 (1983), 184–90, at 189.
11. See P. Zanker, *The Power of Images in the Age of Augustus*, Ann Arbor: University of Michigan Press, 1988. Averil Cameron and Stuart Hall (eds and trans.), *Eusebius, Life of Constantine*, Oxford: Oxford University Press, 1999, 218, describe the recarving of old imperial heads as constituting 'a "quotation" from the repertoire of earlier imperial success.'

of 'pagan' designs, but the general expectation that this was what a triumphal arch should be.[12] In other words, as a communicator, Constantine exploited existing conventions; there were no alternatives and no one suggested that he should do otherwise. At the same time, no one could have been in any doubt that Constantine favoured Christianity; church-building at Rome began within weeks of the battle at the Milvian Bridge, and within months of this, the emperor was closely involved with church disputes in Africa. At no time did Constantine conceal his religious adherence to the 'Saviour God' and Christ (although the latter features less often and, as a rule, less prominently). Perhaps the key to his success and the apparent lack of serious objection from non-Christians lies in the fact that his religious policy in general operated within the boundaries set by previous emperors' involvement with 'religion'.

The 'Christian' legislator

Late in 312, Constantine met with his fellow-Augustus. Licinius at Milan and together they despatched letters to governors clarifying their religious policy.[13] Freedom of worship, already conceded by Galerius in 311, was reaffirmed, 'so that the Deity may show to us in all matters his customary care and favour', and property belonging to the Christians was to be restored to them.[14] Trouble could be anticipated from this last provision, from the new 'owners' of church property. Constantine and Licinius therefore decreed that those who had bought the confiscated assets from the imperial treasury or received them as a gift should return them to the churches, without recompense, and apply to the provincial governor for compensation. The enactment reaffirmed the legal right of the church to own property for meetings and other purposes, and the emperors' confidence that the measure would both further 'public peace' and ensure the continued favour of the Deity.[15] This did no more than guarantee normal religious freedoms to the Christians, while also undoing the economic consequences of the sanctions against them. Licinius, the non-Christian, who would shortly eliminate Maximinus Daza, the foe of Christians, raised no objection.

12. See above, Chapter 5, 118–19.
13. Lactant. *De mort. pers.* 48; Euseb. *Hist. eccl.* 10.5.2.
14. For the church as 'corporate' owner, see Euseb. *Hist. eccl.* 7.13; 7.30.19.
15. Cf. Euseb. *Hist. eccl.* 10.5.15–17.

Among the early beneficiaries of Constantine's goodwill towards Christians, in 313, were the churches of Africa. Writing to Caecilian, whose status as bishop of Carthage was under attack from rigorist followers of rival candidates for the bishopric, Constantine gave him authority to distribute funds held by the local finance officer to named beneficiaries, in line with a schedule drawn up by his principal Christian adviser, Hosius of Corduba;[16] how far Constantine was aware at the time that this could be seen as taking sides against Caecilian's opponents, later to be known as the Donatists, is not known. His apparent enthusiasm for his religion, combined with excessive generosity, also impelled him to offer exemption from public duties to the clergy 'in the catholic church over which Caecilian presides',[17] so that they were not distracted 'from the service due to the Deity'. His justification for the exemption, which would later be revoked, was based on traditional imperial concern for the public welfare, as guaranteed by divine favour: when proper worship was despised, he wrote, public affairs were endangered, whereas, when the Deity was honoured, 'the greatest benefits accrue to the state'. As so often, Constantine was more traditionalist than he appeared; immunities from taxation and *munera* were also traditionally granted to priests of the traditional cults and Constantine extended them to leaders of the Jewish communities in 330.[18]

Constantine's legislative policy towards Christians, though benign, did not feature dramatic departures from past conventions.[19] Because of the imperfect textual transmission and processes of revision of the imperial law-codes of Theodosius (438) and Justinian (529 and 534), the record is incomplete, but it would be unwise to argue for reforms not hinted at in extant literature on the basis of tendentious literary authorities, such as Eusebius, whose aim was to portray Constantine as a 'Christian' lawgiver. Moreover, it is not always possible to detect when Constantine as legislator is in responsive mode, clarifying existing rules, rather than introducing new

16. Euseb. *Hist. eccl.* 10.6.
17. Letter to the proconsul Anullinus (not to be confused with his persecutor namesake), Euseb. *Hist. eccl.*10.7.2.
18. *Cod. Theod.* 16.8.2; 4. See C. Dupont,. 'Les privileges des clercs sous Constantin', *RHE* 62 (1967), 729–52; T. G. Elliot, 'The tax exemptions granted to clerics by Constantine and Constantius II', *Phoenix* 32 (1978), 326–36.
19. For a balanced account, see E. D. Hunt, 'Christianizing the Roman Empire: The evidence of the Code', in Jill Harries and Ian Wood (eds), *The Theodosian Code: Studies in the Imperial Law of Late Antiquity*, London: Duckworth, 1993, reissued 2010, 143–58.

ones. For example, his ruling in July 321 confirming that the church could receive bequests also reassured the dying that their last wishes would be honoured, even if legal formalities were not fully observed; this was in line with his generally permissive attitude on the formulation of all wills, not a concession designed to favour the church at the expense of the family.[20] On manumission of slaves, he wrote on separate occasions to two bishops, Protogenes of Sardica (316) and Hosius of Corduba (321), clarifying the processes of manumission in church, in the presence of the congregation and of the bishop, who was required to set down the transaction in writing 'as a substitute' for public records (*vice actorum*);[21] the response to Hosius provided explicit reassurance that the church formalities were equivalent to the conventional, traditional processes, and, in addition, allowed the clergy to manumit orally or by will, without being required to do so in church.[22] Both these texts are responses to queries, perhaps because of local challenges to the validity of church manumissions; neither is the original law, which Constantine refers to as having been in force for a while, and its precise provisions are unknown.[23] The privilege of religious manumission was not, however, confined to Christians, as various third-century inscriptions on sacral manumissions to pagan deities attest.[24]

Constantine's eagerness to assist the bishops in the carrying out of their duties extended to the workings of the episcopal 'courts' or hearings (*episcopalis audientia*). Again, the record is incomplete, corrupt and perhaps tainted by forgery,[25] but there is no evidence that Constantine created or further empowered episcopal jurisdiction.[26] It had long been the convention within Christian communities

20. *Cod. Theod.* 16.2.4, contra T. D. Barnes, *Constantine and Eusebius*, Cambridge, MA: Harvard University Press, 1981, 50: 'Constantine thereby set the tie of religion above the bonds of family.' For long-term policies on wills, see Jill Harries, 'Constantine the lawgiver', in Scott McGill, Cristiana Sogno and Edward Watts (eds), *From the Tetrarchs to the Theodosians: Late Roman History and Culture, 284–450* CE, Cambridge: Cambridge University Press, 2010, 73–92.
21. *Cod. Just.* 1.13.1.
22. *Cod. Theod.* 4.7.1 = *Cod. Just.* 1.13.2.
23. For the 'three' inscribed laws on manumission, see Sozom. *Hist. eccl.* 1.9.6. For a brief survey, see Claudia Rapp, *Holy Bishops in Late Antiquity: The Nature of Christian Leadership in an Age of Transition*, Berkeley: University of California Press, 2005, 239–42.
24. A. Cameron, 'Inscriptions relating to sacral manumission and confession', *Harv. Theol. Rev.* 32 (1939), 143–79.
25. *Const. Sirm.* 1, ostensibly dated to 333, may be a Merovingian forgery, designed to underpin the authority of episcopal jurisdiction.
26. There is a strong scholarly tradition which favours the view that Constantine in

that the bishop could act as an arbitrator and reconciler in the settlement of disputes, and Constantine did nothing to change that, preferring a policy of deferential non-intervention, which extended to his agreement that the clergy should be tried for clerical offences before an ecclesiastical court.[27] However, when confronted with the question of what should happen if one party to a dispute before the secular courts sought for a transfer to the bishop's 'court', Constantine appears to have ruled that the bishop could conduct a hearing and reach a verdict but that this should then be reported back to the secular judge.[28] A letter to Ablabius, recorded as the questionable *Sirmondian Constitution* 1, allowed the transfer of a lawsuit, in this case concerning protection of the rights of minors from abuse by guardians, from the secular to the episcopal court by one party, regardless of whether or not the other agreed. In line with general arbitration practice, Constantine stated that the bishop's judgement was final and could not be appealed against.[29]

Constantine's innovations with regard to Christians were in line with precedent and consistent with his imperial role as guardian of 'right' religion. He was therefore consistent also in retaining the title of *pontifex maximus*, not as a sop to pagans, nor as an exploitation of the 'ambiguity' attached to the role of a new kind of emperor, but as an affirmation of his right to legislate and adjudicate on religious matters. It was thus to be expected that he should be consulted in c. 321 by the *vicarius* of Rome, Helpidius, on what activities were allowed on the 'Dies Solis'; the reply did not create a new 'Sunday' holiday, the existence of which is assumed in the text, but explained that, although normally legal disputes were not heard on holidays, manumission, being a legal transaction that was a source of joy to all concerned, should be permitted.[30] Similarly in line with imperial fears as to private divination and magic was Constantine's outlawing

some sense formally established *episcopalis audientia*; see, for example, Jean Gaudemet, *Les Institutions de l'antiquité*, Paris: Sirey, 1967 and 1991, 232; G. Vismara, *La giurisdizione civile dei vescovi*, Milan: Giuffré, 1995, 40. For an opposing view, Caroline Humfress, *Orthodoxy and the Courts in Late Antiquity*, Oxford: Oxford University Press, 2007, 156–61; also Jill Harries, *Law and Empire in Late Antiquity*, Cambridge: Cambridge University Press, 1999, 191–211; Rapp, *Holy Bishops*, 242–3.
27. Optatus, *App*endix 5, ed. and trans. Mark Edwards, *Optatus Against the Donatists*, TTH 27, Liverpool: Liverpool University Press 1997, 190.
28. *Cod. Theod.* 1.27.1.
29. For discussion of *Const. Sirm.* 1 (assumed to be genuine) in context, H. A. Drake, *Constantine and the Bishops: The Politics of Intolerance*, Baltimore, MD: Johns Hopkins University Press, 2002, 312–32.
30. *Cod. Theod.* 2.8.1 = *Cod. Just.* 3.12.12.

of both, while retaining the services of religious experts for the public interpretation of omens.[31]

Constantine's exploitation of his pontifical role, combined with the advantages of encouraging the imperial cult as a display of loyalty, may also explain his administration's positive response to an approach from an Italian community, Hispellum, in the early to mid-330s, complaining about the expense caused by sharing priesthoods and public games with the neighbouring community of Volsinii and asking to build a temple to celebrate the cult of the emperor and his family.[32] Permission was granted for the temple but the cult was not to be 'defiled by the conceits of any pestilential superstition'. This amounted to the banning of blood sacrifices, while conceding the right of the people of Hispellum to demonstrate their loyalty to the imperial house in traditional ways.

The policy of toleration of some traditional religious observance in Italy appears to contradict Eusebius' account of the destruction and plundering of temples carried out by Constantine in the east.[33] Eusebius is also undermined by Libanius' observation, made a generation later, that pagan observances were allowed to continue.[34] In this area, the effect of imperial decisions would be localised. Those who lost their temples because they had impinged on Christian requirements, or who came under pressure from enthusiastically Christian governors, would recall Constantine as an oppressor; those unaffected would say the opposite. It can be argued that, of the five specific cases recorded by Eusebius, all can be reckoned as causing offence to Christians for different reasons. Three of the five were temples of Aphrodite, whose cult was associated with licentiousness and ritual prostitution[35] (and of these one was on the reputed site of the Holy Sepulchre at Jerusalem); a fourth was at Mamre, the site of the dwelling of Abraham and Sarah, when they were visited by an angel, where Constantine funded a basilica church;[36] and the temple

31. *Cod. Theod.* 9.16.1–3; John Curran, *Pagan City and Christian Capital: Rome in the Fourth Century*, Oxford: Oxford University Press, 2000, 172–4.
32. Dessau, *ILS* 705; J. Gascou, 'Le Rescrit de Hispellum', *MEFRA* 79 (1967), 609–59; R. Van Dam, *The Roman Revolution of Constantine*, New York: Cambridge University Press, 2007, 23–34; Barnes, *Constantine*, 20–3, redating to the summer of 337. The rescript was issued by Constans, as Caesar in Milan, but reflects the policy of his father's government.
33. Euseb. *Vit. Const.* 3.54, removal of valuable building materials, gold statues etc.
34. Lib. *Or.* 30.6.
35. Euseb. *Vit. Const.* 3.58.1.
36. Letter of Constantine on Mamre, Euseb. *Vit. Const.* 3.51–3. Visitation of Abraham by the angel, Genesis 18.

of Asclepius at Aegae in Cilicia had links with Apollonius of Tyana, the hero of Sosianus Hierocles, and thus a favourite religious role model for persecutors of Christians.[37] How far even these were the results of local initiatives, rather than imperial policy, is uncertain.

So did Constantine at any point ban all pagan sacrifices, as is implied in a law enacted by his youngest son?[38] Constans' law vigorously repudiated what he called *superstitio* and ordered the closure of temples but the extract, as we have it, makes no mention of public funding, the withdrawal of which by Gratian and Theodosius I at the end of the century proved the death blow to pagan rites. Already outlawed by Constantine were nocturnal sacrifices, which had been suspect in the eyes of non-Christian emperors as well, because they were associated with magic and witchcraft; also the domestic sacrifices associated with private divination.[39] Constantine is known as well to have avoided personal participation in blood sacrifices, an aspect of traditional ritual behaviour regularly condemned by Christians but also offensive to some opponents of Christianity, such as Porphyry, who denounced blood sacrifices in the second book of his *De abstinentia*.[40] The regulations in the rescript to Hispellum confirm that Constantine's policy, when he was asked, was not to endorse blood sacrifices. Taken together, the combination of explicit outlawing of some forms of sacrifice and the emperor's known disapproval of sacrificial rites in general would have amounted to a de facto ban – where it was enforced. Working with changed social attitudes and a public willing to follow an emperor's lead, for its own advantage, Constantine sidelined sacrificial rites through a process of incremental change. Nor were there many objections raised. The main source of opposition to Constantine appears to have been not the champions of sacrifice, but those 'Hellenes', Eunapius and perhaps the poet Palladas, who objected to his attacks

37. Eus. *Vit. Const.* 55.5–56; Robin Lane Fox, *Pagans and Christians*, London; Penguin, 1986, 671–2; Cameron and Hall, *Eusebius*, 301–4; A. D. Lee, 'Traditional religions', in Noel Lenski (ed.), *The Cambridge Companion to the Age of Constantine*, Cambridge: Cambridge University Press, 2006, 159–79.
38. *Cod. Theod.* 16.10.2.
39. For various theories, see T. D. Barnes, 'Constantine's prohibition of pagan sacrifice', *AJPhil.* 105 (1984), 69–72; R. M. Errington, 'Constantine and the pagans', *GRBS* 29 (1988), 309–18; Scott Bradbury, 'Constantine and the problem of anti-pagan legislation in the fourth century', *C Phil.* 89 (1994), 120–39; Barnes, *Constantine*, 109–11.
40. See now John North, 'Arnobius and sacrifice', in John Drinkwater and Benet Salway (eds), *Wolf Liebeschuetz Reflected*, *BICS* Supp. 91, London: University of London, 2007, 27–36. For declining enthusiasm among pagans for blood sacrifices, see Scott Bradbury, 'Julian's pagan revival and the decline of blood sacrifice', *Phoenix* 49 (1995), 331–56.

on temple treasures. Their philosophical objections to Christianity would have been strengthened by Constantine's executing for treason, late in his reign, the Platonist philosopher Sopatros, a follower of Iamblichus, and therefore a member of a network of influential pagan thinkers who, in time, would include the emperor Julian.[41]

In the content of his formal legislation, as preserved in the Codes, which edited out much of the rhetoric, Constantine successfully separated the emperor as institution from the emperor as a man with personal religious convictions. However, after 325, the letters and laws, as preserved by Eusebius, are explicit in their formulation of the emperor's confidence in his divine protector. The legal content of edicts or letters, addressed to 'the people' or 'the provincials', is swamped by a plethora of colourful self-justifications – where a 'law' could be said to have existed at all. This was not new; Maximinus Daza's Letter to Tyre, copied by Eusebius, pointed to the successful harvests and general prosperity as 'proof' of divine support, before moving on to a general command to expel the 'impious'.[42]

The purpose of imperial 'letters' was to communicate and there was nothing to prevent emperors from composing 'letters' which made statements of imperial policy or attitudes, but which were devoid of formal legal content. In fact, the focus on legal content, though endorsed by the principles of the Theodosian Code compilers a century later, may be something of an anachronism. As Plato had explained in his dialogue on the *Laws*, a 'law' consisted of its core content, plus sanction, and its justification, which was also essential to the second purpose of law, the education of the virtuous citizen, a principle also endorsed by Cicero in his treatises on law and the state.[43] Constantine's (and Maximinus') rhetoric should not therefore be viewed as optional add-ons; the rhetoric is intrinsic to the purpose of the law as a whole. Thus, while the legal content may be moderate – for example, that non-Christians must be left in peace – the rhetoric, castigating error, sent a contradictory signal. The emperor's communications conveyed his attitude and created opportunities for exploitation by local readers and recipients.

41. For redating of Palladas, see Kevin W. Wilkinson, 'Palladas and the age of Constantine', *JRS* 99 (2009), 36–60. On Sopatros (or Sopater), *PLRE I*, Sopater 1, p. 846. For his death, ascribed to a plot by the Christian praetorian prefect Ablabius, see Zos. *New History* 2.40.3 (derived from Eunapius); Eunap. *VS* 6.2.3.7–11; 3.7.13.
42. Euseb. *Hist. eccl.* 9.7.
43. Plato, *Laws*, 4.719e–723c.

Eusebius' *Life of Constantine* laid out in full Constantine's affirmations of his Christian faith addressed to the eastern provincials in the aftermath of his overthrow of Licinius.[44] In political terms, their purpose was twofold. One purpose was the proclamation of the emperor's religious adherence, with a view to influencing the behaviour of others; a consequence would have been the successful application in 331 of the community of Orcistus in Phrygia for full city status on the grounds, inter alia, that it was devoutly Christian.[45] A second was the integration of proven divine favour with a discourse on legitimacy, already developed by Lactantius. This was based in part on the simple proposition that the victory of an emperor supported by the God of the Christians, who had intervened to protect Christians from persecution, proved the power and favour of that God. The second implication was that the victorious emperor deserved the divine favour – unlike his defeated enemies; their defeat proved their unworthiness to rule and, by extension, that their rule had never been strictly 'lawful' in the first place.

Among the victor's first acts in 325 was a letter to the 'eastern provincials', duly preserved by Eusebius, who read it as a Christian manifesto.[46] The presentation is Christian, perhaps, in the sense in which Constantine understood it, but also reflects ideas familiar to non-Christians. The new emperor asserted the lawfulness of his right to rule by reference to the 'providence' of 'the Supreme God', who had brought him victory; the past atrocities of the persecuting emperors were rejected, along with the fraudulent oracles of Apollo, which had justified the policy. Backed by the one God, to whom, alone among the Tetrarchs, his father had paid honour,[47] and the 'pure light' of his Son, Constantine rejected the past policy of persecution of religious dissidents, relying instead on 'peaceful persuasion' to win the 'diseased' from their errors. As a public statement of faith, it was unambiguous in its adherence to Christianity, with its mention of the 'Son' as a messenger of the supreme 'saviour' deity, while remaining reassuringly traditional in its vague references

44. Euseb. *Vit. Const.* 2.24–42.
45. *MAMA* 7.305; Van Dam, *Roman Revolution*, 150–62.
46. Euseb. *Vit. Const.* 2.48–60.
47. It is uncertain how far eastern provincials would have been aware that Constantius I, Caesar and then Augustus only in the west, was not a Christian monotheist. Euseb. *Vit. Const.* 1.13–18, perhaps on the authority of Constantine's own version of his father's convictions, implies that Constantius prospered because he avoided persecution and correctly identified the 'one God' as that of the Christians.

to light and to the 'deity' in general, and its insistence on religious toleration:[48]

> For the general good of the world and of all mankind, I desire that your people be at peace and free from strife. Let those in error, as well as the believers, gladly receive the benefits of peace and quiet ... May none molest another, may each retain what his soul desires and practise it.

Constantine's most personal Christian manifesto was the rather incoherent text known as the 'Oration to the Saints', an address to an assembly of Christians.[49] The text, originally in Latin, was preserved in a Greek translation as the 'fifth book' of Eusebius' *Life of Constantine*, and its ascription to the emperor has been questioned in the past. Although the general view now is that the text is genuinely 'Constantinian', there is no agreement as to its date or place of delivery.[50] The speech as a whole is an affirmation of the emperor's allegedly unlearned faith, which combines celebration of God and the 'second god' Christ the Saviour with philosophical disquisitions and attacks on the ignorant and impious, who could expect in the afterlife condemnation to 'unquenchable and unceasing fire ... and the precipitous and remote abyss'.[51] Constantine makes a sustained attempt to explain the mission of Christ on earth, his miracles, the Virgin Birth and the relationship of Father to Son, and of both to nature and supreme reason. Despite this focus on the Deity, the text overall can also be read as a justification for a single earthly ruler mirroring the divine order, emphasising the importance of 'one overseer for all existent things' with 'everything subjected to his sole rulership'.[52] Like Lactantius, whose ideas are often reflected in the text,[53] he resorts to pagan witness to the divinity of Christ,

48. Euseb. *Vit. Const.* 2.56.1.
49. Trans. and ed. Mark Edwards, *Constantine and Christendom*, TTH 39, Liverpool: Liverpool University Press, 2003. All quotations are from his translation.
50. R. P. C. Hanson, 'The *Oratio ad Sanctos* attributed to the Emperor Constantine and the Oracle of Apollo at Daphne', *JTS* 24 (1973), 505–11, argues for Antioch but doubts the authenticity of the speech; T. D. Barnes, 'Constantine's speech to the Assembly of the Saints: Date and place of delivery', *JTS* 52 (2001), 26–36, argues for Nicomedia in 321, and has previously suggested Sardica; Edwards, *Constantine and Christendom*, xxiii–xxix, suggests Rome in 315. Also, cautiously, arguing for a revised text, Drake, *Constantine and the Bishops*, 292–7.
51. *Orat. ad Sanct.* 13.
52. *Orat. ad Sanct.* 3.
53. E.g. on the gods' marriages within time (*Orat. ad Sanct.* 4 with Lactant. *Div. inst.* 1.16.5–6); unfavourable (Aristophanic) view of Socrates as deceiver (*Orat. ad Sanct.* 9 with Lactant. *Div. inst.* 3.19–20).

citing and authenticating a Sibylline Oracle,[54] and expounding at length the Christian prophetic content of Virgil's Fourth Eclogue.[55] The peroration reveals the sermon's political purpose, attacking the false beliefs and 'atrocities' of the persecuting 'tyrants',[56] and recording the untimely deaths and overthrow of Decius, Valerian, Aurelian – and Diocletian, whose sumptuous palace at Salonae (Split) is somewhat surprisingly dismissed as a 'contemptible dwelling'.[57] Constantine's own victory was a demonstration of the divine favour (26): '(all men) have witnessed the battles and observed the war, in which God's providence awarded victory to the people'. While demonstrating his theological and philosophical engagement with Christianity, Constantine could not resist exploiting Christian arguments to strengthen and legitimise his position as emperor.

Constantine and the Christians: the search for concord

Constantine's relationship with his patron god differed in one crucial respect from those of his predecessors. Organisation of the cult of the Christian God rested with an empire-wide, city-based network of bishops, clergy and laity. Their theology was distinctive and sophisticated and their reputation for social charity was well established. Feared in the past by some as an 'alternative state', the bishops as a collective and as individuals would exploit their newly won access to the emperor, hoping not only for acts of financial patronage and legal decisions strengthening their institutions and safeguarding their rights, but also for his help in the resolution of internal disputes.[58] For his part, Constantine's priority was the maintenance of the harmony on which he believed the divine favour depended, and he was, as a rule, content that the bishops should sort out their own problems. Despite his apparent wish to be neutral, however, such politic distancing was not always possible.

The schism in North Africa associated with the name of Donatus originated from an apparently technical dispute concerning the

54. *Orat. ad Sanct.* 18–19; an acrostic also cited but ascribed to a different Sibyl by Lactant. *Div. inst.* 1.6.10; 7.19.9.
55. *Orat. ad Sanct.* 19–21.
56. *Orat. ad Sanct.* 22–3.
57. *Orat. ad. Sanct.* 24–5.
58. Celebrated by Euseb. *Vit. Const.* 1.42.1, asserting that bishops dined with Constantine and went everywhere with him.

consecration of Caecilian as bishop of Carthage.[59] It was claimed that one of the consecrating bishops, Felix of Abthungi, had 'handed over' sacred books and objects to imperial officials in the course of the Great Persecution, and that his acts as bishop were therefore invalid. Therefore Caecilian too, although not a *traditor* ('hander over'), was not a true bishop. A further alleged dimension to the controversy was the unbalanced behaviour of a 'factious woman', Lucilla, an over-assertive member of the aristocratic laity. Having been censured by Caecilian for her excessive devotion to saints' bones, she turned against him, and organised the consecration of one of her own servants, Majorinus, as an alternative bishop.[60] While this is a reminder of the important role played by women and by lay Christians in the evolution of late Roman Christianity, the unfavourable depiction of the contumacious Lucilla injected gender stereotyping into the narrative of 'Donatism' developed by its 'catholic' opponents.[61]

   In 313, the challengers to Caecilian appealed to Constantine, who referred the matter to Miltiades, the bishop of Rome, who was to hear the case, with a panel of three Gallic bishops, in Fausta's residence. Miltiades, however, added fifteen Italian bishops to the hearing, and then found against the petitioners, who promptly appealed to Constantine again.[62] Constantine then personally, in a break with precedent, convened a council of Gallic bishops at Arles in 314. This group, which was drawn from all over Gaul, not only ruled decisively again in favour of Caecilian, but also took thought for more general regulation of church matters and the duties of the laity as well: those who took up weapons in peacetime, drove chariots in the circus or performed in theatres, or Christian administrators who flouted the church's rules, should all be subject to excommunication.[63] When the losers appealed to Constantine for

---

59. W. H. C. Frend, *The Donatist Church: A Movement of Protest in Roman North Africa*, Oxford: Clarendon Press, 1952, rev. edn, 1971, is still the standard account. Neither 'Donatists' nor 'Arians' conceded the use of these labels, which their opponents used to categorise them as 'deviant' and separate them from the 'catholic', i.e. universal, Christian community. In the interests of balance I have avoided these terms where possible.
60. Optat. 1.16–19.
61. For assertions that women are susceptible to heresy, see Irenaeus of Lyon (late second century), *Against Heresies*, 1.13.1–4. For allegations about Arius and his women followers, see below, p. 172.
62. Optat. 1.22–4.
63. See Optat. *Appendix* 4; *Conc. Arel.* 1, (314), canons 3, 4, 5 and 7.

a third time in 315, the emperor refused to issue a final ruling and the parties returned to Africa.

The story did not end there. Drawing on a longstanding purist tradition in African Christianity, the followers of Majorinus and Donatus described themselves as the 'church of the martyrs', insisting that martyrdom was preferable to surrender to persecution. Over the next century, down to the time of Augustine, they composed passion literature and set up shrines in celebration of their own martyrs,[64] and, as the 'true' church, established alternative bishops and ecclesiastical organisations in many African cities. After a brief flirtation with military intervention, Constantine seems to have lost interest in the Christians' divisions in Africa. In 330, he received yet another appeal from the bishops of Numidia, complaining that the Donatists 'have, with their wonted shamelessness, thought fit to invade the basilica of that church, which I had ordered to be built in the city of Constantina (Cirta)' and that they had refused to obey orders from the local governors to hand back the site.[65] The petitioners therefore requested confirmation of Constantine's permission to build another church elsewhere, on fiscal land, funded by the emperor's own largess. Constantine's reiterated praises for their patience and Christian willingness to turn the other cheek (a policy he was unlikely to sanction in his own case) is a measure both of his indifference and of the failure of the 'catholics' in parts of North Africa to retain control over the Christian city or rural populations.[66]

While peripheral to Constantine's imperial concerns, the nature of the 'debate' in North Africa about what was required to be a Christian had wider implications. When Optatus, bishop of Milevis, composed his history *Against the Donatists* in or after 384 for the benefit of the schismatic 'brother' Parmenianus, he authenticated his version by the extensive use of documents including letters and court records. Thus the early collaboration of the dissidents who assembled in Cirta in May 303 is 'proved' by the 'writings of Nundinarius, then a deacon ... as is witnessed by the antiquity of the documents, which we shall be able to produce for those who

---

64. See accounts in M. Tilley (ed. and trans.), *Donatist Martyr Stories: The Church in Conflict in Roman North Africa*, TTH 24, Liverpool: Liverpool University Press, 1996. For the martyrs of Abitina, see above, p. 91.
65. Optat. *Appendix* 10.
66. African 'catholics' insisted on their membership of a 'universal' church, by contrast with the schismatic Donatists.

doubt it'.[67] Court records and Constantine's own imperial letters also guaranteed Optatus' veracity.[68] 'Proof' is supplied from the records of a hearing before the governor Zenophilus in 320 that Caecilian's rival, Majorinus, was in fact consecrated by a *traditor*, Silvanus; this included the full testimony of the deacon Nundinarius.[69] Another record, which like the first contained documents, sworn statements and interrogations by both judges and advocates, established that the part of a letter written by Felix which 'proved' him to be a *traditor* was in fact a forgery by one Ingentius, whom we last hear of as being imprisoned on remand 'for stricter interrogation'.[70] The deployment by both sides of official documents to support the 'truth' of their allegations is symptomatic of the legalist and bureaucratic culture of late antiquity – and of the lack of any real doctrinal differences between the factions.

The Council of Nicaea, 325

Once master of the east, Constantine was to find questions of orthodoxy or 'right belief' more widely divisive than the localised schismatic preoccupations of the African churches. Any form of official toleration of diversity, even dissent, was not the preferred option among some Christians in Alexandria, a volatile city with a long history of feuding between its diverse religious and ethnic communities. In 318, a doctrinal controversy had broken out, associated with Arius, a priest in Alexandria.[71] As reported to Constantine, the bishop, Alexander, had asked his priests' opinion in public on a contentious matter, probably the nature of the Trinity,[72] and Arius had 'thoughtlessly replied'.[73] The detail is amplified in the accounts of Athanasius of Alexandria, Alexander's controversial successor as bishop, and in the ecclesiastical histories of Socrates

67. Optat. 1.14.
68. Optat. 1.16.
69. Optat. *Appendix* 1.
70. Optat. *Appendix* 2. Ingentius, whose testimony is inconsistent, is interrogated by the judge, ominously, about his status, preparatory to the possible use of torture if he is unable to establish exemption.
71. On the 'Arian controversy' in general: Rowan Williams, *Arius: Heresy and Tradition*, London: SCM Press, 2000; R. P. C. Hanson, *The Search for the Christian Doctrine of God: The Arian Controversy*, Edinburgh: T. and T. Clark, 1988; D. M. Gwynn, *The Eusebians: The Polemic of Athanasius of Alexandria and the Construction of the 'Arian' Controversy*, Oxford: Oxford University Press, 2007.
72. Socrates, *Hist. eccl.* 1.5.1.
73. Euseb. *Vit. Const.* 2.69.1.

Scholasticus and Sozomen, compiled in Constantinople in the 430s, who preserved a number of self-justifying documents issued by the various parties.[74] On neither side was the tone conciliatory. By 319, Arius, a number of associates and at least three bishops, including Eusebius of Nicomedia, had been denounced by the Alexandrian church leaders as apostates.[75] Arius, however, was not ready to go quietly and retaliated with a complaint to Eusebius of Nicomedia that he had been hounded from the city by his bishop as an atheist, because he could not concur with the bishop's publicly preached doctrines:[76]

> These are impieties, to which we could not listen, even though the heretics should threaten us with a thousand deaths. But as for us, what do we say and believe? That the Son is not unbegotten, nor in any way part of the unbegotten; nor from some lower essence; but that by his own will and counsel, he has subsisted before time and before ages as God ..., only-begotten, unchangeable.

Arius would have hoped that, through these widely circulated statements of his doctrines, the imputations of heresy against him could be refuted, and, indeed, turned against his opponents. But in 324, Alexander widened his attack, accusing his opponents not only of unorthodox belief but also of wicked and deceitful behaviour.[77] Inspired by the devil, Alexander claimed, Arius had 'conspired' with his associates and 'denied the divinity' of Christ, adopting the 'impious' opinions of the 'Greeks and Jews'. And, as was alleged of the Donatists and other heretical movements, they attracted unsuitable women:

> (5) They daily excite disorders and persecutions against us; on the one hand they have courts assembled on the petition of disorderly women, whom they have deceived, on the other they discredit Christianity by the younger women who support them running round every street in an indecent fashion.

74. Cf. Sozomen's wry comment (*Hist. eccl.* 1.1.15) that 'the supporters of both sides in turn made collections of such letters as supported their own standpoints, and omitted those which opposed them'.
75. Socrates, *Hist. eccl.* 1.6.4
76. Theodoret, *Hist. eccl.* 1.5.1–4 = J. Stevenson, *A New Eusebius: Documents Illustrating the History of the Church to AD 337*, 2nd edn, London: SPCK, 1987, 293. See also Arius' letter to Alexander of Alexandria at Stevenson, *New Eusebius*, 294 = Athanasius, *On the synods of Ariminum and Seleucia*, 16.
77. Theodoret, *Hist. eccl.* 1.4 = Stevenson, *New Eusebius*, 295. See Hanson, *Search*, 145: 'Alexander's condemnation of Arius was at least precipitate.'

This frenetic activity was combined with all the trickery of oratory to mislead the unwary and receive acceptance. The result was that some (the bishops who supported Arius) were 'tricked' into signing letters in their support and accepting them into the Christian communion.

For committed Christians, the theological issue was of central importance, but its complexity made it hard to grasp and vulnerable to simplification and misrepresentation. Arius had maintained that 'sons' come after 'fathers' in time and that this must therefore be true of Christ the Son in relation to God the Father – although that relation, as Arius insisted, was established before human time existed. The inference drawn by Alexander (which Arius did not accept) was that therefore Christ was in some sense inferior and not an equal part of the divine entity. But the extreme rhetoric used on both sides soon rendered the initial cause of contention peripheral; the issue between Alexander, and then Athanasius, and Arius, Eusebius of Nicomedia and their followers was in part about Alexandrian episcopal authority, which had been publicly challenged by a mere priest, and partly about who decided the doctrines of the newly universal church.

For Constantine, initially, the dispute was 'extremely trivial and quite unworthy of much controversy'[78] and he advised Alexander and Arius to resolve their differences,[79] offering his 'modest' services as an arbitrator. Constantine's purpose would have been to contain the damage already caused by the public war of words between Arius and Alexander, which had made Christianity a laughing stock. Yet both had behaved in the manner expected of opinion-formers in late Roman cities, exploiting conventional rhetorical techniques to achieve their goal, which, ultimately, was to persuade and to win over their audience, not to educate or inform, still less to engage in a rational discussion about truth. Arius even sought to widen his appeal beyond the ecclesiastical elite by circulating the *Thalia*, a set of simple theological maxims in verse designed to win over the less sophisticated Christians; he also wrote pop songs for sailors, millers and travellers.[80] Therefore, although 'trivial', the affair was liable to

78. Euseb. *Vit. Const.* 2.68.2.
79. It is possible that the letter was addressed to the Council of Antioch, held under the presidency of Hosius of Corduba in spring 325; see Cameron and Hall, *Eusebius, Life of Constantine*, 250. On the Council of Antioch, Hanson, *Search*, 146–51.
80. For the *Thalia*, Athanasius, *On the synods of Ariminum and Seleucia* 15 = (extracts) Stevenson, *New Eusebius*, 296; for the pop songs, Philostorgius, *Hist. eccl.* 2.2.

do disproportionate damage to Christians and disrupt the general harmony by which Constantine set such store. Shrewdly, Constantine drew attention to the divisive effects of public debate, which set a premium on rhetoric and emotion, to the detriment of rational argument. Alexander and Arius should not, in Constantine's view, have debated the matter in public, because of the danger that the audience could be misled.[81] Instead of behaving like philosophers, who also exaggerated the petty differences between them, the Alexandrian Christians should focus on what united them.[82] Constantine's insight would prove unavailing, not only because of what was at stake in Alexandria, but also because what he proposed ran counter to the culture of public debate and controversy which for centuries had helped to decide the outcomes of local power struggles in the cities of the empire.[83]

Other ecclesiastical issues were also pressing, not least a second schism, led by Meletius, the bishop of Lycopolis in Egypt, who, in 304, had deputised for Bishop Peter of Alexandria during the persecution and ordained clergy on his own authority. Excommunicated by Peter on his return, and then sentenced by the secular authorities as a Christian to the mines of Palestine, he returned in 311 and set up an alternative network of bishops. This, and controversy over the date of Easter, spurred the emperor into a fresh initiative, the convening of an 'ecumenical' (world-wide) church council at Nicaea,[84] at which all differences would be resolved. Letters were sent to all bishops and helpful offers were made of free transport by the *cursus publicus* or the use of pack animals; food was also provided for the duration of the council. The bishops' reaction, as reported by Eusebius, was enthusiastic.[85]

> They were drawn by the hope of good things, the opportunity to share in peace and the spectacle of that great marvel, to see such a great Emperor.

81. Euseb. *Vit. Const.* 2.69.2–3.
82. Euseb. *Vit. Const.* 2.71.2–5.
83. On this, see Richard Lim, *Public Disputation, Power and Social Order in Late Antiquity*, Berkeley: University of California Press, 1995.
84. The venue initially chosen was Ancyra, where the impartiality of the bishop Marcellus as an alleged 'Sabellian' was compromised. On being informed of this by Eusebius of Nicomedia, the associate of Arius, Constantine switched to Nicaea, because its location was salubrious and convenient for bishops coming from the west (Stevenson, *New Eusebius*, 298). On Marcellus' career and exile in 336, see Stevenson *New Eusebius*, 316; Socrates, *Hist. eccl.* 1.36; Sozom. *Hist. eccl.* 2.33.
85. Euseb. *Vit. Const.* 3.6.1–2 (*cursus publicus* and enthusiasm of bishops); 3.6.9 (food).

In that ambition the bishops were not disappointed. Eusebius' depiction of Constantine's behaviour at Nicaea is a potent combination of the ceremonial with the conciliatory. All the bishops were assembled in their chosen seats, awaiting Constantine's arrival. Preceded by a few friends, the emperor made his entrance, splendid in purple, gold and precious stones. All rose to their feet and only when Constantine seated himself in the centre on a 'small' chair of gold did the bishops seat themselves likewise. A rhymed speech in praise of God on behalf of Constantine followed, to which the emperor replied 'with a soft and gentle voice' in Latin – the language of power – through an interpreter. However, once the rather heated proceedings were under way, Constantine reverted to Greek, patiently seeking to find agreement 'until he had brought them to be of one mind and one belief on all the matters in dispute'.[86] To underline the emperor's personal dominance, the council was followed by celebrations of Constantine's *vicennalia*, featuring banquets to which the bishops were cordially invited; the whole occasion was compared by Eusebius to the Kingdom of Heaven, a 'dream, not a fact'.[87]

The most enduring legacy of the Council of Nicaea to the Christian church was the Nicene Creed, reported by Eusebius of Caesarea to his own church, and by the later church historians. It also outlawed the beliefs of Arius, as most of those present understood them,[88] and reached agreement on how to calculate the date of Easter. A number of regulations for the churches were agreed: for example, the self-mutilated could not be ordained (canon 1); recent converts should not be elevated to the episcopate (canon 2); no member of the clergy was to share his home with a woman not related to him or 'above all suspicion' (canon 3); and the consecration of any new bishop was to be carried out after proper consultation with colleagues and with the consent of the metropolitan, or head of the ecclesiastical province. The Novatian schismatics at Rome were treated kindly (canon 8), but recent infringements of the convention that a bishop consecrated in one city should not transfer

---

86. Euseb. *Vit. Const.* 3.14.
87. Euseb. *Vit. Const.* 3.15.
88. Socrates, *Hist. eccl* 1.9.3, from the letter from the Council of Nicaea to the Egyptian church (Socrates, *Hist. Eccles.* 1.9.1–4; Theodoret, *Hist. eccl.* 1.9.2–13). But Eusebius of Nicomedia and others refused to anathematise Arius, 'disbelieving the party accused to be such as was represented, having satisfied on this point, both from his own letters to us and from personal conversations' (Eusebius of Nicomedia and Theognius of Nicaea at Socrates, *Hist. eccl.* 1.14.2–6; Sozom. *Hist. eccl.* 2.16.3–6).

to another were ruled out of order for the future (canon 15),[89] as were similar migrations of clergy (canon 16).

Constantine's close personal involvement with the proceedings, while apparently welcomed at the time, would have awkward consequences for himself and even more for his successors. In his concern for harmony, rather than doctrinal purity, Constantine allowed the integrity of his imperial office to be compromised by involvement with ecclesiastical factionalism. In his report to his own church at Caesarea, Eusebius recalled that the emperor had himself been instrumental in the formulation of the creed and had advised the insertion of the word 'co-substantial' into the first draft.[90] This generated another debate and, on the production of a second draft, Eusebius himself asked about the sense in which the phrase 'of the substance of the Father' was used. After further discussion, he acquiesced to avoid trouble, listening without further protest to another speech from Constantine on the matter. Ominously for the future, however, Eusebius concluded his letter with the admission that he had been forced to transmit the resolutions of the Council, showing not only what was agreed, but also 'how reasonably we resisted even to the last minute, so long as we were offended by statements which differed from our own'.

Constantine further mired himself and his office in religious controversy when he conceded the principle that decisions taken by bishops against each other could be enforced by the state – provided that the council, which issued the order, was itself legitimate. Some three months after Nicaea, Eusebius of Nicomedia and his fellow dissidents were exiled by direct imperial order.[91] But there was no legal precedent for the imposition of a criminal sentence for doctrinal dissent. Therefore one ground for this advanced in Constantine's letter to the clergy at Nicomedia was that Eusebius, having been an active supporter of Licinius, was politically suspect. That this was no more than a pretext is confirmed by the fact that, after further negotiations, Eusebius was reinstated three years later. In time, Constantine did evolve a consistent policy towards the exile of bishops: he would set aside the verdict of an episcopal council, if

89. The case of Eusebius of Nicomedia, who had transferred there, controversially, from Beirut, was one such. For Constantine's letter to Eusebius of Caesarea in c. 330, approving his refusal of transfer to the see of Antioch, see Euseb. *Vit. Const.* 3.62.
90. Socrates, *Hist. eccl.* 1.8.4.
91. Stevenson, *New Eusebius*, 304: 'I ordered them to be arrested and banished to the most distant regions possible.'

he was convinced that it was biased or controlled by a faction and would implement a sentence of exile only after hearing both sides. This process did not guarantee impartiality, as Constantine could still be influenced by pressure groups and his own prejudices. However, despite his controversial exile of Athanasius, his preference seems to have been for compromise and conciliation, where possible.

The 'Christian' emperor and his biographer

The portrait of Constantine offered in Eusebius' *Life of Constantine* has provided a yardstick against which the religious policies and even the beliefs of that emperor have been assessed; it is a pity that we have no competing representation from Constantine's eastern adherents, such as Sopatros. It is now recognised that the later historian Socrates had some justification when he commented, apropos of Eusebius' downplaying of the Arian controversy, that he was "more intent on the rhetorical style of his literary work and panegyric of the emperor than accurate statement of fact'.[92] The *Life* is a combination of panegyric with attempts to create an imperial history based on the citation of documentary evidence. Eusebius creates an impression of personal intimacy with Constantine which is not supported by the facts.[93] Even after Constantine's arrival in the east, Eusebius was based at his bishopric in Caesarea in Palestine and was seldom at court. Moreover, his questionable position concerning Nicaea and its sequels, which is suppressed in the *Life*, would not have encouraged privileged access. His version of events after Constantine's death in May 337 has no mention of the murders, in the summer of that year, of almost all the candidates for the purple, other than the three sons of Constantine,[94] and is inaccurate on matters of detail, such as the two wars with Licinius, which he conflates.[95] His argument, often by implication rather than outright statement, that a significant part of Constantine's legislation was driven by a Christian agenda was overstated; much modern

---

92. Socrates, *Hist. eccl.* 1.1, explaining why he will start his history with his own account of Constantine.
93. See for example his claim (*Vit. Const.* 1.28.1) that Constantine told him personally about his vision in 312.
94. *Vit. Const.* 1.1.3; 4.40–52.3; 68; 71.2.
95. For summary of questions of authenticity, see Cameron and Hall, *Eusebius, Life of Constantine*, 4–12

scholarship prefers to situate Constantine's laws in the general moral context of the fourth century,[96] noting also their continuity with the secular legal tradition.[97] But the *Life* can also be read, more sympathetically, as a systematic attempt to create a new kind of biography to match a new kind of emperor, defined by Christian piety and victory, who will provide a model of rule for his sons to imitate.[98]

Eusebius, author also in 336, of the 'Tricennalian Orations' in honour of Constantine's thirty years of rule, is perhaps least appealing in his later years, when he can appear as little more than the sycophantic spokesman of an autocrat.[99] His literary career, however, taken as a whole, is that of a diligent, independent and courageous innovator. Reared in Caesarea, the city of the Christian philosopher Origen, Eusebius celebrated himself as the pupil of one Pamphilus, whose name he took. The most influential aspect of his life's work was his researching of the history of the church, in the context of world history. Late in the third century, he embarked on a two-part work, the *Chronicle*. The first part consisted of a list of dates, collating biblical history with the history of the Chaldeans, Greeks and Romans; this was followed by a list of historical annotations,[100] in part derived from an early third-century chronographer, Sextus Julius Africanus. From this Eusebius moved on to, in effect, create a new literary genre: ecclesiastical historiography. He compiled the *Ecclesiastical History* in several stages. The first seven books date from the late third century and predate the Diocletianic persecution.[101] After 303, faced with the dire consequences of official hostility, Eusebius proceeded, first, to set on record the sufferings of the martyrs of his own province, Palestine. Later his coverage of the persecutions broadened, although he had little to say of the west, and the Palestinian martyrs were incorporated into books 8–9.[102]

96. E.g. J. Evans Grubbs, 'Abduction marriage in antiquity: A law of Constantine (*CTh* ix.24.1) and its social context', *JRS* 79 (1989), 59–83; Grubbs, *Law and Family in Late Antiquity: Emperor Constantine's Marriage Legislation*, Oxford: Oxford University Press, 1995.

97. E.g. Caroline Humfress, 'Civil Law,' in Lenski, *Age of Constantine*, 205–25.

98. *Vit. Const.* 4.51–52.3. For Constantine's 'uniqueness', see the peroration at *Vit. Const.* 4.75.

99. For this text, see H. A. Drake, *In Praise of Constantine: A Historical Study and New Translation of Eusebius' Tricennial Orations*, Berkeley: University of California Press, 1976.

100. Barnes, *Constantine and Eusebius*, 111–25.

101. Barnes, *Constantine and Eusebius*, 126–47.

102. Barnes, *Constantine and Eusebius*, 148–63.

Book 10 celebrates the accession of Constantine, the end of persecution, and imperial favour granted to the restored churches, and
further revisions were made in the light of events, until the issue of
effectively the final version in 325.[103]

Eusebius did not confine himself to history. He was interested in
biblical scholarship and also engaged in debate with pagan thinkers,
writing against the persecutor Hierocles' praises of Apollonius of
Tyana early in the fourth century. His main project after the pro-
visional completion of the *Ecclesiastical History* down to 324 was
to compile, against the writings of Porphyry, an extended analysis
of the Gospels, in two treatises, totalling thirty-five books in all.[104]
Thus, prior to Constantine's conquest of the east, Eusebius would
have been known primarily as a scholar and historian, a theological
controversialist who concentrated his fire on pagans rather than his
fellow Christians. His somewhat hesitant behaviour at Nicaea and
his letter to the clergy at Caesarea, justifying his acquiescence in the
decisions of that council, may reflect the confusion of the cloistered
academic coming to terms with the emotional, as well as the
theological, complexities of the new imperial order.

The biographer presented Constantine as both wished him to
be seen in the last years of his reign. In over thirty years of rule,
Constantine had proved himself to be divinely favoured through a
series of victories over foreign enemies and Roman opponents, who,
in defeat, became automatically categorised as emperors who had
never been.[105] Like his emperor, Eusebius sought to rewrite history,
and thus claim control of the past. Although from 312, Constantine
had been openly favourable to Christianity, the ways in which his
support was demonstrated were largely in line with the practice of
past emperors; where Constantine's situation differed from that of
his predecessors, especially after 325, was that his favoured religion
had an empire-wide organisation of bishops, able and willing to
shape policy through their privileged access to the imperial ear.

103. For discussion in detail of the multiple editions, see T. D. Barnes, 'The editions of
Eusebius' *Ecclesiastical History*', *GRBS* 21 (1980), 191–201.
104. Barnes, *Constantine and Eusebius*, 164–88.
105. Constantine was, like Moses, reared among the 'tyrants' (*Vit. Const.* 1.12), and
both the Tetrarchs and Licinius are consistently labelled as *tyranni*. On Constantine
and Moses, see M Hollerich, 'The comparison of Moses and Constantine in Eusebius of
Caesarea's *Life of Constantine*', *Studia Patristica* 19 (1989), 80–95; for Old Testament
'exemplarity' in general, Claudia Rapp, 'Old Testament models for emperors in early
Byzantium' in Paul Magdalino and Robert Nelson (eds), *The Old Testament in
Byzantium*, Washington, DC: Dumbarton Oaks Collection, 2010, 175–98.

While previous emperors had taken local decisions to finance temples or adjudicate on the membership of a priesthood, Constantine's choices to favour one bishop or sect over another had a wider impact on the opinions and expectations of an increasingly confident and articulate Christian leadership. Though Constantine had successfully kept his imperial distance, the bishops, collectively, were a pressure group that his sons would be unable to ignore.

Can one fairly describe Constantine as a Christian, or as a Christian emperor? He was certainly the first ruler of the Roman world to associate his fortunes with the Christian God and the Christian church, to patronise the Christian establishment and holy sites actively, and to legislate, in however limited or traditional a way, on their behalf. But to call Constantine a 'Christian' without explanation is to beg the question of what his Christianity meant in the context of its times and of his imperial role. Previous emperors had publicly aligned themselves with their tutelary deities and actively promoted their cults. Emperors and gods had a contract; in return for divine favour (as demonstrated by worldly success), the emperor would rule in line with what the 'Divinity' wished of him. In these respects, Constantine did not differ from his predecessors; his success proved that he was indeed 'beloved by God'.

So to set up an artificial modern standard of what Christianity is (or ought to be) and then show that Constantine fell short, both morally (in his murderous dealings with rivals and his own family, his perpetuation of a harsh judicial system etc.) and theologically, in that the utterances on Christianity ascribed to him appear to lack sophistication, is to miss the point.[106] Constantine saw Christianity as useful to him but he also believed in the power of the Christian God. Left to himself, Constantine is unlikely to have exceeded the limits traditionally set for an emperor's patronage of a favoured cult; it was the requirement to respond to Christian requests for legal privilege and pressure from the bishops after 325 which drew him ever closer to implication in the quarrels, as well as the material advances, of a newly ecumenical Christian community. Thus the strengthening of the institutional position of Christianity through a series of small changes happened partly because Constantine reigned for over thirty years. As in the case of Augustus, the length of Constantine's reign in itself made him a revolutionary. His dealings with

106. E.g. Alistair Kee, *Constantine versus Christ: The Triumph of Ideology*, London: SCM, 1982, which systematically 'de-Christianises' Constantine.

the Christian leadership evolved slowly, as his own understanding of his favoured religion and its imperial implications deepened. By 337, when Constantine died, white-robed and baptised into the faith, the relationship between emperor and the 'Divinity' had changed forever.

Figure 43 Bronze pinecone and peacocks, reused in the atrium of Constantine's Church of St Peter, Rome, Italy

Figure 44 Santa Costanza exterior, Rome, Italy

Figure 45 Dionysiac vault mosaic, Santa Costanza, Rome, Italy

Figure 46 Serpent Column, Istanbul, Turkey

Figure 47 Column of Constantine, Istanbul, Turkey

CHAPTER 8

The sons of Constantine

The sons of Constantine reigned in the great shadow of their father, whose name they invoked to legitimise their rule.[1] All four died relatively young, two (Constantine II and Constans) before the age of thirty, and two (Crispus and Constantine II) fell victim to close relations. Crispus was executed in 326, and Constantine II, having been Caesar at Trier from 328 or 330,[2] and Augustus from 337, was killed in a skirmish near Aquileia in 340, having challenged his brother Constans' control of Italy.[3] Reared as the heirs of empire, they were also, by virtue of their appointments as Caesars,[4] the tools through which Constantine's supremacy was exercised. They had their own courts and praetorian prefects, whose power, while the Caesars were still very young, must have been considerable.

From 340, Constantius II and Constans were faced with the task of consolidating the reforms of Constantine in the armies and administration, and of handling the problems of divided rule, a situation which would change the dynamics, again, of the dealings between emperors and bishops. But the period of joint rule is also one with surprisingly poor documentation. The narrative of Ammianus prior to 353 is lost, that of Zosimus, based on Eunapius, is sketchy by comparison and, although useful in parts, often confused, and the epitomators have little to add. Christian sources, though fulsome on their own concerns, do not assist a

1. Dessau, *ILS* 730, 732 (Constantius II); 725 (Constans). Both affirmed their descent from Maximian (through Fausta), Constantius I and (as first alleged by Constantine) Claudius Gothicus.
2. T. D. Barnes, *The New Empire of Diocletian and Constantine*, Cambridge, MA: Harvard University Press, 1982, 84–5 and n. 157.
3. In the initial carve-up, Constantine II received the western provinces of Gaul, Britain and Spain, Constans the central portion, Italy, Illyricum and Africa, and Constantius II the Eastern Empire.
4. Each was accompanied (and effectively supervised) by an experienced praetorian prefect; L. Papius Pacatianus, for example, transferred from Constantine II to serve Constans on the latter's appointment as Caesar in 333 (aged 10 or 13).

comprehensive understanding of the period; the legal texts suffer from poor transmission and confusion over imperial names. This lack affects in particular our perspective on Constans, the youngest of the four, who, although Caesar from 333, Augustus from 337 and ruler of most of Roman Europe as far east as the Aegean Sea for ten years, remains a shadowy and elusive figure.

The struggle for the succession, summer 337

The accession of the sons of Constantine was attended by bloodshed and controversy. In the early 330s, Constantine reversed his previous policy towards the descendants of his father Constantius I and his father's second wife, Theodora. Having kept them all in relative obscurity and far from the centres of power, he promoted his nephew Fl. Dalmatius to the position of fourth Caesar in 335.[5] This move was not popular with Constantine's three surviving sons, all of whom were now Caesars in post; they refused to recognise Dalmatius on their coinage.[6] Despite these indications of opposition, Constantine also promoted Dalmatius' brother, Hannibalianus, to the rank of *nobilissimus* (equivalent to a Caesar) and made him 'King of Kings' – a challenge to the Persian monarchy – and lord of the Pontic shore. The previous generation, Theodora's sons, Julius Constantius and the elder Dalmatius, were also restored to prominence: the former was created patrician and consul for 335; the latter was commander in the east and consul in 333, the year that Constans was made Caesar.[7] The new dispensation was further strengthened by the marriage of Hannibalianus to Constantine's daughter, Constantina (who would later be married to Gallus Caesar).[8]

As the precedent of Constantius I's marriage to Theodora had shown, sons-in-law of emperors could count as sons and therefore heirs. They could also create trouble on their own account. Constantine's first war with Licinius was sparked by an abortive conspiracy on the part of his brother-in-law, Bassianus, who was married to his

5. *PLRE I* Fl. Dalmatius 7, p. 241.
6. An excellent account and new chronology of the struggle for the succession is provided by Richard Burgess, 'The summer of blood: The 'Great Massacre' of 337 and the promotion of the sons of Constantine', *DOP* 62 (2008), 5–51. On the coinage, see 21–2.
7. *PLRE I* Julius Constantius 7, p. 226; Fl. Dalmatius 6, pp. 240–1. The latter held some office in 321, when he received *Cod. Theod.* 12.17.1.
8. Anon. Vales. 6.35; Aur. Vict. *Caes.* 41.20.

half-sister, Constantius I's and Theodora's daughter, Anastasia.[9] It is also possible that the husband of Constantine's other half-sister, Eutropia, one Virius Nepotianus, was implicated in the events of spring and summer, 337. Certainly that branch of the family continued to nurse imperial ambitions: after Constans' murder in 350, the younger Nepotianus, who was also, through his mother, Constantius' and Theodora's grandson, would attempt a military coup at Rome. The suggestion, therefore, that Constantine envisaged a new 'Tetrarchy', consisting of Constantine II and Constantius II as Augusti and Constans and Dalmatius as Caesars, supported by their elders as regents in some sense (a post which has no constitutional or de facto precedent in Roman imperial succession), must be assessed against a background of familial dysfunction, caused by conflicting imperial ambitions, of which all concerned would – or should – have been all too aware.[10]

From Constantine's standpoint, the introduction of more successors, in addition to the three he already had in post, should have been superfluous. It also represented a complete reversal of his previous policy of sidelining the descendants of Theodora. We may infer from this uncharacteristic inconsistency that, in his last years, Constantine, now in his sixties, was perhaps no longer fully in control of events. As the monarch aged, factions flourished, as is usually the case in the dying months and years of an autocratic regime. The reinstatement of the descendants of Theodora, therefore, may be read as a dynastic coup, backed by elements at court opposed to the elevation perhaps of Constantine II, installed at Trier since 328, and certainly of Constantius II, now at Antioch (Constans being still too young to count), which the emperor was unable or unwilling to control.

The prime mover in this is not far to seek. When emperors died, key figures were often retained in post to ease the transition. However, Constantine's long-serving praetorian prefect of the east, Fl. Ablabius, was to be among those killed by the supporters of Constantius II, in June 337. His fate requires explanation. Dominant at court from 330 onwards, he was well positioned, as such power brokers as Septimius Severus' chief minister, Fulvius Plautianus, had been before him, to engineer the promotion of Dalmatius and

9. *PLRE I* Bassianus 1, p. 150; also his brother and co-conspirator, Senecio 1, p. 820.
10. For the 'tetrarchic' hypothesis and support in the coinage, see Burgess, 'Summer', pp. 7–10 and 43–5.

his kindred. The parvenu from Crete had reached the vicariate in Asiana by the mid-320s and held the praetorian prefecture from 329. He had a reputation as an ardent champion of Christianity; he destroyed the pagan philosopher Sopatros and supported the petition from Orcistus in Phrygia for city status on the grounds, inter alia, of its Christianity. He had accumulated great wealth, including estates in Bithynia and a house in Constantinople.[11] Moreover, like Fulvius Plautianus, he had imperial ambitions on his own account. His daughter Olympias was, by 337, betrothed to Constans; the marriage (which never took place) would have allied him with the imperial house and made him potentially the ancestor of future Augusti.[12]

Constantine died in May 337, having failed to designate any of the four Caesars as Augusti. If he did have a 'plan' for the succession, it died with him; we have no option but to note and respect his silence.[13] With Constantine II and Constans both far away, the son on the spot, Constantius II, took quick and decisive action. Soon after the funeral, probably in early June, the descendants of Theodora and their supporters assembled at Constantinople for the occasion were killed and others, Ablabius included, were hunted down and destroyed.[14] The dead included both Dalmatii, Julius Constantius and Hannibalianus and other male aspirants, but their womenfolk were left untouched. Although Julian, who survived along with his older half-brother Gallus, would in time bitterly attack Constantius as being responsible for the deaths of so many of his kindred, the situation at the time may have left Constantius with little choice. If the descendants of Theodora had been promoted not to support but to subvert the sons of Constantine, Constantius (then

11. *PLRE I* Fl. Ablabius, pp. 3–4. He was also the named recipient of a long law of Constantine on the privileges of Christians, *Const. Sirm.* 1, which may be a forgery.
12. Plautianus married his daughter, Plautilla, to Severus' elder son, Caracalla, in 204. According to Dio, this was one reason for Caracalla's successful plot against Plautianus in 205, which resulted in the latter's disgrace and death.
13. The modern hypothesis (above, n. 10) that Constantine intended Constantine II and Constantius II to be the Augusti with Constans and Dalmatius as their Caesars founders on the role expected of Constans; it is unlikely that the youngest brother, or his party, would accept a role inferior to that of his brothers. Constantine did not die suddenly; he had time to name his successor Augusti, had he chosen to do so.
14. The chronology is that convincingly argued by Burgess, 'Summer', 29–43. It should be noted, however, that Dalmatius' probable praetorian prefect, Valerius Maximus, was still in post in August (*Cod. Theod.* 13.4.2); see Barnes, *New Empire*, 8 n. 34 and 135–6. For celebration of the death of Ablabius, Eunap. *VS* 464; Zos. *New History* (deriving from Eunap.), 2.40.3.

aged 19) and his faction would have known that it was a case of his life or theirs.

Late in the summer, Constantine's three sons met in Pannonia to decide on the future governance of the empire. Already cracks had begun to show. Immediately after the purge, Constantine II unilaterally minted coins at Trier, commemorating Helena, his grandmother, and Theodora. As a statement of imperial unity it was unconvincing; perhaps Constantine hoped to dissociate himself from events in the east. Certainly he was assertive of what he saw as the prerogative of seniority, when, in 338, he restored Athanasius to Alexandria, although he had not as Caesar exercised authority in Egypt.[15] It may have been fear of his assertiveness which brought Constantius and Constans together to outvote their brother on the crucial question of territory.[16] Both Constantius, who retained control of the east but acquired Constantinople and Thrace, and Constans, who added Moesia to his existing domains, were gainers, while Constantine was left with Britain, Gaul and Spain, as before. Not the man to accept a setback, Constantine bided his time and, in early 340, invaded Italy. Constans, however, was ready and Constantine was killed in an ambush. Without fuss and with the acquiescence of Constantius, Constans added Constantine's territories to his own, declared the dead Augustus to be 'the public's enemy and our own',[17] and deleted him from the public record – a sentence also carried out in at least some the provinces controlled by Constantius.

Flavius Julius Constans, 337–50

Evidence of Constans' unpopularity with some who controlled the written record is not far to seek. Born in 320 or 323, Constans' elevation as Caesar on 25 December 333, at the age of 10 or 13, was attended by an ominous portent, a 'fire in the sky'.[18] After Constantine II had been disposed of, Constans, we are told, displayed the

---

15. Athanasius, *Apol. contra Ar.* 87.4–7; *Hist. Ar.* 8.2; also Socrates, *Hist. eccl.* 2.3 and Sozom. *Hist. eccl.* 3.2.

16. As a sop, they did agree to issue small sets of the Helena-Theodora coins. The apparent hostility of Constantius II and Constans may be also explained if Constantine was not Fausta's son.

17. *Cod. Theod.* 11.12.1: *publicus et noster inimicus*; T. D. Barnes, *Athanasius and Constantius: Theology and Politics in the Constantinian Empire*, Cambridge, MA: Harvard University Press, 1993, 51–2.

18. Aur. Vict. *Caes.* 41, also the source for other gossip, such as Constans' alleged predilection for beautiful boys handed over as hostages.

arrogance and rashness of youth: his subordinates were corrupt;[19] he personally was greedy and treated his soldiers with contempt; and, along with Constantius, he ruined the cities of the empire by neglect.[20] The sources also suspected him of homosexual leanings (as he did not marry) and of unduly favouring good-looking members of his barbarian bodyguard.[21]

What these stories prove is not that Constans was a bad or even an unpopular emperor but that he generated opposition in influential quarters, especially, as we shall see, at Rome. A contrasting, but equally unreliable, perspective is provided by Libanius, who was forced into delivering a panegyric on both emperors in 344.[22] Libanius would have known little of Constans directly, but his choice of representative stereotype, that of the tireless warrior and hunter, who fought with animals if there were no human foes to hand, is significant. Constans the warrior is represented as a man of exceptional physical strength and endurance, who travelled with a small entourage of picked men at amazing speed and was never where he was expected to be.[23] In going to Britain, he had reached the far edge of the world,[24] while the terror of his name alone was enough to force the Franks – or, as Libanius has it, the Fracti (the 'broken') – into submission.[25] While gifted with the virtues of justice as well as courage, Libanius' Constans is a man of action, not words. Yet emperors – as Constans would find – could not rule through war alone.

Constans' relations with some Romans at Rome deteriorated from the mid-340s. His apparent failure to visit Rome at all, unlike his predecessors, or to acknowledge adequately the importance of the

19. For the alleged abuse of power by Constans' praetorian prefect, Fl. Eugenius (*PLRE I*, Fl. Eugenius 5, p. 292), see Lib. *Or.* 14.10.

20. For Constans' overall record, see Aur. Vict. *Caes.* 41; Eutr. 10.9; Zos. *New History*, 2.42.1; Amm. Marc. 16.7.5. For neglect of the cities by the sons of Constantine, asserted after Constans' death by Fabius Titianus (who joined Magnentius), see Zos. *New History*, 2.49.

21. An accusation also made later against Gratian (Augustus 369–83), who, like Constans, was overthrown by a military coup staged by the army in Gaul. F. Paschoud (ed. with Greek text and French trans.), *Zosime, Histoire Nouvelle. Livres I–II*, Paris; Budé, 1971, 248–9, accepts the homosexuality story as 'confimed' by 'parallel' sources (many of whom in fact derive from a single source or each other).

22. Lib. *Or.* 59, trans. in S. N. C. Lieu and D. Montserrat, *From Constantine to Julian: Pagan and Christian Views. A Source History*, London: Routledge, 1996, 164–209.

23. Lib. *Or.* 59, 144–9. The detail that Constans was in the habit of making journeys with only a small escort may account for his vulnerability in 350.

24. Lib. *Or.* 59, 137–42. See also Amm.Marc. 20.1.1. and 27.8.4.

25. Lib. *Or.* 59, 127–36.

eleven hundredth anniversary in 348 of Rome's foundation rankled with Aurelius Victor and may help to explain his unfavourable opinion of Constans' character and rule.[26] But Rome and its ruling, still pagan, senatorial elite may also have been a source of annoyance to the emperor. An ardent and baptised Christian, who anticipated Gratian by omitting to use his title of *pontifex maximus*,[27] he was confronted with a series of prefects of the city almost all of whom were prominent pagans and members of the pontifical college. After 346, he took drastic action to remedy the situation, by imposing on the Romans in 347 a prefect of his choice, one Ulpius Limenius, previously proconsul of the city of Constantinople. Limenius, exceptionally, was also praetorian prefect of Italy and held the two offices together down to his death in April 349. After an interregnum of forty-one days, Constans made a second outside appointment, Hermogenes, also probably from Greece or further east.

While the Romans at Rome doubtless regarded this as unwarranted interference, Constans' policy reflects a growing confidence on his part, evidenced in other ways in the latter part of the decade.[28] In or after 345, he created the praetorian prefecture of Illyricum, perhaps prompted by an invasion by the Goths of neighbouring Thrace.[29] The first to hold the office was another easterner, Anatolius of Beirut, one of several careerists for whom the 'east–west divide' had little meaning in practice. Ambitious men had a choice of emperors to serve; some, like Ulpius Limenius and Roman senators who also held positions under Constantius, were happy to seize their chances under both. The consul for 340, Septimius Acindynus, had served in Spain under Constantine, but surfaces in the east as prefect of the orient to Constantius II; despite a perhaps prolonged abosence from Italy, he maintained estates there. Two prominent Roman senators, Furius Placidus (consul 343) and Vulcacius Rufinus (consul 347), had largely western careers but both also held, in succession, the short-lived eastern office of *comes per Orientem*

26. For the argument that Constans' coinage with the legend FEL. TEMP. REPARATIO may refer to the eleven hundredth anniversary, see H. Mattingly, '*Fel. temp. reparatio*', *Num. Chron.* (1933), 182–202.
27. Dessau, *ILS*, vol. III.1, lists imperial titulature of Constans at pp. 309–10. While there are obvious risks in an argument from silence, Constans' non-use of the title is also accepted by J. Rüpke, *Fasti Sacerdotum*, Stuttgart: Franz Steiner, 2005.
28. As in his titulature of MAX. AUGUSTUS on a gold medallion from Thessalonica (for Constans' coinage, see J. P. C. Kent, *RIC* 8, 33–9).
29. C. Vogler, *Constance II et l'administation imperiale*, Strasbourg: University of Strasbourg, 1979, 112–23.

Aegypti et Mesopotamiae (count of Egypt and Mesopotamia) under Constantius.

As Constantine alone had nominated consuls, there was no pre-existing convention that there should be an 'eastern' and a 'western' consul. Both consuls in 341 (Antonius Marcellinus and Petronius Probinus) and in 343 (M. Maecius Furius Baburius Caecilianus Placidus and Fl. Romulus) appear to be western nominees. In 349, Ulpius Limenius, although eastern by origin, was again Constans' nominee, along with Aconius Catullinus, a prominent but tactful senatorial pagan.[30] Constans himself, reared as a child in Constantinople and the east, may have had a personal preference for the Greek world. He had already shown interest in the Hellenic culture of old Greece, which was part of his domain. In c. 342, he entertained the Athenian philosopher Prohaeresius royally at Trier, before sending him on to Rome. When the time came for Prohaeresius to return to Athens, Constans granted him the title of *stratopedarch*, or controller of the food supply to Athens, along with control of several grain-producing islands. The appointment was confirmed by Anatolius at a public ceremony at Athens.[31]

What little is known of Constans' administration suggests that he relied on a small group of tried and loyal supporters; this may have annoyed and frustrated other aspirants to high office. His praetorian prefect in Gaul from 341 to, probably, the end of his reign was Fabius Titianus, who was already a senior administrator, having held posts in Italy, Sicily and Asia under Constantine.[32] Consul in 337, he was then prefect of the city of Rome and, as Constantine's man, provided continuity with the previous reign, supporting but perhaps also overshadowing Constantine's son. He did not share his emperors' religious views; his daughter would marry L. Aurelius Avianus Symmachus (prefect of the city, 364–5), and become the mother of one of the last defenders of Roman paganism, Q. Aurelius Symmachus (prefect of the city in 384). Titianus himself would transfer his loyalties, with suspicious ease, to Magnentius and held the city prefecture for the second time in the early 350s.

Almost as durable was Constans' master of the offices, Eugenius,

---

30. He had succeeded in 342 in modifying the emperor's wholesale abolition of 'superstition' by eliciting his consent to temples remaining open for commercial and social purposes (*Cod. Theod.* 16.10.3).
31. Eunap. *VS* 492.
32. *PLRE I* Fabius Titanus 6, pp. 918–19.

who held office from early in the decade to his death in 349.[33] Eugenius may have been one of those officials of Constans suspected of corrupt practices who damaged the reputation of the emperor himself.[34] Whatever Eugenius' failings, Constans stood by his man and honoured him with a statue at Rome in the Forum of Trajan, which was restored by Constantius and Julian Caesar, probably on the occasion of Constantius' visit to Rome in 357.[35] These two exceptionally long tenures contrast with the more normal terms of two or three years in office enjoyed by the chief financial officer, the *comes rei privatae*. One Eusebius 'Mattyocopa' is attested in 342; he survived to plot against Silvanus, the Frankish general in Roman service, in 355.[36] A certain Eustathius is attested in 345;[37] then Orion, perhaps yet another easterner, in 346 and 348;[38] and, at the end of the decade, Marcellinus, the author of Constans' downfall, who precipitated the revolt perhaps to pre-empt his own demotion.

The content of his legal pronouncements confirms the hypothesis that Constans' problems were with personalities rather than policies. Although some laws, such as the outlawing of 'superstition' issued early in his reign,[39] are savage in tone, their approach is in line with conventional imperial priorities. Preservation of revenue was all-important: Titianus was warned that honorary office-holders were not exempt from municipal or tax-collecting duties, and anyone who appealed against this could find his property confiscated;[40] and, contrary to the harsh reputation ascribed to him, Constans ruled

33. *PLRE I*, Fl. Eugenius 5, p. 292.
34. See Lib. *Or*. 14, 10 for Aristophanes of Corinth and below, pp. 288–90.
35. Dessau, *ILS* 1244, referring to the statue as erected by the *divus* (deified emperor) Constans, because of Eugenius' 'most loyal devotion'. It may have been thrown down by the supporters of Magnentius in 350.
36. *PLRE I* Eusebius 6, p. 302; addressee of *Cod. Theod.* 10.10.6 (6 April 342). Like most of Constans' extant laws, this is ascribed in the manuscripts to Constantius: Constans would have followed the practice of issuing his laws in the names of all members of the imperial college, hence the confusion. See also R. Delmaire, *Les Responsables des finances imperiales au bas-empire romain: études prosopographiques*, Brussels: Latomus, 1989, 25–6.
37. *PLRE I* Eustathius 2, pp. 310–11; *Cod. Theod.* 10.10.7 (15 May 345); Delmaire, *Responsables*, 30–1.
38. *PLRE I*, Orion, p. 654, the only entry for this name. *Cod. Theod.* 10.10.8 (5 March 346); *Cod. Theod.* 10.14.2 (17 June 348); Delmaire, *Responsables*, 31–2.
39. *Cod. Theod.* 16.10.2; see below, pp. 278–9. For full discussion of the difficult textual problems of the laws ascribed to Constans and Constantius II, see Paola Cuneo, *La legislazione di Costantino II, Costanzo II e Costante (337–61): materiali per una palingenesia delle costituzioni tardo-imperiali*, Milan: Giuffré, 1997.
40. *Cod. Theod.* 12.1.36 (30 June 343, Trier).

that soldiers could be visited by members of their households, including their slaves, but taxpaying *coloni* were required to remain on the land.[41] A group of laws addressed to his finance officers show a consistent concern to respect due process and restrict the activities of informers, whose allegations must be tested by the lower courts, before being brought before the *comes rei privatae*.[42] The language of his criminal legislation is notably harsh, but not more so than that of his father.[43]

As a Christian from birth, Constans championed the interests of his bishops and supported the ideas and pretensions of Athanasius of Alexandria (see below, Chapter 10). He may also have been one of the first Christian emperors to attend church services in person, an innovation assisted by the unfinished state of some new structures, such as the church at Aquileia, which he attended at Easter 345.[44] But the gratitude of Athanasius' episcopal allies was insufficient to guarantee the survival of the emperor, who had effected Athanasius' restoration to his see in 346. Although Constans had visited Britain and led the Gallic army to victories in the early 340s, his absence from the west from c. 345 onwards[45] provoked feelings of 'neglect' (*incuria*), later recorded by Ammianus. Hoping perhaps to break the control of western elites over government posts, he had relied too much on outsiders and a small core group of trusted advisers and administrators.

But more relevant to the coup that ended his reign and his life may have been the financial difficulties that began to accrue at the end of the decade. Rapid action was required and Magnentius' first act as ruler in Gaul was to levy a property tax of 50 per cent and sell off imperial estates, while there is evidence for debasement in both his gold and silver coin issues.[46] It may thus have been no coincidence

41. *Cod. Theod.* 7.1.3.
42. *Cod. Theod.* 10.10.7; 8.
43. *Cod. Theod.* 9.24.2 (12 November 349), where Constans should be read for Constantius and Titianus for Tatianus, confirms capital punishment for abductors and that slaves guilty of the offence should be burned alive. The rhetoric of deterrence also features in his law against homosexuality (or 'marrying in the manner of a woman'), *Cod. Theod.* 9.7.3.
44. Neil McLynn, 'The transformation of imperial churchgoing in the fourth century,' in Simon Swain. and Mark Edwards (eds), *Approaching Late Antiquity: The Transformation from Early to Late Empire*, Oxford: Oxford University Press, 2005, 235–70.
45. He is last attested at Trier in 345, *Cod. Theod.* 10.10.7; Barnes, *Athanasius and Constantius*, 225.
46. Julian, *Or.* 1. 34ab. Something must be allowed for exaggeration. He also reports

that the prime mover in Constans' fall was his finance officer, Marcellinus. Narratives of the events of January 350 differ but a close reading of the (unreliable) sources suggests that Constans fell victim to a plot by a few, not an organised or wide-scale revolt. In fact the Gallic army could not have initially been involved at all. Autun, where Magnentius was proclaimed Augustus by Marcellinus at a dinner-party on 18 January 350, was not a military centre but probably did contain weapons factories, which were the responsibility of the finance officers.[47] While we may assume that some troops were billeted there for the winter, this was not a centre for the whole army. Magnentius' coup, therefore, was not initially a full-scale revolt and is not in itself evidence for Constans' unpopularity with the military.

More details are supplied by the late Byzantine chronicler Zonaras. These may derive ultimately (and with some interference from several intermediary sources along the way) from Zosimus' source, Eunapius, whose coverage of Constans in his extant work on the *Lives of the Sophists* is neutral to favourable. In Zonaras' account, Marcellinus and Magnentius took advantage of Constans' absence on a hunting trip (a detail also preserved, but not explained, in Zosimus),[48] seized control of Autun, locked the gates and sent out an assassination squad, which intercepted and killed Constans, 'deprived of all assistance',[49] at Helena, modern Elne, near Perpignan. With the emperor dead, Magnentius was able to step into his shoes without opposition.

Several details support this version, at least in outline. Constans' interest in hunting is confirmed by Libanius and its relevance to Marcellinus' plot is also mentioned, in passing, by Zosimus. The Pyrenees were prime hunting territory. Moreover, the secrecy surrounding the coup explains the location of Constans' murder. He would have been descending from the hills, unsuspecting, towards the coast road, on his way either to the Rhine or back through Italy towards the Danube. There is no indication at all that he was

that Magnentius killed Constans' generals and corrupted the soldiers, as well as encouraging slave informers. For the coins, see Kent, *RIC* 8, 41 and 57.
47. As recorded, for later, in the *Not. Dign.* [*occ.*] IX.33 and 34.
48. Zos. *New History*, 2.41, a generally muddled chapter, connected Magnentius' plot with Constans' passion for hunting, without explaining the nature of the connection. On Constans' fall, briefly, Barnes, *Athanasius and Constantius*, 101–2.
49. Zos. *New History*, 2.42.

running away. We are told that he died alone and without friends.[50] That pathetic picture was also not strictly true; as the event would show, the Danube army would have no truck with his killer and, according to Julian, Magnentius had been obliged to kill Constans' generals in Gaul as well. Constans' murder was in fact opportunistic, the result of a private grudge on the part of an apprehensive official and not the outcome of widespread discontent among the military or the wider population.

Thus our verdict on him must be mixed, but perhaps more favourable than that of contemporaries with a grudge like Aurelius Victor or those who took advantage of his fall and lack of heirs to malign his reputation. Constans was in fact the scion of a troubled line, who came to power as Caesar and Augustus when little more than a child. Like all Roman emperors of his time, he had, with a military job to do, a set of administrative responsibilities, which he carried out competently, and some taste for Hellenic culture, as evidenced in his entertainment of Prohaeresius. His slightly bumptious tendency to self-assertion and his tendency to ignore the sensibilities of others are counterbalanced by his effectiveness as a soldier, which ensured for him the loyalty of his Danube legions after his death, by his responsiveness to the wishes of his Christian constituents, and by judgements from sources that, despite the corruption of his officials, he was an able and energetic ruler who controlled his armies without resorting to excessive harshness.[51] Had the lost books of Ammianus, who knew the west, survived, our assessment of Constans' imperial career might be very different.[52]

The fall of Gallus, 354

Constantius II ruled as Augustus for twenty-four years. Unglamorous in appearance, with a long body and short legs, his profile in ancient and modern historians suffers from Ammianus' understandable focus on imperial insecurity and court intrigue, along with the emperor's inability to resolve the high-profile religious controversies of the time, and the more obvious (if also more questionable)

---

50. On Laniogaesus, the *tribunus*, presumably one of the hit squad, as he was the last to see Constans alive, Amm.Marc. 15.5.17 (he was now with Silvanus).
51. Eutr. *Brev.* 10.5; *Epit. de Caes.* 41.24.
52. Ammianus made Constans' visit to Britain the excuse for a digression on that province and was sarcastic on Julian's caution about going to the assistance of 'those across the sea', as Constans had done (Amm. Marc. 20.1.1).

attractions of his successor, Julian. Yet the history of Constantius at war, as we shall see, reveals a man with virtues as a ruler unacknowledged by contemporaries obsessed by the search for glory. He safeguarded the frontiers of the empire, while also conserving Roman resources of money and manpower; his policy against Persia was more successful than that of Julian would prove to be. He also survived challenges to his rule, often with little or no bloodshed. In 350, after Constans' fall, he disposed of Vetranio, briefly proclaimed by the Danube legions, and survived three years of war with Magnentius; in 354, he checked the suspected insubordination of his Caesar Gallus; and in 355, he disposed of a potential rebel, the Frankish-born general Silvanus, by a trick.[53]

Scheming courtiers feature prominently in Ammianus' narrative and contributed to the demise of both Gallus and Silvanus, before turning their baleful attentions to Julian.[54] Notorious among them was 'Paul the Chain', so called because of his skill in complicating matters and 'linking together' chains of accusations to entrap his victims.[55] He actively pursued the followers of Magnentius, and many fell victims to informants without proper investigations. After the Caesar Gallus' fall in 354, Paulus again went into action, this time with an equally nefarious associate, Mercurius, the 'count of dreams' (*comes somniorum*), who reported as true the contents of dreams communicated to him by innocent guests at feasts;[56] later Paulus re-emerges as an informer on associates of Silvanus,[57] before meeting an unlamented end at the hands of Julian.

Ammianus believed that, although individual courtiers were to blame for their own failings, it was Constantius who was responsible for a culture of suspicion. In his concluding assessment of Constantius II's virtues and faults as emperor, Ammianus gave pride of place to the emperor's paranoia:[58]

53. Amm. Marc. 15.5.3–31; John Matthews, *The Roman Empire of Ammianus*, London: Duckworth, 1989, 37–9 and 80–2. For a sceptical (and speculative) view, see J. F. Drinkwater, 'Silvanus, Ursicinus and Ammianus: Fact or fiction?', in C. Deroux (ed.), *Studies in Latin Literature and Roman History* 7, Coll. Lat. 227, Brussels 1994, 568–76.
54. Amm. Marc. 14.5.4 on the 'proximorum cruentae blanditiae', the 'bloodthirsty flattery of those closest to him'; 14.11.2–3, the flatterers advise delaying the recall of Gallus until Urscinus is also neutralised.
55. Amm. Marc. 14.5.6; 15.3.4.
56. Amm. Marc. 15.3.4–6.
57. Amm. Marc. 15.6.1.
58. Amm. Marc. 21.16.8–9; see also 14.5.2–5 (on proscribing the followers of Magnentius).

> If he found any sign of aspiration to supreme power, however false
> or even frivolous, by investigating it endlessly and giving right and
> wrong equal weight, he would easily surpass the monstrous cruelty
> of Caligula and Domitian and Commodus.

Having reproached Constantius for the destruction of all his
relations at the start of his reign, Ammianus reinforced his criticisms
of his methods of investigation:

> And if anything of the kind broke out, charging into investigations
> more eagerly than was in accordance with lawful behaviour, he
> appointed for these legal hearings savage overseers and in punishing
> some he tried to protract their deaths if nature allowed.

As a follower of Ursicinus, who was intermittently suspected of
having imperial ambitions, Ammianus was sensitive to Constantius'
abuse of the judicial system. But he also acknowledged that the
emperor was right to be afraid: what the historian objected to was
not the taking of sensible measures to guarantee imperial security,
but the emperor's abuse of process through the use of torture and
groundless suspicions of the innocent.

Informers out of control, treason charges improperly investigated
and courtiers more interested in their own advancement than the
public interest were a feature of the courts of 'bad emperors';
Tacitus' Tiberius had provided a model and a warning. Yet some
threats were, or could become, real, not least those from – and to –
an unreliable Caesar. The fall of Gallus Caesar in 354 was caused
by Constantius' covert supervision of his appointee, and by Gallus'
own fears of treasonable plots against him, fears in which he
was encouraged by his wife, Constantina. But corrupt courtiers and
unreliable communications were not the only causes of Gallus' fall.
Constantius had been forced into an emergency appointment by
Magnentius' coup in 350. He had had little time to assess Gallus'
suitability for high office; his family connection, as the son of Julius
Constantius and grandson of Constantius I and Theodora, was his
sole qualification.[59]

Constantius' misjudgement became apparent, as Gallus began
to inspire fear on his own account. At Antioch, he ordered the
execution of all the leaders of the local council for opposing a cut
in the price of corn, and was only deterred from carrying out his
threat by the intervention of the *comes Orientis* (count of the East),

---

59. As would also be the case with Julian. For details, see R. C. Blockley, 'Constantius
Gallus and Julian as Caesars of Constantius II', *Latomus* 31 (1972), 433–68.

Honoratus.[60] When the unfortunate people of Antioch petitioned for famine relief, Gallus incited the crowd against the governor, Theophilus, who was duly lynched by the mob. The public warnings of officials whose task it was to restrain him, such as the praetorian prefect, Thalassius, fell on deaf ears. When Constantius despatched Domitianus as Thalassius' successor, the tactless behaviour of the latter and Gallus' 'disordered mind'[61] led to the lynching by the soldiers of both Domitianus and the quaestor Montius, who had urged moderation; other associates of the two were also hunted down and further purges of suspects were triggered by the discovery that a robe of imperial purple had been ordered from the dye-works at Tyre by an unknown person.[62] On receiving reports that his own official had been killed in an apparent army revolt, Constantius would have had little option but to act. After some debate in Constantius' consistory, Gallus was summoned from Antioch to the west by polite messages from the Augustus. Once safely away from his armies, however, he was gradually stripped of his escort and symbols of rank and finally beheaded, hands bound 'in the manner of a guilty bandit'.[63] Such, commented Ammianus, were the workings of Nemesis.[64]

If Ammianus' allegations are to be believed, Gallus was clearly guilty of bad government, if not of treason. But both Augustus and Caesar were arguably the victims of poor communications. Ammianus finds Gallus' violent behaviour inexplicable but it is possible that Gallus failed to appreciate that his officials, being in Constantius' confidence, required tactful handling, a lesson Julian was careful to learn. More sinister, from Constantius' standpoint, was the involvement of the soldiers in the murders of his officials. It seemed that, despite Gallus' wild behaviour, Constantius could not count on the loyalty of elements in his own eastern army.

Senates and spies

Ammianus had little time for discussions of administrative reform, except (as in the case of Julian) where reform also had a moral

60. Amm. Marc. 14.7.2.
61. Amm. Marc. 14.7.21: 'turbidum … ingenium'.
62. Amm. Marc. 14. 7 and 9. Ursicinus was summoned by Gallus from Nisibis and put in charge of the treason trials, a position unlikely to have endeared him to Constantius.
63. Amm. Marc. 14.11.23: 'colligatis manibus in modum noxii latronis'.
64. Amm. Marc. 14.11.25–6. Nemesis also brought about the deaths of those who had conspired against the Caesar.

content. For him, Constantius was little more than an operator of an administrative system set in place by Constantine. The emperor made no substantial alterations to the bureaucratic structures that he inherited from his father but, in Ammianus' view, preserved the distinction between civil and military posts and ensured that those he did appoint to palace jobs or military commands had the proper qualifications and experience. A mediocre leader (the historian continued), he was paranoid about plots against himself.[65] Given the violent deaths of his three brothers and his experience of revolts by Magnentius, Nepotianus, Silvanus and finally Julian, his suspicions were both natural and often justified.

If Constantius preferred the role of consolidator to that of innovator, this should not detract from the significance of his reign for the evolution of late Roman administration, especially in the eastern part of the Roman Empire, as Constantinople became ever more clearly recognised as a capital all but equivalent to Rome. Constantius was seldom in the city himself, preferring to be based at Antioch, from where the Persians could be more easily supervised.[66] However, he did not neglect the physical fabric of the city; he was responsible for building granaries by the harbour to guarantee a steady food supply, the Horrea Constantiana; the erection of baths near the Church of the Holy Apostles, which he also remodelled; and improvements to the water supply. Along with other structures, including colonnades and a public library, he also repaired earlier constructions, which had been erected in too much haste.[67] The orator Themistius, speaking at Rome in 357 (*Oration* 3), was clear that Constantinople was no second city, but a rival to the ancient capital. Increasingly, therefore, not only the officials but also their formal powers mirrored the system in old Rome.

As emperor in the west from 353, Constantius had an opportunity to see for himself how the ancient capital functioned, when he formally visited the city in 357.[68] His contacts with the senators at Rome predated that visit: indeed the Roman elite at Rome may have benefited from direct contact with an emperor more than they had

65. Amm. Marc. 21.6.1–3 and 8–10.
66. For his movements, see G. Dagron, *Naissance d'une capitale: Constantinople et ses institutions de 330 à 451*, Paris: Presses Universitaires de France, 1974, 79–81; Barnes, *Athanasius and Constantius*, 218–24.
67. Julian, *Or*.1.41a; Zos. *New History*, 2.32 for rushed building earlier. For Constantius' building programme in general, see Nick Henck, 'Constantius, *ho philoktistes*', *DOP* 55 (2001), 280–304.
68. See below, Chapter 12, pp. 274–6.

done since the early years of Constantine down to 326. Now, again, they had an emperor to provide guidance and leadership through his responses to officials' queries. The emperor celebrated his visit with the donation of an obelisk to be set up in the Circus Maximus[69] and may also have contributed to the decoration of the churches of St Peter's and perhaps S. Constanze.[70] Performance of public services at Rome was a problem, as it was also in lesser cities, as Constans had acknowledged in letters addressed to Africa, which refused to allow exemptions from curial duties to holders of honorary office.[71] Constantius insisted that senators were to perform their services at Rome in person, laid down rules for a quorum of fifty for public business, and protected them from unauthorised interventions in nominations for office from imperial governors.[72] The form of some of the laws, the *oratio*, a speech covering several subjects and addressed to the senate, could signal that Constantius had a programme of reform in mind, independent of official promptings or proposals. However, the process set out in Symmachus' official correspondence as prefect of Rome in 384 suggests that *orationes*, like letters addressed to officials, were the product of a lengthy process of consultation, involving frequent exchanges of embassies and polite requests from both sides for the implementation of salutary and necessary changes.[73]

On his return to Constantinople from the west in 359, Constantius replaced the proconsul previously in charge of running

69. Amm. Marc. 17.4.13; Dessau, *ILS* 736. Gavin Kelly, *Ammianus Marcellinus, the Allusive Historian*, Cambridge: Cambridge University Press, 2008, 225–30, on the contradictions between Ammianus' account and that of the inscription on the base. For more on the obelisk, which may have pleased non-Christians too, see Garth Fowden, 'Nikagoras of Athens and the Lateran Obelisk,' *JHS* 107 (1987), 51–7.
70. R. Krautheimer, 'A note on the inscription in the apse of Old St Peter's', *DOP* 41 (1987), 317–20.
71. The legislation of Constans on cities in Africa prohibited avoidance of curial duties through acquiring of honorary office (*Cod. Theod.* 6.22.2); honorary officials were to carry out curial duties unless they had contributed real service already (*Cod. Theod.* 6.22.3). The inference is that *honorati* (holders of honorary office) had been seeking exemptions, through the exertion of political pressure; the emperor's response strengthened the hand of those seeking to ensure that the *honorati* did their fair share.
72. *Cod. Theod.* 6.4.7 (353); 8; 9 (357) on the quorum of fifty. *Cod. Theod.* 6.4.3 and 6.4.4.are wrongly dated in the *Cod. Theod.* to 339 (which would make them legislation of Constans): the recipient of both, Mecilius Hilarianus, was praetorian prefect, perhaps of Italy, in 354 (cf. *PLRE* p. 473).
73. See Symmachus, *Relationes* 8; R. H. Barrow, *Prefect and Emperor: The 'Relationes' of Symmachus, AD 384*, Oxford: Clarendon Press, 1973; Jill Harries, *Law and Empire in Late Antiquity*, Cambridge: Cambridge University Press, 1999, 50–1.

the city with its first city prefect, Honoratus.[74] During the same period he overhauled the workings of the eastern senate, set up by Constantine, assimilating it more to the Roman model but also allowing for differences.[75] The proconsul Themistius was put in charge of a recruitment campaign, having himself been adlected into the senate in 355. The letter of Constantius on that occasion celebrated Themistius' qualifications for the office as a man of culture and virtue:[76]

> In receiving from us a Roman dignity, he offers Hellenic wisdom in return, so that for this reason our city is revealed as the summit both of good fortune and of virtue.

A good emperor, the letter continues, will supply walls, buildings and aqueducts for a favoured city as benefits, but

> How much more so is it to augment the senate with such an addition that should improve the souls of those who dwell in her.

The 'augmentations' were carefully selected, combining men drawn from the old elites, with their control of resources, connections and patronage, with 'new men', who would owe their advancement to the emperor.[77] For the first time, the senatorial order was divided on geographical grounds, with the consequence that senators of Rome resident in the east now had to re-register for the senate in Constantinople.[78] The emperor made further changes to the points of entry to the senate, the quaestorship and praetorship, emphasising further the continuity with old Rome. The two magistracies had been an integral part of the *cursus honorum* (ladder of offices) under the Republic, but by late antiquity they were junior

---

74. Socrates, *Hist. eccl.* 2.41.
75. A development entirely ignored by the Antiochene Ammianus. See Gavin Kelly, 'The New Rome and the old: Ammianus' silences on Constantinople', CQ 53 (2003), 588–607; the problem disappears if the arguments for the 340s of A. Skinner, 'The early development of the senate at Constantinople', *Byzantine and Modern Greek Studies* 32 (2008), 148–68, are accepted. On the reform in the context of the recruitment of easterners into a new elite of service, see Peter Heather, 'New men for new Constantines? Creating an imperial elite in the eastern Mediterranean', in P. Magdalino (ed.), *New Constantines: The Rhythm of Imperial Renewal in Byantium, 4th to 13th Centuries*, Aldershot: Variorum, 1994, 11–33, at 17–18.
76. *Letter of Constantius*, 21b, eds and trans. P. Heather and D. Moncur, *Politics, Philosophy and Empire in the Fourth Century: Select Orations of Themistius*, TTH 36, Liverpool: Liverpool University Press, 2001, 108–14.
77. Heather, 'New men', 18.
78. For this reform, Peter Heather, 'Senators and senates', in CAH² 13, 187–8. On a reregistered senator, Lib. *Letter* 70.

posts, held by aspiring senators early in their careers, and often, as in the case of Symmachus late in the fourth century, with expenses paid by their fathers. Twenty years earlier, in his first attempt at reshaping government at Constantinople, Constantius had tightened up the rules on the nomination and selection of the five praetors, who had acquired special titles and ranks.[79] Now he ruled that two of the five, instead of giving public games as had been the custom at Rome, should contribute an equivalent amount in silver for the construction of public works.[80] In addition he made some attempt to replicate the ancient judicial functions of the praetors at Rome by placing his eastern equivalents in charge of cases involving freedom and status, the appointment of guardians, the manumission of slaves, and the emancipation of sons from the legal control of their fathers (*patria potestas*).[81]

As was the practice at Rome, the *oratio* was also the form chosen for Constantius' manifesto to the senate at Constantinople in May 361, setting out in full his proposed changes to their organisation. The speech, which is preserved in multiple extracts in the Theodosian Code, was a wide-ranging description of senatorial privileges and duties. Although the new rules were mostly restatements of existing practice, their collection and reaffirmation acted as a form of codification of laws on status, taxation and exemptions. Senators were not liable for taxes on fugitive *coloni*, unless they actually owned the land tenanted by the fugitives; the *coloni* themselves were not liable to the *collatio lustralis*(trade tax) on the selling of their surplus produce; decurions were excluded from senate membership, though if they succeeded in reaching the praetorship and carrying out its duties they were to be allowed to remain, but had to compensate the cities they had left for expenses incurred; and governors were not permitted to call on senators to fund their local building projects.[82] More controversially, senators as an order were made liable for the *protostasia*, or provision of recruits, out of their own tax assessment; Julian reversed this, arguing that it was an

---

79. *Cod. Theod.* 6.4.5 (340). The top three were the Flavial, the Constantinian and the Triumphal.
80. *Cod. Theod.* 6.4.13 (361); the measure was also an ingenious way of financing construction in a new and expanding city.
81. *Cod. Theod.* 6.4.16. These were the traditional responsibilities of the praetors under the Republic at Rome.
82. *Cod. Theod.* 11.11.5 (*coloni*); *Cod. Theod.* 13.1.13 (*collatio lustralis*); *Cod. Theod.* 12.1.48. (decurions); *Cod. Theod.* 15.1.7. (building projects).

obligation more appropriate for decurions.[83] What is not present in the record but may well also have happened at this stage was the redesignation of the Constantinople senators as *clarissimi*, of equal rank with their counterparts at Rome.

Emerging bureaucracies tend to acquire a life of their own.[84] Constantine had established the master of the offices (*magister officiorum*) as the head of the court bureaucracy.[85] Included in his department were the spy service, or *agentes in rebus*, whose formal job it was to check the validity of passes for the public post (a responsibility which allowed numerous other surreptitious checks as well).[86] While they were entitled to protection from intervention by other departments, there were suspicions as to their honesty and suggestions that not all of their covert (and allegedly extortionate) activities were being reported to their superior. It is presumably because the *agentes* were already levying unauthorised duties on public post transport that Constantius limited the impost to one *solidus* per four-wheeled vehicle, a ruling symptomatic of a general trend in late antiquity for fees or charges to be introduced first on the ground and later by imperial endorsement.[87] Generally dissatisfied with the quality of performance, Constantius ordered his master of the offices to purge the service of unworthy employees, insisting that in future recruitment to the lower ranks should be based on merit, although the plum jobs should still be allocated on the grounds of seniority and reliability.[88]

What the laws did not reveal was that the *agentes* had an evil reputation as informers. Ammianus reported the dire consequences

83. *Cod. Theod.* 11.23.1 (Constantius); 2 (Julian).
84. Hence emperors' longstanding concern with corruption, on which see Ramsay MacMullen, *Corruption and the Decline of Rome*, New Haven; Yale University Press, 1988; on the rhetoric as an unreliable guide to the reality of corruption, Harries, *Law and Empire*, 153–71; Christopher Kelly, *Ruling the Later Roman Empire*, Cambridge, MA: Belknap Press, index s.v. corruption.
85. On the master's temporary acquisition of a new *scrinium* (secretariat) of *dispositiones* (testamentary dispositions), see *Cod. Theod.* 6.26.1; *Cod. Just.* 12.28.2. Vogler, *Constance*, 170–2.
86. *Cod. Theod.* 6.29.4: 'ad cursum regendum et ad curas agendas' ('for the regulation of the public post and other duties'; the *curae*, other duties, are not specified). On the *agentes*, see Vogler, *Constance*, 183–210.
87. *Cod. Theod.* 6.29.5 (359). See, for fees and charges in general, MacMullen, *Corruption*, 150–7.
88. *Cod. Theod.* 1.9.1 (also of October 359). The planned purge anticipates measures against the *agentes* taken by Julian. See also *Cod. Theod.* 3.21.1 and 8.7.4 restricting the right to 'adore the purple' to serving officers under the *magistri* of the horse and infantry; those with only honorary office were to be excluded.

of indiscretions at a feast given by the governor of Pannonia Secunda at Sirmium: on information laid by the *agens* Gaudentius, all at the table were taken into custody, tortured and imprisoned (though one escaped by killing himself). In Aquitaine, an aged informant noticed the wide purple borders to his host's table-cloths, allowing the potential creation of an imperial robe: a 'rich estate was thus ruined'. And in Spain, a spy overheard servants putting out the lights with the word *'vincamus'* ('we'll win'), apparently a local custom: a 'noble house' was thus destroyed.[89] Other officials therefore required protection from abuse of power on the part of the emperor's special agents; Constantius shielded his praetorian prefects from inappropriate requests for free passes on the *cursus publicus* by insisting that they could only be granted by himself or the master of the offices.[90]

Constantius preferred to revise the duties of existing officials rather than create new ones. One exception may have been the imperial quaestor, who would later hold a unique position as the draftsman of imperial laws. Flavius Taurus, named as *quaestor sacri palatii* by Amminaus, is the first attested holder of the office, although the context shows Taurus as a spokesman, the traditional role of the quaestor, not a lawyer. Taurus, however, as some laws addressed to him suggest, may also have been a would-be legal reformer.[91] His imperial master showed a consistent interest in restricting abuse of legal privilege. In an attempt to streamline justice by concentrating judicial power in the hands of the provincial governors (*iudices*), Constantius made hitherto favoured categories of person subject to trial in the governors' courts. This was intended to restrict abuse of the so-called *praescriptio fori*, the practice by which a location for a trial was chosen to benefit one or other party. Those affected included administrators of the imperial estates – of whom governors generally kept clear – and all soldiers in the imperial service; in criminal cases, prosecutions initiated by soldiers were also to be brought before the governor, a measure which denied soldiers the chance of intimidating a civilian defendant before a military tribunal.[92] Thus by insisting that previously privileged categories of litigant were also subject to the governors' jurisdiction,

89. Amm. Marc. 16.8.8 (Aquitaine); 9 (Spain). The structure of the two paragraphs is remarkably similar.
90. *Cod. Theod.* 8.5.9; Vogler, *Constance*, 176–7.
91. For example, *Cod. Theod.* 12.1.49 is a complex system set up for the disposal of property of decurions entering the church. Exemptions are allowed to bishops and those deemed suitable by the council and the people.
92. *Cod. Theod.* 2.1.1 (349); 2 (355).

Constantius would have hoped to limit abuses of the legal system by his own officials.[93] Governors in their turn were also denied the rights of patronage over their own staffs, who were to be selected centrally; governors were not to approve or promote any member of staff.[94]

All this created the illusion of control. In practice confusion, accidental or deliberately engineered, continued. The vicissitudes endured by the Egyptian soldier Abinnaeus reveal the complexities attending what should have been routine matters. Alleged inappropriate exercise of patronage, probable administrative confusion and possible forgery of letters of appointment caused Abinnaeus to approach the emperor on at least three occasions, in order to enhance his career or even retain his job. He first came to Constantius' attention when, after thirty-three years of service, he was chosen in c. 338 by the *comes* Senecio to escort an embassy from a local independent tribe, the Blemmyes, to Constantinople. There he was 'permitted to adore the imperial purple' and granted the rank of a *ducenarius* (middle-grade civil servant). The second communication, addressed to the emperors Constantius and Constans in 341, complained that, on his return to Egypt from his diplomatic mission as escort for the Blemmyes envoys, he found that his routine job as commander of an *ala* (squadron) at Dionysias in the Fayyum had been allocated to others through patronage by the *comes* Valacius, who claimed that 'other men had put forward letters of this kind'.[95] His request that his job be restored to him was based on arguments which combined the services he had already rendered with assumptions that the emperors' response would be consistent with their 'clemency' and 'piety'. Abinnaeus' petition for restitution was, on this occasion, successful but in 344 Valacius tried again to remove Abinnaeus, 'in accordance with imperial orders', as he had served his

93. Contrast a law of Constans (*Cod. Theod.* 2.6.5, of 340), which favoured administrators, allowing four months for a lay litigant to lodge a complaint against the tax authorities, but *six* months for the *fiscus* (treasury) to pursue a claim against a defaulter.
94. *Cod. Theod.* 8.7.7 = *Cod. Just.* 12.57.2; Vogler, *Constance*, 173–6. Governors' staffs were expected to provide their governors with independent advice and prevent them from breaking the rules.
95. *P. Abinn.* 1.12. For texts, see H. I. Bell, V. Martin, E. G. Turner and D. van Berchem (eds), *The Abinnaeus Archive: Papers of a Roman Officer in the Reign of Constantius II*, Oxford: Oxford University Press, 1962. For other examples of duplication or dubious documentation, see *Cod. Theod.* 10.10.5 (Constans, 340) that where more than one imperial grant of the same land is alleged, the one dated earlier is to be deemed valid; and *Cod. Theod.* 15.1.1 that permits for exemptions from public works in Africa issued by governors were to be investigated (Constans, 338).

time and should now, after managing the handover to his successor, 'attend to his own interests'.[96] Once again, Abinnaeus stood his ground and, after a brief period out of office as an ex-*praepositus* (head of unit), was reinstated and continued in post for another five years, from May 346 to early in 351.

Constantius' cautious, incremental approach extended to religious reform. In the mid-350s, he ordered the closure of temples everywhere and forbade access to them, the performance of sacrifice was forbidden, and those who disobeyed were to be executed for their 'crimes' (*facinora*) and have their property confiscated.[97] Governors were charged with the responsibility of seeing the law implemented. The intention was to outlaw all ritual observances based in temples, whether or not they entailed sacrifice, an acknowledgement of the importance of the temples as sites for the celebration of cult, contrasting with Christian flexibility over meeting-places. But, as we have seen, there is evidence for consensus on the ground about religious practices; at Antioch, for example, Libanius and the Christians could agree that blood sacrifice was best avoided.[98]

Constantius' law will therefore have been in line with existing trends. Moreover, the law allowed the continuance of other cultic practices, such as the use of incense or candles, which would later also be adopted in Christian rituals. Despite the confrontational tone of the sources, local compromises were on the whole preferred and enforcement remained patchy.[99] Thus Julian, in 354, on his journey westwards to become Caesar in Gaul, was pleased (and surprised) to find at Ilium, the site of ancient Troy, that the cult statues were brightly polished and the local Christian bishop was happily employed in tending the shrines and tombs of Hector and Achilles.[100] Constantius himself may tacitly have accepted that, as with much imperial legislation, enforcement would depend on local priorities, not action from the centre.

96. *P. Abinn.* 2.9: 'propriis attende utilitatibus'. Abinnaeus' petition (*P. Abinn.* 1) and Valacius' somewhat abrupt letter are the only two documents in Latin; the rest are in Greek and of varying degrees of literacy.
97. *Cod. Theod.* 16.10.4.
98. I. Sandwell, *Religious Identity in Late Antiquity: Greeks, Jews and Christians in Antioch*, Cambridge: Cambridge University Press, 2007, 104–6.
99. As argued for Rome by Michelle Salzman, 'How the west was won: The Christianization of the aristocracy in the west in the years after Constantine', in C. Deroux (ed.), *Studies in Latin Literature and Roman History* 6, Brussels: Latomus, 1992, 451–69.
100. Julian, *Letter* 19 (Wright edition), justifying the retention of the bishop Pelagius in his post. On all this, see Garth Fowden, 'Polytheist religion and philosophy', *CAH*² 13, 538–60 (on Constantius, 539–43).

Figure 48 Equestrian pedestal of Constantius II, Forum Romanum, Rome, Italy

Figure 49 Lateran obelisk, Rome, Italy

CHAPTER 9

Warfare and imperial security, AD 337–61

Warfare shaped the destinies of emperors. From 340 to 350, while Constans campaigned in Gaul and on the Danube, Constantius was kept fully occupied by a resurgent Persia. But after Constans' murder in 350, the threats of civil war, exacerbated by the risk of foreign invasion, would return to haunt both Constantius and his surviving male relatives, his Caesars Gallus and Julian. Emperors would be again at war not only with external enemies but also with each other. How far did they have a choice in the military policies pursued? The story of emperors at war from 284 forms a continuous whole, but also looks back further, to the troubled third century. The two main theatres of warfare were and remained the northern European frontiers along the Rhine and Danube, and the frontier with Persia. However, the precise scale of the threat posed by the new 'barbarian' confederacies, as represented by the Alamanni, the Franks and the Goths, and in Persia the Sasanian kings, fluctuated, as also, within limits, did Roman policies towards them. In their engagement with both, Constantine and his successors worked within an established framework, but also made tactical and strategic choices of their own.

Emperors and armies

What kinds of armies did the emperors lead?[1] Reference has already been made to the two main types of military force, the *comitatenses* (or *comitatus*), the field armies, and the *limitanei*, who were stationed in frontier zones.[2] Although the functions of the two categories appear clearly differentiated, in practice operational distinctions were often blurred: units of *limitanei* were converted

1. For survey, which traces developments from the third century, see R. S. O. Tomlin, 'The army of the late empire', in John Wacher (ed.), *The Roman World*, London: Routledge, 1987, 107–13.
2. See Jones, *LRE*, 607–11.

into *comitatenses* (or *pseudo-comitatenses*) as required, while units from the various field armies were diverted to protect frontiers.[3] Moreover, as subdivisions of the *comitatus* became more closely identified with the regions where they were stationed, soldiers serving with the emperor in person also acquired a separate status from the rest as *palatini* (palace elite troops). Roman military organisation was not fixed or inflexible and, despite its complexity, was designed to adapt to emergencies and changes in imperial priorities.

The late Roman army differed from its predecessors in the first two centuries in the smaller size of its units, especially those who comprised the *comitatenses*. Three main categories of soldier can be identified: the infantry 'legions', which now comprised a thousand men; *vexillationes* (squadrons) of cavalry, about five hundred men strong; and new-style *auxilia* (auxiliaries; c. 500 to 800 men) recruited, perhaps first by Maximian, from across the Rhine. Separate from these were the *scholae*, units attached to the emperor, who, after Constantine's disbanding of the praetorian guard at Rome in 312, formed the bodyguard of the emperor. As palatine troops, they came under the command of the *magister officiorum*; for this reason, the master is sometimes found acting in a military capacity.[4] Another unit of soldiers attached to the emperor, and by extension his most prominent generals, was the *protectores domestici* (soldiers attached to the emperor or his chief generals), an elite corps of which Ammianus was one.

These smaller groupings reflect the greater degree of specialisation to be found in late Roman military organisation. Archers (*sagitarii*) were used in wars against the Persians, as also were slingers, whose shot was well adapted to pierce Persian heavy armour.[5] Heavier artillery pieces, *ballistae*, came in various sizes, ranging from the equivalent of cross-bows (*arcuballistae, manuballistae*) to the machine for the firing of heavy missiles, the *onager* ('wild ass', because it kicked backwards) or *scorpio*, which was used in sieges.[6]

---

3. Jones, *LRE*, 649–54.
4. As in 350, when Magnentius' *magister*, Marcellinus, succeeded in overpowering the forces of Nepotianus at Rome.
5. M. C. Bishop and J. C. N. Coulston, *Roman Military Equipment*, London: Batsford, 1993, 165–6. Lead sling-bullets, probably dating from the fourth century, were also found at Vindolanda on Hadrian's Wall.
6. Amm. Marc. 23.4.1–7 (*ballista, scorpio*); 8–13 (battering ram and *helepolis*, another kind of ram); 14 (fire darts).

Firing the last required specialist knowledge because of the recoil. Ammianus recalled one unfortunate who failed to jump back in time and whose corpse was so disfigured as to be unrecognisable.[7] Cavalry units (*cataphractarii*, *clibanii*) were regularly equipped with heavy armour, and infantry units, especially those in the front line, continued to wear chain mail and helmets.[8] Part of a commander's job was to ensure that the specialist units worked in concert as, separately, the uses to which they could be put were limited. Mistakes could be made: in his first campaigning season, the Caesar Julian made a forced march though a forest, accompanied by *cataphractarii* and *ballistae*, 'who were far from suitable to defend their commander'.[9]

The numbers of soldiers under arms is impossible to ascertain with any certainty. Various numbers are offered by the ancient sources, often rounded up (or down) for dramatic effect.[10] An alternative approach is to reach a 'paper' total by counting up the units listed in the *Notitia Dignitatum*. That document, a list of civil and military offices, probably dates from the early fifth century, but much of its contents were out of date, and therefore, taken as a whole, the list cannot provide a reliable picture of the military establishment at any point in its history. What is known of armies put into the field suggests that there were far fewer soldiers in service than are estimated in the literary sources: the largest army known is that of Julian recruited for the Persian campaign in 363, which numbered 65,000 men. By contrast, he had won the battle of Strasbourg a few years before with a mere 13,000 (although another 25,000 had been routed by the Alamanni, depleting the expected strength of the Romans). Given the lack of reliable statistics, we can only guess at

7. Amm. Marc. 24.4.28; the incident happened at the siege of Maiozamalcha in 363.
8. See Vegetius 1.20 for the assertion that infantry no longer had armour in the late fourth century, refuted by Bishop and Coulston, *Equipment*, 167–79.
9. Amm. Marc. 16.2.5–6, 'parum ad tuendum rectorem idoneis'. Julian arrived safely at his destination, but had been unable to chase down an enemy guerrilla force, 'hindered by the weight of his soldiers' weaponry' ('gravitate praepeditus armorum').
10. A late source, the sixth-century bureaucrat John Lydus (*De mensibus* 1.27), put the Diocletianic figure for soldiers in service at 389, 704, plus 45, 562, in the fleets, a figure so precise as to suggest derivation from official lists, which could themselves be out of date or inaccurate for other reasons. See also Agathias, 5.13.7, recording 645,000 in service at some unspecified 'early' date. Zosimus' figures (*New History* 2.15.1–2) for the forces of Maxentius (188,000) and Constantine (98,000) in 312 cannot be relied on. The Latin panegyrics (*Pan. Lat.* 12 (9).3) are no better, with numbers of 100,000 for Maxentius and a quarter of that for Constantine giving a total western combined force of 125,000.

the real effect on military manpower of wastage in the course of the civil wars of the late third and fourth centuries: as Eutropius and others commented of the havoc wrought by Constantius II's victory over Magnentius at Mursa in 351: it 'destroyed forces which were sufficient for many foreign wars and which might have provided many a triumph and much security'.[11] And, as we have seen, even before Mursa, Constantius was reluctant to risk soldiers' lives unnecessarily against the Persians.

Recruitment of Roman citizens was based on conscription.[12] The provision of recruits was, in effect, a tax, the assessment of which was tied to the land tax (*iugum*); in some years, money (the *aurum tirocinium*) was collected instead. As an account of a Christian military martyr, Maximilian, illustrates, recruits were subjected to a brief interrogation, their height was checked (5′10″ was the required minimum, later reduced to 5′7″) and they were then branded.[13] Life in service was relatively comfortable. The value of basic pay in coin (*stipendium*) was eroded by the debasement of the coinage, but emperors issued regular donatives on their accession and at five-yearly intervals thereafter. More important for everyday prosperity was their receipt of benefits in kind, which were often enhanced by soldiers' extortion from local populations. The billeting of *comitatenses* in towns was a serious grievance, as soldiers demanded bedding and fuel (known as *salganum*) from their hosts, to which they were not legally entitled.[14] It should also be noted that, unlike most Roman citizens, 'barbarians' seem to have volunteered to serve on an individual basis in significant numbers. Units with Germanic titles named in the *Notitia Dignitatum* and elsewhere did not consist entirely of non-Roman peoples, but their names and insignia were a recognition of the contribution made by the friendly 'barbarian' to the Roman military effort.

Loyal service was encouraged by incentives. A string of imperial pronouncements from Constantine and his successors confirmed the fiscal, legal and social privileges of veterans. One, unique legal text

11. Eutr. *Brev.* 10.12; cf. Aur. Vict. *Caes.* 42.9–10; *Epit. Caes.* 42.4; Zos. *New History*, 2.46.
12. Jones, *LRE*, 619–23; A. D. Lee, *War in Late Antiquity: A Social History*, Oxford: Blackwell, 2007, 79–85.
13. *Acts of Maximilian* 1.5.
14. *Cod. Theod.* 7.9.1 (340, Constans suggests that hosts make voluntary contributions, but may not be compelled to do so); *salganum* was forbidden outright in 361, by Constantius II (*Cod. Theod.* 7.9.2), and later emperors agreed.

shows Constantine in direct conversation with his soldiers. Having greeted him with acclamations, the veterans demand reassurance as to their privileges.[15] After some hedging, Constantine delivers a comprehensive list of exemptions, from civic burdens (*munera*), tax payments and tribute (*vectigalia*) and sales taxes in the marketplace. The emperor was concerned that veterans should not be left with time on their hands. They were therefore offered land to farm and start-up grants for farming or, failing that, a business. Two years later, Constantine further defined the scope of tax exemptions and the categories of soldier to which they applied.[16] Their privileges were also legally protected, as were their rights to have their disputes heard in their own courts (*praescriptio fori*). Constantine's concern with veterans' employment prospects was not entirely philanthropic: soldiers without means of support had often resorted to banditry, an outcome such measures were specifically designed to prevent.[17] But if Constantine's famed generosity benefited his soldiers, the effect of such exemptions not only enhanced the suspicion that soldiers were too expensive; it also represented a 'hidden cost' to the Roman and local economies.

Despite these incentives, recruitment could be problematic. Laws of Constantine responded to attempts by sons of soldiers to evade their hereditary obligations by insisting that those who did so, for example by cutting off their fingers, should be forced to serve on town councils. In isolation, these laws are not evidence for a general unwillingness to serve but were designed to deal with problems as they arose. More indicative of a general unwillingness was a report detailing the failure of a recruitment drive in the Egyptian Fayum, addressed to the local commander (*praepositus*), Abinnaeus, in the reign of Constantius II:

> We passed three days together at Karanis and we could not drag away a single man. And we kept the irenarch (local law enforcement officer) under detention, wishing to drag him away. The whole village was ... that we were letting no-one leave the village. They gave you, if you approve, 2 solidi and 50 talents of silver.[18]

15. *Cod. Theod.* 7.20.2, of 326. For the whole collection, *Cod. Theod.* 7.20.1–7. Serena Connolly, 'Constantine answers the veterans,' in Scott McGill, Cristiana Sogno and Edward Watts (eds), *From the Tetrarchs to the Theodosians: Later Roman History and Culture, 284–450 CE*, Cambridge: Cambridge University Press, 2010, 93–114.
16. *Cod. Theod.* 7.20.4.
17. See *Cod. Theod.* 7.20.7, ascribed to Constantius but perhaps earlier.
18. *P. Abinn.* 35. For Abinnaeus and his papyri, see H. I. Bell, V. Martin, E. G. Turner,

Corroboration is offered by Ammianus' analysis of Constantius' ill-advised eagerness in 359 to trust the word of some unreliable Sarmatians, the Limigantes, whom he hoped to recruit, to compensate for his own subjects' preference for providing money rather than men:[19]

> He would grow rich with a future increase in population and be able to conscript recruits very strong in war; for the provincials will cheerfully hand over gold to prevent risk to their bodies, a hope which has more than once seriously damaged Roman interests.

The outcome was unfortunate. When Constantius tried to address them from his tribunal at a parley, the potential recruits rioted and stole his imperial chair with its gold cushion, forcing the emperor himself to flee for his life. Belatedly but effectively, the Romans counterattacked and the Limigantes were driven off with heavy casualties. Such misunderstandings were perhaps inevitable but, as emperors became increasingly dependent on the recruitment of non-Romans to serve in the Roman army, the dangers inherent in such breakdowns of relations could only increase.

Emperors headed a large and complex military organisation. Its pay structure, inherited from the early empire, and his control as legislator over the extent of their rewards, perpetuated the status of the army as, in effect, the emperor's client.[20] But emperors in their turn relied for their position on their popularity with the soldiers. By the late third century, soldiers expected emperors to be 'present' with them, to lead them to 'victories' and to be responsive to their desires. But the loyalties of Roman armies were, primarily, to their generals – and not all generals were emperors. Suspicion on the part of insecure emperors and ambition or fear on the part of their generals risked undermining the effectiveness both of military operations and of the imperial government itself.

Constantius II and Persia

Galerius' treaty of 298 stabilised Rome's eastern frontier for over thirty years. However, from 324, a number of developments under-

and D. van Berchem (eds), *The Abinnaeus Archive: Papers of a Roman Officer in the Reign of Constantius II*, Oxford: Oxford University Press, 1962. Their translation is used here.
19. Amm. Marc. 19.11.7.
20. For emperors' responses to petitions from soldiers, and the need to balance theirs with other interests, see Brian Campbell, *The Emperor and the Roman Army*, Oxford: Clarendon Press, 1984, 264–99.

mined whatever trust had existed between the parties. At some point after 324, Constantine addressed a letter to the young Shapur II, proclaiming himself as God's regent over the world, and deploring the wrongs to the divine will perpetrated by Valerian, who had paid the price for impiety when taken by the Persians.[21] The worrying aspect for the Persians was that in the letter Constantine claimed divine approval for his expansionist designs, and also in effect proclaimed himself the protector of the Christians in Persia. The situation worsened when, in 330, the death of Tiridates III plunged Armenia into a state of uncertainty and made it more vulnerable to Persian intervention. Hannibalianus' proclamation in 335 as 'King of Kings', with overlordship of Armenia and Pontus, would have appeared to the Persians as a clear statement of aggressive intent (whatever Constantine's real motives). In 336, when Shapur invaded Armenia and deposed the king, Tiranes, the pro-Roman faction appealed for help to Constantine. Despite a diplomatic initiative by the Persians in the winter of 336–7, in the spring of 337, Rome and Persia were, once again, on the brink of war.[22]

Thus Constantine's legacy to Constantius was an unstable Armenia and a Mesopotamia threatened by active Persian military aggression. In dealing with Armenia, Constantius displayed what would become the hallmark of his policy, a preference for achieving results without unnecessary expenditure of manpower (although this did not preclude the pursuit of victory-titles, such as Adiabenicus [conqueror of Adiabene], where appropriate). The new king, Arsaces, although a Persian appointee, was encouraged to come over to the Romans – at the expense of the former pro-Roman faction.[23] Likewise, in Mesopotamia, Constantius' policy was to avoid direct confrontation, where possible, relying on the ability of fortified cities under Roman control to resist assault. In the 340s, that confidence appeared well founded. Having assailed Nisibis once in 338, Shapur II subjected the city to two further sieges in 346 (for nine weeks) and in 350 (one hundred days). Later Christian sources, such as the

---

21. Euseb. *Vit. Const.* 4.8–14. In the reign of Constantius, if not earlier, the Persians retaliated with claims of dominion over the empire once controlled by Cyrus the Great and Darius, i.e. as far west as Macedonia and Greece.

22. For ancient views of the causes, see M. H. Dodgeon and S. N. C. Lieu, *The Roman Eastern Frontier and the Persian Wars* AD *226–363: A Documentary Study*, London: Routledge, 1991, 143–63.

23. Julian, *Or.* 1. 20A–21A, suggesting that Constantius won over objectors by handing out lavish presents.

Chronicon Paschale, ascribed the success of Nisibis in resisting Persia to divine intervention: in 350, after failing to breach the defences by diverting a river (which drowned many Persians), the attackers were further deterred by an apparition of Constantius II and an angel, who forced them to withdraw.[24] Constantius may even have achieved a small expansion of Roman control, through the capture of a 'significant' city, perhaps Nineveh, for which he took the title Adiabenicus.[25] Events in the west after the death of Constans took Constantius from the east for ten years after 350. Fortunately for him, Shapur was also distracted by revolts on his northeastern frontier. After the execution of the Caesar Gallus in 354, peace negotiations were opened with Persia, originated, on his own initiative, by the acting head of the eastern administration, Strategius Musonianus, but, although they gave rise to some rhetorical posturing through open letters issued by both sides, the talks came to nothing.

Constantius' policy was not without risk, both to himself and to the security of the frontiers. His failure to win spectacular or decisive victories made him vulnerable to competition from more charismatic military leaders. His master of the horse, Ursicinus, whose following included the loyal Ammianus, *protector domesticus* and future historian, preferred a more direct approach – and was popular with the populations of the eastern cities, who hailed him as their 'defender'.[26] In 358, after some hesitation, Constantius sent Ursicinus to the east to serve alongside a military colleague, Sabinianus, an adherent of the policy of non-confrontation. The collaboration was not a success. In 359, Amida fell to the Persians after a siege of seventy-three days, vividly recorded by Ammianus, who was lucky to escape with his life when the city fell. As Sabinianus and Ursicinus both sought to shift responsibility for the disaster, Ursicinus denounced Constantius' bad advisers and was removed from office. In the meantime, Constantius' personal presence failed to prevent the fall to the Persians of two further

24. *Chronicon Paschale* s.a.350, pp. 537–8: Michael Whitby and Mary Whitby (eds and trans.), *Chronicon Paschale, 284–628 AD*, TTH 7, Liverpool: Liverpool University Press, 1989, 27–8; C. Lightfoot, 'Facts and fiction in the third siege of Nisibis in AD 350', *Historia* 37 (1988), 105–25.
25. Lib. *Or.* 59, 83–7; Amm. Marc. 18.7.1, for Nineveh in Adiabene; Dessau, *ILS* 732 for Constantius II as Adiabenicus.
26. Amm. Marc. 18.6.2; John Matthews, *The Roman Empire of Ammianus*, London: Duckworth, 1989, 40, 405, points out that the acclamations were probably orchestrated by Ursicinus' followers.

frontier cities, Singara and Bezabde, in 360. Not surprisingly, the adherents of Julian would later castigate Constantius for, in effect, assisting the enemy.[27] Yet Constantius had largely succeeded in his main objective: to preserve the frontiers agreed by Galerius in 298.[28]

Ammianus at Amida, AD 359

In late antiquity, siege warfare features prominently, as both Sassanian Persia and, later, northern frontier peoples showed increased (though still sporadic) ability to capture fortified strong points. Sieges were also dramatic events, of defined duration and confined to a limited geographical area. Ammianus' narration of his experiences at Amida is therefore in part a literary set-piece, inviting comparison with, for example, Cassius Dio's account of Septimius Severus' siege of Hatra (at which Dio was not present and of which he knew very little).[29] Ammianus compares Amida by implication to Troy, recalling the fight over the body of Patroclus[30] and the exploits of King Rhesus.[31] The ghost of Thucydides is also invoked with a digression on the plague which afflicted the defenders of Amida for ten days, and which was ended by a shower of rain.[32] But Ammianus' account is of unique value both because, as he empha-sises himself, he was there, and because he provides insight at first hand into siege engines and techniques, the psychology of siege warfare on an unstable frontier, and the wider political and military context of the Amida campaign.

The siege of Amida, which had been fortified by Constantius II as Caesar,[33] lasted seventy-three days, but Ammianus concentrates on selected highlights, while also providing a picture of what happened during periods of waiting and regrouping.[34] He begins with an account of his presence there, as one of thousands of refugees from

27. Lib. Or. 18. 206.
28. Amm. Marc. 25.9.3, from 364, after the frontiers had been adjusted in Persia's favour, following the death of Julian on campaign.
29. For Ammianus' literary technique, see Gavin Kelly, *Ammianus Marcellinus, the Allusive Historian*, Cambridge: Cambridge University Press, 2008.
30. Amm. Marc. 19.1.9.
31. Amm. Marc. 19.6.11, of the Gallic sortie, referring to *Il.* 10. 435.
32. Amm. Marc. 19.4. The *Iliad* is evoked again (3) with the plague compared to the arrows of Apollo raining down on the disobedient Greeks (*Il.* 1.9; 43); and Homer (*Il.* 1.50) is cited (6) as a medical authority.
33. Amm. Marc. 18.9.1. The present 'black walls' date from the sixth century but the foundations of the earlier towers are still visible.
34. On the siege in Ammianus' account, see Matthews, *Ammianus*, 58–66.

the surrounding countryside, who were crammed so closely together on the approaches to the city that the corpses of those killed by enemy fire remained upright, because there was no room for them to fall.[35] Sneaking unobserved through a postern gate (he would later escape by the same means), Ammianus took his station on the walls, from which he could observe the glittering helmets and armour of the besiegers, who covered the ground as far as the eye could see. Among them were elephants, which Ammianus regarded with fear and horror, although in the event they would prove of limited use.

The taking of Amida was not, in fact, a priority for Shapur, who, although present in person, hoped to turn elsewhere. Early in the siege, attempts at negotiation by the Persians failed, and they were pelted with missiles from the walls. The king's plans for breaking off the siege were finally frustrated when the Romans shot dead the young son of his ally, Grumbates of the Chionitae. A brief truce was declared and the youth was given the funeral rites of his own people, which included a lying in state, surrounded by ten effigies of young warriors on couches, who would attend him in the afterlife. After this, Grumbates refused to move from Amida, until his son's spirit was propitiated by the destruction of the city; the besiegers thus became yet more resolute to redeem their own honour by consigning his killers to serve the dead man in the afterlife.[36]

Both sides therefore turned their energies to building devices and counter-devices to break the deadlock. When the Persians constructed a fortified siege tower which would allow their soldiers to fire downwards on the defenders, the Romans created an engine with shot strong enough to break the armour of the siege towers, rendering them useless. Towards the end, while the Persians built up a mound outside the walls, the Romans reinforced the walls from within – only for their mound to collapse, creating a bridge with the Persians' construction, and allowing the enemy access to the city at last.[37]

In his focus on the psychology of siege warfare at Amida, Ammianus, despite the benefit of hindsight, is never overtly defeatist. The defenders are desperate but all the more eager therefore to fight bravely. They had much to put up with. Ammianus repeatedly

35. Amm. Marc. 19.8.11–13.
36. Amm. Marc. 19.1.7 (death of prince); 10–11 (funeral); 19.2.1–2 (Grumbates refuses to move until son avenged by destruction of city).
37. Amm. Marc. 19.8.1–4.

returns to the spectacle of the overwhelming forces which hem the city in on all sides. He also reports on the grim sight of columns of prisoners from a neighbouring fort being led into captivity in Persia.[38] Moreover, within the city there was dispute over tactics. Two Gallic legions which had served Constans' nemesis, Magnentius, in Gaul against Constantius between 351 and 353 had been transferred to the east to keep them out of trouble. Impatient of confinement within the walls, the Gallic soldiers repeatedly begged permission for a night sortie. When this was finally granted, the outcome was unexpectedly positive. The raiders killed many Persians before they were awake, and, but for the alarm being raised in time, could very well have penetrated right through the army to the tent of the Great King himself.[39] Although this made no difference to the respective strengths of the two sides, the achievement of the Gauls provided a temporary boost to the morale of the besieged.

With hindsight, Ammianus was able to report on the wider strategic significance of Amida, and the struggle for influence between Ursicinus, who advocated a raid to relieve Amida, and Sabinianus, 'still among his tombs', who blocked all attempts at action, and who had written backing for his policy in the form of a letter of instructions from Constantius.[40] It is the contrast between the cold, strategic approach of Constantius and Sabinianus, and the horrors which Ammianus had witnessed at first hand, which may explain the sense of anger in his narrative. While other defenders were crucified or led off into captivity,[41] Ammianus slipped out unnoticed and escaped with his life. But he was not yet out of danger. Footsore from walking, to which, 'as a gentleman', he was not accustomed,[42] Ammianus happened on a stray horse – with the mangled body of its dead rider still attached. Then, in desperate need of water, his band came upon a well, with no bucket. Tearing up their own clothes to make a rope, Ammianus and his companions lowered their felt caps into the water to soak it up, then drew them

38. Amm. Marc. 19. 6.1. The fortress is named as Ziata, although Ammianus may have learned that detail later.
39. Amm. Marc.19.6.1–13.
40. Amm. Marc. 19.3.1–2.
41. Amm. Marc. 19.9.2. Aelianus, the *comes* and the tribunes, who had so bravely contributed to the defence, were 'cruelly fixed on stakes' ('patibulis sceleste suffixis') and others, including several *protectores*, were led off as prisoners. On Aelianus at Singara, Amm. Marc. 18.9.3.
42. Amm. Marc. 19.8.7: 'ut insuetus ingenuus'.

back to the surface.[43] Welcoming his good fortune and steering clear of a squadron of Persians in pursuit of some stray Romans, the future historian made his painful way back to Antioch, his native city, which he had never hoped to see again.[44]

Ammianus was not an unbiased historian. He had favourites – notably Ursicinus and the emperor Julian – and he is often opinionated and even uncritical. But he dominates the historiography of the fourth century, for two reasons. One is the sheer amount of detail offered in his account of his own times, and of events of which he was an eyewitness himself or of which he was in a position to receive a privileged account from others. The second is the vividness and immediacy of his writing. While scrupulous in seeking to observe objectivity and impartiality, his failure, on occasion, to do either is part of his attraction; uniquely among the historians of the ancient world, Ammianus the soldier-historian conveys what being at war really meant.

Constans, Magnentius, Julian and the west

Although Ammianus never served, as far as we know, with Constantine's youngest son, he did have access to information on the reign from Constans' minister, Eutherius, who was later to serve as chamberlain to Constantius II, a fact which makes the non-survival of Ammianus' account the more regrettable. As even the disaffected Aurelius Victor conceded, Constans was an effective commander, defeating the Franks in 341 and 342 and the Sarmatians in the winter of 342–3. Writing of Valentinian I (364–75), Ammianus, who had served with Julian in Gaul in the 350s, recollected the fear of Constans still felt by the Alamanni decades later.[45] Moreover, in the winter or early spring of 343, Constans crossed the stormy English Channel to pay a flying visit to Britain. Although his stay lasted only a few weeks, he may have used his time to inspect and perhaps reinforce the forts of the Saxon shore; strong points on the south coast at Portchester, where extensive coin finds date from the 340s to the 370s, and Pevensey, a relatively late addition to the Saxon shoreline, may have benefited from the emperor's presence.[46] From

---

43. Amm. Marc. 19.8.8.
44. Amm. Marc. 19.8.12: 'Antiochiam revisimus insperati'.
45. Amm. Marc. 30.7.5.
46. S. Johnson, *The Roman Forts of the Saxon Shore*, London: Elek, 1976, 137–44. He suggests that Constans may have been responsible for the elevation of the commander

far off Antioch, Libanius, in panegyrical mode,[47] may have exaggerated the significance of the visit. Ammianus' account is lost, but the fact that he combined his account with a digression on the tides and geographical situation of Britain would have served to highlight its importance for his readers. Possibly the historian, writing at Rome forty years after Constans' death, saw in it a significance not apparent at the time – that Constans would be the last emperor of the whole empire to visit Britain in person.

In the years immediately preceding 350, Constans seems to have concentrated on the Danube frontier, perhaps to the detriment of his ties with the armies in Gaul. The Danube had been Constantine's priority for much of the latter part of his reign. A bridge was constructed across the river in 328 from Oescus to Sucidava in Dacia Ripensis, and in the early 330s, he responded to a plea from the Sarmatians for help against the Tervingi, a Gothic group, who were migrating westwards. The result was a lasting treaty with the Tervingi, made in 332, the exact significance of which is disputed,[48] but one consequence may have been an increase in Gothic recruitment into Roman service.[49] Another, which reflects the policy of Constans and Constantius, was an ultimately successful attempt to convert the Goths to Christianity, which was led in the 340s by Ulphilas.[50] Both sides could have perceived this as an attempt to make the Goths more Roman, and Ulphilas was exiled by the anti-Roman factions among the Goths, who also killed some of their Christian converts. But more significant for the future was that the Goths were converted to Constantius' 'Eusebian' or 'Arian' version of Christianity, a fact which would be used against them by their Roman enemies in the later fourth and fifth centuries.

of the Saxon shore to *comes*. Coins of Constans were also found at Bitterne. See also Firmicus Maternus, *On the error of profane religions*, 38.6; Amm. Marc. 20. 1.1. Other later emperors launched their bids for power from Britain, notably Magnus Maximus (383–8) and Constantine III (407–11); neither won clear recognition as a member of an empire-wide imperial college.

47. Lib. *Or.* 59.137–41.

48. Anon. Vales. 6.31; *Consularia Constantinopolitana* s.a. 332, 'the Goths were beaten by the Roman army in the lands of the Sarmatians'; Peter Heather, *Goths and Romans 332–489*, Oxford: Clarendon Press, 1991, 107–15; Heather, *The Goths*, Oxford: Blackwell, 1996, 59–61; M. Kulikowski, *Rome's Gothic Wars*, Cambridge: Cambridge University Press, 2007, 84–7.

49. Euseb. *Vit. Const.* 4.5 (Goths offer tribute but nature not specified); 4.6 (Sarmatians as recruits).

50. Peter Heather and John Matthews, *The Goths in the Fourth Century*, TTH 11, Liverpool: Liverpool University Press, 1991, 133–53.

The military need for Constans' presence on two frontiers at once arguably contributed to a weakening of his ties with the soldiers in Gaul. Although, as we have seen, Constans' death in 350 did not result from a general military uprising,[51] the Gallic army accepted Magnentius, his killer and successor, without apparent difficulty. The immediate result of Constans' death was political and military turbulence – offering opportunities for Rome's external enemies. For a while, the west was split between several local rulers. One Vetranio was proclaimed emperor, while at Rome Constantine's nephew, Nepotianus, mounted a coup and killed Magnentius' praetorian prefect. Nepotianus himself was killed but only after a period of nearly four weeks, during which, we are told, the streets of Rome ran with blood as the partisans of Nepotianus and Magnentius, under the command of his *magister officiorum*, Marcellinus (normally a civilian official), fought for control of the city. Such chaos recalled the bouts of military anarchy which characterised much of the third century. Meanwhile, in the east, Constantius constituted himself Constans' avenger. To cope with the continued threat from Persia, he created his cousin, Fl. Claudius Constantius Gallus, Caesar in the east, to take care of matters in his absence. Neither his march west nor his appointment of Gallus was an option that Constantius would have taken had any other choice been available.

Constantius was to acquire the dubious distinction of being rated as more successful in civil wars than he was against Rome's external enemies. In September 351, he defeated Magnentius at Mursa at a fearful cost in Roman manpower. That disaster overshadows the significance of Constantius' strategy prior to the conflict: to use guile and persuasion, where possible, to avert open war. Constantius' first opponent, Vetranio, was disposed of by peaceful means. Taking advantage of his rival's permission to address the soldiers, Constantius, according to Zosimus/Eunapius, reminded the troops of Constantine's generosity to them, their oaths to be loyal to his sons and how Constans had led and rewarded them in many wars.[52] The soldiers (having been bribed beforehand) acclaimed Constantius and

---

51. See above, pp. 194–6.
52. The view that Constans' attention to his Danubian frontier, which allowed his name to be invoked positively against Vetranio, did alienate some support in Gaul is supported by Philippus' strategy (as reported by Zos. *New History* 2.42) of emphasising Constantine, not Constans, when addressing Magnentius' Gallic army.

deposed Vetranio, who was allowed to retire in safety to Bithynia on a pension.[53]

Would the Gallic army now follow suit and reunite itself with its Danubian associates? Magnentius is alleged to have been worried by approaches made by Philippus, Constantius' envoy, to his Gallic soldiers, reminding them of their (and Magnentius') past loyalty to, not Constans, but Constantine. Magnentius, however, retaliated, to good effect, with a ferocious attack on the dead Constans, combined with assertions of his own unwillingness to take an office which had been forced upon him.[54] The contrasting strategies of Constantius, Philippus and Magnentius, as reported by Zosimus, suggest that the manipulation of soldiers' loyalties was a more complex matter than providing handouts. Money mattered but so too did the emperors' personal presence and relationship with their soldiers. The western armies retained their memories of Constantine; and the Danubian troops, unlike their Gallic counterparts, could still be moved by recollections of Constans. After Magnentius' own death, in 353,[55] and consequent vilification by the victors, his own memory nonetheless conferred status on those who associated themselves with it. Justina, his widow, would marry a rising soldier, Valentinian, who was to be emperor in the west after Julian's death in Persia.

Despite the fall of Magnentius and the purge of his supporters, a sense of crisis remained. In 354, Constantius II campaigned against the Alamanni but his successes were undermined by trouble in his eastern domains, where the Caesar Gallus was deposed and executed for alleged insubordination. The following year provided further evidence of the instability now prevalent in Gaul, due to repeated 'barbarian' incursions and 'long neglect' by emperors.[56] While

---

53. Zos. *New History*, 2. 44. It is possible that Vetranio was a 'plant' by Constantius, assisted by his sister Constantina, to prevent Magnentius from advancing further east. An alternative, which is in line with army behaviour generally and with my view that they were still loyal to the memory of Constans, is that the Danube troops themselves selected a leader, who was not Magnentius, in order to dissociate themselves from his cause.

54. Zos. *New History*, 2.47.

55. For Julian's version of these events, in a panegyric of Constantius, see Julian, *Or.* 1, 30c–32a (Vetranio); 35d–37a (Mursa); 38b–40b (defeats of Magnentius in Italy and Gaul). Ammianus' extant account opens with the purge of Magnentius' supporters after his fall.

56. Amm. Marc. 15.5.2 states that Silvanus' short-lived usurpation in 355 was partly motivated by the unchecked raids of the barbarians and 'long drawn-out lack of attention' (*diuturna incuria*), referring perhaps to Constans (last attested at Trier in 345) and certainly to the distractions caused by Magnentius' efforts to resist Constantius II.

Constantius and his general Arbitio won a further success against a second group of Alamanni, the Lentienses, the internal stability of Gaul was threatened again, albeit briefly, by usurpation. Silvanus, a Frankish leader who had deserted Magnentius for Constantius, revolted, perhaps provoked into action by court intrigue.[57] As ever, Constantius resorted first to deception in preference to open conflict – this time, successfully: his general Ursicinus (and Ammianus) were sent to deal with the problem and Silvanus was killed, having been dragged from a Christian chapel.[58]

In 355, with his presence urgently required elsewhere, Constantius had no option but to appoint yet another Caesar to act as the imperial presence in the west and check the continued raids from across the Rhine into Gaul. His choice was both inevitable and eccentric. Flavius Claudius Julianus, the dead Gallus' half-brother, was Constantius' only surviving relative – but he had no military experience and had spent his life in seclusion, apparently devoted to the study of Greek literature and philosophy. Dressed in imperial purple, the new Caesar was commended publicly to the army by a slightly hesitant Constantius, whose speech was interrupted by, and concluded with, enthusiastic acclamations from the troops. Julian's muttered response, delivered in the original Greek, was less positive: 'purple death has taken me and all-conquering fate'.[59]

Julian had reason to worry. Publicly, Constantius II had welcomed him into the imperial college, associating him with himself in the consulship of 356, and marrying him to Constantius' sister Helena. But Julian's freedom of action was intentionally limited by the continued presence of generals appointed by Constantius, notably Ursicinus (despite doubts at court as to his loyalty) in overall command, the master of the cavalry, Marcellus, and Barbatio, who commanded the infantry. Their presence would counteract Julian's lack of military experience – and any tendency on the Caesar's part to step out of line in other ways. But with several generals in the field simultaneously, operating along an extended frontier, co-ordination was essential, and not invariably forthcoming. After a successful campaigning season in 356, which saw the recapture of Cologne and other towns along the Rhine from the Franks, Julian dispersed his

57. Amm. Marc. 15.5.3–14.
58. Amm. Marc. 15.5.21–31, on Ursicinus and Silvanus. Though forced to act against Silvanus, Ursicinus too would fall victim to scheming courtiers.
59. *Il.* 5. 83; for Julian's alleged unwillingness to abandon his studies at Athens, see also Libanius' funeral oration for the emperor, *Or.* 18, 31.

soldiers for the winter – only to find himself besieged for a month at Sens, with only a small force at his disposal.[60] When Constantius was informed that Marcellus had failed to come to the Caesar's rescue, the master of the cavalry was recalled and sacked, despite his attempts before the consistory to warn his Augustus that Julian was ready to 'fly too high'.[61]

The following year, 357, there was a further failure of two Roman armies to co-operate effectively. A two-pronged attack was launched on the Alamanni by Julian and, from the south, by Barbatio, but the latter's force of 25,000 men was confronted by the enemy before they could link up with the Caesar, and put to flight.[62] The consequence of this military blunder was unexpected. Julian, now with a mere 13,000 men, confronted near Strasbourg a force of Alamanni under seven of their kings, numbering some 35,000. Despite the odds of nearly three to one, and some hesitation on Julian's part about the timing, which was overruled by his advisers,[63] the Romans weighed into the battle, the struggle was fierce and the barbarians were routed; one of their kings, Chonodomarius, was captured after falling off his horse in a bog.[64] The episode had several beneficial consequences. One was that Julian's military reputation in his own right was now fully established in the eyes of his soldiers; doubtless the victory also contributed to his confidence in himself and the favour of his divine protectors (although he was still ostensibly Christian). A second was that he was rid of Barbatio, who took refuge with Constantius at Milan in disgrace. Ammianus' treatment of the 'boorish' Barbatio is uniformly unfavourable. Aside from his 'habitual' slandering of Julian,[65] Barbatio is accused of deliberate incompetence in allowing barbarian raiders to escape unhindered; he even, allegedly, burned part of the Roman fleet deliberately, so that he could not go to Julian's assistance.[66] In Ammianus' narrative, Barbatio, rather than Julian, is made to carry the blame for the two

60. Amm. Marc. 16.3 (Cologne); 16.4.3 (Julian at Sens).
61. Amm. Marc. 16.7.1–3. On Marcellus' vigorous imitation of a bird before the consistory, see Matthews, *Ammianus*, 268, 459–60.
62. Amm. Marc. 16.11.2–15.
63. Amm. Marc. 16.12.8–18 for the debate on the timing (Julian concerned for the effect on soldiers' energy of attacking after long march) and allusions to divine favour.
64. Amm. Marc. 16.12.58–61.
65. Amm. Marc. 16.11.14–15, Barbatio slanders Julian to Constantius 'as usual' (*ut solebat*). He and his wife would be executed on unrelated grounds by Constantius in 359 (Amm. Marc. 16.18.3).
66. Amm. Marc. 16.11.6; 8.

armies' failure to co-ordinate their movements against the Alamanni, a failure which could have cost Rome dear.[67] A third consequence was more long-term. After his victory, Julian was hailed Augustus by his troops. Although he quickly put a stop to the demonstration, news of it would have duly reached Constantius. Constantius had supported Julian against both Marcellus and Barbatio, yet the old story of a tired emperor under threat from a too-successful general was about to be enacted once again.

The culture of war

The Roman *res publica* was, from the beginning, organised for war. In the first part of the fourth century, war was still all-important. Conspicuous splendour, ceremony and hierarchy characterised the late Roman imperial courts and appear far removed from the hardships of military life. But that was not how contemporaries saw it. Discipline, absolute obedience and respect for hierarchies and superiors were values shared by armies and courts alike in the fourth century. Gold-encrusted robes and purple dye impressed the beholder in one sense, but the presence of soldiers with their weapons and standards pressing round the emperor on his tribunal could also be exploited to effect.[68] Even when stationed in a regional capital far from a war zone, the emperor was primarily a war-leader and both he and his court were frequently on the move, prepared to experience on a regular basis the inconveniences, if not the hardships, of travel. Despite the attempts of Constantine, Constantius II, Constans and Julian to take an interest in philosophical and religious controversies, it was not expected that an emperor should also be a philosopher-king; Julian's admiration for Marcus Aurelius, as expressed in his *Caesars*, was a statement of his personal aspirations, not fourth-century reality.[69]

Terminology reinforced the imperial administration's sense of itself as 'military'. The word *militia*, 'service', referred not only to

67. This foreshadows Julian's failure to link up with the army of Procopius in Mesopotamia in 363, the causes of which are unknown. Valens' defeat at Hadrianople in 378 is ascribed to his refusal to await the arrival of the army of Gratian.
68. Cf. Amm. Marc. 20.5.1 on Julian Augustus' appearance before his troops in February 360.
69. E. D. Hunt, 'Julian and Marcus Aurelius', in D. Innes, H. Hine and C Pelling (eds), *Ethics and Rhetoric: Classical Essays for Donald Russell on his 75th Birthday*, Oxford: Oxford University Press, 1995, 287–98. Maxentius' first names were Marcus Aurelius.

the army but to jobs and service at court and in the civilian administration as well. Like the soldiers, administrators were supported by
annona, 'supplies'.[70] Bureaucrats were depicted with belted trousers,
boots and the military cloak (*chlamys*).[71] Most important, as a
symbol of office, was the military-style belt (*cingulum*); one official,
disgraced by Julian, insisted on flaunting his belt, to which he was
no longer entitled, in the emperor's presence,[72] and Valentinian I was
obliged to restore their belts to the *numerarii* (accountants) as a
badge of their military status, after they had been deprived of them
by Julian.[73] Military men and occupants of civilian posts mingled at
court, with varying degrees of co-operation. Predictably, the civilians
coveted the privileges of their military colleagues. Thus, in 326,
Constantine, probably in response to representations from those
affected, declared that his *palatini* were granted the soldiers' legal
right to hold property independently as *peculium castrense* (a
soldier's personal property), because, despite being scholarly
civilians, they endured the dust, toil and long marches which were
the expected hardships of the soldier's life.[74]

Existence on a perpetual war-footing was the product of fear.
Encroaching aliens along the river frontiers of Europe and from
beyond the Tigris and Euphrates were seen as an ever-present threat
to Roman interests. The literary stereotype of the 'barbarian', with
his long hair and attire of animal skins, had little to do with the
integrated Frankish or Gothic recruit in Roman ranks. But 'victory'
was also the most effective means by which an emperor established
his position and undercut the prospects of rivals. To construct a
stable dynasty took time; yet even the sons of Constantine, whose
dynastic position was beyond challenge, were not secure. Therefore
to win victories was one means of ensuring the soldiers' continued
loyalty. But the winning of a series of victories was expensive in
manpower. It is a tribute to the unassuming realism of Constantius
II that he put conservation of manpower consistently, if ingloriously,

70. Ramsay MacMullen, *Soldier and Civilian in the Later Roman Empire*, Cambridgem
MA: Harvard University Press, 1963, 49 (*militia*); 71 (*annona*).
71. Christopher M. Kelly, *Ruling the Later Roman Empire*, Cambridge, MA: Belknap
Press, 2004, 20–1.
72. Amm. Marc. 22.10.5. On belt design in late antiquity, Bishop and Coulston, *Equipment*, 173–9.
73. *Cod. Theod.* 8.1.11 (365).
74. *Cod. Theod.* 6.36.1 (23 May 326). This meant that they had the right to own
independently what they earned in imperial service, even if they had a father, or other
male ascendant, still living.

ahead of accruing victories for their own sake. Yet he had also to live with the consequences. More charismatic or successful generals, like Ursicinus (who was loyal) and Julian (who was not), posed dangers for the incumbent – and for themselves. Constantius was suspicious, because he had to be.

The relative stability of the frontiers for much of the late third and fourth centuries and the military successes of individual emperors, from Diocletian to Galerius to Constantius I, Constantine and his sons, created the sense that the troubles of the third century were left safely behind. But the forces which had undermined imperial unity in the third century had not gone away. These did not consist only of the pressures created by the needs of migrating tribes in Central Europe, the ambitions of the Persian kings or the preference of the areas under most threat, like Gaul and Britain, for local leaders of their own choosing. The effects on the rulers of the Roman Empire itself were ultimately destructive. Emperors could not break themselves of the habit of seeking expensive victories to ensure their own security; the result would be Valens' disastrous defeat by the Goths at Hadrianople in 378, and, ultimately, the permanent political fragmentation of the Western Empire.

CHAPTER 10

Church and empire

From 312, Christian bishops had access to a sympathetic emperor. Naturally, they made the most of it. Constantine's financial contributions to Christian communities strengthened the economic, and thus also the social and political, positions of the favoured bishops and their sees, notably those of Rome and Jerusalem; laws framed in consultation with Christian advisers defined and protected the rights of Christians and their churches. Christians in dispute with non-Christians or with each other were eager to have the emperor on their side, even when, as happened with the Donatists, his intervention was inconclusive. And the rhetoric of his public pronouncements encouraged local self-assertion on the part of Christians and over time diminished support for pagan public cult.

With imperial favour came the risks attendant on increased imperial control, threatening the integrity of institutions which for nearly three centuries had prided themselves on their distance from the imperial order. Lay officials had opportunities to control ecclesiastical process through their involvement as supervisors or observers of church councils and implementers of their decisions. Philagrius of Cappadocia, for example, acted as the imperial hitman against Athanasius, first at the Council of Tyre, then as prefect of Egypt, when Athanasius was expelled in 338, then as escort to the eastern bishops at Sardica in 343.[1] The exercise of imperial patronage could reduce the bishops collectively and individually to the status of clients, expected to express their gratitude, perhaps inappropriately, for emperors' support. The extent of the Christian emperors' active concern with the convening of councils, for example at Nicaea in 325 or Sardica in 343, at which state officials like Strategius Musonianus – or even the emperor – presided, and their insistence that agreement be reached and enforced on matters of doctrine and church discipline, raise the question of how far the church

---

1. *PLRE I* Philagrius 5, p. 694.

allowed itself to be 'absorbed' into the state,[2] and how far the growth of the monastic movement in the Egyptian countryside and of lay devotion to a life of Christian self-denial in the towns was a reaction to the increased 'worldliness' of the church establishment. In fact, as we shall see, Christians retained their right to independent self-regulation, while the beginnings of the monastic movement predate the accession of Constantine.

Bishops, councils and provinces

Early Christian organisation was based on the cities of the Greek Eastern Empire, where the polis had for centuries been the main civic unit. Bishops, their clergy and their congregations were defined by their city and evolved independently of formal central control. Uniformity of belief was maintained, with difficulty, through the exchange of letters between sees, the circulation of writings by those, such as Irenaeus of Lyon in the late second century, who became recognised as spokesmen for orthodox or 'universal' (Catholic) Christianity, and the convening of special synods, such as the meeting of over sixty bishops assembled at Rome to try the case of the Novatians in 250.[3] As time went on, bishops in provinces began to meet together to decide on matters of shared concern. As we shall see,[4] the canons of the council of Elvira, in Spain, dating from sometime in the early fourth century, of the roughly contemporary council of Ancyra, and of Arles, attended by all Gallic bishops in 314, provide important evidence for ecclesiastical self-regulation on a local, provincial level, and for how the Christian communities viewed themselves. They also assume a right to ecclesiastical self-governance incompatible with assumptions that the church was – or ever could be – absorbed into the Roman state.

Although pre-Constantinian Christian organisation was rooted in the secular civic and provincial context, because it was convenient that it should be so, there was no formal agreement that this should

2. See E. D. Hunt, 'The church as a public institution', in *CAH*[2] 13, 238–76, at 239: 'none could be under any illusion that the gathering (at Sardica) was other than an instrument of imperial policy, with the object of forging ecclesiastical unity, especially in the presence of a senior *comes* (Strategius Musonianus) and palace official (Hesychius, *castrensis*) from Constantius' court'; also (on Liberius and Athanasius in 355), p. 249, 'the bishop of Rome was thus no more immune than other church leaders from absorption into the contemporary Roman state'.
3. Euseb. *Hist. eccl.* 6.43.
4. Below, pp. 232–4.

always be the case. Indeed western bishops, who attended Nicaea only in small numbers,[5] would express doubts at Sardica eighteen years later as to whether villages or very small cities should be entitled to a bishop at all; in their opinion, a congregation had to be sufficiently large to merit a bishop, whether it was based in a city or not.[6] This caveat reflects the more limited spread of Christianity particularly in Gaul, where, according to Sulpicius Severus late in the fourth century, Christianity arrived late,[7] and where the north of the region remained largely un-Christianised down to the sixth century.

At Nicaea, in 325, the bishops, who came mostly from the east, confirmed and strengthened the existing organisation by province, by recognising the power of the metropolitan bishop, the bishop of the provincial capital, to give consent to all consecrations of bishops within his province; the metropolitans were also to convene two provincial councils per year to resolve disputes and discuss matters of common concern. But where there was a divergence between the existing ecclesiastical sphere of metropolitan authority and the secular structure, the ecclesiastical prevailed. Rome remained the metropolitan of all of Italy south of Rome (Italia Suburbicaria) and over the next decades, as the 'apostolic' see, acquired increased authority as a court of appeal in ecclesiastical matters.[8] Alexandria retained control not only over all Egypt, despite the Diocletianic provincial subdivisions, but also over 'Libya' and the Pentapolis (Cyrenaica). The see of Jerusalem, not as yet the beneficiary of the imperial largess that would make it one of the principal pilgrimage centres of the east, was treated differently and remained in subordination to Palestinian Caesarea, albeit in an honourable second place. It did not occur to the bishops to consider what might happen if the secular status of metropolitan sees were to be affected by future provincial reorganisations.[9]

5. The Gallic representative came from the small see of Die (Dea Vocontiorum) and was probably selected because of his seniority – certainly not because of the standing of his see.
6. Sardica, Canon 6 (Latin). Such a community might still be entitled to a presbyter of its own, subject to the local bishop. In the east *chorepiscopi*, 'country bishops', were routinely subject to the bishop of the nearest full city.
7. Sulpicius Severus, *Chronicle* 2.32: *serius trans Alpes Dei religione suscepta* ('the religion of God (Christianity) was adopted late on the far side of the Alps').
8. See Amm. Marc. 15.7.10, on Constantius' referral of Athanasius' case to Liberius in 355.
9. As was Basil of Caesarea in the 370s, with the creation of Cappadocia Secunda; and all the bishops of southern Gaul by the elevation of Arles to the status of Gallic metropolitan in 407.

Provincial church councils regulated the behaviour of clergy and
laity within the Christian community, and, on occasion, commented
on issues of wider significance; the bishops at Arles, for example,
briefly signalled their support for the consecration of Caecilian and
their rejection of the Donatist case. The primary concern of provincial councils was with local issues, but regulation of behaviour
which, under Roman law, would incur penal sanctions was also
agreed. The Spanish bishops who met early in the fourth century
at Elvira in Baetica in southern Spain under the chairmanship of
Hosius of Corduba, Constantine's most influential episcopal adviser,
condemned those who committed homicide by magic to perpetual
exclusion from the community;[10] under Roman law, the penalty for
homicide, with or without the assistance of magic, was death, but
for the bishops, the use of magic was an aggravating factor, because
it implied idolatry as well. Sanctions imposed on other forms of
delinquency reveal social assumptions shared by Constantine. Both
Constantine and the bishops believed in the permanence of marriage.
However, while Constantine excluded adultery by a husband from
his list of just causes for a woman to initiate divorce proceedings
unilaterally,[11] the bishops at Elvira, perhaps reflecting a situation
prior to Constantine's law, permitted a woman to leave her adulter-
ous husband, but not to remarry until after he was dead.[12] The
bishops at Ancyra early in the joint reign of Constantine and Licinius
agreed that the private use of soothsayers and divination was unlawful; the bishops imposed excommunication for five years, the
emperor ordered the execution of all concerned.[13] On matters of
detail, the clergy asked the same questions as did Roman lawyers.
The bishops at Elvira excommunicated a mistress who whipped a
slave-girl to death for a fixed period,[14] allowing two years' remission
if the death was accidental and specifying the implement (the lash)
used. A roughly contemporary law of Constantine focuses on the
weapon or other means used by a master to kill a slave to determine
whether or not the death was intentional; if the latter, the master

10. *Conc. Elvira*, canon 6. The date is uncertain. John Richardson, *The Romans in
Spain*, Oxford: Blackwell, 1996, 241–5, believes that the lack of reference to the Great
Persecution or the Edict of Milan, supports a date pre-303.
11. *Cod. Theod.* 3.16.1.
12. *Conc. Elvira*, canon 9.
13. *Conc. Ancyra*, canon 24; *Cod. Theod.* 9.16.1–2.
14. *Conc. Elvira*, canon 5. The canon also specified that the slave must have died within
three days of the beating, thus guaranteeing that the beating was the cause of death.

could be prosecuted (and potentially executed) for homicide.[15] There was thus consensus between emperor and bishops on how the law should work in principle, reflecting the shared culture of ecclesiastical and Roman lawyers. On penal policy, the church, unlike the Roman state system, allowed space for reform and repentance; failure to do both endangered not only the body but also the soul.

Church council regulations are not merely evidence for the content of the *lex Christiana*: it was assumed that they worked in practice. As might be expected, the efficacy of church regulations depended on their wider civic and social context. Christians' formulation of an alternative penal system could be viable only if it was able to function separately from, and independently of, that of the state. For the penances imposed by the churches to have meaning, there could be no invoking of the state penal system by accusers. It was obvious that, for example, the person who consulted a soothsayer could not be both executed and excommunicated by the church for five years. Similarly, the penances stipulated by the church for adulterers could apply only if the guilty parties (the married woman and her lover) did not experience the criminal penalties, exile and perhaps death, imposed by the state under the Lex Julia on adulteries.

How, then, was it possible for the ecclesiastical process to sideline that of the state? For the 'public' criminal process to be activated, individuals, not the state, were obliged to initiate a criminal process before the governor. The accuser was solely responsible for constructing the case against the accused, which would then be tested in court by the presiding judge and opposing advocates. Ancient Rome had no concept of a police force as such, still less detective agencies or bureaux of investigation. If no accuser took action, the person suspected of a criminal act suffered no consequences. The disciplines imposed by the bishops therefore, while they reflected assumptions similar to those of Romans in general, also presupposed that resort to the state's courts was not automatic. 'Criminal' acts could be controlled and penalised by alternative means. The line between state and church jurisdiction was thus very carefully drawn and state process and penalties were kept rigorously separate from their

---

15. *Cod. Theod.* 9.12.1, of 319. A later law (*Cod. Theod.* 9.12.2) appears to give intention less prominence, concentrating instead on the legitimacy of the punitive function of a master's chastisement of slaves.

ecclesiastical equivalents. One may suspect that the separation of jurisdictions also worked because the penal policies adopted by the church councils accorded with a wider social desire for alternative forms of regulation to those of the state, which acknowledged human fallibility and permitted space for repentance and reconciliation.

Bishops and cities

The numbers of clergy in each city establishment and the wealth of local churches varied widely. In a letter written in the mid-third century and cited in extracts by Eusebius, the church at Rome is described as having:[16]

> Forty-six presbyters, seven deacons, seven subdeacons, forty-two acolytes, fifty-two exorcists, readers and janitors and over fifteen hundred widows and persons in distress, all supported by the grace and kindness of our Lord.

This establishment was exceptionally large, a response in part to the size of a city which, at its height, contained over a million people, but also a reflection of the offerings made by the wealthy laity, which permitted the operation to grow and fund itself. Expansion was assisted by the convention that priests and clergy should be self-supporting, while not allowing their need to make a living to override their religious duties. Canons of provincial councils restricted the trading activities of bishops and clergy to the province within which they were resident; they could be economically active beyond the provincial boundaries, but only through agents.[17]

The powers of the bishop over clergy and congregation were extensive.[18] He controlled the finances of his church, allocating funds to charity and almsgiving, building and maintenance of churches and the support of clergy where appropriate. He also had a role as a fund-raiser, soliciting and receiving offerings (*oblationes*) from the laity.[19] The most powerful of all the Christian laity was the

---

16. Euseb. *Hist. eccl.* 6.43.11.
17. *Conc. Elvira*, canon 19.
18. Claudia Rapp, *Holy Bishops in Late Antiquity: The Nature of Christian Leadership in an Age of Transition*, Berkeley: University of California Press, 2005, 23–55; also 208–34.
19. R. Finn, *Almsgiving in the Later Roman Empire: Christian Promotion and Practice, 313–450*, Oxford: Oxford University Press, 2006, 35–56.

emperor.[20] In the *Liber Pontificalis*, a history of the bishops of Rome compiled in the early Middle Ages,[21] a list is provided of the donations made by Constantine and later emperors for the endowments of churches at Rome. For the earliest Constantinian church, St John Lateran, built on the site of the camp of Maxentius' loyal *equites singulares*, the gifts included gold decoration for the building itself, along with chandeliers of silver and gold, hung with dolphins, and numerous liturgical vessels made of precious metal.[22] Each is listed by weight. Provision was also made for the lighting and other running costs by the gifting to the church of named estates, identified also by location, and their revenues. The gifts may have been the proceeds of conquest. St John Lateran was funded by revenues from estates in Italy and Africa, formerly controlled by Maxentius. By contrast, the later endowments of St Peter's date from after Constantine's conquest of Licinius and were drawn from the suburbs of Antioch and Alexandria and elsewhere in Egypt 'given' to Constantine by their owners.[23] Many such benefactions were tied to specific purposes and provided no assistance to the 'poor of Christ' who were theoretically the church's main responsibility.[24]

The connection between foundation, endowment and pre-existing imperial property emerges from other Constantinian foundations. Among them was the mausoleum of Helena, his mother, who was interred in a porphyry sarcophagus with 'medallions', initially intended for him. The site of Helena's burial place was the basilica of Marcellinus and Peter the exorcist, which was partly funded by Helena's own estate at Laurentum. Its precious metal endowments included four silver candelabra (200 lb each); a gold chandelier shaped like a crown with 120 dolphins (30 lb) and twenty silver chandeliers (20 lb each); three gold chalices, decorated with jewels (10 lb each); and in front of Helena's grave, a silver altar weighing 200 lb. Although the lists sound impressive, the total revenues for the church at Rome from these endowments was less than a quarter of the revenues ascribed to the wealthy Christian senatorial woman

20. Finn, *Almsgiving*, 56–8.
21. See Raymond Davis, *The Book of Pontiffs (Liber Pontificalis)*, TTH 5, Liverpool: Liverpool University Press, 1989, rev. edn 2010.
22. Davis, *Pontiffs*, 16–18.
23. On St Peter's on the Vatican Hill, see John Curran, *Pagan City and Christian Capital: Rome in the Fourth Century*, Oxford: Oxford University Press, 2000, 109–15, with full bibliography at 109, n.197.
24. Finn, *Almsgiving*, 60–5.

Melania the Younger in the early fifth century, and a mere tenth of what the wealthiest senators could dispose of as annual income.[25]

The bishop's public persona as a preacher was key to the perceptions held of his church in the wider community.[26] The frequent occurrence of Christian festivals, along with the celebration of Sunday (the Lord's Day). gave the bishop regular opportunities to display his skills as a public speaker to all comers, and the theatrical potential of the office was further enhanced by the role of spectacle in the processions held in honour of saints and other Christian holy days. As the number of saints' days in the calendar expanded, so the shape of the year also changed. Many saints were favoured by their cities because they were 'local', in the sense that they were martyred, or lived and died as confessors of the faith, in the community of which they were now invited to be patrons. Although this development accelerated in the latter part of the fourth century, the variety of the entries in the Roman Calendar of 354, which range from depictions of City Fortunes and the planets to lists of the birthdays of emperors, consuls, urban prefects and bishops of Rome, show that Christian institutions were already coexisting with traditional observances.[27]

Bishops were chosen by election and confirmed by consecration.[28] The high public profile of bishops and the potential for the exercise of patronage and influence through control of the local church revenues made the role an attractive one for careerists of a perhaps less spiritual bent. The overnight transformation of powerful laymen into bishops was inhibited by rules which insisted that a potential bishop must first pass through the lower clerical orders of reader, deacon and priest.[29] Despite this, the filling of an episcopal vacancy, especially in a metropolitan or imperial capital, could provoke unwelcome outside interest and internal strife. The 'constituencies' in episcopal elections consisted of the clergy, sometimes the local

---

25. Hunt, 'Church as public institution', 261; on rich senators, Olympiodorus, Fragment 41, 2.
26. See M. P. Cunninghman and P. Allen (eds), *Preacher and Audience: Studies in Early Christian and Byzantine Homilies*, Leiden: Brill, 1998.
27. For contents of Calendar, see Michelle Salzman, *On Roman Time: The Codex-Calendar of 354 and the Rhythms of Urban Life in Late Antiquity*, Berkeley: University of California Press, 1990, 23–60. It should be noted that no Christian holidays are listed in the calendar section (VI) itself.
28. See Peter Norton, *Episcopal Elections 250–600: Hierarchy and Popular Will in Late Antiquity*, Oxford: Oxford University Press, 2007.
29. *Conc. Sardica* (Latin), canon 13.

nobility, and the 'plebs Dei', the ordinary laity, including the poor, for whom the church was responsible. Popular endorsement, or the appearance of it, was necessary if a bishop was to be effective as an arbitrator of disputes among his laity or a fund-raiser to finance his church and clergy. A second stage in the creation of a bishop was his consecration by at least three other bishops in his province, including the metropolitan;[30] the Donatist opponents of Caecilian claimed not that he had handed over sacred books but that one of his consecrating bishops had done so, thus making Caecilian's consecration at Carthage invalid.

Although there were some high-profile imperial interventions in the process of choosing a bishop, these were largely confined to the capital cities in which the emperors took a special interest. Constantine, for example, meddled with the election of a bishop at Antioch, by sending a letter of advice,[31] and his son Constantius II went further, transferring his favourite Eusebius of Nicomedia to Constantinople, in contravention of the canons which forbade such translations. In cities where crowd violence was a traditional, even accepted, way of expressing public opinion, episcopal elections could be attended by mob violence. In 342, at Constantinople, an imperial official sent to impose a candidate was lynched by a mob;[32] and in 367, according to Ammianus, the corpses of 137 people were left in a basilica, the consequence of street battles between the supporters of the two contenders, Damasus and Ursinus, for the bishopric of Rome.[33]

The bishop had long exercised judicial functions within his Christian community, which expanded as the fourth century progressed. The aim of the 'bishop's hearing' (*episcopalis audientia*) was to reconcile the parties to a dispute, rather than to impose a settlement on them. Bishops thus conducted themselves in the manner of what the Romans saw as an arbitrator, an adjudicator, whose authority was agreed by the parties, who also agreed to abide by his verdict and thus 'end' their dispute, rather than pursuing it further through various appeal procedures. As congregations grew larger and the

30. *Conc. Nicaea*, canons 4 and 6.
31. Euseb. *Vit. Const.* 3.59.
32. Amm. Marc. 14.10.2 (on the son of the official); Socrates, *Hist. eccl.* 2.13; Sozom. *Hist. eccl.* 3.7. *PLRE I*, Hermogenes 1, pp. 422–3.
33. Amm. Marc. 27.3.13. See also *Collectio Avellana*, 1.7. In the end, order was restored by the prefect of the city, Vettius Agorius Praetextatus, a noted supporter of traditional Roman religion and mystery cults.

influence of Christian leaders in cities became more pervasive, resort to the bishop's hearing became more commonplace. The bishop thus came to exercise a jurisdiction in civil matters that provided an alternative, cheaper and often more expeditious means of achieving dispute resolution than was offered by the secular power.[34]

Less is known about the lay townsfolk, who provided the funds for the support of the churches' activities and audiences for the public activities of the bishops and clergy. The active involvement of the Spanish-born lay patron Lucilla in the opening stages of the Donatist controversy at Carthage shows that individual members of the laity were not passive recipients of episcopal instruction;[35] they could also seek to control events. The resolutions of provincial synods illustrate the problems of lay, as well as clerical, behaviour that bishops might be obliged to address. There were, for example, converts from disreputable professions, such as charioteers or touring actors; both were warned to give up their professional activities or be excluded from communion.[36] Outright exclusion was prescribed for those who broke the commandment about bearing false witness against another. The practice of usury was banned, although the laity were excommunicated only if they had failed to respond to a formal warning.

The criminalisation of dissent

The status of clergy in relation to the law is one of the areas in which we can see most clearly the extent to which Christianity was, or was not, absorbed into the state. As we shall see, alleged criminal offences featured prominently in the rhetoric of churchmen eager to blacken the characters of opponents in the eyes of their fellow Christians, the emperor and the secular authorities. These allegations were intended to be taken seriously and their deployment in the service of ecclesiastical rivalries raised the issue of whether offences against Christianity or right belief, however defined, could themselves become subject to the Roman secular criminal process.

---

34. Rapp, *Holy Bishops*, 242–52; Jill Harries, *Law and Empire in Late Antiquity*, Cambridge: Cambridge University Press, 1999, 191–211.
35. Optat. 1, 16. On Lucilla, described as a 'senatorial lady' (*clarissima femina*), see A. Mandouze, *Prosopographie Chrétienne du bas-empire. I: Afrique (303–533)*, Paris: CNRS, 1982, Lucilla 1, p. 649.
36. *Conc. Arelate*, canons 4–5.

The problem became urgent in the aftermath of Nicaea. Increasingly, feuding bishops sought to enlist the power of the emperor and the state on their own behalf. Ecclesiastical polemic came to focus not solely or even mainly on doctrinal differences but on the alleged criminal behaviour of opponents, behaviour which, if formally brought to trial in a law court and proved, would result in punishment by the secular authorities. The crucible for conflict was the city of Alexandria, which had a long history of inter-community conflict between Jews and Greeks, now further complicated by the presence of the Christian congregation and its turbulent leaders. The bishops of Alexandria faced multiple challenges to their authority from the followers of Arius and their supporters elsewhere in the Eastern Empire; from the followers of Meletius of Lycopolis, who even established an alternative bishopric in Alexandria in the 330s; and from the highly educated and articulate non-Christians. The city's general ambience encouraged a culture of direct action, even of physical violence against opponents, which was to persist through the fourth century, culminating in the lynching of the pagan philosopher Hypatia in 415. From the imperial standpoint, the safeguarding of public order was a priority and those, including bishops, who were shown to be responsible for violence, riots and other disturbances were unlikely to receive a favourable hearing at the imperial court.

This background helps to explain the problems encountered by Alexander's successor as bishop, Athanasius, throughout his long and turbulent career, down to his death in 371.[37] On succeeding his mentor in June 328, Athanasius received a direct command from Constantine to reinstate bona fide Christians, including, by implication, Arius and his supporters, and the Melitians:[38]

> Having therefore knowledge of my will, grant free admission to all
> who wish to enter the church. For if I learn that you have hindered
> any who lay claim to membership, or debarred them from entrance,

37. On Athanasius and Constantine in the context of the power politics of the time, see T. D. Barnes, *Athanasius and Constantius: Theology and Politics in the Constantinian Empire*, Cambridge, MA: Harvard University Press, 1993, 19–33; on Athanasius' 'misconduct', resulting in schism, R. P. C. Hanson, *The Search for the Christian Doctrine of God: The Arian Controversy*, Edinburgh: T. and T. Clark, 1988, 239–73.
38. Cited by Athanasius, *Apology against the Arians* 59 = J. Stevenson, *A New Eusebius: Documents Illustrating the History of the Church to* AD *337*, 2nd edn, London: SPCK, 1987, 310.

> I will immediately send someone to depose you at my command and remove you from your place.

In the years that followed, Athanasius had also to handle challenges from the followers of Meletius. One letter from a distressed Melitian, Callistus, complained bitterly of violence inflicted by Athanasian partisans, backed by elements of the military, on his colleagues, during the course of which a bishop was allegedly confined in the meat market, monks were beaten and temporarily imprisoned, and clergy flung into prison.[39]

More credence may be attached to Callistus' complaint than to the multiple charges of violence which had accumulated against Athanasius by 335. In that year, the Council of Tyre, which consisted largely of bishops opposed to Athanasius, heard that the bishop of Alexandria was guilty inter alia of breaking the sacred chalice of one Ischyras through his agent the priest Macarius, overturning an episcopal chair, false imprisonment of, and assaults on, various bishops and clergy, and the murder of one bishop, Arsenius. Inconveniently for the accusers, Arsenius had been discovered alive and well – but, they alleged, had nonetheless been the victim of serious violence:

> A bishop under the jurisdiction of Athanasius named Plusian had, at the command of his chief, burnt the house of Arsenius, fastened him to a column, and maltreated him with thongs and then imprisoned him in a cell. They further stated that Arsenius escaped from the cell through a window and, while he was sought for, remained for a while in hiding; that, as he did not appear, they naturally supposed him to be dead.

This indictment of Athanasius reflects a change in the character of conflict between the bishops. Athanasius was not accused, as Arius had been, of heresy but of serious crimes, including magic and violence, for which he would be liable to capital punishment if accused in the public secular courts. Moreover, the assembly at Tyre was packed with opponents of Athanasius. In desperation, the bishop fled to Constantinople and attempted to intercept Constantine on his return from a riding expedition.[40] When Constantine, after some hesitation, instituted further inquiries, the opponents of

---

39. For analysis of this episode, Barnes, *Athanasius and Constantius*, 32.
40. Athanasius, *Apology against the Arians* 36; Socrates, *Hist. eccl.* 1.34–5; Sozom. *Hist. eccl.* 2.28.

Athanasius dropped most of the charges examined at Tyre but added a further accusation, that the bishop planned to intercept the grain ships sailing from Alexandria to Constantinople. These opponents would doubtless have recollected that the pagan philosopher Sopatros, previously on friendly terms with Constantine, had been executed a few years before on the grounds that he had sought to disrupt the corn supply by magic.[41] Perhaps worn out by the constant trickle of accusations, Constantine ordered Athanasius to leave Alexandria and go into exile in Gaul, but did not replace him as bishop.

In classical law, doctrinal incorrectness was not a crime. But, as we have seen above, a depraved *mens* could be identified by the bad behaviour of its owner. Although it was the latter which was punishable in law, it was the former which gave rise to it. As was also true of the enforcement of legal sanctions against the Christians under Diocletian, it was not obvious how a process directed against theological dissidence should work. Athanasius, though accused of crimes of violence punishable under the Lex Julia *de vi*, never faced a secular court; he was judged by councils of his peers. One consequence of this contamination of the ecclesiastical by the secular, perhaps not fully appreciated at the time, was the beginnings of the assimilation of ecclesiastical offences to secular forms of wrongdoing, and their resultant punishments. In an undated decree against Arius, addressed 'to the bishops and people', Constantine branded him and his followers with the Roman legal disability of *infamia* (loss of civil rights and legal status) and ordered the burning of all his books.[42] Moreover, in an exercise in labelling which shows complete disregard for the difference between a pagan and a heretic, Constantine ordered the 'Arians' to be designated as 'Porphyrians', people who accepted Porphyry's arguments against the Christians:

> Since Arius had imitated wicked and impious persons, it is just that he should undergo the like *infamia*. Since Porphyry, that enemy of piety, having composed licentious treatises against religion, found a suitable recompense, such as from that time onward branded

41. Eunap. *VS* 462; Socrates, *Hist. eccl.* 1.1.5 on the story that he refused Constantine's plea for forgiveness from the old gods for the killing of Fausta and Crispus.
42. Socrates, *Hist. eccl.* 1.9.30–31; Caroline Humfress, *Orthodoxy and the Courts in Late Antiquity*, Oxford: Oxford University Press, 2007, 225–7; the reading of *infamia* here as being the legal term and not a vague threat of a bad reputation is confirmed by reference to the measure by Theodosius II in 425 against the heretic Nestorius (*Cod. Theod.* 16.5.66 = *Cod. Just.* 1.5.6.)

him with *infamia*, overwhelming him with deserved reproach, his impious writings also having been destroyed; so now it seems fit that Arius and such as hold his sentiments should be named as Porphyrians, that they may take their appellation from those whose conduct they have imitated. And in addition to this, if any treatise composed by Arius should be discovered, let it be consigned to the flames.

The intrusion of the secular criminal law into ecclesiastical disputes was potentially catastrophic.[43] Other factors, however, mitigated the effects of this development. In a culture very aware of the characters and locations of the different courts that could be selected for the hearing of disputes, Constantine and his successors observed the convention that ecclesiastical and civil offences alleged against the clergy should be a matter only for the church courts and councils, but backed by the emperor as enforcer. Church leaders themselves became more insistent that clergy could be judged only in church courts, and should avoid becoming entangled with the state's courts.[44] Moreover, the risks of engaging in the secular process, paradoxically, provided a safeguard. The rhetoric of criminal accusation indulged in by the feuding bishops did not extend to the lodging of formal accusations before the secular courts, because frivolous charges were discouraged by the rule that the accuser, if he failed, was liable to the same penalty which 'threatened' the accused.[45] In that respect at least, therefore, the emperor – and the fearsome penal apparatus at his disposal – was kept at a safe distance.

The increased intensity of episcopal feuding after Nicaea cannot be blamed on any one action of Constantine or of individual bishops. Whatever the real character of Athanasius – whose version of events was to dominate the record – the divisions in the Alexandrian church, the involvement of other bishops on both sides, and the schism in rural Egypt caused by Melitius all predated Constantine's victory in the east in 324, and Athanasius' disputed consecration in 328. But the close intellectual interest taken by

43. As shown by the execution of the Priscillianists on charges of magic by the local Augustus, Magnus Maximus, in Gaul in 386. The bishops who accused Priscillian were themselves excommunicated by a section of the Gallic church. See H. Chadwick, *Priscillian of Avila: The Occult and the Charismatic in the Early Church*, Oxford: Oxford University Press, 1976.
44. The *Liber Pontificalis*' entry for Julius (bishop of Rome, 336–52), *Lib. Pont.* 36, mentions that he issued a decree ordering that no cleric should take part in any lawsuit, but should litigate only in a church.
45. Riccobono, *FIRA* 1, 459–60, lines 10–23 (edict on accusations).

Constantine in the deliberations at Nicaea raised the stakes: the ecclesiastical faction which could gain imperial backing would also enjoy a decisive advantage over its opponents. The techniques of the factions used to gain that support therefore became more extreme, the accusations against opponents more damaging. To Constantine's credit, he appears to have understood the motivations behind the rhetorical denunciations of one faction by the other; he therefore, as a rule, took a prudently sceptical approach. In the end, Athanasius fell victim not to the specific accusations made against him but to the accumulated evidence that he was a trouble-maker.

Constans, Constantius II and the bishops

The accession of Constantine's three sons, quickly reduced to two, changed the dynamic of the relationship between bishops and emperors. For the first time, feuding Christian leaders could approach two emperors, offering alternative, and equal, sources of authority and patronage. Constantine II had allowed Athanasius to return to Alexandra as its bishop, perhaps unaware of Athanasius' condemnation at Tyre a few years before (335); by setting aside an inconvenient decision of a council of bishops, he created a precedent (perhaps inadvertently) for imperial intervention in the churches' internal disciplinary processes. Athanasius' two associates, Paul of Constantinople and Marcellus of Ancyra, were also allowed back, but were quickly thrown out again. After two attempts, Constantius succeeded in 338 in evicting Athanasius, who took refuge in Rome; he was replaced in Alexandria by George of Cappadocia. Constantius' justification would have been that he was upholding the verdict against the bishop reached by the Council of Tyre in 335; he may also have wished to assert himself against Constantine II's intervention outside his agreed sphere of authority.

In 341, however, a council at Rome cleared Athanasius of the charges made against him at Tyre and ordered his restoration to Alexandria – in direct contravention of the verdict reached by Constantius II. The backing of Constans was key to the confidence of the Roman bishops and Athanasius. No council of bishops in Constantine's lifetime had ever openly defied the will of that emperor (although the Donatists resisted successfully in other ways) and the constitutional position was unprecedented. In an effort to avoid further uncertainty, Constans called a group of eastern bishops to Trier to hear their side of the case, while Julius, the bishop of Rome, asked for a general council to be convened under the joint auspices of the two emperors. In 343, some seventy-six 'Eusebian' bishops and ninety-four 'Nicene' or 'Athanasian' bishops met at Sardica to resolve their differences.[46]

The outcome of Sardica was a disaster for church unity, so prized by Constantine and (in theory) by his sons as the bedrock of their religious policy. The western bishops, who arrived first, endorsed the decisions of the Rome council and admitted Athanasius and his associates to communion with them. The eastern bishops, who had first assembled at Philippopolis, just within Constantius' domains, under the aegis of various lay notables, including the prefect Strategius Musonianus, were furious that decisions had been pre-empted, and congregated in the imperial palace at Sardica. Despite attempts by Constantine's favourite bishop, the aged Hosius of Corduba, to bring the sides together, no serious discussions took place. Instead, separate councils were held, both at Sardica, resulting in two distinct sets of resolutions, both claiming to represent the view of the Christian community as a whole. The western group, confident in the support of Constans, was especially assertive, insisting in a letter to Constantius that provincial governors, whose responsibility was public business, should avoid interference with lawsuits involving the clergy, and any form of intimidation of innocent Christians.[47]

At the heart of the crisis was the unresolved question of where authority for ecclesiastical decisions ultimately lay in a divided empire. The clear status of Nicaea as a world council and the presence there of Constantine, the sole Augustus, made open attacks on its authority difficult. But the effects on Christian unity of an ecclesiastical establishment divided on the same territorial lines as the imperial college itself was revealed in the aftermath of Sardica. The two emperors came close to war, as Constans insisted, with characteristic bluntness, on the rapid restoration of Athanasius and his allies to their sees: 'if you were to refuse to take this action, be assured that I will come in person and restore them to the thrones which were theirs, even against your will'.[48] Constantius backed down, restored Athanasius and bided his time.

The increased confidence of groupings of church leaders in their defiance of emperors was directly due to those emperors' failure

46. For the numbers, see H. Hess, *The Early Development of Canon Law and the Council of Serdica*, Oxford: Oxford University Press, 2002, 101–2.
47. Cited by Hilary of Poitiers, *To Constantius* I = *CSEL* 65, 181–2.
48. Socrates, *Hist. eccl.* 2.22.5.

to present a united front. It was an irony that both Constantius II and Constans were motivated by the same desire as had actuated Constantine – the preservation of harmony and 'concord' in the church. Both were eager for harmony, in their terms, and they differed profoundly over what the terms were. The reason was partly that, whatever their personal views may have been, each believed that he represented the balance of church opinion within his domain: the east may well have had a majority of Eusebians at this stage, while the west, which contained far fewer Christians, was almost solidly for Athanasius. The territorial division of authority between the two emperors provided justification and support for those bishops under the rule of each who thought like him. Divisions thus became self-reinforcing, widening the gap between east and west. Moreover, because a choice of imperial patron was available, it became acceptable, as it had not been under Constantine, openly to challenge imperial authority in the matter of 'right' religion. Sardica and its aftermath were not the cause but the expression of deep-rooted divisions which were unlikely to be resolved while both emperors remained alive.

The murder of Constans by Magnentius in 350 was, as later church historians observed, a blow to Athanasius' supporters, made worse by Constantius' close engagement with the minutiae of ecclesiastical feuding. Observing Constantius' policies towards the Christians from the outside, Ammianus concluded that the emperor was too taken up with superstition and tiny points of dispute; he also complained about the burden on the public post created by numerous bishops in transit to councils.[49] In fact, there were only three 'oecumenical' councils in Constantius' reign: Sardica in 343, at which, as we have seen, the eastern and western delegations failed to co-operate on anything, and the joint councils at Rimini and Seleucia in 359. However, there were smaller gatherings also and frequent journeys taken by bishops on embassies to each other or to the emperor – or perhaps into enforced exile.

The Christian perspective on their arguments over orthodoxy differed. It may seem strange to us that disputes over 'Arianism' (or, more accurately, 'Eusebians')[50] should have proved so divisive for so long after the main players were dead (Alexander of Alexandria in

49. Amm. Marc. 21.16.18.
50. As argued by David M. Gwynn, *The Eusebians: The Polemic of Athanasius of Alexandria and the Construction of the 'Arian' Controversy*, Oxford: Oxford University Press, 2007.

328, Arius in 335). But, underlying the apparently technical disputes concerning the nature of God the Father and God the Son (and, in due course, the Holy Spirit as well) was a deep conviction that the truth was all-important, because it was on its ownership of the truth that the claims of Christianity to be the sole 'right religion' rested. As the bishops on all sides argued, truth lay ultimately in a right reading of the Gospels. Each side claimed that its reading of scripture was correct and that the other had imported new ideas not authorised by the texts, thus corrupting and abandoning the truth as revealed through Jesus. In their relentless ideological war on *superstitio*, or the false religions practised by polytheists and pagan monotheists, Christians could not allow those who had 'chosen' the wrong path ('heresy' derives from the Greek word for choice) to spread 'false religion' within their own ranks. From their own perspective, the positions of Athanasius and his adherents on the one side and the 'Eusebians' and their successors on the other differed more profoundly than the rather specialised nature of their differences might suggest. On a more practical level, there were livelihoods at stake, as those bishops convicted by their peers of heresy or other misdemeanours were liable to be expelled from their sees into internal exile, a sentence enforced by state intervention.

By 349, Constantius was ready to reassert his authority and both Athanasius and his crony Paul of Constantinople were again sentenced to exile. Paul was spirited out of Constantinople by the prefect Philippus, prominent among Constantius' lay partisans, imprisoned in Cucusus in Cappadocia and killed there in 351. Athanasius, however, confident in the strength of his local support, simply ignored the order and played for time. Only in 355, after Magnentius had been suppressed and several more abortive councils had been held at Sirmium (351), Arles (353) and Milan (355), was Athanasius finally removed from his see. He would spend the rest of Constantius' reign in hiding, emerging once again in the 360s to reclaim his right in Alexandria. In 359, two further councils were held in parallel at Rimini (Ariminum) and Seleucia and the bishops were obliged, at last, to agree to a creed drafted by the emperor himself at Sirmium in May that year. Those who openly dissented were, again, deposed and exiled.[51]

The change in what was acceptable in ecclesiastical discourse,

51. For spirited narratives from a later perspective, see Socrates, *Hist. eccl.* 2.6–47, and Sozom. *Hist. eccl.* books 3 and 4.

when directed to or at emperors, became apparent after the death of Constans, whose authority in life had upheld the decisions of the western councils. As ruler of the west, Constantius, the opponent of Athanasius, found himself in a minority. Few bishops came out in his support: two only, Saturninus of Arles and Paternus of Périgueux, are certainly attested for Gaul. And in Milan, when the see fell vacant, Constantius was obliged to import an easterner, Auxentius, as no local Eusebian was available. Without consensus between east and west, his attempts to impose an empire-wide uniformity of belief on his fractious bishops depended ultimately on the open use of force and intimidation. Although even Athanasius tried to restrain his language, while there was hope of reconciliation with Constantius, he and others finally turned on the emperor, labelling him the Antichrist, because he persecuted Christians as Nero, Decius and Galerius had done before him.[52] Harking back to the rhetoric of usurpation and legitimation which had characterised Christian writings on the persecuting *tyranni*, Maximinus Daza, Maxentius and the rest, Athanasius, Hilary of Poitiers (a signatory of Seleucia under protest) and others challenged the right of Constantius, as another persecutor of Christians, to rule at all. For an emperor dogged by insecurity, to be labelled a *tyrannus* and usurper would have struck a sensitive chord.[53]

The accusations levelled by Christians against each other fuelled conflict and adversely affected the perceptions of outsiders. Athanasius, who maintained his position against opponents in Alexandria by 'the systematic use of violence and intimidation',[54] alleged similar behaviour on the part of the bishops who had condemned him. After Sardica, the eastern bishops were accused of causing the execution of innocent arms workers at Hadrianople and the unlawful exiling of bishops and priests, who were also subjected to gratuitous violence, and even killed. The eastern bishops counterattacked with denunciations not only of Athanasius but also of his associates, such as Marcellus of Ancyra:[55]

---

52. Barnes, *Athanasius and Constantius*, 127; 150–1.
53. See Sonia Laconi, *Costanzo II: ritratto di un imperatore eretico*, Rome: Herder Editrice, 2004, 87–118, on Constantius as the *tyrannus* of all *tyranni* in the invective of Lucifer of Cagliari. Lucifer, whose invective was based on Cicero and who also described Constantius as the new Catiline, was an extreme Athanasian.
54. Barnes, *Athanasius and Constantius*, 32; P. Lond. 1914.
55. Hilary of Poitiers, *Against Valens and Ursacius* 1.9, trans. Lionel Wickham (1997), 26.

> There took place ... after Marcellus the heretic's return, house-
> burnings and various kinds of aggressive act. He dragged naked
> presbyters into the forum and ... openly and publicly profaned the
> consecrated body of the Lord hanging round the bishops' necks.
> Holy virgins vowed to God and Christ, their clothes dragged off, he
> exposed with horrifying foulness in the forum and the city centre to
> the gathered populace.

These accusations of public violence and assaults on the values at the
heart of Christianity are in part characteristic of the late antique
rhetoric of victimhood, by which the speaker routinely but not
always truthfully represented himself as the innocent victim of
violence and oppression.[56] However, as we have seen, they imported
allegations of criminal behaviour that were traditionally handled by
the secular courts.[57] Despite the violence of the language (and of the
acts alleged), the bishops avoided resort to the state's courts, when
dealing with their own.

Ammianus' account of the expulsion of bishop Liberius from
Rome in 355 for supporting Athanasius makes a characteristically
careful distinction between offences alleged by rumour and proved
in a court of law.[58] In Ammianus' account, Liberius was accused
formally before Constantius of opposing the emperor's commands
and the 'decrees' of a majority of his fellow bishops. The reason
for the decrees had been the behaviour of Athanasius, who was
'persistently rumoured' to have meddled with matters outside his
province, and had therefore been deposed. Liberius' offence against
Constantius was his failure to endorse the exile of Athanasius, on the
grounds that no one should be condemned in absentia, which
amounted to disobedience to an imperial order. But Athanasius
was also tainted by 'rumours' that he had practised magic; he had
reportedly told the future by divination from birds, as well as having
done other things inconsistent with Christianity. All this, wrote
Ammianus, was no more than rumour or report; the canny historian
knew better than to believe everything he was told.

---

56. Harries, *Law and Empire*, 166.
57. Cf. Humfress, *Orthodoxy and the Courts*, 226, on Constantine's denunciation of
Porphyry in 324 (Socrates, *Hist. eccl.* 1.9) and his branding with *infamia*: 'the *legal*
censure of divergent theological belief was achieved by defining a new group (Arius and
his supporters) and branding it with an old name'.
58. Amm. Marc. 15.7.6–10.

'The desert made a city'

In the midst of ecclesiastical turmoil, there emerged a celebration of the virtues of silence, a *Life* of the Egyptian holy man Antony, written soon after his death at the age of 105 in 356 and ascribed, probably wrongly, to Athanasius.[59] Antony, as represented in the *Life*, became the model which future seekers after personal sanctity would try to imitate. Although militant in its advocacy of Athanasian orthodoxy, the *Life* was also an exercise in bridge-building between forms of Christianity which were rooted in different social milieux. Alexandria, where Antony visited but did not reside, was urban, Greek-speaking, cosmopolitan, literate and versed in the techniques of dispute. Antony, however, is a man of the villages, the countryside and the desert; he is Coptic-speaking and addresses visitors through an interpreter;[60] he does not read books but knows the Scriptures from memory,[61] and his holy wisdom allows him to out-argue all opponents. Antony therefore dealt with a divided society, urban versus rural, Coptic versus Greek, learned versus illiterate. Although the differences are repeatedly drawn out, the author of the *Life* also shows how they can be bridged. Antony receives visitors from the cities, preaches sermons (of the author's composition),[62] and visits Alexandria to spectacular effect, when required to lend support to the victims of Maximinus Daza's persecution of the local Christians.[63] His miracles of healing benefit named individuals, lending these an air of authenticity;[64] another character, an imperial official acting on behalf of the Arians, has his death accurately foretold (he was fatally bitten by a horse).[65] Antony receives gifts, including a sheepskin later returned to the donor to be

59. For 'the desert made a city', see *Life of Antony*, 14. On ascetic authority, Rapp, *Holy Bishops*, 100–52. On Egyptian and Syrian monasticism in general (Syria, though important, was less influential), see D. J. Chitty, *The Desert a City: An Introduction to the Study of Egyptian and Palestinian Monasticism under the Christian Empire*, London: Mowbrays, 1977; J. E. Goehring, *Ascetics, Society and the Desert: Studies in Early Egyptian Monasticism*, Harrisburg: Trinity Press International, 1999; Peter Brown, *The Making of Late Antiquity*, Cambridge, MA: Harvard University Press, 1978, 81–101.
60. *Life of Antony*, 16 (A. delivers a sermon in 'Egyptian'); 72 (interpreter).
61. *Life of Antony*, 3 (memory 'takes the place' of books).
62. *Life of Antony*, 16–43 (to monks); 74–80 (to 'those accounted wise').
63. *Life of Antony*, 46–7.
64. *Life of Antony*, 48 (daughter of Martinianus); 57 (Fronto); 61 (Archelaus, *comes*, on behalf of the holy virgin Polycratia of Laodicea).
65. *Life of Antony*, 86. The Arian was called Balacius.

treasured as a relic,[66] and condemns Athanasius' 'Arian' enemies.[67]

Antony is portrayed as a Christian phenomenon; no interest is shown in his pagan antecedents or rural background. But disposal of worldly goods, withdrawal from the city and rejection of conventional social mores on marriage, family and slavery in favour of freedom in an idealised rural setting were not new. In the first century AD, the Jewish writer Philo of Alexandria explored the 'contemplative life' through discussion of the Therapeutai, who renounced their property, marriage and children and withdrew from Alexandria to live in the rural hinterland in 'free' communities, which met together regularly to receive instruction from the group leader; so great were the similarities with Christian asceticism that Eusebius believed that the Therapeutai were in fact Christian all along.[68] Moreover, in economic terms, for an Egyptian village-dweller to adopt the austere lifestyle of a monk, engaging during the working day in small-scale manufacture of baskets or other goods, meant simply exchanging one kind of rural community for another.[69]

Although Antony withdraws from centres of population, there is no sense in the *Life* that he was motivated by dislike of the worldliness of the Constantinian or post-Constantinian church. The conflicts acknowledged in the *Life* are those present in Egypt between urban and rural cultures. In fact, the *Life* provides evidence that Christians were already seeking spiritual comfort in or on the edges of villages, long before Constantine's triumph in 312. Born in c. 250, Antony lost his parents at the age of 18, and, after placing his sister with a group of holy virgins, he adopted a long-established teacher resident in a nearby village. About fifteen years later, he moved further away from the village, to live among the tombs, and would subsequently make further journeys in search (vainly) of total isolation. Repeatedly, he found himself the centre of groups of monks demanding further enlightenment. At no point did he try

---

66. *Life of Antony*, 91–2; the sheepskin, now worn out, is bequeathed, to be treasured as a relic.

67. On 'Arianism', a recurrent theme in the latter part, see *Life of Antony*, 69, 82, 86, 89, 91. On the 'social' role of the holy man in general, see Peter Brown, 'The rise and function of the holy man in late antiquity', *JRS* 61 (1971), 80–101 = Brown, *Society and the Holy in Late Antiquity*, London: Faber, 1982, 103–52.

68. Philo, *On the contemplative life* (trans. in the Loeb Classical Library, Philo, vol. 9) claimed as Christian by Euseb. *Hist. eccl.* 2.16–17. Philip Rousseau, *Pachomius: The Making of a Community in Fourth Century Egypt*, Berkeley: University of California Press, 1985, rev. 1999, 13–18.

69. Rousseau, *Pachomius*, 13.

to generate interest in establishing communities or rules; the monks were there already. Further corroboration is supplied from the early life of Pachomius, who began to receive instruction from the *abbas* (father) Palamon in c. 316; Palamon was already well established as a teacher of monks and the ascetic life.

Monastic life in Egypt offered residents of rural communities a lifestyle of greater status and perhaps security, because of its communal and spiritual values, in surroundings which remained familiar. Pachomius' first monastery was founded in the deserted Nile valley village of Tabennesi, in effect bringing life to a dead village, abandoned, like many others, due to agricultural and economic failure. As his communities expanded, more foundations followed; on his death, he was, according to a later source, the leader of some three thousand monks.[70] Pachomius was the author of the first monastic rule, presented to him, so the legend went, by an angel, inscribed on a bronze tablet (as also, though not by angels, were some Roman statutes).[71] But in the early decades of the monastic movement, conventions were not yet fully established or agreed, practices varied, even within communities,[72] and obedience depended on the charismatic qualities of the 'fathers' more than on written codes of conduct. But the rule shows what would be expected of monks in terms of dress, food (two meals per day) and deportment, as well as the kinds of work they would do; in the early fifth century, Palladius saw groups of monks working as diggers, gardeners, smiths, bakers, laundry-workers, basket and reed-weavers, cobblers and copyists.[73] Admirers laid great stress on the appearance of the ascetic as the outward indicator of inner holiness; however, the show-off who lacked the inner gift, despite his outward display of ascetic virtue, would always be unmasked.[74]

Despite much attention having been paid to women ascetics at Rome and elsewhere later in the fourth century, less has been said of the role of women in the early development of devotion to the Christian life. Yet there were already communities of celibate women, such as the one to which the young Antony consigned his sister in c. 270; years later, he met her again, to find her still a virgin

70. Palladius, *Hist. Laus.* (c. AD 420), 7.6.
71. Palladius, *Hist. Laus.* 32.; Rousseau, *Pachomius*, 87–104.
72. Palladius, *Hist. Laus.* 14, on ascetics in a monastery doing their own thing.
73. Palladius, *Hist. Laus.* 32.12.
74. T. Shaw, '*Askesis* and the appearance of holiness', *JECS* 6 (1998), 485–99.

and acting as a 'guide' to the rest.[75] There were also individual religious women, such as Juliana of Caesarea, who gave shelter to Origen at a time of persecution and who, if she lived alone, was probably financially independent. Other urban virgins conducted a religious life, while continuing to live with, and be dependent on, their families, who had presumably acquiesced in the consequent loss of descendants and perhaps heirs. If such a woman entered a public contract of virginity and then broke it by marrying, she was deemed by the bishops at the council of Ancyra to have married twice. This was less heinous, in the bishops' eyes, than the behaviour of holy virgins who lived as 'sisters' with men to whom they were not related.[76]

There were also women in the desert, despite the physical hardships and dangers of assault entailed. After Pachomius' first monastery was established, his sister Maria arrived and, after a suitable delay, was allowed to found a parallel community for women, subject to the same rule and supervised by designated senior monks. In return for the monks' manual labour and food, the nuns engaged in the most conventional of female house industries, the manufacture of textiles, for use by both communities. Although there were safeguards to prevent unsupervised contact between the sexes, tensions were bound to arise. Accounts dating from later in the century show 'mothers' (*ammas*) refusing to accept the dictates of the male supervisors.[77] And a feud within a convent, intensified by the isolation of a closed community of women, led to tragedy: a nun was denounced by another for fornication and killed herself; the false accuser then hanged herself; and full Christian rites of burial were denied to both.[78]

The participation of women in Christian activities could not be ignored and by some was both welcomed and honoured. For women of modest means (or none at all), life in a convent offered security and companionship; it had also long been the convention that Christian communities had a special duty to look after widows (including all types of single women) and orphans. But for some, in influential roles, inappropriate self-assertion by the daughters of

75. *Life of Antony*, 3 and 54.
76. *Conc. Ancyra*, canon 19. Susanna Elm, *'Virgins of God': The Making of Asceticism in Late Antiquity*, Oxford: Clarendon Press, 1994, 25–59.
77. Elm, *'Virgins'*, 304–10.
78. Palladius, *Hist. Laus.* 33.

Eve, whose temptation of Adam caused the Fall,[79] was deeply suspect. Male-authored hagiography recorded that male ascetics in the desert, Antony included, struggled constantly and painfully against the temptations of the flesh, inflicted on them by the Devil in the shape of apparitions of beautiful women. It would not have helped that women were in fact there, in communities of their own. Moreover, the fact that ascetic activities took place independently of the control of the local bishops made asceticism itself a questionable form of Christianity – perhaps even tinged with heresy. In 340/1, a small group of bishops assembled at Gangra in Paphlagonia condemned the activities of a freelance cleric, Eustathius of Sebaste, who had set up monasteries and encouraged women to leave their husbands, dress like men and shave their heads. Although all this accorded with ascetic conventions, the bishops would have none of it. Women were ordered to stay with their husbands, dress like women and not cut their hair, 'which God gave them to remind them of their subordination'.[80] The bishops at Gangra, though chaired by the bishop of Constantinople, were not necessarily representative of their colleagues, empire-wide; Gangra, like the councils of Elvira and Ancyra, records a local reaction to specific developments which affected the region directly. But they provide a corrective to the promotion of the ascetic ideal indulged in by the celebrants of Antony, Pachomius and others. Monasteries were, formally, outside episcopal control and were therefore potentially a threat to bishops' authority. And they represented values which subverted conventional respect for family and property, and thus threatened to bring Christianity into disrepute among the very classes among the laity whose patronage supported ecclesiastical prestige and power.

The ascetic and monastic movements were thus not a reaction against a worldly church, seduced by the blandishments of Constantine. The roots of asceticism went deeper and the search for spiritual fulfilment provided new models of saintliness for the emergent fourth-century church. The vision expressed in the *Life of Antony* (which would be surprising if it were that of Athanasius, so divisive a figure in other respects) was that both brands of (orthodox) Christianity, the episcopal, based on the city, and the monastic or ascetic, could complement and reinforce each other. For

79. For the history of Eve as the Christian equivalent of Pandora, see E. Pagels, *Adam, Eve and the Serpent*, London: Weidenfeld and Nicolson, 1988.
80. *Conc. Gangra*, 13 (female transvestites); 14 (not to leave husbands); 17 (hair). On subordination, see Paul, 1 Cor. 11; 5–16.

the sceptics, however, uncontrolled asceticism smacked of heresy and threatened episcopal primacy. In time, too, some ascetics, such as the Pannonian Martin, bishop of Tours in the late fourth century (372–97), would openly assert that the holiness of the monk was superior to that of the bishop, and the ascetic teachings and activities of Jerome, secretary to Pope Damasus at Rome in the 380s, and his female coterie would provoke suspicion, gossip and even riots. As the dynasty of Constantius I came to an end, with the reign of Julian, in 363, the question of whether the holy man (and woman) was to be tamed and institutionalised, or rejected and discarded as divisive and heretical, remained unresolved.

CHAPTER 11

Images of women

The period of the emergence of the 'new empire' is not, at first sight, propitious for the history of elite women in the ancient Roman world. The courts of emperors were peripatetic and militaristic in their culture and women were debarred, as they always had been, from the holding of formal public office in imperial administration. Within court society, the wives and daughters of emperors failed to assert any form of public individuality, still less exert active power. Their sphere remained the household. Within the private space of the *domus* (home) they appear, unnamed, on wall-paintings and mosaics, dressed as noblewomen with nothing to denote imperial status. In the literary sources they are represented almost solely in terms of their role as the daughters, wives and mothers of future emperors, their characters reshaped as a commentary on their husbands or sons. Thus Galerius' alleged barbarian character is made by Lactantius to derive from his mother; and Magnentius' misjudgement in taking on Constantius at Mursa is, in Zosimus' account, the more culpable because he ignored his mother's wise advice. Even when Helena Augusta emerges from the shadows as the first and most prominent female pilgrim to, and patron of, the religious sites of the Holy Land, she is presented by Eusebius as Constantine's 'mother', engaged in supporting her son's Christian mission.[1] When women were over-assertive, the men who wrote about them were quick to castigate their inappropriate behaviour.[2]

Nor do we find much expansion of women's freedoms in the legislative policies of Diocletian, Constantine or the succeeding generation of emperors. Instead, as we have seen, Constantine blocked the escape of women (as well as men) from unhappy marriages by limiting the availability of unilateral divorce and

1. Euseb. *Vit. Const.* 33.42.1–47.3.
2. For example, Ammianus on Constantina, wife of Gallus, who predeceases him: 14.7.4; 9.3 11.22. See also Optatus of Milevis 1.16 on the inappropriate behaviour of the Donatist supporting *clarissima femina* Lucilla.

imposed the threat of heavy penalties on lovers who eloped. Beyond the court, the expansion of the power and influence of Christian bishops under imperial patronage brought no corresponding benefit to women, who were debarred from holding positions in the official church hierarchy. The voices of women are largely silent in the sources, except, as we shall see, as petitioners to governors; we are left with men's perceptions or 'images' of women and denied access to the reality of their lives.

Despite appearances, what was said by lawmakers or church leaders about what women ought to be is not borne out by what is known of women as they were – as far as can be ascertained. Although their marriages were still, officially, arranged by their fathers or heads of household, *patres familias*, who also made the decision for their male descendants, the shape of the family had changed since the time of Augustus, with greater legal recognition offered to the relationship of mother and child in the law of succession which, from the second century onwards, allowed mothers and children to inherit from each other.[3] By the late fourth century, women could even act as guardians of their under-age children, provided that they entered into the public records a declaration that they would not remarry; this change, designed to safeguard the interests of the children, is significant for the legal empowerment of women, whose ability to administer assets reliably and independently was thus enshrined in law.[4]

One element in legal changes which benefited women in the longer term was driven by the fact that financially independent women had the power to control their personal wealth, even when nominally under the supervision of guardians, whom they could change at will, and to act as patrons in their own right. In the Greek east, it was already accepted that women could hold magistracies and act as patrons of their cities, although their individual independence was restricted by the convention that they always acted on behalf of their families as a whole.[5] In late antiquity, emperors declared that, although women could not hold the praetorship, they were bound to carry out the financial obligations of the office, if required. The legal

3. For the Senatus Consultum Tertullianum and the Senatus Consultum Orphitianum, which allowed this, see Jane Gardner, *Women in Roman Law and Society*, London: Croom Helm, 1986, 196–200.
4. *Cod. Theod.* 3.17.4 (390).
5. As argued by R. van Bremen, *The Limits of Participation*, Amsterdam: J. C. Gieben, 1996.

right to inherit, own and bequeath property gave to female lay Christians considerable financial, and by extension social, leverage on their bishops and favoured members of the clergy; the wealth of the churches, especially those outside the main capitals, depended on the generosity of the laity, not least its female members. Although the era of the great female patrons of Christian bishops and writers was still to come – that of the senatorial women at Rome who patronised Jerome and Pelagius, the deaconess Olympias, who gave comfort to John Chrysostom at Constantinople, and, in the fifth century, the pious sisters of Theodosius II – the beginnings of self-assertion on the part of female Christians can be detected already in the reign of Diocletian.

Imperial women I: The Tetrarchy and Constantine

The role of the wives and daughters of emperors in cementing political alliances and lending support to dynastic legitimacy was crucial. Though unable to be emperors themselves, they were potential mothers of emperors and essential to the formation of dynasties. Their role as conduits for imperial dynastic continuity was not new: the claims to the succession of Augustus' successors Gaius (37–41) and Nero (54–68) had derived from their descent from Augustus by the female line. In default of heirs male, the men that imperial daughters married and their children gave them the potential to be serious power players, whether they liked it or not. Thus Diocletian's two Caesars were the sons-in-law of their respective Augusti; Maxentius married Valeria Maximilla, daughter of Galerius, although the relationship did not, in the event, guarantee Maxentius' claims as successor;[6] and the alliances of the successors to the Tetrarchy with each other were confirmed by the marriages of Constantine with Fausta and of Licinius with Constantia, sister of Constantine.

But late third-century empresses, though essential for the propagation of dynasties of men, had no profile in their own right, existing in the public record only as adjuncts of their menfolk. Power rested entirely with the soldier-emperors, whose militaristic ethos left no

6. Dessau, *ILS* 667, 671. T. D. Barnes, *Constantine: Dynasty, Religion and Power in the Later Roman Empire*, Oxford: Wiley-Blackwell, 2011, pp. 48–9, suggests, speculatively, that Minervina, Constantine's first wife, may have been a close female relation of Diocletian, perhaps a niece.

room for (anachronistic) notions of chivalry. The private experience of Constantine's empress Fausta, married for nearly twenty years to the man responsible for the deaths and posthumous degradation of her father (Maximian) and brother (Maxentius), can only be guessed at; the story in Lactantius that she informed Constantine of one of her father's plots to assassinate him may have been framed to account for her remaining in favour, or indeed alive at all.[7] In 312, Maxentius' (and Fausta's) mother, Eutropia, was forced to make a public statement that she had been unfaithful to her husband: the real father of Maxentius, she alleged, had been a Syrian.[8] We are not told what the consequences would have been had she refused.

The survival of imperial women could depend on the success of their men. The mothers, widows and daughters of losers were dangerous to the victors because of the threat their present, or even future, offspring could pose as foci for the disaffected; even young children were not spared. In 313, the victorious Licinius summarily killed Candidianus, Galerius' son by a concubine who had been adopted by Galerius' widow, Valeria; Severianus, son of the short-lived and by then dead Augustus Severus, who was disposed of because he had allegedly hoped to succeed Maximinus Daza; and the two children of Maximinus Daza, a boy aged eight and a girl aged seven.[9] Prisca, Diocletian's widow, and Valeria also fell victim to Licinius' purge. Lactantius, who may have recognised, but does not acknowledge, their Christian sympathies, recalled of Valeria's execution that 'many watched with pity, for so great a fall', commenting grimly that their modesty (*pudicitia*) and station in life had been their undoing.[10] By contrast, Constantius II's purge of rival claimants in 337 did not extend to the womenfolk and the lives of the children of Julius Constantius, Gallus and Julian were spared. However, in 350, the younger Eutropia, half-sister of Constantine, fell victim to the carnage at Rome attending the overthrow of her son, Nepotianus (her husband, the senator Virius Nepotianus, may have been killed in the summer of 337).

Rumour and scandal attended Constantine's alleged murder of his wife Fausta in 326, soon after his execution of his son Crispus.[11]

---

7. Lactant. *De mort. pers.* 30.1–5.
8. Anon. Vales. 4.12. Maxentius was thus not only illegitimate but also 'foreign'.
9. Lactant. *De mort. pers.* 50.2–6.
10. Lactant. *De mort. pers.* 51.2. See also Maximim Daza's overtures to Valeria (*De mort. pers.* 39), his persecution of friends of Valeria (40) and her exile to Syria (41).
11. Aur. Vict. *Caes.* 41.11 states that Crispus was executed 'iudicio patris' ('by judicial

While it is assumed that Fausta was an adult (at least 12 years old) at the time of her marriage to Constantine in 307,[12] it is possible that the union was in reality a betrothal. The absence of children for the next decade and Fausta's comparative fecundity thereafter (she was the mother of two or three sons and two daughters) suggest a delay in the consummation of the marriage. The generations are confused: Fausta was the younger sister of Theodora, and Constantine's marriage with her made him his own father's brother in law. Perhaps she was closer in age to Crispus than to her husband. Her religious affiliations are unknown; the use of the *Domus Faustae* for the Council of Rome in 313 merely demonstrates that Constantine used his wife's property as if it were his own. Her life as empress could have caused her both resentment and fear. If Constantine II, born in 316, was indeed a concubine's son, this can hardly have contributed to harmonious marital relations. Nor would the delay in elevating Fausta and Helena to the status of Augusta in c. 324, a step taken to advertise the strength of the Constantinian dynasty, have helped.

The cause of Fausta's disappearance in 326 was unknown at the time and has defied elucidation since – a tribute to the secrecy which enfolded the happenings in the Constantinian *domus*. Ancient writers filled the gap in their knowledge with fictions based on the stories of Phaedra and Hippolytus or Joseph and Potiphar's wife: the young man, they alleged, had rejected the advances of his step-mother, who denounced him to his father, resulting in the execution of the one and the death of the other.[13] Another version derived from a tradition hostile to Constantine himself, which depicted him as a second Nero; the alleged manner of Fausta's death, that she was suffocated by steam in a bath, can be read as an echo of the killing by Nero of his blameless wife, Octavia (Seneca, credited with a tragedy on that event, was much read in late antiquity). A Latin epigram, preserved by the fifth-century Gallic aristocrat and bishop Sidonius Apollinaris, lamented the arrival of a 'Neronian age', re-placing that of Saturn, a reference evoking Lactantius' interest in the Saturnian age, which, in the *Divine institutes*, he contrasted with

process conducted by his father'), implying a formal, though in this case secret, court hearing.
12. See T. D. Barnes, *The New Empire of Diocletian and Constantine*, Cambridge, MA: Harvard University Press, 1982, 34.
13. Philostorgius, *Hist. eccl.* 2.4.4a–b; Zos. *New History* 2.29.2. On Octavia's death, Tac. *Ann* 14.64, 'perfervidi balnei vapore enecatur'. For a view of Fausta and Crispus which respects this dubious evidence more than I do, see Barnes, *Constantine*, 144–9.

that of the parricidal Jupiter, patron of Diocletian. The pagan historian Eunapius, followed by Zosimus, took a different tack, arguing that Constantine's guilt at the murders of his wife and son brought about his conversion to Christianity, a religion which forgave anything.[14] Ignorance, the inevitable consequence of secrecy, as always, generated both fantasy and polemic.

Contradictory hypotheses can be offered: that Fausta was in league with Crispus; or that she was plotting against him. Closer in age to Crispus than she was to Constantine, she could offer dynastic legitimacy to the rising military star, through her descent from Maximian, by exchanging the father for the stepson. Equally plausible is the alternative, that Fausta was concerned that Crispus, now an active military commander, might pose a threat to her own sons, all (or both) of whom were under 10 years of age. Tensions were inherent in the customary recognition of the sons of first wives; Constantine, son of Helena, made Augusta in c. 324, had effectively blocked the elevation of the sons of Constantius by his second wife, Theodora, daughter of Maximian; and Crispus, Constantine's son by Minervina, was by 326 acquiring a military reputation of his own. As we have seen, in 337 there was no love lost between the descendants of Helena and of Constantius I's second (and imperial) wife Theodora.[15]

The family crisis in 326 marked a turning point. Constantine visited Rome for the last time, to celebrate his twenty years of rule (as he had done the previous year at Nicaea), before returning to a court now permanently based in the east which, like that of Shakespeare's *Richard III*, was now full of widows: Helena, repudiated wife and now widow of Constantius I; Eutropia, widow of Maximian and mother of the dead Maxentius and Fausta; and Constantia, who had vainly pleaded with her brother Constantine to spare the life of her husband Licinius.[16] All three now emerged as active patrons of Christianity. Reverting to the traditional feminine role of intercessor and mediator, Constantia involved herself with

14. Zos. *New History*, 2.29; cf. the emperor Julian's satirical take on Constantine and amoral Christianity, at Julian, *Caesars* 336. For Fausta's death, see references at *PLRE*, Fl. Maxima Fausta, pp. 325–6.

15. Fausta's memory does not seem to have suffered as a result of her death: see Julian, *Or.* 1.9b–d, in praise of Fausta as mother of Constantius II. For speculation on the plot, Robert Frakes, 'The dynasty of Constantine down to 363' in Noel Lenski (ed.), *The Cambridge Companion to the Age of Constantine*, Cambridge: Cambridge University Press, 2006, 91–107.

16. Zos. *New History*, 2.28.2; Anon. Vales. 5.28

the aftermath of Nicaea, seeking to reconcile her brother with the followers of Eusebius of Nicomedia.[17] Helena and Eutropia went further, departing from court on pilgrimage to the Holy Land. There Eutropia would write a 'report' to Constantine complaining about the slow pace of modernisation at the religious site of Mamre,[18] while Helena, as her son's representative, would contribute to the transformation of Jerusalem as a metropolis for religious tourism.[19]

The death of Fausta, whatever the reason, represented a nadir in the fortunes of imperial women. Thereafter, women who lost out in court power struggles lived on, but turned their energies elsewhere. Most notably, in the 440s, the empress Aelia Eudocia, the estranged wife of Theodosius II, whose power struggle with the emperor's sister Pulcheria had ended in stalemate, journeyed to the Holy Land, acquiring fresh prestige and public plaudits for her patronage of sacred sites.[20] Before her, empresses had already become more assertive and the public profile of many had become higher (although we are still dependent on the vagaries of the sources for details).

Christian patronage provided an outlet for the energies of Helena, Eutropia and numerous later wealthy women. But it also removed inconvenient empresses from the centre of power. Although, with hindsight, we can appreciate the achievement of Helena and other patronesses of Christianity as financiers and promoters of the sacred shrines, their removal from court, whether voluntary or not, could also be read as a failure to hold their own in the power game. The appearance of family unity at the top was preserved – we may note Constantine's deference to his 'mother-in-law' on the subject of Mamre – but only on condition that the family lived apart.

This argument, that patronage of Christianity by (some) women was encouraged by lack of openings elsewhere, is supported by better-documented examples from later in the century.[21] The lack of documentation for the long years Helena spent at Rome, in her

17. Sozom. *Hist. eccl.* 2.27; 3.19.
18. Euseb. *Vit. Const.* 3.51–2.
19. On Helena, see J. W. Drijvers, *Helena Augusta: The Mother of Constantine the Great and the Legend of her Finding of the True Cross*, Leiden: Brill, 1992. For a more sceptical view, see E. D. Hunt, *Holy Land Pilgrimage in the Later Roman Empire, AD 312–460*, Oxford: Oxford University Press, 1982, 28–39.
20. See Kenneth G. Holum, *Theodosian Empresses: Women and Imperial Dominion in Late Antiquity*, Berkeley: University of California Press, 1982, 217–25.
21. E.g. at *Letter* 108, 5–6, Jerome claims of Paula that she adopted a holy life out of weariness of the Roman social scene.

Sessorian Palace on the Esquiline Hill, where she constructed baths and shrines and where she would choose to be buried, denies us direct knowledge of what her influence may have been on the women she encountered in the Eternal City. The first Roman noble-woman to adopt the ascetic life, we are told, was Marcella, who refused a second marriage with the Christian senator Neratius Cerealis[22] and took up Bible studies in her house on the Aventine.[23] On the assumption that the co-religionists Cerealis and Marcella were not strangers when their marriage was planned, this connects Marcella with the imperial house: Cerealis' sister, Galla,[24] had been the mother of the Caesar Gallus, husband to Constantina, who would share with her sister, the younger Helena, a devotion to the cult and shrine of St Agnes at Rome.

Marcella's choice of lifestyle may thus have been inspired by her experience of the Christianity practised at Rome, that of Helena, perhaps Eutropia or Constantia and certainly Constantina, the pious, but underemployed, widows and single women at the courts of Constantine and his sons. In the 380s, Marcella became the role model for a coterie of senatorial women at Rome, who succumbed to the persuasions of the charismatic Christian Jerome and 'gave up' their wealth, or rather passed it on to their natural heirs, in order to pursue the ascetic life and the enhanced status, 'noble by birth, nobler still in holiness', which came with it.[25] For widows, who had lost the status of married women, and girls, who had not yet acquired it, the ascetic vocation was a way out, as Jerome explicitly acknowledged. So too, on a more illustrious level, was Christian patronage, for the ladies of Constantine's troubled court.

Imperial women II: Eusebia

Ammianus' overall perception of Constantius' court was that it was dysfunctional. Imperial suspicion was reinforced by intrigues and failures to receive or process information correctly. To this toxic mix was added the emperor's excessive dependence on flatterers, women

22. *PLRE I* Neratius Cerealis 2, pp. 197–9. He erected baths on the Esquiline, next door to the basilica of Liberius, later S. Maria Maggiore.
23. Jerome, *Letter* 127, 2 for Marcella as the 'first'.
24. *PLRE I* Galla 1, p. 382.
25. For the safeguarding of property rights of heirs, see Jill Harries, '"Treasure in heaven": Property and inheritance among senators of late Rome', in E. Craik (ed.), *Marriage and Property*, Aberdeen: Aberdeen University Press, 1984, 54–70.

and eunuchs. All were equally unacceptable, although arguably in fact both women and eunuchs helped to mediate conflicts and absorb or divert hostility from the emperors and their chief advisers. Ammianus comments that eunuchs hid away 'like bats and exercised their influence in secret'.[26] While expressing approval of Eutherius, who served Constans and later defended Julian against Marcellus in Constantius' consistory, Ammianus had nothing good to say for Eusebius, the *praepositus* of the imperial bedchamber, who intervened in ecclesiastical affairs under both Constantine and Constantius, acted as one of Gallus' judges at Pola and was finally sentenced to death at Chalcedon in 361.[27] From the standpoint of emperors, however, the physical state of eunuchs allowed them to act as personal attendants without causing allegations of impropriety, and their inability to have children ensured that they could entertain no dynastic ambitions.

Despite Ammianus' general criticism of the influence of women, he sympathised with the interventions of Constantius' second wife, Eusebia, on behalf of his hero, Julian.[28] These predated Julian's appointment as Caesar: allegations that Julian had met with the traitor Gallus at Constantinople, having left his refuge at Macellum in Cappadocia with covert designs, were rebutted by the empress and Julian was permitted to travel on to Athens, to complete his education.[29] It was also due to her favour, according to Ammianus, that Julian was called to serve as Caesar in 355 and married to Helena, another sister of Constantius. But in his account of the relationship between the childless Eusebia and Helena, suspicions of women as poisoners, embedded in the literary tradition, resurface: Eusebia, Ammianus claimed, first bribed a midwife to kill Helena's first son, then gave her a drug which caused her to miscarry of all her

26. Amm. Marc. 16.7.7. See M. K. Hopkins, 'The political power of eunuchs', in Hopkins, *Conquerors and Slaves* 1, Cambridge: Cambridge University Press, 1978, 172–96. Also S. Tougher, 'Ammianus and the eunuchs', in J. W. Drijvers and D. Hunt (eds), *The Late Roman World and its Historian: Interpreting Ammianus Marcellinus*, London: Routledge, 1999, 64–73.
27. Amm. Marc. 20.2.3 (influence on military policy); 21.15.4 (organises aftermath of death of Constantius II); 22.3.12 (execution, celebrated as Justice hurling him down over a cliff).
28. On Ammianus and women, see G. Sabbah, 'Présences féminins dans l'histoire d'Ammien Marcellin: les rôles politiques', in J. den Boeft, D. den Hengst and H. C. Teitler (eds), *Cognitio gestorum: The Historiographic Art of Ammianus Marcelllinus*, Amsterdam: N. Jork, 1992, 91–105.
29. Amm. Marc. 15.2.7–8; Julian, *Or.* 3.118A–C.

other children.[30] Eusebia herself, daughter of the consul of 347 and
sister to the two consuls of 359, died young and Constantius
then married Faustina, who became the mother of his posthumous
daughter, the future wife of the emperor Gratian.[31]

Given the suspicions that existed between Constantius and Julian,
most of whose relatives, including his half-brother Gallus, the
Augustus had destroyed, Eusebia could usefully have acted as a
mediator and confidence-builder on behalf of her husband.[32] Whatever her motive, Eusebia, unlike her predeceessor Fausta, exercised
visible influence. The speech of thanks composed in her honour by
Julian to demonstrate publicly his gratitude for her support in the
dangerous last months of Gallus' Caesarship reveals something of
the potential of the office of empress, while still constructing the role
in traditional terms.[33] Some justification was required for the act of
addressing an encomium to a woman at all. Julian's answer, characteristically, was to evolve an argument based on Greek philosophy
and Homer. Gratitude was to be expected in return for great services
and those who failed to express their thanks in public were failing
in their duty. Plato, Aristotle and Xenophon had offered eulogies to
men they admired. Women too were admirable:

> I should think it strange indeed if we shall be eager to applaud men
> of high character and not think fit to give our tribute of praise to a
> noble woman, believing as we do that excellence is the attribute of
> women no less than of men.[34]

Homer, Julian declared, provided a precedent for encomia of
women: Odysseus had been a suppliant in Phaeacia to the princess
Nausicaa and the queen Arete, who had persuaded the king Alcinoos
to help him, and the poet himself had praised Penelope as the ideal
wife. Eusebia, therefore, deserved the same tribute of gratitude as a
man would.

Despite his professed aim to glorify Eusebia, Julian is vague on

30. Amm. Marc. 16.10.18–19. Cf. allegations that Livia poisoned the heirs of Augustus
to pave the way for the succession of her son, Tiberius.
31. Amm. Marc. 21.6.4.
32. S. Tougher, 'The advocacy of an empress: Julian and Eusebia', *CQ* 48 (1998),
595–9.
33. In general see S. Tougher, 'In praise of an empress: Julian's speech of thanks to
Eusebia', in Mary Whitby (ed.), *The Propaganda of Power: The Role of Panegyric in
Late Antiquity*, Leiden: Brill, 1998, 105–23. On the rhetorical rules for the *Gratiarum
actio* (speech of thanks), see Quint. *Inst.* 3.7.10.
34. Julian, *Or.* 3.104B.

details. In line with the conventions of panegyric, Eusebia's home-
land, Macedon, is praised, with predictable references to Philip II
and Alexander the Great; on her lineage, another standard topic, her
father had been consul, an office which even emperors desired, and
her mother was also of noble Greek descent. Constantius' qualities
as emperor and husband are given full but general coverage, and the
example of Penelope resurfaces: Odysseus (Constantius) preferred
his Penelope to all the goddesses (Circe, Calypso) that he might have
married.[35] Amid the fulsome rhetoric three services of Eusebia to
Julian stand out: her intercession in his favour with Constantius; the
grant of permission to retire to Athens (which evokes a disquisition
on the wonders of Hellenic culture); and a gift of books, the more
appreciated because he habitually took a book with him even on
campaigns. The encomium itself may be characterised as cautious
innovation. Eusebia's virtues are those of the 'good empress' –
beauty, virtue, modesty and the ability to persuade her husband
to show mercy – but they are also those of the philosopher: good-
ness, temperance and wisdom. In his literary construction of a
'philosopher-queen' who shows the kindness of the ruler in patron-
ising another philosopher, Julian the panegyricist creates an
apolitical world of culture and philanthropy, and of notional
female equality, far removed from the political intrigues and power
struggles which in the real world surrounded both.

Eusebia was represented as active in promoting the interests of
Julian at court, and received warm public praise for her pains, but
she remains a stereotype, denied a voice of her own. Later, more
assertive women came to the fore. Justina, wife first of Magnentius
then of Valentinian I, exploited the power which accrued to her as
virtual regent in her son Valentinian II's minority, to assert herself
against Ambrose of Milan in Italy in the 380s, and in the fifth
century Galla Placidia acted as regent for her son, the child
Valentinian III, and corresponded with Theodosius II's sister,
Pulcheria.[36] Christian piety enhanced the influence of empresses such
as Arcadius' wife, Eudoxia, who helped to destroy John Chrysostom
early in the fifth century, and Pulcheria, whose enmity to Nestorius
contributed to the latter's downfall. The dynastic policy of the

35. Julian, *Or.* 3.112D–114B.
36. On Justina, Neil McLynn, *Ambrose of Milan: Church and Court in a Christian Capital*, Berkeley: University of California Press, 1994, 171–96; Placidia's letter discussed by Fergus Millar, *A Greek Roman Empire: Power and Belief under Theodosius II (408–450)*, Berkeley: University of California Press, 2006, 37–8.

children of Arcadius was itself original; a combination of teenage vows of virginity on the part of the emperor's sisters and Theodosius' choice as a wife of a professor's daughter, rather than a scion of the eastern aristocracies, denied the opportunities afforded by political alliances but also kept potential rivals at a safe distance.

Child emperors could not rule without help and the older female relatives of child emperors, like Valentinian II and, in the fifth century, Theodosius II and Valentinian III, had a potential role as unofficial rulers not available to the wives or mothers of adult (and efficient) emperors. But on a more profound level other factors were at work. One was the new opportunity for self-assertion afforded by Christianity not only to imperial women but to aristocrats in general. The second was that the Roman Empire of the fourth century became more settled, as the immediate threat of military or political disintegration receded. As emperors travelled less, courts became less frenetically mobile and by the early fifth century, eastern Roman emperors were so well settled in Constantinople that the complaint against them was that they were too 'shut away'.[37] The machismo of the mobile military camp was superseded by a more intricate, ornate and ceremonious court culture. Although still debarred from office-holding or the formal decision-making processes, which formed the bedrock of imperial government, empresses now had space to exert influence both behind the scenes and through Christian patronage. Their changed role, therefore, was the product of broader developments affecting not only the status and powers of imperial women but also the nature of imperial government as a whole.

The most significant benefactor of the Roman churches in the 350s was Constantina, daughter of Constantine and married first to Hannibalianus, who was killed in the purge of June 337, and then, many years later, to Gallus Caesar, whom she predeceased. On imperial property, she erected a funerary basilica for herself close to the reputed tomb of St Agnes and commemorated her benefaction with an inscription, celebrating her own generosity, the help of Christ and the triumph of Agnes, the 'victorious virgin' over paganism and 'all earthly things'.[38] The first letters of the lines of

37. Synesius of Cyrene, *De regno* 12b–14b. Cf. Claudian, *On the IVth consulate of Honorius*, 320–52, and, from the 380s, Pacatus, *Panegyric of Theodosius* (= *Pan. Lat.* 2(12)), 21.
38. *Inscriptiones Latinae Christianae Veteres* 1768, 1–6. 'Sacravi tempum *victricis* virginis Agnes, Templorum quod *vincit* opus terraneque cuncta.' The present tense of

the poem form the words 'Constantina Deo', 'Constantina to God': this empress had no doubt of her right to address the Divinity directly. When Julian's wife, Helena, died in 360, she too was laid to rest in the St Agnes burial site: Agnes was now the accepted guardian saint of the women of the imperial house.[39]

In life, Constantina shared her husband Gallus' reputation for cruelty and fear of conspiracies.[40] Mediation on her part between her husband and brother was prevented by her death in Bithynia in 354 and Gallus did not long survive her. How far Constantina was guilty by association cannot be known; Ammianus is regrettably prone to report adverse rumours concerning powerful women.[41] But Constantina's patronage of a (female) saint is a continuation of the self-assertion of imperial women, such as Helena and Eutropia, through Christian building. Moreover, her presence on the Roman scene is part of a fragmentary picture of growing aristocratic female lay involvement with the Roman church, perhaps encouraged by Helena's long and undocumented sojourn in the capital. A late source reports that, in 357, Constantius was harassed by devout women who petitioned for the restoration of Liberius, and openly expressed their frustration when their petitions were rejected.[42] The story may be an invention but it reflects the evolution of a collective, Christian identity among the elite women of Rome, which would find fuller expression later in the century but which originated with the imperial women of the house of Constantine.

Women and the law

Legal discourse assumed that women were 'weak' and 'frivolous'. Although this assumption had been explicitly rejected by the jurist Gaius in the second century,[43] it still acted as a justification

---

vincit is worth noting: Agnes' victories are in the present, not in the past of her martyr-dom on earth.

39. Contrast the triumphal emphasis of Constantina's tribute with that of Prudentius, *Peristephanon* 14, with the emphasis on, inter alia, the penetration of Agnes by the executioner's sword.

40. Amm Marc. 14.7.4; 9.3 (she listens in on treason trials); 11.22 (Gallus blames the now dead Constantina for executions).

41. Such as Eusebia's alleged drugging of Helena, to prevent her having children.

42. Theodoret, *Hist. eccl.* 2.14.

43. Gaius, *Institutes* 1.144 (justification); 190 (rejects case as 'more specious than true'). See Gillian Clark, *Women in Late Antiquity: Pagan and Christian Lifestyles*, Oxford: Oxford University Press, 1993, 56–62; Antti Arjava, *Women and Law in Late Antiquity*,

for debarring women from certain kinds of legal activity; they could act on behalf of their own families, in limited ways, but not for third parties. Paradoxically, the 'weak' stereotype also provided opportunities for women petitioners to act more effectively as litigants and petitioners, by recycling the rhetoric of their rulers to support their case. In 297, Aurelia Didyme petitioned for the restoration of her maternal inheritance, stolen, she alleged, by her two uncles: 'the race of women', she informed the governor, 'is easily despised on account of the weakness of our nature'.[44] Another Aurelia had more clout, as she was the owner of large estates and a taxpayer, with children in army service; alleging that she had been cheated by her agents, she too claimed special consideration, being 'a weak woman and a widow'.[45] Claims of 'weakness' were in fact part of a wider rhetoric of victimhood, employed to win the attention and sympathy of judges by emphasising the petitioner's vulnerability: Aurelia Atiaris of Hermopolis complained that, when she went to collect payment of a debt, she was imprisoned in a house and whipped by three named people, one of whom was a known bad character, the nocturnal sheep-shearer, Apion.[46] Apion's nefarious character is confirmed by a male petitioner, Aurelius Aboul, who complained that eleven sheep were shorn by night by Paul, a soldier, and three other named individuals, including Apion, now revealed as the son of the local police chief, Horion.[47]

In the legislation of Constantine, the rhetoric of 'weakness' is replaced by an emphasis not found in earlier imperial texts on the 'modesty' expected of women, which both protected and restricted them. The home, the *domus*, acted as both a refuge and a prison. Two imperial pronouncements sent to Africa early in the reign (and perhaps reflecting local expectations) gave husbands overall supervision of their wives' affairs, to prevent the women from violating 'matronly modesty' (*matronalis pudor*) by going to court and being present at 'assemblies of men', and insisted that law officers were not

Oxford: Oxford University Press, 1996, 231–7; J. Beaucamp, 'Le vocabulaire de la faiblesse feminine dans les texts juridiques romains du IIIe au VIe siècle', *RHDFE* 54 (1976), 485–508.

44. *P.Oxy.* 34.2713, trans. J. Evans Grubbs, *Women and the Law in the Roman Empire*, London: Routledge, 2002, 54.

45. *P.Oxy.* 1.71, Grubbs, *Women and the Law*, 54.

46. *P. Abinn.* 51 and 52. For text and translations see H. I. Bell, V. Martin, E. G. Turner, and D. van Berchem (eds), *The Abinnaeus Archive: Papers of a Roman Officer in the Reign of Constantius II*, Oxford: Oxford University Press, 1962.

47. *P. Abinn.* 48, 7–12.

to arrest women in their own homes and drag them out in public.[48] Even where the right to act as an adult in legal terms had been granted to 18-year-old women on grounds of good character, they were expected to stay at home and be represented in public by their procurator or agent.[49] Respect for their modesty was even accorded to bad women, convicted of crimes; a ruling of Constantius II enforced the segregations of the sexes in closed prisons.[50]

As noted above, Constantine took a strict line over morality and marriage, reflecting not so much Christianity as the mood of the times.[51] The convention which obtained throughout Roman history was that marriage was a voluntary contract between the two parties, based on the intention to be married (*affectio maritalis*), a principle reiterated as late as 428 by the lawyers of Theodosius II.[52] In theory, therefore, either party was free to end the marriage, although Constantine, as we have seen, severely limited the grounds for unilateral divorce.[53] The apparent liberality of 'no-fault' divorces under classical law was modified by the financial consequences, which did take account of who initiated the divorce and who was to blame for the end of the marriage.

Changes in the rules came about because of social needs. *Affectio maritalis* in isolation required a high degree of trust between the parties and their families. In practice, women in particular were wise to ensure that there were witnesses to the 'intention' of both; the institution of concubinage, often a long-lasting union, was superficially similar to marriage, the essential difference being the status of the children as illegitimate or not.[54] Constantine reinforced the respect he felt due to marriage by restating the convention that a man should not bring his concubine under the same roof with his

---

48. *Cod. Just.* 2.12.21 (12 March 315); *Cod. Theod.* 1.22.1 (11 January 316).
49. *Cod. Theod.* 2.17.1.1 (9 April 324, to prefect of the city of Rome), 'propter pudorem ac verecundiam' ('due to their modesty and respect for decency'). Young men were allowed this at 20, because they matured physically later than women did.
50. *Cod. Theod.* 9.3.3 = *Cod. Just.* 9.4.3.
51. Cf. Diocletian's denunciation of close-kin marriage or incest in the Damascus Edict, trans. Grubbs, *Women and the Law*, 140–3, and discussed by Simon Corcoran, 'The sins of the fathers: A neglected constitution of Diocletian on incest', *Journal of Legal History* 21 (2000), 1–34.
52. *Cod. Theod.* 3.7.3, stating that a marriage did not depend on legal formalities but on legal capacity and the intention of the parties, confirmed by their friends.
53. Susan Treggiari, *Roman Marriage: Iusti coniuges from the Time of Cicero to the Time of Ulpian*, Oxford: Oxford University Press, 1991, 52–7.
54. Susan Treggiari, '*Concubinae*', PBSR 49 (1981), 59–81; Arjava, *Women and Law*, 205–10; Clark, *Women in Late Antiquity*, 31–3.

wife.[55] He also tightened up the rules for the contracting of marriage. Betrothal, previously an informal arrangement, became more important. Constantine laid down regulations about the return, or not, of betrothal gifts, if one party resiled from the contract or died.[56] It was also assumed that the marriage would normally take place within two years of the betrothal and that a failure to do so released the parties from their obligation, allowing a new relationship to be formed.[57] Late in his reign a further formality, 'the kiss', complicated the proceedings, as the exchange of a 'kiss' was held to make the betrothal still more binding.

Constantine also redrew the boundaries of what was acceptable as a marriage between people of different status. Augustus' marriage legislation had prevented senators from marrying freedwomen, and Constantine expanded the prohibition to include members of the curial order and provincial priests, as well as senators, and added explanations of the lower end of the social scale, which clarified that people such as actresses and tavern keepers, and others classed as 'humble and abject' persons, were forbidden to marry with their betters (although they could presumably live with them as concubines).[58] The law failed to mention slaves (who could not be 'married' in a legally recognised sense) and was not comprehensive in its definition of who the humble and abject might be, creating problems of definition revisited by a later emperor. As so often, the aim was to state a principle – that the wealthier classes should not marry beneath themselves – rather than provide watertight legal definitions of what was or was not permitted.

Assertive women

Women were often in reality not the 'weak' or passive victims of wrongdoers. The petitions from Egypt show them eager to asset their rights; like men, women constantly tested the law. Aurelia Maria, for example, lost three sheep and had nine shorn by night and could identify two alleged culprits from information supplied by the field-guards; she expected Abinnaeus, as the local judge, to take action on the evidence she had provided.[59] She illustrates a regular

55. *Cod. Just.* 5.26.1 (14 June 326).
56. *Cod. Theod.* 3.5.2 (319), modified by 3.5.6 (334/5)
57. *Cod. Theod.* 3.5.4 + 5 (332).
58. *Cod. Theod.* 4.6.3.
59. *P. Abinn.* 49, 11–15.

feature of the petitions papyri, from Hermopolis and elsewhere: the willingness of women to petition in their own names for their rights. As property owners in their own right and prominent members of village societies, women used the same techniques as their menfolk to achieve their ends – and more. Exploiting the stereotype of female weakness, they presented themselves as victims of brutality, beaten until 'at the door of death'.[60] Nor was lack of literacy a deterrent. Both men and women took their complaints to the local scribes, who often had a repertoire of formulae for the reporting of grievances, designed to have maximum impact on the recipient; the complainant then attested his or her agreement to the text. Just as, on a higher social level, public orators ascribed imperial virtues of philanthropy, mercy and generosity to emperors as a means of persuading emperors to act consistently with these qualities, so the village petitioners played back governmental rhetoric to their judges, in the hope of ensuring that they too would judge justly.

They were not alone. A quarter of the petitioners recorded in the surviving parts of the Diocletianic Codex Hermogenianus were women, eager to make their presence felt at the highest level. The well-meaning Asclepiodota is advised not to 'intercede' over debts incurred by her husband (the first-century SC Velleianum had limited women's involvement with third-party transactions);[61] Philotera is reassured that she is not liable for the debts of her son (even if she had helped him);[62] Faustina, disinherited by her father for refusing to divorce her husband at the father's request, is allowed to petition for the will to be overturned on the grounds that it is 'undutiful';[63] a husband, Alexander, who has been forcibly separated from his wife by her relations is allowed to sue for her return – provided she states publicly that she agrees.[64]

60. Cf. *P. Cair. Isid.* 63 'they attacked me with blows, [dragged] me around by the hair, tore my clothing to pieces and left me lying on the ground'. For more on the techniques employed by the redoubtable Taesis of Karanis to achieve restitution of property, see Jill Harries, *Law and Empire in Late Antiquity*, Cambridge: Cambridge University Press, 1999, 185–7.
61. *Cod. Just.* 4.12.1. For this and the texts that follow, see Grubbs *Women and the Law*, 66–8; 197–8.
62. *Cod. Just.* 9.22.19.
63. *Cod. Just.* 3.28.18. On the *querela inofficiosi testamenti* ('complaint of unduteous will') see Gardner, *Women in Roman Law and Society*, 183–90; B. W. Frier and T. A. J. McGinn, *A Casebook on Roman Family Law*, American Philological Association, New York: Oxford University Press, 2004, 377–85.
64. *Cod. Just.* 5.4.11.

Predictably, they also asked too much. There were limits to concessions to womanly 'weakness', as it was not right that the law
should be exploited by the allegedly disadvantaged. Not all imperial
replies, therefore, were favourable or helpful. In a property dispute
one Frontina had claimed ignorance of the law, a claim correctly
disallowed (although the excuse was still open to minors).[65] Nor
were women to litigate inappropriately: Cosmia is censured for
trying to bring a prosecution for forgery (women were not permitted
to bring criminal prosecutions except where family interests were
directly involved).[66] On occasion, a petitioner might offer a helpful
suggestion on how the law might be modified. When one Caelestina,
who was finalising divorce arrangements, suggested, perhaps on the
basis of local custom, that the children of her marriage should be
allocated to the parents by gender, Diocletian responded that there
was no precedent for this in Roman law; instead, the local governor
must adjudicate on the placement of the children.[67]

There was also one category of woman who had no need to
invoke 'weakness' to get her way – the woman philosopher. Elite
women were often well educated[68] and there was a long tradition of
active female involvement in philosophy, going back to Theano, the
wife of Pythagoras, and forward to the Alexandrian philosopher
Hypatia, who would be lynched by a Christian mob in 415; under
the early empire, philosophers like the Stoic Musonius Rufus
and Plutarch took women's intellectual attainments seriously. In the
mid-fourth century, the Neo-Platonist Sosipatra[69] went further and
asserted her personal superiority over her husband in the impending
afterlife. The unfortunate spouse, Eustathius, who was also an established philosopher, would, she said, die within five years of their
marriage (he did) and would thereafter ascend to a state of being
inferior to hers.[70] Despite this demonstration of supernatural insight
(she was also able to pre-empt and cure a young lover's passion for
her), Sosipatra's financial and social arrangements depended on a

---

65. *Cod. Just.* 6.9.6.
66. *Cod. Just.* 9.1.12. See Constantine's affirmation at *Cod. Theod.* 9.1.3.9 that women
could bring criminal prosecutions only in response to injury or damage (*iniuria*) to their
family.
67. *Cod. Just.* 5.24.1. In classical law, legitimate children normally remained with the
father.
68. Emily Hemelrijk, *Matrona docta: Educated Women in the Roman Elite from
Cornelia to Julia Domna*, London: Routledge, 1999.
69. *PLRE I*, Sosipatra, p. 849.
70. *PLRE I*, Eustathius I, p. 310.

relation of her husband, Aedesius,[71] head of a school of philosophers at Pergamon, who supervised her material assets and may have determined her places of residence.

The figure of the woman philosopher also provided precedent for the active participation of Christian women in theological discussion, and more. While the senatorial patronesses of Jerome and Pelagius appeared to concede their need for a teacher, their studies were pursued sometimes at such a pace that even Jerome found it hard to keep up. The popularity of female saints with women worshippers also suggests a newfound confidence in women's collective identity (previously also a feature of networks based on women-only cults, such as that of the Bona Dea under the Republic). As well as Agnes, already noted, whose shrine became a burial ground for the women of Constantine's house, women could also have found inspiration from the (apocryphal) story of Thecla, who rejected marriage for the sake of following Paul, was rescued from the arena by a sympathetic queen and subsequently became a teacher in her own right.

By the end of the fourth century, Helena Augusta was re-emerging from the shadows as a new type of imperial patron, reflecting the higher profile enjoyed by imperial women of the house of Theodosius. Not only Augusta now, but also the *bona stabularia*, the virtuous innkeeper, Helena the legend reflected the change in the fortunes of elite women since her time.[72] The picture of women in Constantine's laws as restrained at home by modesty had been reflected in his conduct of his own household, the affairs of which had been shrouded in secrecy and have remained so ever since. But that picture could never reflect the reality of women's lives. For those empowered by the independent possession of wealth, opportunities for patronage and active influence were many, and increased with the expansion of Christianity, despite their being debarred from priestly functions. But also, as had always been the case, women of less exalted rank evolved strategies to protect their modest assets and livelihoods, pestering governors and even emperors with their petitions for redress. By the early fifth century, as the Theodosian dynasty settled itself at Constantinople, the era of the new Helenas, of the Augustae Eudoxia, Galla Placidia, Pulcheria and Eudocia, was about to begin.

71. *PLRE I* Aedesius 2, p. 15. His students included Julian and Maximus of Ephesus.
72. For the legend of Helena as the discoverer of the True Cross, first expressed in Ambrose's funeral oration for Theodosius I, see Drijvers, *Helena Augusta*, 95–117.

CHAPTER 12

Rome and Antioch

While Constantinople would evolve slowly to be capital of the
east, Antioch remained the centre of operations against Persia
for Constantius II, as it would be also for his successor Julian. A
city with a long history, a flourishing local elite and a vigorous
intellectual life, Antioch was also a vibrant political, military and
administrative centre, shaped by its longstanding relationship with
emperors and their officials. By contrast, 'Eternal Rome', the ancient
heart of empire, was a backwater, remote from the power plays
of the imperial court. But the Romans at Rome continued to exert
both symbolic and practical influence. Although the requirements
of imperial security drew emperors towards the borders, and
Ammianus, writing at Rome in c. 390, maintained, in satirical vein,
that nothing serious or important was ever done there,[1] its symbolic
status as the heart of empire ensured a special place for the eternal
city. Both cities, in very different ways, illustrate how civic identity
in capital cities was shaped by the presence – and absence – of
emperors.

Rome

Constantius' one visit to Rome in 357 was a memorable event,
which publicly and successfully celebrated the relationship of city
and emperor.[2] Ammianus' description of the formal ceremonial
arrival and subsequent public actions by the emperor has literary
elements, but also reveals what was expected of an imperial visitor
to the 'Eternal City'. The military procession was designed to
impress, as Constantius himself sat in a golden, jewel-encrusted

1. Amm. Marc. 14.6.26: *Haec ... memorabile nihil vel serium agi Romae permittunt.*
2. See chapter on late antiquity in Jon Coulston and Hazel Dodge (eds), *Ancient Rome: The Archaeology of the Eternal City*, Oxford: Oxford School of Archaeology, 2000; R. Krautheimer, *Rome: Portrait of a City, 312–1308*, Princeton, NJ: Princeton University Press, 1980.

chariot, surrounded by columns of armed men and military standards, the 'dragons woven of purple thread, bound to the golden and
jewelled spear-points, their mouths wide open and inflated by the
wind and thus hissing as if provoked by anger'.[3] As he approached
the city, applause rang out on all sides, but Constantius, with the
dignity which characterised his behaviour throughout his reign,
never moved but remained calm: 'not seen to be nodding when the
wheel jolted, nor spitting, nor wiping or rubbing his face or nose'.[4]
Once inside the city, he addressed the senators in the senate
house and the people from the tribunal (the venues were in line
with ancient republican practice). At the horse races, according to
Ammianus a favourite entertainment of the plebeians,[5] Constantius
exchanged badinage with the crowd, respecting their traditional
freedom of speech.[6]

Through his public actions, Constantius acknowledged Rome's
historical and symbolic identity. Both senate and people have a place
in the pageant and the locations of the emperor's addresses to
both recall the institutions of the Roman Republic. Although, in
Ammianus' phrase, Rome had consigned the government to the
Caesars as to her children, the Eternal City was still, symbolically,
the source of all authority. By conforming to Roman expectations,
Constantius not only won friends in the city – the senate would
openly rebuke Julian's pretensions to empire in 361[7] – but also
legitimised his position as the 'Caesar' (meaning emperor) to whom
the government had been entrusted.

Constantius' idea of Rome, as projected by Ammianus, was also
constructed in terms of the buildings. As Constantius viewed the city
from the Rostra, he marvelled at the massive temple of Jupiter,
the huge baths and amphitheatre, the Pantheon, various temples, the
Theatre of Pompey, dedicated in 55 BC, and the Forum of Trajan.
Most Roman monuments listed by Ammianus were the work of
emperors: Hadrian had erected the Pantheon (originally built by
Agrippa) and a temple of Venus and Rome; Domitian had built an
Odeon, and Vespasian the Forum of Peace. This Rome is a city of

---

3. Amm. Marc. 16.10.7.
4. Amm. Marc. 16.10.10.
5. Amm. Marc. 14.6.25, where he also reports the plebs' vulgar habit of sniffing loudly
while checking out the form of horses and charioteers.
6. Amm. Marc. 16.10.13. Contrast Diocletian's lack of ease with the *libertas* (freedom)
of the Roman plebs in 303, as reported by Lactantius *De mort. pers.* 17.2.
7. Amm. Marc. 21.10.7.

massive public monuments, reflecting the benefactions of emperors over the centuries and the presence of the ancient gods. The amazement expressed by Constantius, the Christian imperial tourist, was a fitting response to the grandeur of the past and his Roman heritage.

In this snapshot, by a classicising historian, Christian Rome is invisible. Yet, as we have seen, Constantine had already contributed to the transformation of the cityscape through his building of the Lateran on the Caelian Hill, St Peters on the Vatican, and other significant churches, which were tied largely to imperial sites, often previously associated with Maxentius. Neither Constans nor Constantius seems to have taken any active interest in further promoting imperial patronage of the Roman churches; the *Liber Pontificalis* (*Book of Popes*) entry for Pope Julius (336–52) has no information on imperial donations. The *Liber Pontificalis* is not entirely trustworthy and reliable archaeological evidence is scarce. However, the bishops of Rome seem to have actively engaged in the building of several smaller churches. Marcus, bishop for a few months in 336, is said to have built two churches, one within the city walls; Constantine seems to have provided these foundations with property for their upkeep and liturgical vessels but did not interfere with their design. His successor, Julius, was credited with no fewer than seven basilicas and three funerary churches. Again, some were in the centre (one was 'close to the Forum') and, if the traditions are credible, they show a determination on the part of the bishops of Rome to expand the Christian topography of the city.[8]

The involvement of Bishop Liberius with the controversies concerning Athanasius, resulted in schism at Rome. Liberius succeeded Julius in May 352 but was exiled by Constantius in 355. The emperor appointed his archdeacon, Felix, as his successor, but many Roman clergy and laity remained loyal to Liberius and refused to accept his replacement.[9] The schism also seems to have had a geographical dimension, as Felix based himself in the southwest of the city, seizing control of a basilica built by Julius in Trastevere, but was unable to assert himself elsewhere. On his return to Rome in 358 (having reached agreement with Constantius), Liberius tried to reconcile his opponents, with some success, although further violence would erupt on his death in 366.

8. For documentation and location of Marcus' and Julius' churches, see John Curran, *Pagan City and Christian Capital: Rome in the Fourth Century*, Oxford: Oxford University Press, 2000, 181–94.
9. *Collectio Avellana* 1.2 for the oath of loyalty taken to Liberius by Christians at Rome.

In the reigns of Constantius and Julian, there is only limited evidence for the involvement of the Roman aristocracy in Christian religious patronage. A prominent Christian senator, Iulius Bassus, died while holding the city prefecture in 359: his epitaph recorded that he was widely mourned by the Roman people, and his sarcophagus demonstrates how Christian symbolism could be assimilated to traditional iconography.[10] As we have seen, Rome also acquired status as the preferred burial site for imperial women. Both Constantina and Julian's wife, the younger Helena, invoked, posthumously, the patronage of St Agnes, the 'living' and victorious virgin; one senses a collective self-assertion on the part of the wives of Caesars, choosing to endow and be laid to rest in a city which was the symbolic heart of empire, but also geographically distanced from where emperors tended to be.

Aside from Cerealis and Bassus, the only other holder of the Roman urban prefecture known to be Christian in the 340s and 350s was one Flavius Leontius in 355–6.[11] Pagan holders included the *pontifex maior*, M. Maecius Memmius Furius Baburius Caecilianus Placidus, who was prefect of the city under Constans in 346–7, having been praetorian prefect of Italy and consul (343) under the same emperor. More controversial was Q. Flavius Maesius Egnatius Lollianus, named Mavortius, whose career began under Constantine: having lost favour in the mid-330s, when he was denied the consulship, he was Constans' prefect of the city in 342, before serving Constantius II as praetorian prefect of Italy and, finally, consul in 355. Being interested in astrology, Mavortius had, perhaps tactlessly, proposed a work on that subject (the *Mathesis*) to the writer Firmicus Maternus; that writer would soon convert, perhaps opportunistically, to Christianity and deploy his polemical talents in his attack on the *Errors of pagan religions*, exhorting Constans and Constantius to take a hard line on pagan rituals. One pagan holder of the office even had reason to be grateful for apparent divine intervention: in 348, the prefect Tertullus, who had earlier faced down a food riot by offering his two small sons to the crowd, found himself offering sacrifice at the temple of Castor at

10. E. S. Malbon, *The Iconography of the Sarcophagus of Iulius Bassus*, Princeton, NJ: Princeton University Press, 1990.
11. T. D. Barnes, 'Statistics and the conversion of the Roman aristocracy', *JRS* 85 (1995), 135–47 at 147. There were six prefects known to be Christian in the reign of Constantine, of whom five also held the consulship.

Ostia at the very moment when the delayed grain ships arrived in port.[12]

Perhaps the most prominent upholder of the ancient religions to act as prefect of Rome was Memmius Vitrasius Orfitus, priest of Vesta and devotee of Apollo, whose daughter, Rusticiana, was to be married to Q. Aurelius Symmachus, one of the last and most eloquent defenders of traditional cult at Rome.[13] Orfitus rose through the senate's ranks by holding the offices of the ancient senatorial *cursus honorum*, as *quaestor candidatus* (recipient of the emperor's *orationes*), praetor and suffect (lesser) consul. In 350, in defiance of the looming threat of Magnentius, he declared for Constantius II and represented the senate on embassies to that emperor. His loyalty to the ruling house was rewarded with the rank of count of the first order (*comes primi ordinis*) and he served on the emperor's consistory, an instance of a prominent senator also winning recognition in the context of court administration. Once Magnentius had been expelled from Italy, Orfitus returned to his senatorial career as proconsul of Africa in 352. After this he held the city prefecture twice, from the end of 353 to mid-355, and then again from January 357 to March 359. He would thus have presided in the senate when Constantius addressed it on the occasion of his visit in 357.

How these religious affiliations affected the general culture and behaviour of the Roman aristocracy is harder to establish.[14] Although Constantius removed the Altar of Victory from the senate house in 357, as a concession to the religious sensibilities of the Christian element in the senate, it was restored soon after, perhaps before Julian succeeded as Augustus.[15] But Roman senators preferred to request laws from emperors, rather than have laws imposed upon them. Although views on religious observance varied, senators were also influenced by a strong sense of collective solidarity; conflict therefore might be vigorous but its worst effects were contained. In 341, Constans had instructed the *vicarius* of Italy to

12. Amm. Marc. 19.10.2–4.
13. For references, see *PLRE I* Memmius Vitrasius Orfitus 3, pp. 651–3.
14. For a gradualist view applied to the 'conversion' of the senatorial aristocracy, see Michelle Salzman, 'How the west was won: The Christianization of the aristocracy in the west in the years after Constantine', in C. Deroux (ed.), *Studies in Latin Literature and Roman History* 6, Brussels: Latomus, 1992, 451–69.
15. B. Croke and J. Harries, *Religious Conflict in Fourth Century Rome: A Documentary Study*, Sydney: Sydney University Press, 1982, ch. 2.

'abolish sacrifices' in line with a previous law of Constantine, but he stopped short of removing public funding from the priestly colleges or their cultic celebrations.[16] In response, the prefect and senate required clarification as to whether temples could remain open for non-sacrificial events, and Constans obliged with a regulation, perhaps suggested by the prefect himself, which protected them from damage, on the grounds that the temples were also venues for festivals.[17]

Constans' legislation reflects the input of advisers with different agendas, perhaps more sensitive than he was to the feelings of religious traditionalists at Rome. For at Rome, the ancient priestly college of the *pontifices*, in charge of ritual regulation (and various aspects of family law) since Rome's earliest times, still carried out its age-old tasks. This was recognised by Constans, despite his stance against 'superstition'; in 349, the *pontifices* received confirmation of their right to vet the demolition of tombs for purposes of reconstruction. If their consent was withheld, penalties would be enforced in line with tradition on those who removed building material from structures, which it was impious (*nefas*) to touch.[18] Respect for burial places was common ground for Christians and non-Christians alike. But the deference to the role of the *pontifices* suggests that the most Christian of emperors still found it wise to defer to the traditional priestly establishment at Rome, of which, despite his apparent refusal to use his title of *pontifex maximus*, he was still nominally the head.

Constans' dealings with Rome on religion thus show the process of negotiation and compromise at work. His chief correspondent as representative of the senate was the prefect of the city, who handled matters related to the senate or the city.[19] As is documented by the far better-attested career of Symmachus, prefect in 384, the prefect of the city presided over, and represented to the emperor the views

16. *Cod. Theod.* 16.10.2. The fact that the *vicarius* was the addressee of the version preserved in the Code does not mean that the prefect of the city did (or did not) also receive a copy. Public funding for Roman pagan cult and the colleges was removed by Gratian in 383.
17. *Cod. Theod.* 16.10.3 (November 342).
18. *Cod. Theod.* 9.17.2 (March 349).
19. On the Roman urban prefecture, see A. Chastagnol, *La Préfecture urbaine à Rome sous le bas-empire*, Paris: Presses Universitaires de France, 1960. Older but still good is W. G. Sinnigen, *The Officium of the Urban Prefecture during the Later Roman Empire*, Papers of the American Academy at Rome 12, Rome: American Academy in Rome, 1957.

of, the Roman senate.[20] He was responsible for the adlection of new senators and their carrying out of their duties properly; absentee senators who failed to perform their public services were liable to be recalled and fined.[21] He had overall charge of the city's food supply, the distribution of wine and the revenues concerning both. These tasks could prove problematic. Vagaries of weather could delay the grain ships on their voyages from Africa and, despite the creation of extensive storage facilities over the centuries, supplies could run low, resulting in riots, as Tertullus found to his cost in 348. In 365, the elder Symmachus faced rioters angry at what they saw as the high price of wine; Symmachus retorted that he would use the wine supply to quench his lime-kilns rather than sell it off cheap to the plebs. Wine proved problematic for the family again when, after his second prefecture, Orfitus was accused of failing to pay what was due to the wine treasury, a debt which emperors tried to claim from Orfitus' successor Tertullus and subsequently from the younger Symmachus, who insisted that he had inherited nothing from his father-in-law.[22]

As Rome's most eminent judge, the prefect also had the power to deal with appeals and pass judgement *vice sacra iudicans* (in the emperor's stead) as if he were the emperor himself – although the experience of Symmachus in 384 suggests that politically sensitive cases or those which presented special legal difficulties were referred upwards, regardless of the prefect's official powers.[23] There seems to have been no official 'court room'. The prefect moved round the city, using various sites to hold sessions in the open air, a practice consistent with the longstanding tradition that justice should be public and be seen to be done. The peripatetic nature of the prefect's jurisdiction allowed him also to respond to emergencies as they arose. In 356, Leontius was prefect, 'swift in hearing cases, most just

20. In *Relatio* (state paper) 3, petitioning for the restoration of the Altar of Victory in 384, Symmachus claimed to represent majority senatorial opinion. This was contradicted by Christian senators and by Ambrose of Milan. For translation of *Relatio* 3, and the other state papers, see R. H. Barrow, *Prefect and Emperor: The 'Relationes' of Symmachus*, Oxford: Clarendon Press, 1973.
21. *Cod. Theod.* 6,4,7 to Orfitus, notifying him of a letter on the matter to the praetorian prefect, Hilarianus. Hilarianus' involvement suggests a doubt as to whether the city prefect could or would enforce sanctions on his fellow senators.
22. Symmachus, *Letters* 9.150; *Relatio* 34. For wine riots in Orfitus' time as prefect, see Amm. Marc. 14.6.1.
23. Symmachus, *Relatio* 49, on referral of a technically unlawful appeal of an *agens in rebus*, about to be penalised for an unsuccessful prosecution.

in reaching judgements and by nature kind', although over-prone
to exert his authority by excessive severity.[24] Without other means
of expressing their views, the right of the Roman mob to riot was
tacitly recognised, but the responsibility for preserving order rested,
still, with the prefect. Having faced down one protest over the arrest
of a charioteer, Leontius confronted a further disturbance over an
alleged wine shortage. On recognising the ringleader, one Petrus
Valvomeres, Leontius, after a public altercation, ordered his immediate arrest and had him flogged, despite his protests and those
of the mob; the summary action worked and the crowd dispersed
without further ado.[25]

Inevitably, as they exercised their jurisdiction at Rome, prefects
faced legal problems where imperial clarification was required and
wealthy senators had a vested interest in family and property law.
Gifts between families and households featured in the correspondence between Orfitus and Constantius II in the 350s more conspic-
uously than did religion. What happened, for example, if a patron
without children gave away substantial gifts to freedmen, then
acquired children later? The answer was that the gifts would revert
to the donor. What happened if mothers, as well as fathers, unwisely
gave presents to feckless children? After some hesitation, in 358,
Constantius declared to Orfitus that an undutiful child must return
a gift to his mother in its entirety (and not half as previously stipulated). However, mothers who remarried could not then claim back
gifts from their children, and mothers of low status or bad character
(the two were often equated) were not allowed to reclaim presents
under any circumstances.[26] Law was made by consultation and
response, but it was also shaped by the vagaries of human nature.

Policies on gifts show the functioning of the system in other ways
too. Good intentions could become clouded with legal chicanery,
as imperial rulings were tested to destruction in the courts. Constantine's ruling that gifts between parents and childen (but not others)
were exempt from the normal formalities of sale (*mancipatio*),
delivery and entry of the transaction in the public records, was
consistent with his desire to simplify procedure but ran counter to

24. Amm. Marc. 14.7.1–5.
25. See John Matthews, 'Petrus Valvomeres rearrested', in Michael Whitby, Philip
R. Hardie and Mary Whitby (eds), *Homo viator: Classical Essays for John Bramble*,
Bristol: Bristol Classical Press, 1987, 277–84.
26. *Cod. Theod.* 8.13.4 (358), modifying *Cod. Theod.* 8.13.1 (349). The meaning of
'undutifulness', if contested, would require definition in a court of law.

the interests of gift-givers other than parents who had omitted the formalities.[27] It thus caused predictable confusion. Did this exemption apply more widely? In courts, advocates would have tried to extend the application of the law by use of analogy, an accepted technique in legal and forensic argumentation. So in 341, Constans reconfirmed to the city prefect Celsinus that all gifts were to be entered in the public archives, in line with the general principle of Constantine's rule (to which parents and children were the exception);[28] but a decade later Orfitus required further assurance that gifts between people who were not close relations (*extranei*) must be formally registered and that Constantine's exemption applied *only* to parents and children.[29]

Emperor and senate therefore corresponded regularly on problems concerning the senate and its city. The physical distance of emperors from Rome rendered personal contacts between individual senators and emperors more difficult and limited the extent to which senators could exploit access to the emperor's ear to influence events. Distance could also distort the information emperors received and thus also the decisions made; only with difficulty in 370, for example, was Valentinian I persuaded to ensure that senators were not made liable to torture in treason trials. But the fact that the emperor was far away also helped senators at Rome to maintain a measure of independence, despite the oversight exercised by the imperially appointed *vicarius* of Rome and praetorian prefect of Italy. The often vast personal fortunes of senators, their ownership of extensive lands in Italy, Africa and beyond, the cultural self-assurance of the Eternal City based on its long history and cultivated upper class, and the increasing prominence of Rome as a Christian centre, whose 'founders' Peter and Paul would symbolically supplant Romulus and Remus, all contributed to a continuing (albeit misplaced) confidence that Rome would indeed last forever.

Libanius and Antioch

In the reigns of Constantius II and Julian, Antioch in Syria was an imperial capital,[30] in the sense that the emperor was frequently in

---

27. *Cod. Theod.* 8.12.4 9(319); and 5 (333).
28. *Cod. Theod.* 8.12.6 (December 341). Characteristically, Constans buttresses his policy with his father's authority.
29. *Cod. Theod.* 8.12.7. Clearly some senator had been trying to argue otherwise.
30. On the city and topography, see Glanville Downey, *A History of Antioch in*

residence. Its 'imperial' status depended, however, on its usefulness as a military base for eastern campaigning and thus on the state of Rome's relations with Persia. In times of peace, its location was too far removed both from the heartlands of the Eastern Empire and from the Danube frontier. In the longer term, therefore, the more central position of Constantinople would favour its development as the fixed capital of the east and the main seat of government and bureaucracy. Even when emperors were absent, however, Antioch was an administrative hub, as the headquarters of the praetorian prefect, the governor of Syria (*consularis Syriae*), the count of the east (*comes orientis*) and the master of the soldiers for the eastern sector (*magister militum per orientem*).[31]

One fruitful source for the life of Antiochenes in the fourth century is the orator and sophist, or teacher of rhetoric, Libanius. Often controversial and cantankerous, especially when confronting other teachers of rhetoric in competition with him, Libanius spent his life championing the values of Hellenic culture, the traditional philosophy, history and language of the wider Greek world. This made him, in due course, a natural ally of the emperor Julian, whose devotion to Hellenism he shared. Although his position as a public professor in Antioch exempted him from curial services, he identified with the local curial class, some of whom were related to him, and was active in the politics of the city. His career is a demonstration of the continuing social importance in late antiquity of both the spoken and the written word. As 'public orator', he celebrated the virtues of his city (*Oration* 11, the *Antiochikos*), and the emperors Constantius and Constans (*Oration* 59) and Julian (*Orations* 12 and 13), whose virtues he also commemorated after his death (*Oration* 18). In later life he continued to deliver speeches on public issues, such as, under Theodosius I (379–95), a defence of pagan temples (*Oration* 30), and, in 386, a vigorous attack on the iniquities of a governor, Tisamenos (*Oration* 33), who is portrayed as venal, incompetent and unjust. But Libanius also composed works in the form of speeches which were never delivered but sent as pamphlets to appropriate recipients, including emperors at Constantinople. In the meantime, through his letters, he cultivated an extensive network of useful contacts and former pupils. Much of his correspondence has

Syria, Princeton, NJ: Princeton University Press, 1961; on administration, J. H. W. G. Liebeschuetz, *Antioch: City and Imperial Administration in the Later Roman Empire*, Oxford: Clarendon Press, 1972.
31. Liebeschuetz, *Antioch*, 110–18.

to do with his school, as he protects its reputation, furthers the careers of his students through letters of recommendation, bends the ears of officials in Antioch and elsewhere, or seeks to influence the outcome of a lawsuit by a carefully crafted appeal to the judge. The aim of the letters was practical but they were also designed to be expressions of the writer's culture, an affirmation of the importance of civilised behaviour.[32]

Libanius' early life is known from his eloquent and self-justifying *Autobiography* (*Oration* 1), which paints a vivid picture of the insecurities and bitter rivalries of the educational profession.[33] Only comparatively late in life, in 355, did Libanius at last find safe harbour in Antioch, after many vicissitudes. His parents came from the city and Libanius might have expected to follow his father onto the council. But, at the age of 15, Libanius, to the amazement of his friends and relations, abandoned chariot races, the theatre, gladiatorial shows and even his pet pigeons for the life of a sophist; the language of dedication to a vocation echoes that of Christian renunciation of worldly pleasures. At the age of 22, in 336, Libanius left home for Athens, later to be the intellectual sanctuary for the young Julian. Four years later, goaded by the plots of rivals (he states), Libanius moved on and thereafter spent time educating students in Constantinople (where his life was threatened by rivals, supported by the city's proconsul), Nicaea and Nicomedia in Bithynia, and again, in 349, Constantinople. Now in imperial favour, Libanius found himself unable to settle and, after some delay, was allowed to give up his salaried post at Constantinople for a permanent position as teacher of rhetoric at Antioch. Thereafter he used his position to advocate educational values at Antioch, including official salaries for his four assistants (*Oration* 31).

A year later, in 356, the topography and living conditions of the city were eloquently, if selectively, invoked when Libanius' panegyric of Antioch was delivered at the Olympic festival (a grandiose

---

32. For context, see Raffaella Cribiore, *The School of Libanius in Late Antique Antioch*, Princeton, NJ: Princeton University Press, 2007; Isabella Sandwell and Janet Huskison (eds), *Culture and Society in Late Roman Antioch*, Oxford: Oxbow Books, 2004.
33. Greek text edited with translation and notes by A. F. Norman, *Libanius' Autobiography (Oration 1)*, Oxford: Oxford University Press, 1965; later edition by A. F. Norman with selection of Libanius' letters in the Loeb Classical Library, Cambridge, MA: Harvard University Press, 1992. On his life and work, briefly, Liebeschuetz, *Antioch*, 1–39.

occasion, maintained only with difficulty). For the speaker, the city had everything a citizen could desire:[34]

> She is more prosperous than the oldest states, while to the rest she is superior either in size or origin or fertility of the land. Moreover, if she be inferior to any (city) in respect of her walls, she yet surpasses that city in her supply of water, her mild winters, the wit of her inhabitants, the pursuit of philosophy and in the most noble feature of all, in Greek education and oratory, she rises superior to a city still greater (sc. Rome) … if you leave our city to go elsewhere, you will remember it, while if you come here from elsewhere, you will forget those towns you knew before.

Although it was expected that a panegyricist of a city should draw on standard themes when making his speech, allowing him to idealise his subject and omit inconvenient truths, the speaker could not include anything that too obviously contradicted the experience of his local audience. As Libanius stated, Antioch did indeed benefit from its situation on the navigable river Orontes, a morning's ride inland from its port at Seleucia, where a harbour was constructed by Diocletian for military as much as commercial purposes. Antiochene lifestyles are enhanced by 'the choicest products of every land', as the citizens 'reap the fruits of the whole world'.[35] Its agricultural hinterland was fertile, growing olives, vines and grain, which provisioned a large and prosperous population.[36] The water supply was both plentiful and pure. Celebrating the springs of Daphne, the 'palace of the Nymphs', Libanius described the waters as 'cold, clear and sweet, redolent of charm and soothing for the body to touch'. These waters flowed from the suburb of Daphne into the main city, assisting the Orontes in supplying fountains to every house and public and private baths in abundance. Real life was not so ideal. As Libanius did not mention, the numbers requiring food were not stable. As Julian would discover in 362, the mustering of any large force against Persia inevitably disrupted the balance of supply and demand celebrated by the orator, resulting in shortages, higher prices and social unrest.

---

34. Lib. *Ant.* 271–2, trans. A. F. Norman, *Antioch as a Centre of Hellenic Culture as Observed by Libanius*, TTH 34, Liverpool: Liverpool University Press, 2000, 64. All the translations below are taken from this. The speech *To the Antiochenes for the teachers* (*Oration* 31) is also translated in this volume (66–83).
35. Lib. *Ant.* 264. Despite this, the Antiochene upper class consisted of estate owners, not traders.
36. Lib. *Ant.* 174–5.

Physical amenity, Libanius asserted, gave rise to a flourishing civic society. The long main street, for example, with its colonnades and front doors opening directly onto the thoroughfare, allowed the inhabitants to socialise, even in bad weather. It followed that the people of the city were well behaved, honouring the ruling city council as children do their parents,[37] and the local council was a model of its kind, where members of the same families had served over the generations and were glad to spend their money on services to the city, even to the point of nearly bankrupting themselves. Baths, theatres, the grain supply, horse races and other public entertainments received funding from the councillors, beyond the call of duty; so public spirited were they (alleged Libanius) that they even refused to take advantage of the exemptions for which they were eligible.[38]

> It is a point of honour for each of them in the performance of their duties to surpass their predecessors, to preclude their successors from competing with them, to make a finer show in every one they give, and to provide novelties in addition to the usual attractions.[39]

Such too (as Libanius did not recall) had been the behaviour of the cities in second-century Bithynia, as celebrated by Dio Chrysostom, the sophist from Prusa – and castigated by the harassed governor and imperial representative, the younger Pliny. Competition to stage prestige shows by cash-strapped councillors was, in times of hardship, simply not affordable, but old habits died hard.[40]

Finally, the educator celebrates the wisdom and rhetorical gifts of his councillors. These, he said, not only improved the quality of public debate, attracting admiring audiences 'as though to regular seats of instruction', but also allowed the council to challenge imperial governors more effectively. Governors invited the eloquent and learned councillors to be present at their deliberations; the councillors in their turn were outspoken in according praise or blame. Such expressions of opinion did indeed matter. A law of Constantine had ordered acclamations of governors to be reported to him as part of his assessment of their performance in office,

37. Lib. *Ant.* 150–6.
38. For the more complex behaviour of councillors, many of whom dodged liturgies, while a few very rich families still revelled in euergetism, see Liebeschuetz, *Antioch*, 132–49.
39. Lib. *Ant.* 136.
40. For excessive competition in giving of games at Rome and failed attempts by the senate at self-regulation, see Symmachus, *Relatio* 8.3.

and Libanius echoed his reasoning: 'it counts a great deal for a governor's career that the council should be of the opinion that his decisions have been just'.[41]

This was Antioch as it would have liked to see itself, not as it was. The occasion of Libanius' speech, the Olympic Games, was already becoming an anachronism, albeit, still, a very popular one. Participation and training in athletics were on the wane and it would become increasingly inappropriate for the city, with its assertive Christian population, to celebrate a festival in honour of Olympian Zeus.[42] Moreover, councillors were far less casual about exemptions and more eager to better themselves by abandoning curial duties altogether than Libanius concedes. Given the lack of information on the council in general, statistical certainty is impossible, but Libanius' letters show a consistent willingness to help friends to avoid liability for curial duties. One fugitive, Dianius from Bithynia, was housed in Antioch until the governorship of his native province fell into the hands of a relative: Libanius corresponded both with the relative, who died, and with his successor, scheming to get Dianius onto the legal staff of the praetorian prefect.

The significant Christian population, its churches and clergy are entirely missing from Libanius' word-portrait.[43] Yet 'Christians' were first heard of under that name in Antioch in the first century and the church was ancient. In the third century, Paul of Samosata had been accused of flaunting himself as if he were a secular ruler, and under Constantine and Constantius, Antioch had been the venue for ecclesiastical councils and a battleground for schismatic bishops. As Julian would find to his cost in 362, Antiochene Christians were prepared publicly to defy the emperor in defence of their local martyr, a sign of their confidence in their numbers. Julian's satiric attack on the city, the *Beard-Hater* (*Misopogon*), was in part a response to the contumaciousness of the Christians in Antioch. In

41. Lib. *Ant.* 142. For Constantine's law, see *Cod. Theod.* 6.16.1. For Libanius' attack on the governor Tisamenos in 386 for paying too much attention to acclamations, see Lib. *Or.* 33.11. Peter Brown, *Power and Persuasion in Late Antiquity: Towards a Christian Empire*, Madison: University of Wisconsin Press, 1992, explains how rhetoric, skilfully deployed by subjects, also created expectations of the rulers.
42. Liebeschuetz, *Antioch*, 136–40.
43. This accords with classicising criteria. Libanius was not personally anti-Christian and protected Christian associates during the reign of Julian. For Libanius' (and John Chrysostom's) religious culture and the meaning of religious affiliation, see I. Sandwell, *Religious Identity in Late Antiquity: Greeks, Jews and Christians in Antioch*, Cambridge: Cambridge University Press, 2007.

the latter part of the fourth century, John Chrysostom would inspire his congregation with sermons celebrating the holy life of a Christian community, which he too saw as representing the people of Antioch as a whole.[44]

Libanius' Antioch was a place where things happened, a city with a buzz, commercial, financial and even frivolous, illuminated all the hours of the night, a city which indeed never slept.[45] Even in the absence of emperors, Antioch was the residence of three civilian imperial representatives, the praetorian prefect, the *comes orientis* and the *consularis* of Syria, along with their staffs. The duties of the count, whose main function was to supply support to the military effort in the east, were wide-ranging. Prominent in the letters of Libanius is Domitus Modestus,[46] later Valens' praetorian prefect of the east, who acted as judge in court cases and kept order in the city; in the hierarchy of governors, he outranked all but the proconsuls of Asia and Africa (who had precedence for historical reasons) and frequently the counts went on to hold higher offices.[47] The *consulares* of Syria were less elevated and seem to have been men of modest ambitions who held office for relatively short periods, often for less than a year. As was generally the case, the civil governors presided over court cases, but could be appealed from to a higher authority. They were also responsible for supervising the collection of taxes, and the methods of the collectors could be mistaken for those of bandits grabbing loot.[48]

The case of one Aristophanes of Corinth, a client of Libanius, is representative of the problems with which the governors as judges had to deal and the role of patronage in alleviating the plight of the condemned. The purpose of Libanius' rhetorical petition, delivered not in person but in writing to Julian in 362 (*Oration* 14), was to persuade the emperor to award to Aristophanes some form of honour or exemption which would allow him to return to his native Corinth free of the reproach of having been subjected to judicial interrogation as an accessory to treason. Libanius' intervention

44. Liebeschuetz, *Antioch*, 224–42, for Christian and pagan festivals and religious developments.
45. Lib. *Ant.* 265–7.
46. Lib. *Letters* 46, 49, 58 (358–9); For the *comes* Honoratus Nebridius' military operations in Isauria in 354 see Amm. Marc. 14.2.20.
47. *Not. Dign.* [*or.*] 22.17.33. Asia and Africa were the core senatorial provinces and (with different boundaries) had been 'senatorial' from the time of Augustus.
48. Cf. Amm. Marc. 28.2.13, on bandits, the Maratocupremi, who successfully plundered villages by masquerading as tax collectors.

was, in his eyes, justified because he sought to remedy an alleged miscarriage of justice. But the willingness of eminent patrons to intervene in the judicial process, either in the course of legal hearings and trials or afterwards, highlights the potential incompatibility of a rule-based justice system with a culture of patronage, the exercise of which depended on discretion and having the right contacts. Much of the alleged 'corruption' of the late antique system can be ascribed to the tension between these two competing cultural claims. Nor were Christians exempt from the urge to interfere in the judicial process, although their involvement was generally in the direction of mercy.

Aristophanes' story is that of a minor player caught up in great events. His misfortunes, as Libanius represented them, went back a long way. A member of the curial order at Corinth, Aristophanes' ownership of his property was challenged by Constans' corrupt official Eugenius, and Aristophanes was forced to flee to Syria. There he took refuge with the philosopher Fortunatianus and was enlisted by Constantius II as an *agens in rebus*, a job he carried out energetically but (allegedly) without profiting from corrupt dealings. Aristophanes' wanderings show the mobility of the late antique man on the make; resembling those of the young Libanius, but for less positive reasons. He had also moved, as many others would do, from curial to imperial service, although his change of career was dictated by necessity rather than fulfilled ambition. Imperial service was no guarantee of safety. While on the staff of Parnasius, prefect of Egypt (also subject to the *comes orientis*), he was accused of a minor act of peculation and disgraced. Moreover, Parnasius himself had fallen under suspicion of treason and, along with his staff, was investigated by the notorious 'Paul the Chain'.[49] Aristophanes, naively, admitted that he had introduced a soothsayer to Parnasius but maintained that the consultation referred only to Parnasius' private affairs. For Paul, this would have provided a useful 'link' in the 'chain' of evidence against both; Constantine's law had outlawed private consultation of diviners on any matter at all. Although Domitius Modestus, as the final judge in the case, spared Aristophanes interrogation under torture because of his curial status, he was sent into internal exile. To secure Aristophanes' recall, Libanius played on Julian's known preference for philosophers, as well as his client's (alleged) good character, innocence of wrongdoing and general

---

49. *Or*. 14.15. Amm. Marc. 19.12 for the treason trials at Scythopolis.

misfortunes. Despite Aristophanes' conviction for peculation and possible involvement with treason, Julian's own dislike of Paul the Chain, whom he had executed, doubtless assisted him in his decision to listen sympathetically to Libanius' request.[50]

Julian and Antioch

Julian's relationship as emperor with Antioch in 362–3 was far from easy. His own, satirical, opinion of the city was set out in a New Year address to the citizens early in 363, entitled *Beard-Hater* (*Misopogon*) or (perhaps ironically) *Antiochikos*. From this at times jaundiced production emerges a depiction of Antioch and its people which can be set alongside that of Libanius. Although the two had much in common, the attitudes of emperor and sophist also differed in fundamental respects. While Libanius wrote as a lover of his city and long-time resident, Julian's prickly satire shows his increasing difficulties in coping with a world with which he was out of step.

The *Misopogon* was Julian's reply to various lampoons about his appearance, character and policies composed by the citizens in the context of their New Year festival, which, like the Saturnalia at Rome, turned the conventional social order upside down. Their targets included his beard, which they suggested he should twist into ropes, his distaste for public entertainments and his religious policies, especially as regarded Christianity. Part of the game was to speak in riddles:

> 'The *Chi*', say the citizens, 'never harmed the city in any way, nor did the *Kappa*'. Now the meaning of the riddle, which your wisdom has invented, is hard to understand but I obtained interpreters from your city and I was informed that these are the first letters of names, and that the former is intended to represent Christ and the latter Constantius.

Julian's response was to declare sarcastically that Constantius had indeed wronged them – by not putting Julian to death. As for Christ (*Chi*), Julian observed that the people of Emesa had burned Christian 'tombs', though Julian 'had never annoyed them', while the Antiochene common people had chosen 'atheism' and hated Julian for his devotion to the old gods. At every stage, Julian uses

---

50. Julian, *Letter* 53 (number in Wright's Loeb edition). Julian does not specify a solution but promises to consult Libanius further.

vocabulary in reverse – an acknowledgement of the conventions of the festival of which his pronouncement was part.

Julian's attitude to public entertainments did him no favours with the pleasure-loving Antiochenes. Where Libanius celebrated a city where the lights never went out, Julian was a kill-joy:[51]

> I banish myself from the theatres, such a dolt am I ... And even when I do enter the theatre I look like a man who is expiating a crime. Then again, although I am entitled a mighty Emperor, I employ no one to govern the mimes and chariot-drivers as my lieutenant or general throughout the inhabited world. ... I hate horse-races as men who owe money hate the market-place. Therefore I seldom attend them, only during the festivals of the gods; and I do not stay the whole day as my cousin (Constantius) used to do, and my uncle (Julianus, *comes Orientis*) and my brother by the same father (Gallus). Six races are all I stay to see, and not even those with the air of one who loves the sport.

Julian thus fitted himself into a long tradition of emperors who openly despised public entertainments, not least his model Marcus Aurelius;[52] he would also find himself in agreement with prominent Christians who deplored the moral effect of gladiatorial and other spectacles. But however virtuous, this behaviour was not a route to popularity with the people at large.

Equally unappealing in a now very Christian city was Julian's religious policy. The Antiochenes found Julian's expressions of devotion to the gods excessive:[53]

> 'The Emperor sacrificed once in the temple of Zeus, then in the temple of Fortune; he visited the temple of Demeter three times in succession ... The Syrian New Year arrived and again the Emperor went to the temple of Zeus the Friendly One. Then came the general festival and the Emperor went to the shrine of Fortune. Then, after refraining on the forbidden day, again he goes to the temple of Zeus the Friendly One and offers up prayers according to the custom of our ancestors. Now who could put up with an Emperor who goes to the temples so often ...?

51. Lib. *Ant.*, 266–7; Julian, *Misopogon* 342B, reflecting also on the 'unmanliness' of the Antiochenes.
52. Claimed for Marcus by SHA, *Marcus* 15.1; 22.5,6. It should be noted that the SHA went in for 'in-jokes' about Julian, and that it is possible that Julian's character is here imposed on Marcus.
53. Julian, *Misopogon* 339D–340C, Wright translation (Loeb), modified.

Nor were Julian's 'misdeeds' confined to excessive sacrifice. In a public clash with Christian devotees, Julian removed the body of the martyr Babylas, formerly bishop of Antioch, from his new funerary church, erected on the shrine of Apollo at Daphne. From Julian's perspective he was justified: the holiness of the sanctuary, where the rites had already been largely abandoned,[54] was damaged by its pollution by a corpse. However, the angry Christians were quick to retaliate. In a public demonstration of defiance, the relics were moved in solemn procession to a different resting place, and soon after, the temple of Apollo was itself destroyed by fire.[55]

Julian's response to the Antiochenes was in line with a tradition of imperial tolerance, of 'freedom of speech', especially as exercised by the people in imperial capitals. As we have seen, Diocletian and Constantius II both encountered and, to a point, tolerated, the free-speaking of the plebs at Rome, although Ammianus is careful to observe of Constantius' visit that neither side went too far. Libanius recalled an anecdote of Constantine, who had wisely ignored hostile demonstrations at Rome, rejecting a suggestion that he should loose the troops on the mob;[56] in the same vein, he recalled that Constantius II, too, on learning that his imperial statue at Edessa had been overturned and spanked, chose to ignore the incident.[57] Later emperors formally conceded that not all insults directed against emperors by individuals deserved prosecution; the per-petrator might be drunk or benefit from other extenuating circum-stances. Naturally, a tolerant response on the part of emperors to provocation was the preferred option – in the opinion of subjects.

But Julian's satire also had a serious point. As his readers well knew, he did have other options, ranging from executions of offenders, as had been threatened by Gallus against the Antioch city council, to loss of city status[58] or confiscations of property,[59] which he chose not to exercise. Moreover, Julian's punishment of cities, or factions within cities, like Caesarea, Edessa or Bostra, was connected to the activities of Christians within those cities; justice was

54. Julian, *Misopogon* 361D–362B.
55. Julian, *Misopogon* 361B–D. Julian argues that Apollo had already abandoned the temple.
56. Lib. *Or.* 19. 19.
57. Lib. *Or.* 19. 48–9.
58. Socrates, *Hist. eccl.* 5.4 on forfeiture of metropolitan status of Caesarea in Cappa-docia.
59. Julian, *Letter* 40 (of Christian Edessa).

exploited to serve a religious feud. In this context, Julian's response to the Antiochenes, that he would remove the favour of his imperial presence from them, by relocating to Tarsus, was mild in comparison but in fact implied worse consequences to come. For the transfer of imperial favour to an alternative city could have long-term implications for both status and prosperity. Moreover, the *Misopogon* was not only a satire. It may also be termed an 'edict of chastisement' (which could take the form of a letter), a means of communication used by emperors from the first century onwards to improve the behaviour of provincials and castigate wrongdoing.[60]

Despite its satirical content and the restraint shown by Julian in his response to what he saw as multiple provocations, Julian's response to Antiochene protests and his perspective on the city as a whole draws attention to his weaknesses as emperor. By contrast with the patriotic and tolerant Libanius, Julian flaunts his divergence from the values of the frivolous and 'unmanly' people of the city, making a virtue of his austere lifestyle – so much more appreciated by his former Gallic subjects than by the decadent easterners – and his contempt for public amusements and the cheerfully chaotic street life of the Syrian metropolis. Unlike Constantius and even Gallus, he made no concessions to popularity – and prided himself on that fact. Most damaging for his long-term hopes of restoring the ancient cults was his total failure to understand or deal with the Christian allegiances of the ordinary people of the city. Where Libanius was happy to tolerate Christians as one among many religions (although he would vigorously protest against temple destruction in the 380s), for Julian the Christians remained the 'Galilaeans' and works of charity on their part merely fuelled among the poor 'an admiration for godlessness'.[61]

60. Maud W. Gleason, 'Festive satire: Julian's *Misopogon* and the New Year at Antioch', *JRS* 76 (1986), 106–119 at 116–18.
61. Julian, *Misopogon* 363A.

CHAPTER 13

Julian Augustus

The impact of the nineteen-month reign of Julian as sole Augustus on contemporary observers[1] and later writers[2] was out of all proportion to its length. Opinion was polarised. His admirers included Ammianus (with reservations), his panegyricists Claudius Mamertinus (consul 362)[3] and Libanius and, a little later, the historian Eunapius, who drew on the notes of Julian's friend, the doctor Oribasius, and the gist of whose work was preserved by Zosimus. Critics included Christian writers, such as Gregory Nazianzus, who shared Julian's studies in Athens in the 350s, and the Syrian hymn-writer Ephrem, an eyewitness of the surrender of Nisibis to the Persians after Julian's death on campaign.[4] Nor was religious policy the only bone of contention. The ambitious Persian campaign of 363 and its perceived failure bewildered observers like Libanius; and Ammianus' frequent criticisms of Julian's public demeanour, his dependence on 'philosophers' and his excessive devotion to blood sacrifices, show that doubts over Julian were not confined to Christians.

Julian's self-representation in his literary works is unique among writings authored by emperors. Previous emperors had tried their

1. Cf. Claudius Mamertinus' *Speech of thanks for his consulship* (= *Pan. Lat.* 3(11)) delivered on his taking office in January 362, 14.4: 'Thus his reign will already seem long to those who do not measure its length by the tally of the days or months but by the number of his deeds and achievements' ('itaque grandaevum iam imperium videbitur, his qui non ratione dierum aut mensium sed operum multitudine et effectarum rerum modo Iuliani tempora metientur').
2. Two short but useful biographies of Julian are R. Browning, *The Emperor Julian*, London: Weidenfeld and Nicolson, 1975, and G. W. Bowersock, *Julian the Apostate*, London: Duckworth, 1978; S. Tougher, *Julian the Apostate*, Edinburgh: Edinburgh University Press, 2007, provides a useful survey of important issues.
3. See his *Pan. Lat.* 3 (11), delivered in 362.
4. See translations of Mamertinus, Chrysostom's *Homily on St Babylas* (extract) and Ephrem's *Hymns*, in Samuel N. C. Lieu, *The Emperor Julian: Panegyric and Polemic. Claudius Mamertinus, John Chrysostom, Ephrem the Syrian*, TTH Greek ser. 2, Liverpool: Liverpool University Press, 1989.

hands at literature, notably Hadrian, who dabbled in poetry, Marcus Aurelius (Julian's hero)[5] in his Stoic *Meditations*, Constantine in sermons to his courtiers and the *Oration to the Saints* ascribed to him, and even Constantius with his bad poetry. But Julian was far the most prolific and versatile imperial author of antiquity. His surviving work includes panegyrics (of questionable sincerity) of Constantius II and, more credibly, of Eusebia,[6] satire (the *Caesars, Misopogon*), hymns, for example to Helios, philosophical treatises, often in the form of letters,[7] and an extensive official or quasi-official correspondence with friends, administrators and public organis-ations. Despite his highly personal tone, Julian wrote always as Caesar or Augustus. His letters and even his philosophical treatises, like Constantine's disquisitions on Christianity, were designed to have a public impact, and could be read as guides to policy.[8] The rhetoric was all-important: ostensible claims of support for religious toleration could not be interpreted as advocacy of equality among religions when 'error' was denounced and the emperor's personal religious preferences vigorously and extensively justified.

Has Julian received more attention than he deserves? The last 'pagan' emperor has potent symbolic significance. Reared as a Christian, in c. 351 Julian converted to an esoteric form of pagan-ism, although his true convictions were not publicly known until 361. As Augustus he attempted to reverse the rise of Christianity and reinvigorate the city-based organisation of traditional cults. His accession thus posed an unforeseen threat to Christians and their leaders, who could not be confident that the gains over the previous decades were secure. The question of whether Julian would have succeeded in frustrating the 'Galilaeans', had he lived, is hypotheti-cal but, as we shall see, relevant to the reasons for the expansion of Christianity in the fourth century.

Julian had also to respond to the military challenges from abroad and the internal stresses at home inherited from the third century by the 'new' empire of late antiquity. His campaigns as Caesar in Gaul appeared to have stabilised the western frontiers for the duration of

5. As stated at Julian, *Letter to Themistius* 253A, *Caesars* 328C–D, 335C.
6. She is also given honourable mention at Julian, *Letter to the Athenians* 274A–B, 275B.
7. For example, *Against the Cynics* and (in the same vein) *To the Cynic Heracleios*. His treatise *Against the Galilaeans* survives only through citations by Cyril of Alexandria, who sought to refute it.
8. Euseb. *Vit. Const.* 2. 47–61 for Constantine's *Letter to the eastern provincials* on his religious beliefs/policy.

his short reign. Julian the Caesar had been impelled towards revolt by the explosive combination of his own distrust of his cousin Constantius, who had been party to the destruction in 337 of most of his family, the mischief-making of Constantius' courtiers, the effects on his confidence (and Constantius' fears) of his own success in Gaul following his victory at Strasbourg, and the aspirations of his Gallic army. Such difficulties were personal, but also systemic; armies were loyal to the leaders and comrades they knew, not to an imperial abstraction. In 361, Julian, to his amazement, acquired an empire 'by the normal law of succession', which he and his army 'had expected to snatch by force'.[9] Once in the east, Julian was forced in his turn to conciliate the regional loyalties of the eastern armies, loyal to the dead Constantius II; his war on Persia was in part motivated by his need to win their trust. For his own reasons too, he sought a decisive outcome against the Persians, perhaps in imitation of Galerius, some sixty years earlier; after Julian's failure, imperial management of the eastern frontier became more restrained (and less expensive). Thus, while Julian's differences from his immediate predecessors have attracted most attention, his similarities to them were no less significant.

Education

Unlike the sons of Constantine, Julian was educated away from the imperial court. Born in, probably, 331 at Constantinople, he was the son of Julius Constantius and his second wife Basilina, who died soon after Julian's birth. His paternal grandparents were Constantius I and Constantius' second wife, Theodora, the daughter of Maximian. His half-brother Gallus, by a different mother, was five years older than he. Although Julian referred to Constantine as his uncle, his allegiance lay with the line of Theodora, not that of the Christian Helena. However, for polemical purposes, when justifying his revolt against Constantius to the Athenians, family ties mattered:

> For it is public knowledge that on the father's side my descent is the same as that of Constantius (II) on his father's side. For both our fathers were born as brothers, the sons of the same father.[10]

In Julian's version of events, Constantius' actions in 337 were the

9. Amm. Marc. 22.2.3: 'advertebant enim imperium, quod ereptum ibant ... praeter spem ordinario iure concessum'.
10. Julian, *Letter to the Athenians* 270C.

more heinous because directed against close kin. Julian was six
when his father, uncle Dalmatius and cousins Hannibalianus and
Dalmatius were killed in the coup at Constantinople, which
confirmed the three sons of Constantine as sole Augusti. All were
young and would have expected to produce heirs in due course.
With the empire apparently secured for the house of Constantine,
Gallus and Julian were allowed to live; it may have helped that
Constantius was married to their sister. Julian had no doubt as to
Constantius' personal responsibility for the deaths in 337:

> And such close kin as we were, see how this philanthropic monarch
> behaved, for he killed six of my cousins, who were also his, and my
> own father, his uncle, and in addition an uncle common to us both
> on the father's side, and my own eldest brother – all without trial,
> and me and my other brother (Gallus) he wished to kill but finally
> sentenced us to exile.

Julian's early education, then, was not that of a man expected
to succeed to the purple. By his own account, he was fortunate in
his first tutor, Mardonius, who from 338 instructed Julian in the
classics, especially Homer and Hesiod. Observers credited
Mardonius with using the ancient Greek authors as examples of
morality, a significant example of the connection between the
classical authors and right moral (and religious) belief which was to
be central to Julian's later thinking.[11] In 342, Gallus and Julian were
comfortably confined on the estate of Macellum in Cappadocia.
According to Julian, they were under constant supervision, denied
the company of boys of their own age and any access to serious
structured learning. Julian, however, continued to read voraciously
as he accessed the books of the eunuch supervisors and the library of
George of Cappadocia, a resource which, in 362, after that bishop's
violent death in Alexandria, Julian would claim as his own property
by law.

In 348, a new and more peripatetic phase began. Now aged 17,
Julian left Macellum for the city of his birth, Constantinople. Next,
his first, indirect contact with Libanius was made at Nicomedia,
where he also may have read Plato with Themistius. Oratory and the
writings of Plato and Aristotle were supplemented by exposure
to Platonic ideas, which would have a profound influence on his
policies as emperor, as he encountered Aedesius, the pupil of the

---

11. Cf. Lib. *Or.* 18. 157 for the connections between classical literature and morality.

Platonist Iamblichus of Syria, also the mentor of the ill-fated Sopatros, executed by Constantine. Julian would encounter too the controversial theurgist Maximus at Ephesus and Priscus at Athens. Under Maximus' influence, in 351, Julian repudiated his Christianity, although he continued to profess the faith publicly for a further ten years.

In the view of many who criticised Julian's excessive devotion to sacrifices and 'philosophers' (of the wrong kind), his educational experience was far from beneficial. The ideas furthered by the followers of Iamblichus, building on a tradition going back through Porphyry (who was also a bitter opponent of the Christians) and the third-century thinker Plotinus to Plato and Pythagoras, were not easily explained for the general reader, then or now.[12] No 'introduction' or short guide to late Roman Platonic thought survives from antiquity, an omission the more significant given the taste of the age for epitomes, chronicles and other useful summary collections of knowledge. Instead, the Platonists concentrated largely, though not exclusively, on commentaries, a format which can encourage a focus on minutiae at the expense of the broader picture. However, underlying all later Platonic writing is an interest in the various levels of being and perception, ranging from appearances through a hierarchy of intellectual and 'intelligible' levels to ultimate union with the One. The emphasis is on the journey to perfection of the individual; the philosophers had little interest in public life or the citizen's duty to the community.

As emperor, Julian devoted time to writing to friends, expounding his version of Platonic theology. The Hymn to Helios (the Sun), addressed to his friend and counsellor Sallustius, seeks to assimilate different 'levels of being' to the Sun; the highest or 'intelligible' world consists of Platonic Forms, now called 'the intelligible gods'; in the 'middle world' were the intellectual gods (here the Sun becomes Helios-Mithras); and in the world as perceived by the senses, Helios, the Sun as we see it, is all-supreme and all-giving: Helios-Mithras was midway 'between the visible gods, who inhabit the cosmos, and the immaterial and intelligible gods who surround the Good [*t'agathon*]'.[13] So supreme and all-giving is Helios that

12. See, for example, Gillian Clark (ed. and trans.), *Iamblichus, On the Pythagorean Life*, TTH Greek ser. 8, Liverpool: Liverpool University Press, 1989; J. M. Dillon and W. Polleichtner (eds and trans.), *Iamblichus of Chalcis, The Letters*, Atlanta, GA: Society of Biblical Literature, 2009.
13. Julian, *Hymn to Helios* 138D.

he subsumes the functions of the other gods, Apollo, Dionysus, Asclepios and even Zeus himself.[14] This Helios is a more sophisticated creation than the Sol Invictus of Aurelian[15] or (in certain moods) Constantine, but the choice of the Sun as favoured or supreme deity at least had precedent.[16]

The emperor's religion could never be a purely private matter. For Julian, the bridge between public cultic observance and private conviction was the Iamblichean connection of right belief with right religious action, that is, ritual. Iamblichus combined a system of education in the different levels of reality with a distinctive theology based on the 'Chaldean Oracles', a religious compilation by one Julianus in the reign of Marcus Aurelius.[17] If the devout seeker after truth performed the right ritual actions towards the gods, the gods would do what he wanted of them. Moreover, he (or she)[18] would acquire something of the nature of the divine. This was known as 'theurgy', the 'working of the gods'. However, a promise that the success of a petition was guaranteed if the right ritual acts were done also resembled magic, and the expertise of Julian's favourite teacher, Maximus, lay precisely in that area. Maximus could 'work' the gods' statues to produce visible 'miracles' and strange signs. For Platonists more interested in the other strand of late Roman philosophy, the integration of Aristotelean logic into Platonic thought, Iamblichus and his followers (Julian perhaps included) represented a dangerous departure from the path of reason. Julian's personal religion, therefore, was not simply 'pagan' but a version of 'paganism' that was suspect in the eyes of many and the doctrines of which were esoteric and therefore unlikely to command wide popular support.[19]

14. Julian, *Hymn to Helios* 143C–144C.
15. Julian, *Hymn to Helios* 156C, connects with Aurelian's cult-based approach when he describes the festivals of the Sun at Rome, including Sol Invictus.
16. On Julian's Hellenism and philosophy, see P. Athanassiadi, *Julian: An Intellectual Biography*, Oxford: Oxford University Press, 1992, derived from her *Julian and Hellenism*, Oxford: Clarendon Press, 1981. For Julian's domestic shrine to the Sun-god, see Lib. *Or.* 12.80–2; *Or.* 18.127. For the broader cultural context, see G. W. Bowersock, *Hellenism in Late Antiquity*, Cambridge: Cambridge University Press, 1990; P. Athanassiadi and M. Frede (eds), *Pagan Monotheism in Late Antiquity*, Oxford: Oxford University Press, 1999; S. Mitchell and P. van Nuffeln (eds), *One God: Pagan Monotheism in the Roman Empire*, Cambridge: Cambridge University Press, 2010.
17. See P. Athanassiadi, 'The Chaldean Oracles', in Athanassiadi and Frede, *Pagan Monotheism*, 149–82; Rowland Smith, *Julian's Gods: Religion and Philosophy in the Thought and Action of Julian the Apostate*, London: Routledge, 1995, 91–113.
18. For the pagan philosopher Sosipatra, see Eunap. *VS* 466–70 and above, pp. 272–3.
19. Cf. Amm. Marc. 22.12.6–7 and, on excessive sacrifices, 25.4.16–17, describing

Accession

Julian's period as Caesar in Gaul laid the foundation for his accession as Augustus through military victories, notably at Strasbourg, and a tax-cutting administration. During these years he fell out with several officials appointed by Constantius II, not least Barbatio and the praetorian prefect Florentius; for these he substituted men he could trust, such as his finance officer (*comes sacrarum largitionum*) Claudius Mamertinus[20] and his master of the horse, Fl. Nevitta,[21] who would share the consulship of 362. Surprisingly for a man represented as chronically suspicious, Constantius backed his Caesar where he felt Julian to be in the right: it is largely due to Julian's propaganda, backed by Ammianus, that we see Constantius as too quick to seize on the artful imputations of the designing courtiers.[22]

In 360, Julian was proclaimed Augustus for the second time at Paris. By now, there was no going back. His rise to this point illustrates the close and perhaps inevitable relationship between military victory and imperial aspiration. Julian had used the two years following his Strasbourg victory to consolidate Roman military superiority, making raids into the territories of the Franks and Alamanni to force the 'barbarians' to terms. His relationships with the officials appointed by Constantius had also been difficult; in particular, Julian disapproved of the revenue-raising policies of the praetorian prefect, Florentius, whose attempts to raise the level of taxation asked were countermanded by Julian's insistence that special levies should not be implemented.[23]

By 359, Constantius looked to Julian to supply reinforcements to fend off a resurgent Persia after the fall of Amida. Julian was therefore required to send four named military units to Persia, with detachments from other units as well. The envoy, Decentius, arrived

Julian as '*superstitiosus magis quam sacrorum legitimus observator*' ('superstitious in his religious observance rather than one who acts in accordance with religious law').
20. Amm. Marc. 21.8.1; in 365, he was sacked by Valentinian I and Valens for peculation in office as praetorian prefect (Amm. Marc. 27.7.1–2).
21. Amm. Marc. 21.8.3.
22. Julian, *Letter to the Athenians* 277D–278D; 280D–282D.
23. Amm. Marc. 17.3.2–5; also 25.4.15 for Julian's generosity. For Florentius' correct advice, for which he got no credit, to attack promptly at Strasbourg, see Amm. Marc. 16.12.14. Julian, *Letter to the Athenians* 280A–B, accused Florentius of poor judgement; his advice to offer 2000 lb of silver to the Franks for safe passage across the Rhine was overruled by Julian, who then crossed unharmed.

in Gaul in February 360. Julian's response was to arrange the departure eastwards of two units, the Celtae and the Petulantes. The other
two, however, the Aeruli and Batavians, were absent in Britain,
under the command of Lupicinus, the 'master of arms', who had
been sent as Julian's deputy to quell an uprising of the Picts and
Scots.[24] But the Caesar was already aware that trouble was to be
anticipated, as he had pledged his word that the soldiers, many of
whom were barbarian recruits, would not be required to leave
Gaul.[25] And so it proved. An anonymous leaflet was dropped on the
ground in the camp of the Petulantes, warning that they would be
'despatched to the ends of the earth, like criminals and condemned
men, leaving their loved ones to be enslaved by the Alamanni'.[26]
Then, when they arrived at Paris, they were met by Julian in person.
After an emollient speech, the Caesar invited their officers to
dinner:[27]

> So that he could offer greater honour to those about to go so far
> away, having invited their chiefs (*proceres*) to dinner he asked them
> outright to make such requests as were most urgently on their minds.

Later the same evening, the soldiers rioted and surrounded the
palace, proclaiming Julian Augustus. When Julian finally appeared
before them the next day, he publicly disavowed any wish for the
new title, but his resistance was overcome, and he was raised
high on a shield and 'crowned' with the neck-chain belonging to
a standard-bearer of the Petulantes. The new 'Augustus' then
rewarded his followers with promises of a donative of five *aurei* and
a pound of silver, accompanied by promises of good government and
reforms.[28] Dissidents were disposed of: Lupicinus was arrested on his
return from Britain, while Florentius fled across the Alps.[29]
   Julian's version of these events was that he was coerced by the

24. Amm. Marc. 20.1.
25. Amm. Marc. 20.4.4.
26. Amm. Marc. 20.4.10: 'Nos quidem ad orbis terrarum extrema ut noxii pellimur et
damnati, caritates vero nostrae Alamannis denuo servient.' Also, Julian, *Letter to the
Athenians* 283b; Zos. *New History* 3.9.1.
27. Amm. Marc. 20.4.13: 'Utque honoratius procul abituros tractaret, ad convivium
proceribus corrogatis, petere siquid in promptu esset edixit'; for omission of dinner,
Julian, *Letter to the Athenians* 284B–285A.
28. Amm. Marc. 20.4.14–8 (acclamation); 5.3–7 (speech to soldiers).
29. Amm. Marc. 21.6.5. Florentius succeeds Anatolius as praetorian prefect of Illyricum
and is appointed consul for 361 by Constantius. Amm. Marc. 22.3.6: on Julian's
accession, Florentius goes into hiding with his family and is condemned to death in
absentia at Chalcedon. He re-emerged after Julian's death.

soldiers into accepting the title of Augustus, without prior consultation or agreement from Constantius. But how far did he personally connive at his own elevation? Like Magnentius ten years earlier, he denied that he was influenced by personal ambition. A further similarity with Magnentius' coup, which Julian omits from his public self-justification in the *Letter to the Athenians*, was the dinner with the officers, which led directly to the outbreak. Moreover, Julian put into circulation a 'confidence' shared with his 'close friends' that, on the night before his acceptance of the title, he had been visited in a dream by the 'Genius of the public', who declared his longstanding support for Julian's ambitions but threatened to withdraw his favour if Julian did not accede, 'given that the vote of so many was in accord'.[30] In stressing this proof of divine favour as grounds for his legitimacy as ruler, Julian followed the precedent of Constantine and the Tetrarchs before him. But at this stage, the identity of the gods in whose support Julian trusted in secret was known only to a few.[31]

Although he refused to endorse Julian's elevation,[32] Constantius II took no immediate action against him. Julian himself moved cautiously to consolidate his position in the west. He conducted a successful campaign on the Rhine, against the Atthuarian Franks, and made his own appointments, sidelining those of Constantius.[33] He also held games at Vienne to mark the fifth anniversary of his reign, publicly wearing the insignia of an Augustus. More insidiously, he would seek, in spring 361, to blacken the reputation of his absent colleague by arresting a king of the Alamanni, Vadomarius, alleging that Constantius had corresponded with the king and had incited the Alamanni to launch raids into the Roman province of Raetia in order to prevent Julian from leaving Gaul.[34]

In 361, believing that he had secured Gaul, Julian at last went on the offensive against his cousin, attacking on three fronts. He himself

---

30. Amm. Marc. 20.5.10: 'sententia concordante multorum'. For the withdrawal of the Genius, prior to Julian's death, see Amm. Marc. 25.2.3.
31. At this stage, Julian was publicly still Christian but had already indicated secretly that his religious allegiance lay elsewhere.
32. Amm. Marc. 20.8 (Julian's letter to Constantius); 9.4–5 (Constantius' response, including new appointments of Nebridius as praetorian prefect and Felix as *magister officiorum*).
33. Amm. Marc. 20.10.1–2 (Franks); 20.9.8 (Anatolius as *magister officiorum*); 21.5.11–12 (Constantius' prefect, Nebridius, refuses to support Julian but is allowed to leave unharmed).
34. Amm. Marc. 21.3 and 4; Julian, *Letter to the Athenians* 286A–B.

moved eastwards, along the Danube, while another army struck through Raetia and Noricum, and a third through northern Italy. He reached Sirmium without encountering serious resistance, and secured the pass of Succi into Thrace. But the impression of rapid success was illusory; Julian had neither the time nor the strength to consolidate his gains. Moreover, the tendency of Gallic and Danubian armies to go their separate ways, already evidenced in the aftermath of Constans' death, resurfaced. Julian's attempt to neutralise two Danube legions loyal to Constantius by stationing them in Gaul backfired when they marched into northern Italy instead and besieged Aquileia, which declared for Constantius. Moreover, the senate at Rome refused to receive Julian's diplomatic overtures, responding with the reproachful slogan, 'We demand respect for your creator.'[35] Resistance to the pretender would have been strengthened by the news that Constantius, proverbially more successful in civil wars than he was against foreign enemies,[36] had now at last set out for the west. But at the point where Julian's attempt seemed to falter, his guardian gods again intervened. In November 361, at the age of 44, Constantius II died of illness in Cilicia, having (or so it was rumoured) named Julian as his heir,[37] although other reports mentioned only that he was acclaimed by the armies.[38] Julian drew the inevitable lesson from Constantius' opportune demise: his gods had brought about his accession and guaranteed his legitimacy.[39] He entered Constantinople in triumph on 11 December 361,[40] to find a city in mourning for the previous emperor, whom Julian now honoured with a state funeral.[41] Julian thus became undisputed and sole Augustus of the whole Roman world.

Though a hero to his western followers, Julian was entirely unknown to the armies of the east and their leaders. Moreover, prominent members of the previous administration were still in place with whom Julian too had scores to settle. The result of military

35. Amm.Marc. 21.10.7: 'auctori tuo reverentiam rogamus'.
36. Amm. Marc. 21.16.15.
37. Amm. Marc. 21.15: 'Fama tamen rumorque loquebatur incertus' ('Gossip, however, and rumour were reporting').
38. Amm. Marc. 21.15.2–5; 22.2.1–2.
39. Cf. Mamertinus, *Speech of thanks*, *Pan. Lat.* 3 (11).27.5 (on death of Constantius), that the safety of the state was perpetuated by heavenly assistance ('caelesti ope salutem rei publicae propagatam').
40. Amm. Marc. 22.2.4.
41. See, ungraciously, Gregory Nazianzus, *Or.* 5.16–17.

pressure and perhaps Julian's personal inclinations was a series of military trials held at Chalcedon and presided over by a board of judges, drawn from supporters of both Constantius and Julian.[42] Prominent court officials, including both the counts of the finances, Evagrius the *comes rei privatae*, Ursulus, the *comes sacrarum largitionum*,[43] and another Florentius, the master of the offices, were exiled or executed, as also were some of the men implicated in the plots which had led to the fall of Gallus (whose memory Julian, at least in public, always treated with respect).[44] Ammianus protested bitterly at the execution of the count Ursulus, who had sought to protect Julian, but was delighted to see the last of the more infamous informers, notably Paul 'the Chain' and the corrupt eunuch and former *cubicularius*, Eusebius.

Worries among his entourage over the insecurity of Julian's position underlie the 'speech of thanks' (*Gratiarum actio*) delivered by the new consul Mamertinus in Constantinople early in 362.[45] The speaker's task was to praise and justify both his emperor and his own elevation; as Julian's *comes sacrarum largitionum*, praetorian prefect (of Illyricum) and now consul, he was Julian's man, not Constantius'. His speech combined fairly conventional praise of Julian with rebuttal of implied criticisms and covert attacks on the behaviour of 'previous emperors', meaning Constantius II. Julian is honoured for his military achievements in Gaul, although little detail is given.[46] He is praised too for the protection he offered his people from barbarians – and from the depredations of the provincial governors, whom Constantius (by implication) was unable or unwilling to control.[47] Julian's march eastwards is represented as a further attack on the barbarians, this time of the Danube; as he progressed past cowering barbarians on one bank and rejoicing

---

42. The judges were Julian's adherents Salutius Secundus (praetorian prefect), Cl. Mamertinus and Nevitta, along with Constantius' ministers Arbitio, Agilo and Jovinus.
43. For anger at Ursulus' execution, despite his past support of Julian, see Amm. Marc. 22.3.7. For the suggestion that Julian could not control the verdicts, see Gregory Nazianzus, *Or.* 4.64; Socrates, *Hist. eccl.* 3.1.43.
44. Palladius, former master of the offices, and Fl. Taurus, former praetorian prefect and consul, were exiled; Apodemius, former *agens in rebus* who denounced Gallus, and Silvanus were executed; Pentadius, however, who took down Gallus' interrogation in shorthand, was acquitted.
45. See R. C. Blockley, 'The panegyric of Claudius Mamertinus on the emperor Julian', *AJPhil.* 93 (1972), 437–50.
46. *Pan. Lat.* 3 (11).3.1; 4.3.
47. *Pan. Lat.* 3 (11).1.4; 4.2–4.

Romans on the other, he restored cities,[48] supplied the people of Rome with grain[49] (the unco-operative response of the Roman senate is not mentioned) and treated all comers with generosity, while he himself preserved a frugal mode of living. Turning to his own situation, Mamertinus maintained that his consulship was the more legitimate as the unasked gift of a lawful emperor than it would have been had the recipient been required to engage in the degrading process of canvassing required under the Roman Republic.

Mamertinus' stress on Julian's legitimacy was a response to those in Constantinople who thought otherwise. Given that Julian was the closest surviving kin to the dead emperor, the lawfulness of his accession should have been beyond doubt. Moreover, as Julian was, allegedly, the successor named by Constantius himself, Mamertinus might have been expected to emphasise continuity with the previous regime. Indeed, as Mamertinus acknowledged, Julian had given Constantius a state funeral.[50] However, Mamertinus chose a modified version of the option more often taken by emperors who had displaced a predecessor by force – vilification. By indirectly attacking 'previous emperors', Julian's spokesman challenged the legitimacy of Constantius himself and, by extension, the house of Constantine. Constantius' offences are a familiar catalogue. He had sought to destroy Julian and failed to check his courtiers' plots against his Caesar; he had failed to control bad governors and had allowed a culture of extravagance and greed to prevail at court, so that offices could be acquired not by merit but only by bribery of corrupt courtiers, women and eunuchs.[51] Most heinous was the accusation, now publicly aired by Mamertinus, that Constantius had conspired with the Alamannic king Vadomarius to attack Julian in Gaul, thus imperilling the security of the empire in order to protect his own.[52]

To express such views before an audience consisting in part of Constantius' former supporters was hardly an effective way to conciliate their goodwill. On the assumption that Mamertinus echoed his master's voice, we may ask why this line was taken.

48. *Pan. Lat.* 3 (11).9.1–10.3.
49. *Pan. Lat.* 3 (11).14.1–2.
50. *Pan. Lat.* 3 (11).27.5. This was because Julian had 'forgiven' his predecessor.
51. *Pan. Lat.* 3 (11).17–20.
52. *Pan. Lat.* 3 (11).6.1. For references on Vadomarius, see C. E. V. Nixon and B. S. Rodgers (eds and trans.), *In Praise of Later Roman Emperors: The Panegyrici Latini. Introduction, Translation and Historical Commentary,*, Berkeley: University of California Press, 1994, 401–2, n.38.

Certainly, it is symptomatic of some political naivety on the part
of the new regime. However, the divisive tone was no accident. In
his legislation, as we shall see, Julian was to take great delight in
reversing some of the legal decisions of Constantine, to whose
mistaken views he explicitly refers. This was not simply self-
assertion or lack of tact. If emperors reversed decisions of their
predecessors it was customary to do so with discretion. The
exception was the routine abolition by new emperors of the acts of
predecessors overthrown by force and thus designated usurpers
(*tyranni*) by the victors;[53] to treat the policies of previous rulers with
open contempt was to subvert their status as rulers in the first place.
Mamertinus as orator and Julian as legislator were therefore of
one mind. An open declaration that Constantine or Constantius II
was a *tyrannus* would incur ridicule; however, in celebrating the
triumphant return of (pagan) Philosophy, 'clothed in purple',
Mamertinus and his master proclaimed the end of the domination of
Constantine's divine patron, the Christian God.[54]

Julian the reformer

Like emperors before him, Julian promised a new beginning. The
style of the new emperor was deliberately and consciously austere
and informal.[55] The overpaid palatine officials who had cluttered up
the court of Constantius II were summarily dismissed and the ornate
ceremonial beloved by his predecessor was curtailed.[56] Mamertinus
celebrated Julian's egalitarian behaviour at his own consular in-
auguration and Julian himself, having improperly intervened to give
the signal to start Mamertinus' games, promptly fined himself
ten pounds of gold for misconduct.[57] While in Constantinople he
deferred to the senate and often attended its meetings. But not all
were enraptured by the new informality. Ammianus criticised Julian
for abandoning a senate meeting to rush out and embrace Maximus;
such conduct detracted from the majesty and dignity necessary for

---

53. Examples given at *Cod. Theod.* 15.14.
54. *Pan. Lat.* 3 (11).23.4.
55. Amm.Marc. 22.4; Lib. *Or.* 18.130.
56. Amm. Marc. 22.4.9 on the allowances paid the emperor's barber; *Cod. Theod.*
6.24.1, restriction of fifty on number of court functionaries entitled to rations; *Cod.
Theod.* 8.1.6–7, accountants made liable to torture if suspected of corruption.
57. Amm. Marc. 22.7.2.

a ruler.[58] Readers of the *Misopogon*, addressed to the Antiochenes early in 363, would note its savagely ironic and satirical tone; although now understood as part of the burlesque expected of New Year celebrations, Julian's choice of embarking on satire at all reflects his lack of instinctive understanding of how an emperor was expected to project himself in public.[59]

Julian did not confine his economy drive to his personal expenses or the court. A series of laws on the *cursus publicus*, perhaps in response to questions about expenditure raised by officials, show a consistent determination to cut back on abuse of post warrants. To that end, he limited the total number that could be issued by praetorian prefects, but allowed the creation of a small surplus, to be handwritten by himself, and delivered to governors by *vicarii* in the event of emergencies.[60] The series suggests that Julian's enthusiasm to cut out the *cursus* altogether where it was under-used caused alarm among the tax-collecting authorities, which feared they might come to lack the means to transport taxes in kind to the ports. Thus, when Julian abolished the *cursus publicus* in Sardinia – a small place with little use for it – he informed officials that they would have to pay for themselves in future, but also conceded that a residual service was required for transport of the *annona*.[61]

Not all, or perhaps even most, of the laws preserved in the Theodosian Code came directly from Julian in person, but he would have had to endorse at least the outlines of a policy.[62] One wonders who was responsible for an endearing excursus on the right definition of a 'supernumerary horse' or *parhippus*: the law's insistence that if the post warrant said 'one', then a second was 'supplementary', but if the warrant specified 'two', then the third was the supernumerary might appear too obvious to be stated (as the law conceded); yet its preservation by both Theodosius II and Justinian shows that lawyers both at the time and later thought the point

58. Amm. Marc. 22.7.1 (consular celebrations); 22.7.3; Socrates, *Hist. eccl.* 3.1.53 (detraction from majesty of ruler). Also Eunap. *VS* 7.3.16 and 4.1, Lib. *Or.* 18. 155–6.
59. On the *Misopogon* as satire, see Maud W. Gleason, 'Festive satire: Julian's *Misopogon* and the New Year at Antioch', *JRS* 76 (1986), 106–19.
60. *Cod. Theod.* 8.5.12 (22 February 363; 13 (20 June 362); both to Mamertinus as praetorian prefect, the latter in response to reactions from the *comes sacrarum largitionum*.
61. *Cod. Theod.* 8.5.16 (25 November 362).
62. For an attempt to contextualise Julian's laws, centred on his law on teaching, see J-M. Carrié, 'Julien législateur: un mélange de genres', in Carrié (ed.), *L'Empereur Julien et son temps*, *Antiquité Tardive* 17 (2009), 175–84.

worth making.[63] And Julian himself administered the restrictions in the law, allowing a prospective visitor to the court the privilege of one *parhippos*.[64]

Contemporaries took note of Julian's unavailing efforts to restore the prosperity of cities and, in particular, to restock the benches of the city councils. Libanius (who was not averse to assisting favoured colleagues wishing to edge out of curial duties) celebrated Julian's removal of exemptions; it was clearly right that those who evaded their responsibilities should be recalled.[65] Ammianus, however, perhaps on behalf of his fellow Antiochene decurions, took a more critical stance, blaming Julian for abolishing exemptions from curial service to which veterans were entitled and for giving inconsistent decisions in response to appeals.[66] In fact, there was little that Julian could do to arrest the haemorrhaging of talent from the cities of the east. The new and expanding administration at Constantinople offered opportunities for the talented and ambitious, which were unlikely to be choked off by emperors in need of their services.

Julian's concern for the cities was underpinned by a policy of generosity (*liberalitas*), combined with tax-cutting.[67] He had already shown a penchant for reducing the burdens on cities while still in Gaul, and as he moved eastwards in 361, Julian is said to have brought relief to the cities of Illyricum and Greece; his letters also show him responding favourably to requests for relief, for example from the cities of Thrace.[68] An early reform of the *aurum coronarium* formally reinstated its voluntary status, a concession quickly repealed, as it applied to decurions, by Valentinian I and Valens.[69] Decurions were also reassured that they did not have to pay, or make up the shortfall in, the *collatio lustralis*, or trade tax – unless, of course, they were traders; exemptions from curial service for those with large numbers of children (in this case, thirteen) were also confirmed.[70] Civic life would be reinvigorated by the creation of new

63. *Cod. Theod.* 8.5.14 (9 September 363) and *Cod. Just.* 12.50.4.
64. Julian, *Letter* 15, to Aëtius.
65. Lib. *Or.* 18, 147–8; J. H. W. G. Liebeschuetz, *Antioch: City and Imperial Administration in the Later Roman Empire*, Oxford: Clarendon Press, 1972, 174–86.
66. Amm. Marc. 22.9.12.
67. Praised by Amm. Marc. 25.4.15. Ironically, this was also one of Constantine's most celebrated virtues, dismissed by Julian in his *Caesars* as wasteful prodigality.
68. Julian, *Letter* 27.
69. *Cod. Theod.* 12.13.1 (voluntary nature of crown gold); 2 (repeal by Valentinian and Valens).
70. *Cod. Theod.* 12.1.50.1, in line with previous policy; *Cod. Theod.* 12.1.55 (children), well-known exemption, which should not have been challenged.

officials, including a city-based official, the *zygostates*, who was to be in charge of assessing the worth of chipped or damaged *solidi*, the last an innovation which outlasted Julian's reign.[71]

Much of the legislation ascribed to him in the legal collections reflects the routine ongoing nature of the emperor's job. Advised by officials, Julian quietly conformed to many of the legal conventions observed by his predecessors. Thus, for example, existing rights to retention of dowries under binding agreements were to be upheld; betrothal gifts in the form of land to under-age girls were to be valid, provided they were properly attested in the public records;[72] *vicarii* were not to be bypassed in the appeals process;[73] and a fine would be imposed if appeals were not forwarded within thirty days.[74] Yet even in areas of civil law, where religion was not an issue, Julian openly subverted Constantine's authority. He objected to Constantine's rulings on rights to sue (or not) named co-parties to a lawsuit;[75] and, in a boost to state authority as against that of the family head, he reinstated the 'ancient law' which insisted that an under-age wife could not sell property without authorisation from a magistrate – a transaction which Constantine had permitted subject only to the consent of the husband.[76]

The new Augustus openly challenged the Christians, whom he consistently labelled 'Galilaeans'. Special privileges, such as clerical immunity from curial service,[77] were removed and exiles recalled, but not reinstated in their previous ecclesiastical posts.[78] The public celebrations of martyrs were curtailed, when the emperor banned the holding of funeral processions in cities during daylight hours because

71. *Cod. Theod.* 12.7.2 = *Cod. Just.* 10.73.2, to Mamertinus. On the *zygostates*, see Jairus Banaji, *Agrarian Change in Late Antiquity: Gold, Labour and Aristocratic Dominance*, Oxford: Oxford University Press, 2001, 62–3; 70.
72. *Cod. Theod.* 3.5.8 (to Hypatius, *vicarius* of Rome).
73. *Cod. Theod.* 1.15.4, reiterating the practice of Constantius (see sections 2 and 3).
74. *Cod. Theod.* 11.30.29 and 31.
75. *Cod.Theod.* 2.4.2, where Julian accuses Constantine of encouraging legal chicanery on the part of defendants.
76. *Cod. Theod.* 3.1.3. Cf. Amm. Marc. 21.10.8, where Julian criticises Constantine for promoting 'barbarians' to high office, while doing the same himself. On Julian's attitude to his predecessors in general, see G. W. Bowersock, 'The Emperor Julian on his predecessors', *Yale Classical Studies* 27 (1982), 159–72.
77. Julian, *Letter* 39 to the citizens of Byzacium; the Galilaeans are the sole named exemption among all those now withdrawn.
78. Julian, *Letter* 41, 436B. His *Letter* 24 warns that Athanasius of Alexandria had been allowed back to the city, but not to his office as bishop. *Letter* 46 to Ecdicius (431B–C) exiles Athanasius again; the emperor complained, in his own hand, that Athanasius had baptised Greek aristocratic women.

of the pollution incurred by those who came into contact with the dead.[79] One otherwise obscure martyr proved exceptionally awkward. At Antioch, the Caesar Gallus had installed the relics of the martyr Babylas in the precinct of Apollo at Daphne.[80] Julian ordered the removal of the relics, and the Christians responded by organising a large and joyous public procession to escort their martyr to his new resting place.[81] Subsequently, the temple of Apollo burned down and Julian, accusing the Christians, without proof, of arson, confiscated the funds of the Great Church of the city.[82]

His policy also alienated some non-Christian opinion. Ammianus criticised the edict which banned the appointment of Christians by councils as official teachers of the pagan classics; it should be buried, he wrote, in 'perpetual silence'.[83] Nevertheless, the thinking behind it was coherent (if, in the view of many, mistaken). For Julian, the works of the ancient authors, especially the Greeks, were not simply literature but guides to the moral values and behaviour advocated by traditional religion. It followed that if Christians, who rejected the old gods, were to act as official teachers of the pagan classics (which also taught pagan morality), they would be guilty of double standards, as they would be going against the exclusivist principles of their own religion. Instead, they would confine themselves to the exposition of Mark and Luke.

For Christian devotees of the ancient classics, such as Gregory of Nazianus, this was potentially a disaster, as it drove a wedge between their Christian religion and their Hellenic culture, which, hitherto, had been compatible.[84] The immediate practical effects of the law are unknown; two eminent Christian teachers, Prohaeresius

79. *Cod. Theod.* 9.17.5 = *Cod. Just.* 9.19.5; Julian, *Letter* 56. On Julian and relics, see J. Torres, 'Emperor Julian and the veneration of relics', in Carrié, *L'Empereur Julien*, 205–14.
80. Sozom. *Hist. eccl.* 5.19.12–13.
81. Sozom. *Hist. eccl.* 5.19.18–19; John Chrysostom, *Homily on St Babylas*, 16–90.
82. Julian, *Misopogon* 346B; 361B; Amm. Marc. 22.13.2; Sozom. *Hist eccles.* 5.20.5.
83. For the *koinos nomos* ('general law') banning the teaching of pagan classics by officially appointed teachers, see Julian, *Letter* 38 (Wright); Amm. Marc. 22.10.7: 'obruendum perenni silentio', and 25.4.21; Socrates, *Hist. eccl.* 3.16.1; Sozom. *Hist. eccl.* 5.18; Theodoret, *Hist. eccl.* 3.8. For the related constitution, a different extract from the lost Latin original, see *Cod. Theod.* 13.3.5. See also T. M. Banchich, 'Julian's school laws: *Cod. Theod.* 13.3.5 and *Ep.* 42', *Ancient World* 24 (1990), 5–14.
84. For argument for Julian as 'politically tolerant' see Mar Marcos, '"He forced with gentleness": Emperor Julian's attitude to religious coercion', in Carrié, *L'Empereur Julien*, 191–204; for context of his policy in Julian's thought, see Smith, *Julian's Gods*, 179–218.

at Athens and Marius Victorinus at Rome, resigned from their posts but others, such as Ausonius of Bordeaux, seem to have been unaffected. For the longer term, Julian had posed a question which would perplex conscientious Christians for decades to come. Jerome's insistence, when secretary to Pope Damasus at Rome in the 380s, that one could not be both a 'Ciceronian' and a 'Christian' would be one echo in the Latin-speaking world of a widespread concern in the later fourth century over the relationship of Christianity and the 'pagan classics', and whether the two could in fact coexist peacefully.

Julian's strategy against the hated religion was pursued on many fronts. Like Maximinus Daza before him, he planned to set up a provincial priesthood.[85] This would take over the functions which made the Christians appear praiseworthy, namely their kindness to strangers, their care for their dead and the professed holiness of their lives. Supplies of grain and wine were to be made available to the high priests at public cost, one fifth for distribution to the priests' servants and the rest to be given to strangers and beggars. Christians would have noted that Julian's charity was funded by the state, while theirs came, still, from the offerings of the faithful; it was unlikely that the poor of Christ were to be superseded by the poor of Julian. The priests themselves were to worship with their entire households, and were not to attend theatres, drink in pubs or engage in disreputable occupations. In line with the edict on the teaching of the pagan classics, the priests were advised not to read saucy lyric poets like Archilochus or Hipponax; wrong-headed philosophers such as Epicurus were also off limits, as reading bad authors corrupted the soul.[86] Those who fell short were to be disciplined by the provincial high priest and even dismissed. Dissent within the households of the priests would also not be tolerated.[87]

Christians, though not formally disadvantaged, could hope for nothing from the new regime. Although impartial as a judge in court, Julian could not resist inquiring after the litigants' religious allegiance, a disconcerting departure from convention for those likely to be disadvantaged, although Ammianus claimed that

---

85. See Julian, *Letter* 22 to Arsacius, high priest of Galatia, for his expectations of provincial high priests; also *Letter* 20 to Theodorus, appointing him high priest of Asia, with a schedule of regulations to follow.
86. Julian, *Letter to a Priest*, passim.
87. Julian, *Letter* 32, to the priestess Theodora.

nothing came of it.[88] Moreover, Christians were openly discriminated against wherever the emperor had discretion. In palace appointments, Julian instructed that the 'god-fearing' were to be preferred over the 'Galilaeans'.[89] While proclaiming a policy of toleration – no Christian was to be dragged into a temple or forced to sacrifice – Julian used every opportunity to weaken their organisation and discredit their doctrines. Favours for the shrine of the Great Mother at Pessinus were made conditional on the adherence of *all* its people to the cult.[90] When two Christian factions came to blows in Edessa, Julian confiscated their assets, giving part of the proceeds to the soldiers; the purpose of this, he said, was so that, being poor, they had a better chance of reaching Heaven.[91] Christians were also blamed for public disorders at Bostra, and castigated as sacrilegious, 'tyrants' and so sick that they had rejected the gods for corpses and relics.[92] The signal to the populations of the empire was stark: the emperor would pay lip-service to toleration but in practice would limit the Christians' opportunities for career advancement and do nothing to protect them from their enemies.[93]

Julian in Persia

In the spring of 363, Julian travelled from Antioch to rendezvous with a massive army of 65,000 men, assembled at Carrhae in preparation for a decisive blow against the Persians.[94] Julian's precise intentions and motivations were mixed. In his public propaganda, he distanced himself from the over-cautious policy of containment adopted by his predecessor, which had resulted in the loss of several border cities (although of recent acquisitions only Bezabde now remained in Persian hands).[95] The aim therefore was to achieve a

88. Amm. Marc. 22.10.2.
89. *Letter* 37, to Atarbius.
90. Julian, *Letter* 22, 432A.
91. Julian, *Letter* 40, 424D.
92. Julian, *Letter* 41, 438C.
93. Sozom., *Hist. eccl.* 5.9.12: Julian fails to show anger against the killers of three Christians. R. J. Penella, 'Julian the persecutor in fifth century church historians', *Ancient World* 24 (1990), 31–43. Julian also, notoriously, failed to punish the Alexandrians for the lynching of George of Cappadocia.
94. In addition to Ammianus' account in books 23–5, see Zos. *New History* 3.12–29, based on Eunapius' access to the notebooks of the physician Oribasius, with Eunap. fr. 8 (*FHG* 4, 15). The account of Magnus of Carrhae is a possible influence, although this is debatable.
95. Lib. *Or.* 18.205–11.

victory which, like that of Galerius in 298, would result in a lasting settlement favourable to the Romans.[96] But Galerius' victory had been won in Greater Armenia: Julian's ambitions in marching south and east to Ctesiphon were more grandiose. In his retinue travelled a pretender to the Persian throne, the prince Hormizdas, who would prove his usefulness on the march in the course of local negotiations;[97] the implication was that Julian's aim was to overthrow Shapur himself. It is possible that Julian may not have had fixed plans beyond the assault on Ctesiphon, an apparently viable goal as the city had fallen to Septimius Severus in 198. Julian's motives were also more personal. Although his military talents had already been displayed to good effect in Gaul, he had still to conciliate a sceptical eastern Roman army. As a man driven by the ideas and ideals absorbed in his isolated youth, the figures of Alexander the Great and Trajan, Lucius Verus and Septimius Severus, provided inspiration for his project.[98] Moreover, the favour of the gods required further demonstration. Julian, the Persian victor and thus the clear favourite of the gods, could hope to return to his unfinished war with the Christians with greater hopes of success.

Not all were as confident as he. Ammianus castigated the 'lazy and malevolent' critics who objected to the unnecessary confusion caused by an emperor pursuing a personal agenda. Pride, said the critics, came before a fall.[99] After Julian's death, Libanius admitted that there had been disaffection among the military, although nothing came of it.[100] And from Gaul, newly settled by Julian but still unstable, came a warning from the prefect Sallustius against

---

96. Amm. Marc. 24.1.10 reports an encounter with a former soldier of Galerius, settled in Mesopotamia with a harem, and now an old man.

97. Amm. Marc. 24.1.8 (Hormizdas negotiates surrender of Anatha); 24.2.11 (abused by defenders of Pirisabora), but 24.2.20–1 (negotiates surrender of Pirisabora).

98. On Alexander, Julian, *Caesars* 323D; on Trajan, *Caesars* 333A. Amm. Marc. 23.5.17 has Julian recalling the victories of Trajan, Verus and Severus over Persia, but adds, with ironic effect, mention of Gordian III, who was betrayed and killed by his own side, perhaps an anticipation of the rumour that Julian was killed by one of his own soldiers. On the aims and outcomes of Julian's enterprise, see R. C. Blockley, *East Roman Foreign Policy: Formation and Conduct from Diocletian to Anastasius*, ARCA 30, Leeds: Francis Cairns, 1992, 24–30.

99. Amm. Marc. 22.12.3. On the value of Ammianus as an 'eyewitness', whose version is also shaped by literary criteria, see Gavin Kelly, *Ammianus Marcellinus, the Allusive Historian*, Cambridge: Cambridge University Press, 2008, 65–101; also 296–317 on Ammianus' construction of Julian as *exemplum* ('exemplary', not always in a positive sense).

100. Lib. *Or.* 18.199.

over-extension.[101] Even the gods, it seemed, had their reservations. Julian's Etruscan diviners (whom Ammianus also approved of) proclaimed through their observation of the omens that the gods were opposed to the war.[102] They, however, were themselves opposed by Julian's 'philosophers', a group which, according to Ammianus, had great authority but were often wrong and were very stubborn 'over matters not clearly understood by them'.[103]

At Carrhae, the force was split and a smaller army of 30,000 men, jointly commanded by Julian's relative Procopius and Sebastianus,[104] was sent eastwards to join Arsaces of Armenia and deceive Shapur into believing that this was the main invasion, a diversionary tactic which proved successful in the short term.[105] In the meantime, Julian, with the main force, met the fleet near Callinicum and then followed the line of the river Euphrates south and east in the direction of the first main military objective, Ctesiphon on the Tigris. But as the army slowly advanced, so the advantage of surprise grew less. Spread over ten miles, to maximise its effect, the column moved slowly in tandem with the fleet on the river. Fortresses on the way were stormed, persuaded to surrender or bypassed.[106] The Roman army suffered increasing damage from the guerrilla tactics of the local Persian and Saracen defenders. Conditions worsened as the Persians flooded the fields along the Romans' route by breaking down the dykes. Having tracked down the canal dug out by Trajan and Severus through which the fleet could be transported from the Euphrates to the Tigris waterway, the Romans fetched up before the walls of Ctesiphon.[107] Although cheered by an initial success when a Persian force was driven back within the walls, for the Romans the

101. Amm. Marc. 23.5.4.
102. John Matthews, *The Roman Empire of Ammianus*, London: Duckworth, 1989, 176–9; Amm. Marc. 25.2.7–8, warning over shooting star.
103. Amm. Marc. 23.5.1: 'in parum cognitis perseverantium diu'. That even success was a delusion is suggested in Ammianus' account of events at Ctesiphon (24.6.17), when a minor victory is immediately followed by a disastrous (non-)sacrifice of ten bulls to Mars Ultor, an omen perversely ignored by Julian, who promises (correctly) never to sacrifice to Mars again.
104. Amm. Marc. 23.3.5.
105. On Julian's strategy, see Matthews, *Ammianus*, 130–83; C. W. Fornara, 'Julian's Persian expedition in Ammianus and Zosimus', *JHS* 111 (1991), 1–15.
106. Amm. Marc. 24.1.6–9 (Anatha); 24.2.9–22 (Pirisabora); 24.4.2–26 (Maiozamalcha).
107. Amm. Marc. 24.5.1–2.

moment of truth had arrived.[108] Ctesiphon was well fortified and could not be taken.[109]

Yet Julian, apparently, had no 'Plan B'. The generals debated the option of advancing further into the interior, east of the Tigris, and agreed that the fleet could not make headway against the river current and was now surplus to requirements. All the boats, therefore, with the exception of twelve retained for bridge-building, were burned. The effect on morale of the destruction of the ships was disastrous and rumours began to circulate that Persian infiltrators were distorting Roman military planning.[110] On 16 June, the army began to march, not into the interior but alongside the Tigris northwards towards Roman territory in Corduene. Harassed by Persian and Saracen horsemen, the Romans waited apprehensively for the appearance of the Persian king's army. One evening a cloud of dust was spotted; as the next day dawned, it was revealed that the king's army had indeed arrived.[111] Despite this, Julian refused negotiations and continued the march. Ten days after the army's departure from Ctesiphon, the emperor rushed, incompletely armed, into a skirmish and received a fatal wound from a cavalry spear.[112] The night after, he died. Almost immediately, his death became the subject of speculation, with responsibility ascribed variously to a Saracen horseman, a Christian or a soldier on his own side.[113] His friends were quick to disseminate the picture of Julian dying as a true philosopher, debating with his friends Maximus and Priscus, in the manner of Socrates in Plato's *Phaedo*, the nature of the immortal soul.[114]

This moving portrait did nothing to rescue the Roman army from its plight. A new emperor, Jovian, a tall man in his early thirties unrelated to his predecessor, was quickly acclaimed by the army.[115] His first job was to extricate his force by reaching agreement with Persia. The treaty, predictably bewailed by Ammianus, allowed the Romans to withdraw unscathed, but Singara and the key market town of

---

108. Amm. Marc. 24.6.4–16. Julian's tactics in the battle were based on *Il.* 4.297 (Amm. Marc. 6.4.9).
109. Amm. Marc. 24.7.1.
110. Amm. Marc. 24.7.2–6.
111. Amm.Marc. 24.8.7 (dust cloud); 25.1.1 (Persian army revealed).
112. Amm. Marc. 25.3.6–9.
113. For the last, Amm. Marc. 25.6.6.
114. Amm. Marc. 25.3.15–23.
115. Amm. Marc. 25.5.4–6.

Nisibis were returned to Persian control, although their populations
were allowed to depart and take refuge in Roman territory. For the
Christian Ephrem of Nisibis, the juxtaposition of Julian's dead body
outside the walls and the Persian standard flying over the city was
a vivid demonstration of the retribution that would overtake the
impious.[116] For Ammianus, the fault lay entirely with the pusillani-
mous Jovian.[117] Whatever might be urged on Julian's behalf – that
he had taken many towns on the Euphrates, seriously panicked the
Persians and depleted the king's stock of elephants[118] – the terms of
the treaty make clear the perceptions of both sides as to where
victory lay. After Julian, there were periodic surges in activity on
the frontiers and the kingship of Armenia remained a bone of
contention, but the redrawing of boundaries would stabilise the
border for many decades to come and there would be no further
wars on the scale experienced by Constantius and Julian until the
sixth century.

   Julian possessed in abundance the charismatic qualities that his
cousin Constantius lacked. Eloquent and impassioned (if occasionally verbose), he inspired devotion and dislike in equal measure.
Although a reporter rather than an independent thinker, he engaged
with characteristic enthusiasm in the war of ideas with the newly
dominant Christianity, bringing to the fray a new dimension; while
Platonism focused on private virtue, Julian sought to explain in
both his writings and his life how the philosopher could be a good
ruler, albeit an unwilling one, as well.[119] Yet, even before the Persian
debacle, his long-term success in checking the advance of the
'Galilaeans' was in doubt. He correctly identified Christian social
and civic organisation as one source of its strength and planned
to sideline it with parallel pagan structures, yet his own version of
paganism was idiosyncratic and elitist (in that only intellectuals
could engage with it) and its rituals, especially those involving large-
scale blood sacrifices, no longer commanded popular respect, as his
experience at Antioch showed. Even had he been capable of outlawing Christianity outright, a process for which there was no legislative
precedent, he had nothing viable to put in its place.

116. Ephrem, *Hymn* 3, 1–19. See also Amm. Marc. 25.8.13–14 (lamentation at Nisibis)
and 25.9.1–11 (evacuation and handover of city).
117. Amm. Marc. 25.10.4.
118. Amm. Marc. 25.7.1.
119. Cf. his *Letter to Themistius*, of uncertain date, but recording his response to his
elevation as either Caesar or Augustus.

As emperor, Julian's record was mixed. He made a serious effort to cut administrative costs, but so had others done, to little long-term effect. Like other emperors, he tried and failed to sustain the strengths of city councils, oblivious of the facts that other forms of local leadership, by bishops and returning imperial administrators, were becoming more attractive and that his own Constantinople was a magnet for talented administrators. Aside from his attempts at religious reform, it was the style of Julian's government which attracted most attention. Spontaneous by nature, he lacked sensitivity to the expectations of his audiences; and did not appreciate the dignity required of an emperor in his public behaviour. The manner of his accession, as celebrated by Mamertinus, was divisive, as also were his gratuitous attacks on Constantine's legislation. By impugning his predecessors, Julian undermined the office of emperor itself. His failure in Persia was not entirely of his own making. The conciliation of the eastern army was a political imperative, but Julian's reversion to the 'Alexander' mode of outright conquest is also a comment on the compulsion on the part of Roman emperors to prove their right to rule by spectacular victories in battle, a compulsion which Constantius had, in his latter years, consistently and courageously resisted. That it was the boring Constantius who better understood the role of emperor was something that Julian's adherent Ammianus would be unlikely to acknowledge.

Figure 50 Column of Julian, Ankara, Turkey

CHAPTER 14

The funeral director

Jovian, known unkindly as the funeral director because of his association with the obsequies of both Constantius II and Julian,[1] died
unexpectedly in February 364 and the eastern army selected a new
emperor, Valentinian I, who, with his brother Valens, inaugurated a
new dynasty.[2] When Theodosius I was appointed to succeed Valens
in the east, after the latter's death at the battle of Hadrianople in
378, a second imperial house was founded, which would survive in
the east to 450 and in the west to 455. An attempt by a man related
to the previous dynasty, Procopius, in 365 to overthrow the new
emperors failed ignominiously and such descendants of Constantine
as survived faded into obscurity, although Constantius II's daughter,
born posthumously, became the wife of Gratian, Valentian's eldest
son (Augustus 367–83).[3]

The deaths of Julian and Jovian mark the end not only of a
dynasty but also of the 'long third century'. Diocletian, Constantine
and their colleagues and successors kept the frontiers of the Roman
Empire secure and avoided a repetition of the fragmentation which
had seriously threatened imperial unity in the 250s to 270s. They
also exploited the perceived danger from the 'barbarians' of the
north and the Persians to the east to project themselves as effective
military leaders, Augusti 'ever victorious'. This guaranteed the
support of the armies they led and of the gods, or God, whose
favour was demonstrated through their success as generals and the
prosperity of the empire they ruled. How far the repeated sorties
against the Franks, Alamanni or Sarmatians were in fact necessary
for frontier security, rather than imperial prestige, cannot be known.

1. Amm. Marc. 21.16.21, Jovian receives 'imperial' rations while escorting the body of
Constantius II, anticipating an *imperium* that was 'empty' (*cassum*) and like a shadow
(*umbratile*).
2. Amm. Marc. 25.10.12–13, suggesting the death was suspicious.
3. Amm. Marc. 21.5.6. Constantius' women were exploited by Procopius in 365 (Amm.
Marc. 26.7.10).

Nor can the cost to the empire over time in lives and resources of maintaining several standing armies on a war-footing be accurately assessed. In any event, emperors lacked the power to control the effects of migrations far beyond their frontiers. In the later fourth century, disruption caused by the presence of unassimilated federate armies within the empire and the appearance beyond the frontiers of a new Asiatic people, the Huns,[4] exacerbated pressures on the Roman military establishment and led, in the early fifth century, to the collapse of the Rhine frontier and the partitioning of much of Gaul, Spain and Africa among the Germanic peoples.

Julian's death marks the effective end of the old unified imperial order. It was also a stage in the gradual drifting apart of 'east' and 'west' which, in the fifth century, would enable the Greek Roman Empire to survive and prosper, while the west fragmented and the political map of Europe was redrawn. A few emperors after Julian and Jovian would reign, briefly, as sole Augusti but, under the Theodosian emperors from 379, Constantinople acquired a more assertive separate identity as a powerful magnet for Greek-speaking talent, although Latin would remain the language of administration and law down to the early sixth century. But if the east–west division became more apparent in the fifth century, it should not be retrojected onto the situation in the fourth century, nor should assumptions of separation distort the lived experience of those who served emperors in east and west, or who travelled the empire from Bordeaux to the Holy Land as traders, tourists or pilgrims, or who transported their goods ranging from horses to amphorae across the Mediterranean.

As administrative reformers, Diocletian and Constantine built on the work of their predecessors, but had more time to see their changes take effect. Through a series of ad hoc changes, Diocletian streamlined provincial organisation, the structures of taxation and the collection of revenues, but he left the refinement of the court bureaucracy to Constantine. The imperial court administrations thus created were rule-bound, hierarchical and competitive. Though often underrated, the consolidation carried out by the sons of Constantine, especially Constantius II, was also significant; his reign saw a notable rise in the standing of Constantinople, with the

4. Peter Heather, 'The Huns and the end of the Roman Empire in western Europe', *English Historical Review* 110 (1995), 4–41; also Heather, *The Fall of the Roman Empire: A New History*, London: Macmillan, 2005, 202–5; 343–8.

upgrading of its senate. He may also have been responsible for the creation of a new chief law officer, the imperial quaestor, who would later mastermind one of the most significant cultural legacies of the ancient world to modern Europe: the Justinianic *Corpus Iuris Civilis* (529–34).[5] And, as Justinian's enterprise illustrates, the framework created by the emperors of the early fourth century would survive, with some modification, into the fifth, and beyond into the Byzantine Empire. The administrative environment of the quaestor Tribonian and of John Lydus[6] in the sixth century would have been recognisable to their bureaucratic forebears in the fourth.

It is in the context of emperors as cautious and incremental reformers, responding to prompts from officials and subjects, that we should view the pivotal figure of Constantine and his relations with the religion that he patronised and promoted, Christianity. To work at all, laws had to be specific. Laws against religious deviance therefore banned not a named religion but the practices associated with it (such as, in the case of Christians, meetings for the Eucharist); the authorities also confiscated the books where belief was enshrined and the other assets of the deviant community and, most important, signalled disapproval through the rhetoric of their public pronouncements. So when Constantine turned against sacrifice, he was able to do so in terms of precedent and changed social mores; sacrifices associated with bad magic and divination were already banned or suspect and the killing of animals as sacrifices, especially in large numbers, no longer suited the mood of the times. It is a measure of Constantine's political shrewdness that he could promote an agenda which Christians like Eusebius could claim as their own but to which many non-Christians could also subscribe.

The comparison of Constantine with Julian is instructive. Both insisted that those in 'error' should not be persecuted; both discoursed publicly and at some length about their philosophy; both, to a point, favoured, or were seen to favour, adherents of their preferred religion; and both backed their chosen god(s) with public

5. The first quaestor documented as giving legal advice was in the time of Valentinian; the first official to be described as *quaestor sacri palatii* was Fl. Taurus, acting as imperial spokesman on an embassy but without obvious legal duties. For the evolution of the spokesman into the legal adviser, see Jill Harries, 'The Roman imperial quaestor from Constantine to Theodosius II', *JRS* 78 (1988), 148–72. On the quaestor Tribonian and the Corpus Iuris Civilis, see Tony Honoré, *Tribonian*, London: Duckworth, 1978.
6. On John Lydus' treatise *On the magistracies (De magistratibus)*, see M. Maas, *John Lydus and the Roman Past*, London: Routledge, 1992, 53–66 (with especial focus on the praetorian prefecture).

money. But the differences between them are more striking. Constantine dealt with an organisation already rooted in the civic life of the empire and confident, despite its many vigorous and bitter disputes, in its own identity; Julian in 362 was forced to create, in effect, a new priesthood, teach it how to behave and provide public funds to kick-start its operations. Moreover, Constantine, unlike Julian, kept his personal beliefs separate from his conduct of imperial business in general; Julian too often allowed his resentment of 'Galilaeans' and others who had annoyed him to surface in inappropriate contexts. And, crucially, Constantine was more in tune with the wider religious culture of an empire increasingly monotheist, sceptical of the rites of the old gods, and prepared to assess religions in terms of their beliefs, rather than their rites. Julian did not want simply to turn back the clock; he sought to recreate a past religious order that had never existed and which lacked broad appeal.

Throughout the period, the Christian churches preserved their separate identity. Neither Constantine nor his sons attempted to interfere in ecclesiastical self-regulation; the clergy and laity were subject to rules and penalties which existed in parallel with those of the state. The exception was the formulation of right belief by church councils and the imperial enforcement of sanctions against those 'heretics' who lost out in the argument. While Constantine's authority went unchallenged, the theological divisions in the 340s between the two emperors, Constantius II and Constans, created conflicting foci of authority and, even after the death of the latter, emboldened some bishops openly to challenge imperial decisions. Thereafter, the relationship between church and state became more openly one to be negotiated rather than taken for granted. In particular, from the 370s, Ambrose of Milan exploited his position as bishop of the imperial capital to assert ecclesiastical autonomy and even his right as bishop to deny access to his church to sinful emperors. Questions surrounding the adoption of the ascetic life also moved to centre stage: the high-profile 'conversions' of members of the senatorial elite at Rome would create division and controversy within the order and beyond; the relationship of the independent holy man or community of holy men with the episcopate, and the implied criticism of the latter as corrupted by 'the world', would require resolution; in some quarters asceticism would become tainted with socially deviant behaviour and heresy.

This was not a gentle age, and it did not favour the aspirations of those denied access to office and power. Yet, as we have seen, the women of the imperial house, though lacking voices of their own, by no means acquiesced in their lot and Helena would provide the precedent and the exemplar for female patronage of Christianity. By c. 400, as the eastern court became settled in Constantinople, the influence of women was more openly acknowledged and courted. But this was accompanied by a development which, in the west, proved more dangerous: the accession to power of child emperors, who could not act in person as military leaders. Constantine's experiment with his sons as child-Caesars had depended for its success on his own longevity; his authority as father and Augustus both controlled and protected them. But the reigns in the west in the late fourth and fifth centuries of the child-emperors Valentinian II and, initially, Valentinian III (Augustus aged four) allowed scope for imperial mothers, who could not lead armies, to take control. More importantly, it permitted the unofficial 'colleges of generals', which had dominated government in the third century, to reassert themselves. Although not emperors themselves, it was men like Stilicho, the minister of Honorius, overthrown by rival courtiers in 408, Aetius, the chief general of Valentinian III, killed by his imperial master in 454, and, from the 450s, Ricimer, the arch-kingmaker, who controlled policy and could make or unmake emperors.

The 'new empire' of Diocletian, Constantine and their successors was a paradox. A new military, governmental and administrative structure was created but its framework was already present in provinces which had existed for centuries and in cities which, despite increased intervention from the centre, preserved much of their autonomy and a fierce pride in their civic identities. A 'new' religion, Christianity, came to the fore, but it drew on ancient Jewish and Graeco-Roman philosophical traditions and was in many respects already compatible with contemporary religious culture. The Tetrarchy and the house of Constantine created the semblance of a new dynastic stability, but the old sources of disruption remained; emperors had to work hard to establish their right to rule; the loyalties of locally based armies remained volatile; rival generals eyed supreme power, or could be suspected of doing so. The heads that wore the crown could not rest easy. And, as it had done from Augustus onwards, the imperial Roman autocracy depended on the consent of those it governed, a consent maintained by constant communication between emperors and subjects and a lawmaking system traditional in character but responsive in operation.

Chronology

Political/Military	Religious/Cultural	Events elsewhere
284 Death of Numerian; accession of Diocletian		
285 Carinus killed at battle of the Margus; Maximian campaigns against Bagaudae and repels German incursion		
286 Maximian made joint Augustus with Diocletian; Carausius seizes power in Britain		
287 Diocletian imposes Tiridates as client king in Armenia; restructuring of Syria frontier; Maximian crosses the Rhine		
290/1 Conference of Diocletian and Maximian at Milan		
293 Constantius I and Galerius created Caesars; Narses becomes king of Persia		
293–5 Galerius in Egypt		
	295 Edict on incest; completion of Codex of Hermogenian	
296 Constantius defeats Allectus, the successor of Carausius		

Political/Military	Religious/Cultural	Events elsewhere
297–8 Revolt in Egypt, suppressed by Diocletian; Maximian visits Africa		
298 Galerius defeats the Persians and imposes terms on Narses		
299 Maximian returns from Africa to Italy; Galerius and Diocletian meet at Nisibis		
	c. 300 Council of Elvira (Spain)	c. 300 Tiridates of Armenia converted to Christianity
301 Constantius I wins victory over Franks	301 (1 September) Currency Revaluation Decree; (November) Edict on Maximum Prices	
	302 Imperial letter to Julianus against the Manicheans	302 Hormizdas II king of Persia
303 (late in year) Diocletian's *vicennalia* celebrated at Rome	303 (February) Inauguration of the 'Great Persecution' of the Christians	
305 (1 May) Diocletian and Maximian abdicate; Constantius and Galerius Augusti, with Severus and Maximim Daza as Caesars		
306 (25 July) Death of Constantius I at York: Constantine proclaimed Augustus but later accepts rank of Caesar, while Severus promoted to Augustus (October) Maxentius proclaimed Augustus at Rome (winter) Constantine campaigns against the Franks		
307 Maxentius defeats Severus, who abdicates at Ravenna, and successfully defies Galerius; Constantine visits Britain and, on return to Gaul, marries Fausta and accepts title of Augustus from Maximian	307 Building programme of Maxentius at Rome (to 312)	

Political/Military	Religious/Cultural	Events elsewhere
308 Constantine bridges Rhine at Cologne (11 November) Meeting of Galerius, Diocletian and Maximian at Carnuntum; Maximian retires again, Licinius proclaimed Augustus		
		309 Shapur II becomes king of Persia; he will reign for seventy years to 379
310 Maximian challenges Constantine, is defeated and forced to take his own life	310 Lactantius writes the Divine Institutes, to be revised later	
311 (1 May) Death of Galerius	311 (spring) Edict of Toleration	
312 (28 October) Battle of the Milvian Bridge; death of Maxentius Constantine and Licinius Augusti		
313 (February) Licinius marries Constantia at Milan Licinius later publishes agreement reached with Constantine at Milan on Christians' property (30 April) Maximinus Daza defeated by Licinius near Hadrianople; kills himself at Tarsus (July)		
	c. 314 Lactantius writes On the deaths of the persecutors; birth of Libanius at Antioch Silvester bishop of Rome	
315 (July–September) Constantine at Rome; celebrates decennalia	315 Dedication of Arch of Constantine at Rome; first monastery of Pachomius in Egypt	
316 First war between Constantine and Licinius; defeat of Licinius at Cibalae (8 October)		

Political/Military	Religious/Cultural	Events elsewhere
317 (1 March) Crispus and Constantine, sons of Constantine, and Licinianus, the son of Licinius and Constantia, proclaimed Caesars		
	323 Council of Ancyra	
324 Second war between Constantine and Licinius (3 July) Licinius defeated at Hadrianople; Hellespont fleet destroyed by Crispus (19 September) Licinius abdicates (8 November) Constantius II proclaimed Caesar	324 Foundation of Constantinople	
325 Death of Licinius; Council of Nicaea; first celebration of Constantine's *vicennalia*	325 Final revised version of Eusebius, *Church History*	
326 Constantine at Rome to celebrate *vicennalia* (May) Execution of Crispus Death of Fausta		
	328 Athanasius succeeds Alexander as bishop of Alexandria	
	330 Dedication of Constantinople; death of Iamblichus the philosopher	
332 Constantine concludes treaty with the Goths		
333 Constans proclaimed Caesar		
335 Dalmatius proclaimed Caesar	335 Council of Tyre; Firmicus Maternus writes *Mathesis*, on astrology	

Political/Military	Religious/Cultural	Events elsewhere
337 (May) Death of Constantine (June) Purge of rival claimants at Constantinople (September) Constantine II, Constantius II and Constans Augusti		
338 Shapur attacks Nisibis but withdraws after two months	338 Restoration to Alexandria by Constantine II of Athanasius, later expelled again by Constantius II; Eusebius writes his *Life of Constantine*	
340 Death of Constantine II near Aquileia; Constantius II begins reform of Constantinople senate	340 Libanius teaches at Constantinople	
	342 Prohaeresius of Athens entertained by Constans at Trier; Bishop Paul restored at Constantinople	
343 Constans' visit to Britain	343 Council of Sardica	
	344 Libanius professor at Nicomedia	
346 Second assault on Nisibis by Shapur	346 Athanasius restored again to Alexandria	
348 Battle with Persians at Singara	348 Rome's eleven hundredth anniversary largely ignored	
	349 Bishop Paul deposed and exiled from Constantinople by Constantius II	
350 (January) Proclamation of Magnentius at Autun; murder of Constans Proclamation of Vetranio by Danube legions (June) Nepotianus briefly Augustus at Rome but killed by Magnentius Shapur besieges Nisibis for the third time		

Political/Military	Religious/Cultural	Events elsewhere
351 Gallus proclaimed Caesar; is based at Antioch; Vetranio yields to Constantius II; defeat of Magnentius at the battle of Mursa		
353 Death of Magnentius and his brother Decentius		
354 Execution of Gallus Caesar	354 Libanius appointed official teacher at Antioch	
355 Abortive revolt of Silvanus; Julian created Caesar in Gaul by Constantius II		
357 Constantius II's visit to Rome; Julian wins battle of Strasbourg		
359 Siege of Amida, which falls to Persians		
360 Julian proclaimed Augustus at Paris; Bezabde and Singara taken by Persians		
361 Constantius II completes reform of Constantinople senate; Julian moves east against Constantius but the latter dies of illness (3 November); Julian sole Augustus		
362 (late in year) Julian at Antioch	362 (January) Mamertinus, speech of thanks to Julian at Constantinople	
363 Julian's Persian expedition; death of Julian and proclamation of Jovian; Singara and Nisibis ceded to Persia by treaty		
364 (February) Death of Jovian; Valentinian I proclaimed by troops and his brother Valens appointed by him as joint Augustus		

Guide to further reading

Ancient texts and modern translations

For Ammianus Marcellinus, see J. den Boeft and others (eds and comm.) in a series down to 2009, Leiden: Brill; also available with English translation in the Loeb Classical Library, ed. J. Rolfe, 1939. An abbreviated English translation by W. Hamilton is available in the Penguin edition, 1986; see major studies by John Matthews, *The Roman Empire of Ammianus*, London: Duckworth, 1989; Gavin Kelly, *Ammianus, the Allusive Historian*, Cambridge: Cambridge University Press, 2008.

For text and illustrations of the Anonymous *De Rebus Bellicis*, see M. W. C. Hassall and R. I. Ireland, *De Rebus Bellicis*, Oxford: British Archaeological Reports Int. Ser. 63, 1979.

Aurelius Victor is translated in H. W. Bird (ed. and trans.), *Aurelius Victor: De Caesaribus*, TTH 17, Liverpool: Liverpool University Press, 1994; Latin text, along with that of the *Epitome de Caesaribus*, can be found in *Sex. Aurelius Victor*, ed. F. Pichlmayr (Tubingen: Teubner, rev. 1993). *Eutropius: Breviarium*, is translated by H. W. Bird, TTH 14, Liverpool: Liverpool University Press, 1993.

Eusebius, *Ecclesiastical History*, is accessible through the Loeb Classical Library; Greek text at E. Schwarz (ed.), *Eusebius Werke. II: Die Kirchengeschichte* (vol. 1, 1903; vol. 2, 1908); for his *Life of Constantine*, see English translation and commentary by Averil Cameron and Stuart Hall, Oxford: Clarendon Press, 1999. For the *Oration to the Saints* ascribed to Constantine, see Mark Edwards (ed. and trans.), with commentary, in *Constantine and Christendom*, TTH 39, Liverpool: Liverpool University Press, 2003. For Lactantius, see *On the Deaths of the Persecutors*, ed. and trans. J. L. Creed, Oxford: Oxford University Press, 1984; texts also in S. Brandt (ed.), *CSEL* 27 (1897), and J. Moreau (ed.), *Sources Chrétiennes* 39 (1954). For his *Divine Institutes* see A. Bowen and Peter Garnsey (eds and trans.), TTH 40, Liverpool: Liverpool University Press, 2003. For the popes, as remembered later, Raymond Davis, *The Book of Pontiffs (Liber Pontificalis)*, TTH 5, Liverpool: Liverpool University Press, 1989. The Donatists can be followed up in M. Tilley (ed. and trans.), *Donatist Martyr Stories: The Church in Conflict in Roman North Africa*, TTH 24, Liverpool: Liverpool University Press, 1996, and in Mark

Edwards (ed. and trans.), *Optatus Against the Donatists*, TTH 27, Liverpool: Liverpool University Press, 1997.

For the *Latin Panegyrics*, see C. E. V. Nixon and B. S. Rodgers (eds and trans.), *In Praise of Later Roman Emperors: The Panegyrici Latini. Introduction, Translation and Historical Commentary*, Berkeley: University of California Press, 1994. For Libanius, *Antiochikos* 271–2, see A. F. Norman, *Antioch as a Centre of Hellenic Culture as Observed by Libanius*. TTH 34 Liverpool: Liverpool University Press, 2000. For Themistius, see P. Heather and D. Moncur (eds and trans.), *Politics, Philosophy and Empire in the Fourth Century: Select Orations of Themistius*, TTH 36, Liverpool: Liverpool University Press, 2001.

For Zosimus, *New History*, the Greek text is available in the Budé edition, ed. F. Paschoud, 1975, and translated with commentary by R. T. Ridley, Sydney: Sydney University Press, 1982. A seventeenth-century commentator wrote that Zosimus, despite his hostility to Christian emperors, should be believed 'even in those Relations, there being no doubt but that the Christian princes were guilty of many enormities' (Leunclavius, who translated Zosimus into Latin, as reported later in *The History of Count Zosimus*, London, 1684). Moderns are more sceptical.

For Abinnaeus and his papyri, see H. I. Bell, V. Martin, E. G. Turner and D. Van Berchem, *The Abinnaeus Archive: Papers of a Roman Officer in the Reign of Constantius II*, Oxford: Oxford University Press, 1962. There are also useful source collections in translation, for example: M. H. Dodgeon and S. N. C. Lieu, *The Roman Eastern Frontier and the Persian Wars AD 226–363: A Documentary Study*, London: Routledge, 1991; A. D. Lee, *Pagans and Christians in Late Antiquity: A Sourcebook*, London: Routledge, 2000; M. Maas, *Readings in Late Antiquity*, 2nd edn, London: Routledge, 2010; Peter Heather and John Matthews, *The Goths in the Fourth Century*, TTH 11, Liverpool: Liverpool University Press,1991; and S. N. C. Lieu, *The Emperor Julian; Panegyric and Polemic. Claudius Mamertinus, John Chrysostom, Ephrem the Syrian*, TTH Greek ser. 2, Liverpool: Liverpool University Press, 1989.

Modern works

General

Introductions to the period are offered by Peter Brown, *The World of Late Antiquity: From Marcus Aurelius to Muhammed*, London: Thames and Hudson, 1971, and *The Making of Late Antiquity*, Cambridge, MA: Harvard University Press, 1978; Averil Cameron, *The Later Roman Empire*, London: Routledge, 1993; Peter Garnsey and Caroline Humfress, *The Evolution of the Late Antique World*, Cambridge: Orchard Academic, 2001.

For more detailed coverage of all aspects of the period see Alan Bowman, Peter Garnsey and Averil Cameron (eds), *Cambridge Ancient History. Vol. 12: The Crisis of Empire, AD 235–337*, 2nd edn, Cambridge: Cambridge University Press, 2005; and volume 13, Cameron and Garnsey (eds), *The Late Empire, AD 337–425*, 1998; also the monumental classic by A. H. M. Jones, *The Later Roman Empire: A Social, Economic and Administrative Survey*, London: Blackwell, 1964.

Third century

On aspects of the third century, see L. de Blois, *The Policy of the Emperor Gallienus*, Leiden: Brill, 1976; J. F. Drinkwater, *The Gallic Empire: Separation and Continuity in the North-Western Provinces of the Roman Empire, AD 260–274*, Historia Einzelschriften 52, Stuttgart: Steiner, 1987; A. Watson, *Aurelian and the Third Century*, London: Routledge, 1999.

Covering the third and later centuries are the essays in Simon Swain and Mark Edwards (eds), *Approaching Late Antiquity: The Transformation from Early to Late Empire*, Oxford: Oxford University Press, 2005.

Diocletian and the Tetrarchy

On Diocletian, see W. Kuhoff, *Diokletian und die Epoche der Tetrarchie*, Frankfurt: Peter Lang, 2001. R. Rees, *Diocletian and the Tetrarchy*, Edinburgh: Edinburgh University Press, 2004. For a provocative take on Galerius, see Bill Leadbetter, *Galerius and the Will of Diocletian*, London: Routledge, 2009. On the 'Great Persecution' see essays in D. V. Twomey and M. Humphries (eds), *The Great Persecution*, Dublin: Four Courts Press, 2009. For the laws, see S. Corcoran, *The Empire of the Tetrarchs: Imperial Pronouncements and Government, AD 284–324*, Oxford: Oxford University Press, 2nd edn, 2002; and on the Gregorius and Hermogenian project, Serena Connolly, *Lives Behind the Laws: The World of the Codex Hermogenianus*, Bloomington: Indiana University Press, 2010.

On Maxentius as emperor, see (in German but with numerous useful references) E. Groag in the first edition of the *RE* (Pauly-Wissowa), 14, 2417–84; also, in English, M. Culhed, *Conservator urbis suae: Studies in the Politics and Propaganda of the Emperor Maxentius*, Stockhom: Svenska Institutet, Rome, 1994.

Constantine, his sons and Julian

On Constantine, there are numerous studies, but T. D. Barnes, *Constantine and Eusebius*, Cambridge, MA: Harvard University Press, 1981, *The New Empire of Diocletian and Constantine*, Cambridge, MA: Harvard University Press, 1982, and *Constantine: Dynasty, Religion and Power in the Later Roman Empire*, Oxford: Wiley-Blackwell, 2011, stand out for rigorous research and controversial interpretations. See also H. A. Drake, *Constantine and the Bishops: The Politics of Intolerance*, Baltimore, MD: Johns Hopkins University Press, 2002, and R. Van Dam, *The Roman Revolution of Constantine*, New York: Cambridge University Press, 2007. Valuable contributions are contained in S. Lieu and D. Montserrat (eds), *Constantine: History, Historiography and Legend*, London: Routledge, 1998; Noel Lenski (ed.), *Cambridge Companion to the Age of Constantine*, Cambridge: Cambridge University Press, 2006; and E. Hartley, J. Hawkes, M. Henig and F. Mee (eds), *Constantine the Great: York's Roman Emperor*, York: York Museums and Galleries Trust, 2006.

On Constantius, T. D. Barnes, *Athanasius and Constantius: Theology and Politics in the Constantinian Empire*, Cambridge, MA: Harvard University Press, 1993. On Julian, R. Browning, *The Emperor Julian*, London: Weidenfeld and Nicolson, 1975, and G. W. Bowersock, *Julian the Apostate*, London: Duckworth, 1978, are still useful; S. Tougher, *Julian the Apostate*, Edinburgh: Edinburgh University Press, 2007, provides an up-to-date survey of important issues. Rowland Smith, *Julian's Gods: Religion and Philosophy in the Thought and Action of Julian the Apostate*, London: Routledge, 1995, is central for Julian's thought.

Government, administration and cities

On Roman government, see Christopher M. Kelly, *Ruling the Later Roman Empire*, Cambridge, MA: Belknap Press, 2004. For a less rosy view, Ramsay MacMullen, *Corruption and the Decline of Rome*, New Haven: Yale University Press, 1988. Much has still to be learned from and about the Theodosian Code, on which see John Matthews, *Laying Down the Law: A Study of the Theodosian Code*, New Haven: Yale University Press, 2000. On the functioning of law see also Jill Harries, *Law and Empire in Late Antiquity*, Cambridge: Cambridge University Press, 1999; and Caroline Humfress, *Orthodoxy and the Courts in Late Antiquity*, Oxford: Oxford University Press, 2007. For Constantius' underrated role as an administrative reformer, see C. Vogler, *Constance II et l'administation imperiale*, Strasbourg: University of Strasbourg, 1979.

On the cities of the empire, see articles in John Rich (ed.), *The City in Late Antiquity*, London: Routledge, 1992; Fergus Millar, 'Empire and city, Augustus to Julian: Obligations, excuses and status', *JRS* 73 (1983), 76–96. On Rome, N. Morley, *Metropolis and Hinterland: The City of Rome and the Italian Economy*, Cambridge: Cambridge University Press, 1996; W. V. Harris (ed.), *The Transformations of Urbs Roma in Late Antiquity*, *JRA* Supp. 33, 1999, 23–33; John Curran, *Pagan City and Christian Capital: Rome in the Fourth Century*, Oxford: Oxford University Press, 2000, 43–6; Jon Coulston and Hazel Dodge (eds), *Ancient Rome: The*

Archaeology of the Eternal City, Oxford: Oxford School of Archaeology, 2000; R. Krautheimer, *Rome: Portrait of a City, 312–1308*, Princeton, NJ: Princeton University Press, 1980. On Rome's administration, A. Chastagnol, *La Préfecture urbaine à Rome sous le bas-empire*, Paris: Presses Universitaires de France, 1960. On other cities, Glanville Downey, *A History of Antioch in Syria*, Princeton. NJ: Princeton University Press, 1961; J. H. W. G. Liebeschuetz, *Antioch. City and Imperial Administration in the Later Roman Empire*, Oxford: Clarendon Press, 1972; Charlotte Roueché, *Aphrodisias in Late Antiquity: The Late Roman and Byzantine Inscriptions*, JRS Monographs 5, London: Society for the Promotion of Roman Studies, 1989, rev. 2004; S. Basset, *The Urban Image of Late Antique Constantinople*, Cambridge: Cambridge University Press, 2004.

Foreign relations

On Persia and Rome see R. N. Frye, 'The political history of Iran under the Sasanians', in E. Yarshater (ed.), *Cambridge History of Iran. Vol. 3, part 1: The Seleucid, Parthian and Sasanian Periods*, Cambridge: Cambridge University Press, 2000, 116–80. The frontier is also discussed by B. Isaacs, *The Limits of Empire: The Roman Army in the East*, Oxford: Oxford University Press, 1990; R. C. Blockley, *East Roman Foreign Policy: Formation and Conduct from Diocletian to Anastasius*, ARCA 30, Leeds: Francis Cairns, 1992; A. D. Lee, *Information and Frontiers: Roman Foreign Relations in Late Antiquity*, Cambridge: Cambridge University Press, 1993.

On Rome and the Germanic peoples, T. S. Burns, *Rome and the Barbarians, 100 B.C. to A.D. 400*, Baltimore, MD: Johns Hopkins University Press, 2004; Peter Heather, *Goths and Romans, 332–489*, Oxford: Clarendon Press, 1991, and *The Goths*, Oxford: Blackwell, 1996; J. F. Drinkwater, *The Alamanni and Rome, 213–496 (Caracalla to Clovis)*, Oxford: Oxford University Press, 2007; M. Kulikowski, *Rome's Gothic Wars*, Cambridge: Cambridge University Press, 2007.

Religions, culture and social relations

On religious background, S. Mitchell and P. van Nuffelen (eds), *One God: Pagan Monotheism in the Roman Empire*, Cambridge: Cambridge University Press, 2010; more philosophically, P. Athanassiadi and M. Frede (eds), *Pagan Monotheism in Late Antiquity*, Oxford: Oxford University Press, 1999; also Garth Fowden, *Empire to Commonwealth: Consequences of Monotheism in Late Antiquity*, Princeton. NJ: Princeton University Press, 1993; Robin Lane Fox, *Pagans and Christians*, London: Penguin, 1986; Samuel N. C. Lieu (ed.), *Manichaeism in the Roman Empire and the Near East*, Leiden: Brill, 1994.

On Christian organisation and leadership, Claudia Rapp, *Holy Bishops* in *Late Antiquity: The Nature of Christian Leadership in an Age of Transition*, Berkeley: University of California Press, 2005; Peter Norton, *Episcopal Elections 250–600: Hierarchy and Popular Will in Late Antiquity*, Oxford: Oxford University Press, 2007; R. Finn, *Almsgiving in the Later Roman Empire: Christian Promotion and Practice, 313-450*, Oxford: Oxford University Press, 2006.

On the 'Arian' controversy, R. P. C. Hanson, *The Search for the Christian Doctrine of God: The Arian Controversy*, Edinburgh: T. and T. Clark, 1988; D. M. Gwynn, *The Eusebians: The Polemic of Athanasius of Alexandria and the Construction of the 'Arian' Controvers*, Oxford: Oxford University Press, 2007.

On monasticism see D. J. Chitty, *The Desert a City: An Introduction to the Study of Egyptian and Palestinian Monasticism under the Christian Empire*, London: Mowbrays, 1977; J. E. Goehring, *Ascetics, Society and the Desert: Studies in Early Egyptian Monasticism*, Harrisburg: Trinity Press International, 1999; Philip Rousseau, *Pachomius: The Making of a Community in Fourth Century Egypt*, Berkeley: University of California Press, 1985, rev. 1999; Susanna Elm, *'Virgins of God': The Making of Asceticism in Late Antiquity*, Oxford: Clarendon Press, 1994.

On women in late antiquity, see J. W. Drijvers, *Helena Augusta: The Mother of Constantine the Great and the Finding of the True Cross*, Leiden: Brill, 1992; J. Evans Grubbs, *Law and Family in Late Antiquity: Emperor Constantine's Marriage Legislation*, Oxford: Oxford University Press, 1995; Gillian Clark, *Women in Late Antiquity: Pagan and Christian Lifestyles*, Oxford: Oxford University Press, 1993; Antti Arjava, *Women and Law in Late Antiquity*, Oxford: Oxford University Press, 1996.

On cultural background see Averil Cameron, *Christianity and the Rhetoric of Empire: The Development of Christian Discourse*, Berkeley: University of California Press, 1991; G. W. Bowersock, *Hellenism in Late Antiquity*, Cambridge: Cambridge University Press, 1990; and at Antioch, Raffaella Cribiore, *The School of Libanius in Late Antique Antioch*, Princeton, NJ: Princeton University Press, 2007; Isabella Sandwell and Janet Huskison (eds), *Culture and Society in Late Roman Antioch*, Oxford: Oxbow Books, 2004.

Bibliography of modern works cited

R. Abdy, 'In the pay of the emperor: Coins from the Beaurains (Arras) Treasure', in E. Hartley, J. Hawkes, M. Henig and F. Mee (eds), *Constantine the Great: York's Roman Emperor*, York: York Museums and Galleries Trust, 2006, 52–8.

R. Alston, 'Roman military pay from Caesar to Diocletian', *JRS* 84 (1994), 113–23.

Clifford Ando, *The Matter of the Gods: Religion and the Roman Empire*, Berkeley: University of California Press, 2008.

Antti Arjava, *Women and Law in Late Antiquity*, Oxford: Oxford University Press, 1996.

P. Athanassiadi, *Julian and Hellenism*, Oxford: Clarendon Press, 1981.

— *Julian: An Intellectual Biography*, Oxford: Oxford University Press, 1992.

— 'The Chaldean Oracles', in P. Athanassiadi and M. Frede (eds), *Pagan Monotheism in Late Antiquity*, Oxford: Oxford University Press, 1999, 149–82.

P. Athanassiadi and M. Frede (eds), *Pagan Monotheism in Late Antiquity*, Oxford: Oxford University Press, 1999.

R. S. Bagnall, *Egypt in Late Antiquity*, Princeton, NJ: Princeton University Press, 1993.

Jairus Banaji, *Agrarian Change in Late Antiquity: Gold, Labour and Aristocratic Dominance*, Oxford: Oxford University Press, 2001.

T. M. Banchich, 'Julian's school laws: *Cod. Theod.* 13.3.5 and *Ep.* 42', *Ancient World* 24 (1990), 5–14.

T. D. Barnes, 'Lactantius and Constantine', *JRS* 63 (1973), 29–46.

— 'Sossianus Hierocles and the antecedents of the Great Persecution', *Harvard Studies in Classical Philology* 80 (1976), 239–52.

— 'The editions of Eusebius' *Ecclesiastical History*', *GRBS* 21 (1980), 191–201.

— *Constantine and Eusebius*, Cambridge, MA: Harvard University Press, 1981.

— *The New Empire of Diocletian and Constantine*, Cambridge, MA: Harvard University Press, 1982.

— 'Constantine's prohibition of pagan sacrifice', *AJPhil.* 105 (1984), 69–72.

— 'Constantine and the Christians of Persia', *JRS* 75 (1985), 126–36.
— *Athanasius and Constantius; Theology and Politics in the Constantinian Empire*, Cambridge, MA: Harvard University Press, 1993.
— 'Scholarship or propaganda? Porphyry, *Against the Christians*, and its historical setting', *BICS* 39 (1994), 53–65.
— 'Statistics and the conversion of the Roman aristocracy', *JRS* 85 (1995), 135–47.
— 'Emperors, panegyrics, prefects, provinces and palaces (284–317)', *JRA* 9 (1996), 532–58.
— 'The Franci before Diocletian', in G. Bonamente and F. Paschoud (eds), *Historia Augusta Colloquium Genavense* 2 (1996), 11–18.
— 'Constantine's speech to the Assembly of the Saints: Date and place of delivery', *JTS* 52 (2001), 26–36.
— *Constantine: Dynasty, Religion and Power in the Later Roman Empire*, Oxford: Wiley-Blackwell, 2011.
R. H. Barrow, *Prefect and Emperor: The 'Relationes' of Symmachus, AD 384*, Oxford: Clarendon Press, 1973.
S. Bassett, 'The antiquities in the hippodrome at Constantinople', *DOP* 45 (1991), 87–96.
— *The Urban Image of Late Antique Constantinople*, Cambridge: Cambridge University Press, 2004.
J. Beaucamp, 'Le vocabulaire de la faiblesse feminine dans les texts juridiques romains du IIIe au VIe siècle', *RHDFE* 54 (1976), 485–508.
H. I. Bell, V. Martin, E. G. Turner and D. van Berchem (eds), *The Abinnaeus Archive: Papers of a Roman Officer in the Reign of Constantius II*, Oxford: Oxford University Press, 1962.
H. W. Bird (ed. and trans.), *Eutropius: Breviarium*, TTH 14, Liverpool: Liverpool University Press, 1993.
— (ed. and trans.), *Aurelius Victor: De Caesaribus*, TTH 17, Liverpool: Liverpool University Press, 1994.
M. C. Bishop and J. C. N. Coulston, *Roman Military Equipment*, London: Batsford, 1993.
R. C. Blockley, 'Constantius Gallus and Julian as Caesars of Constantius II', *Latomus* 31 (1972), 433–68.
— 'The panegyric of Claudius Mamertinus on the emperor Julian', *AJPhil.* 93 (1972), 437–50.
— 'The Romano-Persian treaties of 299 and 363', *Florilegium* 6 (1984), 28–49.
— *East Roman Foreign Policy: Formation and Conduct from Diocletian to Anastasius*, ARCA 30, Leeds: Francis Cairns, 1992.
L. de Blois, *The Policy of the Emperor Gallienus*, Leiden: Brill, 1976.
A. Bowen and P. Garnsey (eds and trans.), *Lactantius, Divine Institutes*, TTH 40, Liverpool: Liverpool University Press, 2003.
G. W. Bowersock, *Julian the Apostate*, London: Duckworth, 1978.

— 'The Emperor Julian on his predecessors', *Yale Classical Studies* 27 (1982), 159–72.

— *Hellenism in Late Antiquity*, Cambridge: Cambridge University Press, 1990.

Alan Bowman, Peter Garnsey and Averil Cameron (eds), *Cambridge Ancient History. Vol. 12: The Crisis of Empire, AD 235–337*, 2nd edn, Cambridge: Cambridge University Press, 2005.

Scott Bradbury, 'Constantine and the problem of anti-pagan legislation in the fourth century', *C Phil.* 89 (1994), 120–39.

— 'Julian's pagan revival and the decline of blood sacrifice', *Phoenix* 49 (1995), 331–56.

Peter Brown, 'The rise and function of the holy man in late antiquity', *JRS* 61 (1971), 80–101 = Peter Brown, *Society and the Holy in Late Antiquity*, London: Faber, 1982, 103–52.

— *The World of Late Antiquity: From Marcus Aurelius to Muhammed*, London: Thames and Hudson, 1971.

— *The Making of Late Antiquity*, Cambridge, MA: Harvard University Press, 1978.

— *Society and the Holy in Late Antiquity*, London: Faber, 1982.

— *Power and Persuasion in Late Antiquity: Towards a Christian Empire*, Madison: University of Wisconsin Press,1992.

R. Browning, *The Emperor Julian*, London: Weidenfeld and Nicolson, 1975.

W. W. Buckland, *Textbook of Roman Law*, ed. Peter Stein, 3rd edn, Cambridge: Cambridge University Press, 1966.

Richard Burgess, *Studies in Eusebian and Post-Eusebian Chronology*, Historia Einzelschriften 135, Stuttgart: Franz Steiner, 1999.

— 'The summer of blood: The "Great Massacre" of 337 and the promotion of the sons of Constantine', *DOP* 62 (2008), 5–51.

A. Cameron, 'Inscriptions relating to sacral manumission and confession', *Harv. Theol. Rev.* 32 (1939), 143–79.

Averil Cameron, 'Constantinus Christianus', *JRS* 73 (1983), 184–90.

— *Christianity and the Rhetoric of Empire: The Development of Christian Discourse*, Berkeley: University of California Press, 1991.

— 'Constantius and Constantine: An exercise in publicity', in E. Hartley, J. Hawkes, M. Henig and F. Mee (eds), *Constantine the Great: York's Roman Emperor*, York: York Museums and Galleries Trust, 2006, 18–30.

Averil Cameron and Peter Garnsey (eds), *Cambridge Ancient History. Vol. 13: The Late Empire, AD 337–425*, 2nd edn, Cambridge: Cambridge University Press, 1996.

Averil Cameron and Stuart Hall (eds and trans.), *Eusebius, Life of Constantine*, Oxford: Oxford University Press, 1999.

Brian Campbell, *The Emperor and the Roman Army*, Oxford: Clarendon

Press, 1984.

— 'The army II: The military reforms of Diocletian and Constantine', in *CAH*² 12, 120–30.

J-M. Carrié (ed.), *L'Empereur Julien et son temps*, *Antiquité Tardive* 17 (2009).

— 'Julien législateur: un mélange de genres', in J-M. Carrié (ed.), *L'Empereur Julien et son temps*, *Antiquité Tardive* 17 (2009), 175–84.

Elio Lo Cascio, 'The new state of Diocletian and Constantine: From the Tetrarchy to the reunification of the empire', in *CAH*² 12, 170–81.

P. J. Casey, 'Carausius and Allectus: Rulers in Gaul?', *Britannia* 8 (1977), 283–301.

— *Carausius and Allectus: The British Usurpers*, London: Batsford, 1994.

H. Chadwick, *Priscillian of Avila: The Occult and the Charismatic in the Early Church*, Oxford: Oxford University Press, 1976.

A. Chastagnol, *La Préfecture urbaine à Rome sous le bas-empire*, Paris: Presses Universitaires de France, 1960.

— 'L'Inscription constantinienne d'Orcistus', *MEFRA* 93 (1981), 381–416.

— 'Un nouveau préfet de Dioclétien', *ZPE* 79 (1989), 165–8.

D. J. Chitty, *The Desert a City: An Introduction to the Study of Egyptian and Palestinian Monasticism under the Christian Empire*, London: Mowbrays, 1977.

Emma C. Clark, J. M. Dillon and J. P. Herschbell (eds and trans.), *Iamblichus, De Mysteriis*, Atlanta, GA: Society of Biblical Literature, 2003.

Gillian Clark (ed. and trans.), *Iamblichus, On the Pythagorean Life*, TTH Greek ser. 8, Liverpool: Liverpool University Press, 1989.

— *Women in Late Antiquity: Pagan and Christian Lifestyles*, Oxford: Oxford University Press, 1993.

Manfred Clauss, *The Roman Cult of Mithras: The God and his Mysteries*, trans. Richard Gordon, Edinburgh: Edinburgh University Press, 2000.

F. Coarelli, 'L'edilizia pubblica a Roma in età tetrarchica', in W. V. Harris (ed.), *The Transformations of Urbs Roma in Late Antiquity*, *JRA* Supp. 33, 1999, 23–33.

— *Rome and Environs: An Archaeological Guide*, Berkeley: University of California Press, 2007.

Serena Connolly, 'Constantine answers the veterans', in Scott McGill, Cristiana Sogno and Edward Watts (eds), *From the Tetrarchs to the Theodosians: Late Roman History and Culture, 284–450* CE, Cambridge: Cambridge University Press, 2010, 93–114.

— *Lives Behind the Laws: The World of the Codex Hermogenianus*, Bloomington: Indiana University Press, 2010.

M. Corbier, 'Coinage and taxation: The state's point of view', in *CAH*² 12, 327–92.

Simon Corcoran, 'Hidden from history: The legislation of Licinius', in

Jill Harries and Ian Wood (eds), *The Theodosian Code: Studies in the Imperial Law of Late Antiquity*, London: Duckworth, 1993, reissued 2010, 97–119.

— 'The sins of the fathers: A neglected constitution of Diocletian on incest', *Journal of Legal History* 21 (2000), 1–34.

— *The Empire of the Tetrarchs: Imperial Pronouncements and Government, AD 284–324*, Oxford: Oxford University Press, 2000; 2nd edn, 2002.

Jon Coulston and Hazel Dodge (eds), *Ancient Rome: The Archaeology of the Eternal City*, Oxford: Oxford School of Archaeology, 2000.

M. H. Crawford, 'Discovery, autopsy and progress: Diocletian's jigsaw puzzles', in T. P. Wiseman (ed.), *Classics in Progress: Essays on Ancient Greece and Rome*, Oxford: British Academy and Oxford University Press, 2002, 144–63.

Raffaella Cribiore, *The School of Libanius in Late Antique Antioch*, Princeton. NJ: Princeton University Press, 2007.

B. Croke and J. Harries, *Religious Conflict in Fourth Century Rome: A Documentary Study*, Sydney: Sydney University Press, 1982.

M. Culhed, *Conservator urbis suae: Studies in the Politics and Propaganda of the Emperor Maxentius*, Stockholm: Svenska Institutet, 1994.

Paula Cuneo, *La legislazione di Costantino II, Costanzo II e Costante (337–61): materiali per una palingenesia delle costituzioni tardo-imperiali*, Milan: Giuffré, 1997.

M. P. Cunninghan and P. Allen (eds), *Preacher and Audience: Studies in Early Christian and Byzantine Homilies*, Leiden: Brill, 1998.

John Curran, *Pagan City and Christian Capital: Rome in the Fourth Century*, Oxford: Oxford University Press, 2000.

G. Dagron, *Naissance d'une capitale: Constantinople et ses institutions de 330 à 451*, Paris: Presses Universitaires de France, 1974.

P. S. Davies, 'The origins and purpose of the persecution of 303', *JTS* 40 (1989), 66–94.

Raymond Davis, *The Book of Pontiffs (Liber Pontificalis)*, TTH 5, Liverpool: Liverpool University Press, 1989, rev. edn 2010.

A. Dearn, 'The Abitinian martyrs and the outbreak of the Donatist schism', *Journal of Ecclesiastical History* 55 (2004), 1–18.

D. de Decker, 'La politique religieuse de Maxence', *Byzantion* 38 (1968), 472–562.

R. Delmaire, *Largesses sacrées et res privata: l'aerarium imperiale et son administration du IVe au Vie siècle*, Paris: Ecole Française de Rome, 1989.

— *Les Responsables des finances imperiales au bas-empire romain: études prosopographiques*, Brussels: Latomus, 1989.

E. dePalma Digeser, *The Making of a Christian Empire: Lactantius and Rome*, Ithaca, NY: Cornell University Press, 2000.

G. Depeyrot, 'Economy and society', in Noel Lenski (ed.), *Cambridge Companion to the Age of Constantine*, Cambridge: Cambridge University Press, 2006, 237–9.

J. M. Dillon and W. Polleichter (eds and trans.), *Iamblichus of Chalcis, the Letters*, Atlanta, GA: Society of Biblical Literature, 2009.

S. Dmitriev, *City Government in Hellenistic and Roman Asia Minor*, New York: Oxford University Press, 2004.

M. H. Dodgeon and S. N. C. Lieu, *The Roman Eastern Frontier and the Persian Wars AD 226–363: A Documentary Study*, London: Routledge, 1991.

Glanville Downey, *A History of Antioch in Syria*, Princeton, NJ: Princeton University Press, 1961.

H. A. Drake, *In Praise of Constantine: A Historical Study and New Translation of Eusebius' Tricennial Orations*, Berkeley: University of California Press, 1976.

— *Constantine and the Bishops: The Politics of Intolerance*, Baltimore, MD: Johns Hopkins University Press, 2002.

— 'Lessons from Diocletian's persecution', in D. V. Twomey and M. Humphries (eds), *The Great Persecution*, Dublin: Four Courts Press, 2009, 49–60.

J. W. Drijvers, *Helena Augusta: The Mother of Constantine the Great and the Legend of her Finding of the True Cross*, Leiden: Brill, 1992.

J. F. Drinkwater, *The Gallic Empire: Separation and Continuity in the North-Western Provinces of the Roman Empire, AD 260–274*, Historia Einzelschriften 52, Stuttgart: Steiner, 1987.

— 'Silvanus, Ursicinus and Ammianus: Fact or fiction?', in C. Deroux (ed.), *Studies in Latin Literature and Roman History* 7, Coll. Lat. 227, Brussels 1994, 568–76.

— 'The Germanic threat on the Rhine frontier: A Romano-Gallic artefact?', in R. Mathisen and H. Sivan (eds), *Shifting Frontiers in Late Antiquity*, Aldershot: Variorum, 1996, 20–30.

— *The Alamanni and Rome, 213–496 (Caracalla to Clovis)*, Oxford: Oxford University Press, 2007.

R. Duncan Jones, *The Economy of the Roman Empire*, 2nd edn, Cambridge: Cambridge University Press, 1982, 366–9.

— *Structure and Scale in the Roman Economy*, Cambridge: Cambridge University Press, 1990.

— *Money and Government in the Roman Empire*, Cambridge: Cambridge University Press, 1994.

— 'Economic change and the transition to late antiquity', in Simon Swain and Mark Edwards (eds), *Approaching Late Antiquity: The Transformation from Early to Late Empire*, Oxford: Oxford University Press, 2005, 20–52.

C. Dupont, 'Les privileges des clercs sous Constantin', *RHE* 62 (1967),

729–52.

Mark Edwards (ed. and trans.), *Optatus Against the Donatists*, TTH 27, Liverpool: Liverpool University Press, 1997.

— (ed. and trans.), *Constantine and Christendom*, TTH 39, Liverpool: Liverpool University Press, 2003.

— *Culture and Philosophy in the Age of Plotinus*, London: Duckworth, 2006.

T. G. Elliot, 'The tax exemptions granted to clerics by Constantine and Constantius II', *Phoenix* 32 (1978), 326–36.

Susanna Elm, *'Virgins of God': The Making of Asceticism in Late Antiquity*, Oxford: Clarendon Press, 1994.

Jas Elsner, *Imperial Rome and Christian Triumph*, Oxford: Oxford University Press, 1998.

— 'Perspectives in art' in Noel Lenski (ed.), *Cambridge Companion to the Age of Constantine*, Cambridge: Cambridge University Press, 2006, pp. 255–77.

K. T. Erim,, J. Reynolds and M. H. Crawford, 'Diocletian's currency reform: A new inscription', *JRS* 61 (1971), 171–7.

R. M. Errington, 'Constantine and the pagans', *GRBS* 29 (1988), 309–18.

A. Ferrua, *Epigrapmmata Damasiana*, Rome: Pontificio Istituto di archaeologia cristiana, 1942.

R. Finn, *Almsgiving in the Later Roman Empire: Christian Promotion and Practice, 313–450*, Oxford: Oxford University Press, 2006, 255–77.

C. W. Fornara, 'Julian's Persian expedition in Ammianus and Zosimus', *JHS* 111 (1991), 1–15.

Garth Fowden, 'Nikagoras of Athens and the Lateran obelisk,' *JHS* 107 (1987), 51–7.

— *Empire to Commonwealth: Consequences of Monotheism in Late Antiquity*, Princeton, NJ: Princeton University Press, 1993.

— 'The last days of Constantine: Oppositional versions and their influence', *JRS* 84 (1994), 146–70.

— 'Late polytheism', *CAH*² 12, 521–72.

— 'Polytheist religion and philosophy', *CAH*² 13, 538–60.

Robert Frakes, 'The dynasty of Constantine down to 363', in Noel Lenski (ed.), *Cambridge Companion to the Age of Constantine*, Cambridge: Cambridge University Press, 2006, 91–107.

M. Frede, 'Celsus' attack on the Christians', in Jonathan Barnes and Miriam Griffin (eds), *Philosophia Togata* II, Oxford: Oxford University Press, 1997, 218–40.

— 'Origen's response against Celsus', in M. Edwards, M. Goodman and S. Price (eds), *Apologetics in the Roman Empire*, Oxford: Oxford University Press, 1999, 131–56.

W. H. C. Frend, *The Donatist Church: A Movement of Protest in Roman North Africa*, Oxford: Clarendon Press, 1952, rev. edn 1971.

B. W. Frier and T. A. J. McGinn, *A Casebook on Roman Family Law*,

American Philological Association, New York: Oxford University Press, 2004.

R. N. Frye, 'The political history of Iran under the Sasanians', in E. Yarshater (ed.), *Cambridge History of Iran. Vol. 3, part 1: The Seleucid, Parthian and Sasanian Periods*, Cambridge: Cambridge University Press, 2000, 116–80.

Jane Gardner, *Women in Roman Law and Society*, London: Croom Helm, 1986.

Peter Garnsey, *Social Status and Legal Privilege in the Roman Empire*, Oxford: Oxford University Press, 1970.

Peter Garnsey and Caroline Humfress, *The Evolution of the Late Antique World*, Cambridge: Orchard Academic, 2001.

J. Gascou, 'Le Rescrit de Hispellum', *MEFRA* 79 (1967), 609–59.

Jean Gaudemet, *Les Institutions de l'antiquité*, Paris: Sirey, 1967 and 1991.

Lloyd P. Gerson (ed.), *The Cambridge Companion to Plotinus*, Cambridge: Cambridge University Press, 1996.

A. Giardina, 'La formazione dell'Italia provinciale', in A. Schiavone (ed.), *Storia di Roma. Vol. III.1: L'eta tardoantica: crisi e transformazione*, Turin: Giulio Einardi, 1993.

Maud W. Gleason, 'Festive satire: Julian's *Misopogon* and the New Year at Antioch', *JRS* 76 (1986), 106–19.

J. E. Goehring, *Ascetics, Society and the Desert: Studies in Early Egyptian Monasticism*, Harrisburg: Trinity Press International, 1999.

Cam Grey, 'Contextualising *colonatus*: The *origo* of the late Roman empire', *JRS* 97 (2007), 155–75.

Lucy Grig, *Making Martyrs in Late Antiquity*, London: Duckworth, 2004.

R. Grigg, 'Constantine the Great and the cult without images', *Viator* 8 (1977), 1–32.

J. Evans Grubbs, 'Abduction marriage in antiquity: A law of Constantine (*CTh* ix.24.1) and its social context', *JRS* 79 (1989), 59–83.

— *Law and Family in Late Antiquity: Emperor Constantine's Marriage Legislation*, Oxford: Oxford University Press, 1995.

— *Women and the Law in the Roman Empire*, London: Routledge, 2002.

D. M. Gwynn, *The Eusebians: The Polemic of Athanasius of Alexandria and the Construction of the 'Arian' Controversy*, Oxford: Oxford University Press, 2007.

R. P. C. Hanson, 'The *Oratio ad Sanctos* attributed to the Emperor Constantine and the Oracle of Apollo at Daphne', *JTS* 24 (1973), 505–11.

— *The Search for the Christian Doctrine of God: The Arian Controversy*, Edinburgh: T. and T. Clark, 1988.

Jill Harries, '"Treasure in heaven": Property and inheritance among senators of late Rome', in E. Craik (ed.), *Marriage and Property*,

Aberdeen: Aberdeen University Press, 1984, 54–70.

— 'The Roman imperial quaestor from Constantine to Theodosius II', *JRS* 78 (1988), 148–72.

— 'Constructing the judge: Judicial accountability and the culture of criticism in late antiquity', in Richard Miles (ed.), *Constructing Identities in Late Antiquity*, London: Routledge, 1999, 214–33.

— *Law and Empire in Late Antiquity*, Cambridge: Cambridge University Press, 1999.

— 'Creating legal space: The settlement of disputes in the Roman Empire', in C. Hezser (ed.), *Rabbinic Law in its Roman and Near Eastern Context*, Tubingen: Mohr Siebeck, 2003, 62–81.

— '*Favor populi*: Patronage and public entertainment in late antiquity', in Kathryn Lomas and Tim Cornell (eds), *Bread and Circuses: Euergetism and Municipal Patronage in Roman Italy*, London: Routledge, 2003, 125–41.

— *Cicero and the Jurists*, London: Duckworth, 2006.

— 'Violence, victims and the legal tradition', in Hal Drake (ed.), *Violence in Late Antiquity: Perceptions and Practices*, Aldershot: Variorum, 2006, 85–102.

— *Law and Crime in the Roman World*, Cambridge: Cambridge University Press, 2007.

— 'Roman law codes and the Roman legal tradition', in J. W. Cairns and P. du Plessis (eds), *Beyond Dogmatics: Law and Society in the Roman World*, Edinburgh: Edinburgh University Press, 2007, 85–104.

— 'Constantine the lawgiver', in Scott McGill, Cristiana Sogno and Edward Watts (eds), *From the Tetrarchs to the Theodosians: Late Roman History and Culture, 284–450 CE*, Cambridge: Cambridge University Press, 2010, 73–92.

Jill Harries and Ian Wood (eds), *The Theodosian Code: Studies in the Imperial Law of Late Antiquity*, London: Duckworth, 1993, reissued 2010.

W. V. Harris (ed.), *The Transformations of Urbs Roma in Late Antiquity*, *JRA* Supp. 33, 1999.

E. Hartley, J. Hawkes, M. Henig and F. Mee (eds), *Constantine the Great: York's Roman Emperor*, York: York Museums and Galleries Trust, 2006.

M. W. C. Hassall and R. I. Ireland, *De Rebus Bellicis*, Oxford: British Archaeological Reports Int. Ser. 63, 1979.

M. Heath, 'Rhetoric in mid-antiquity', in T. P. Wiseman (ed.), *Classics in Progress: Essays on Ancient Greece and Rome*, Oxford: Oxford University Press, 2002, 419–39.

Peter Heather, *Goths and Romans 332–489*, Oxford: Clarendon Press, 1991.

— 'New men for new Constantines? Creating an imperial elite in the eastern Mediterranean', in P. Magdalino (ed.), *New Constantines:*

The Rhythm of Imperial Renewal in Byzantium, 4th–13th Centuries, Aldershot: Variorum, 1994, 11–33.

— 'The Huns and the end of the Roman Empire in western Europe', *English Historical Review* 110 (1995), 4–41.

— *The Goths*, Oxford: Blackwell, 1996.

— 'Senators and senates', in *CAH*² 13, 187–8.

— *The Fall of the Roman Empire: A New History*, London: Macmillan, 2005.

Peter Heather and John Matthews, *The Goths in the Fourth Century*, TTH 11, Liverpool: Liverpool University Press, 1991.

P. Heather and D. Moncur (eds and trans.), *Politics, Philosophy and Empire in the Fourth Century: Select Orations of Themistius*, TTH 36, Liverpool: Liverpool University Press, 2001.

Emily A. Hemelrijk, *Matrona docta: Educated Women in the Roman Elite from Cornelia to Julia Domna*, London: Routledge, 1999.

Nick Henck, 'Constantius, *ho philoktistes*', *DOP* 55 (2001), 280–304.

M. Hendy, *Studies in the Byzantine Monetary Economy, AD 300–1450*, Cambridge: Cambridge University Press, 1985, 371–95.

H. Hess, *The Early Development of Canon Law and the Council of Serdica*, Oxford: Oxford University Press, 2002.

M. Hollerich, 'The comparison of Moses and Constantine in Eusebius of Caesarea's *Life of Constantine*', *Studia Patristica* 19 (1989), 80–95.

Kenneth G. Holum, *Theodosian Empresses: Women and Imperial Dominion in Late Antiquity*, Berkeley: University of California Press, 1982.

Tony Honoré, *Tribonian*, London: Duckworth, 1978.

— 'The making of the Theodosian Code', *ZSS RA* 104 (1986), 133–222.

M. K. Hopkins, 'The political power of eunuchs', in M. K. Hopkins, *Conquerors and Slaves* 1, Cambridge: Cambridge University Press, 1978, 172–96.

Caroline Humfress, 'Civil law and social life', in Noel Lenski (ed.), *Cambridge Companion to the Age of Constantine*, Cambridge: Cambridge University Press, 2006, 205–25.

— *Orthodoxy and the Courts in Late Antiquity*, Oxford: Oxford University Press, 2007.

M. Humphries, 'From usurper to emperor? The politics of legitimation in the age of Constantine', *Journal of Late Antiquity*, 1 (2008), 82–100.

— 'The mind of the persecutors: "By the gracious favour of the gods"', in D. V. Twomey and M. Humphries (eds), *The Great Persecution*, Dublin: Four Courts Press, 2009, 11–32.

E. D. Hunt, *Holy Land Pilgrimage in the Later Roman Empire, AD 312–460*, Oxford: Oxford University Press, 1982.

— 'Christianizing the Roman Empire: The evidence of the Code', in Jill Harries and Ian Wood (eds), *The Theodosian Code: Studies in the*

Imperial Law of Late Antiquity, London: Duckworth 1993, reissued 2010, 143–58.

— 'Julian and Marcus Aurelius', in D. Innes, H. Hine and C Pelling (eds), *Ethics and Rhetoric: Classical Essays for Donald Russell on his 75th Birthday*, Oxford: Oxford University Press, 1995, 287–98.

— 'The church as a public institution', in *CAH*[2] 13, 238–76.

B. Isaac, *The Limits of Empire: The Roman Army in the East*, Oxford: Oxford University Press, 1990; 2nd edn, 1992.

S. Johnson, *The Roman Forts of the Saxon Shore*, London: Elek, 1976, 2nd edn 1979.

— *Late Roman Fortifications*, London: Batsford, 1983.

David Johnston, 'Epi-classical law', in *CAH*[2] 12, 200–7.

A. H. M. Jones, *The Greek City from Alexander to Justinian*, Oxford: Oxford University Press, 1940.

— 'Census records of the later Roman Empire', *JRS* 43 (1953), 49–64.

— 'The date and value of the Verona List', *JRS* 44 (1954), 21–9.

— '*Capitatio* and *iugatio*', *JRS* 47 (1957), 88–94.

— *The Later Roman Empire: A Social, Economic and Administrative Survey*, London: Blackwell, 1964. [Use Jones, *LRE*]

Alistair Kee, *Constantine versus Christ: The Triumph of Ideology*, London: SCM, 1982.

Christopher M. Kelly, 'Emperors, government and bureaucracy', in *CAH*[2] 13, 138–83.

— *Ruling the Later Roman Empire*, Cambridge, MA: Belknap Press, 2004.

— 'Bureaucracy and government', in Noel Lenski (ed.), *Cambridge Companion to the Age of Constantine*, Cambridge: Cambridge University Press, 2006, 183–204.

Gavin Kelly, 'The New Rome and the old: Ammianus' silences on Constantinople', *CQ* 53 (2003), 588–607.

— *Ammianus Marcellinus, the Allusive Historian*, Cambridge: Cambridge University Press, 2008.

J. P. C. Kent, *RIC* 8, 33–9.

C. E. King, 'The Maxentian mints', *Num. Chron.* 19 (1959), 47–78.

I. König, 'Die Berufung des Constantius Chlorus under des Galerius zu Caesaren: Gedanken zur Entstehung des ersten Tetrarchie', *Chiron* 4 (1974), 567–76.

R. Krautheimer, *Rome: Portrait of a City, 312–1308*, Princeton, NJ: Princeton University Press, 1980

— 'A note on the inscription in the apse of Old St Peter's', *DOP* 41 (1987), 317–20.

W. Kuhoff, *Diokletian und die Epoche der Tetrarchie*, Frankfurt: Peter Lang, 2001.

M. Kulikowski, 'Constantine and the northern barbarians', in Noel Lenski (ed.), *Cambridge Companion to the Age of Constantine*, Cambridge:

Cambridge University Press, 2006, 347–76
— Kulikowski, *Rome's Gothic Wars*, Cambridge: Cambridge University Press, 2007.
Sonia Laconi, *Costanzo II: ritratto di un imperatore eretico*, Rome: Herder Editrice, 2004.
Robin Lane Fox, *Pagans and Christians*, London: Penguin, 1986.
Bill Leadbetter, 'The illegitimacy of Constantine and the birth of the Tetrarchy', in S. Lieu and D. Montserrat (eds), *Constantine: History, Historiography and Legend*, London: Routledge, 1998, 71–85.
— 'Patrimonium indivisum? The empire of Diocletian and Maximian', *Chiron* 28 (1998), 213–28.
— *Galerius and the Will of Diocletian*, London: Routledge, 2009.
A. D. Lee, *Information and Frontiers: Roman Foreign Relations in Late Antiquity*, Cambridge: Cambridge University Press, 1993.
— 'Traditional religions', in Noel Lenski (ed.), *Cambridge Companion to the Age of Constantine*, Cambridge: Cambridge University Press, 2006, 159–79.
— *War in Late Antiquity: A Social History*, Oxford: Blackwell, 2007.
Noel Lenski (ed.), *Cambridge Companion to the Age of Constantine*, Cambridge: Cambridge University Press, 2006.
— 'The reign of Constantine', in Noel Lenski (ed.), *The Cambridge Companion to the Age of Constantine*, Cambridge: Cambridge University Press, 2006, 72–5.
C. Lepelley, *Les Cités de l'Afrique romaine au bas-empire*, 2 vols, Paris: Etudes Augustiniennes, 1979–81.
E. Levy, *West Roman Vulgar Law: The Law of Property*, Philadelphia: American Philosophical Society, 1951.
J. H. W. G. Liebeschuetz, *Antioch: City and Imperial Administration in the Later Roman Empire*, Oxford: Clarendon Press, 1972.
Samuel N. C. Lieu, *The Emperor Julian: Panegyric and Polemic. Claudius Mamertinus, John Chrysostom, Ephrem the Syrian*, TTH Greek ser. 2, Liverpool: Liverpool University Press, 1989.
— *Manichaeism in the Roman Empire and the Near East*, Leiden: Brill, 1994.
S. N. C. Lieu and D. Montserrat, *From Constantine to Julian: Pagan and Christian Views. A Source History*, London: Routledge, 1996.
C. Lightfoot, 'Facts and fiction in the third siege of Nisibis in AD 350', *Historia* 37 (1988), 105–25.
Richard Lim, *Public Disputation, Power and Social Order in Late Antiquity*, Berkeley: University of California Press, 1995.
Andrew Louth, 'Philosophical objections to Christianity on the eve of the Great Persecution', in D. V. Twomey and M. Humphries (eds), *The Great Persecution*, Dublin: Four Courts Press, 2009, 33–48.
M. Maas, *John Lydus and the Roman Past*, London: Routledge, 1992.

S. MacCormack, *Art and Ceremony in Late Antiquity*, Berkeley: University of California Press, 1981.

M. McCormick, *Eternal Victory: Triumphal Renewal in Late Antiquity, Byzantium and the Early Mediaeval West*, Cambridge: Cambridge University Press, 1986.

Scott McGill, Cristiana Sogno and Edward Watts (eds), *From the Tetrarchs to the Theodosians: Late Roman History and Culture, 284–450 CE*, Cambridge: Cambridge University Press, 2010.

Neil McLynn, *Ambrose of Milan: Church and Court in a Christian Capital*, Berkeley: University of California Press, 1994.

— 'The transformation of imperial churchgoing in the fourth century,' in Simon Swain. and Mark Edwards (eds), *Approaching Late Antiquity: The Transformation from Early to Late Empire*, Oxford: Oxford University Press, 2005

Ramsay MacMullen, *Soldier and Civilian in the Later Roman Empire*, Cambridge, MA: Harvard University Press, 1963.

— 'Constantine and the miraculous', *GRBS* 9 (1968), 81–96.

— 'Judicial savagery in the Roman Empire', *Chiron* 19 (1986), 147–66.

— *Corruption and the Decline of Rome*, New Haven: Yale University Press, 1988.

E. S. Malbon, *The Iconography of the Sarcophagus of Iulius Bassus*, Princeton, NJ: Princeton University Press, 1990.

A. Mandouze, *Prosopographie Chrétienne du bas-empire. I: Afrique (303–533)*, Paris: CNRS, 1982.

M. M. Mango, 'The porticoed street at Constantinople', in N. Necipoglu (ed.), *Byzantine Constantinople: Monuments, Topography and Everyday Life*, Leiden: Brill, 2001, 29–51.

J. C. Mann, '*Duces* and *comites* in the fourth century', in D. E. Johnston (ed.), *The Saxon Shore*, London: Council for British Archaeology, 1977, 11–15.

Mar Marcos, '"He forced with gentleness": Emperor Julian's attitude to religious coercion', in J-M. Carrié (ed.), *L'Empereur Julien et son temps, Antiquité Tardive* 17 (2009), 191–204.

John Matthews, 'Petrus Valvomeres rearrested', in Michael Whitby, Philip R. Hardie and Mary Whitby (eds), *Homo viator: Classical Essays for John Bramble*, Bristol: Bristol Classical Press, 1987, 277–84.

— *The Roman Empire of Ammianus*, London: Duckworth, 1989.

— *Laying Down the Law: A Study of the Theodosian Code*, New Haven: Yale University Press, 2000.

— *The Journey of Theophanes: Travel, Business and Daily Life in the Roman East*, New Haven: Yale University Press, 2006.

H. Mattingly, '*Fel. temp. reparatio*', *Num. Chron.* (1933), 182–202.

Fergus Millar, 'P. Herennius Dexippus, the Greek world and the third century crisis', *JRS* 59 (1969), 12–29.

— 'Paul of Samosata, Zenobia and Aurelian: The church, local culture and political allegiances in third-century Syria', *JRS* 61 (1971), 52–83.

— *The Emperor in the Roman World*, London: Duckworth, 1977.

— 'Empire and city, Augustus to Julian: Obligations, excuses and status', *JRS* 73 (1983), 76–96.

— *A Greek Roman Empire: Power and Belief under Theodosius II (408–450)*, Berkeley: University of California Press, 2006.

S. Mitchell, 'Maximinus and the Christians in AD 312: A new Latin inscription', *JRS* 78 (1988), 105–24.

— *Anatolia: Land, Men and Gods in Asia Minor*, I, Oxford: Oxford University Press, 1993.

S. Mitchell and P. van Nuffelen (eds), *One God: Pagan Monotheism in the Roman Empire*, Cambridge: Cambridge University Press, 2010.

N. Morley, *Metropolis and Hinterland: The City of Rome and the Italian Economy*, Cambridge: Cambridge University Press, 1996.

C. Müller, *Fragmenta Historicorum Graecorum*, Paris: Didot, 1841–72. [Use *FHG*]

Stuart Munro-Hay, *Aksum: An African Civilisation of Late Antiquity*, Edinburgh: Edinburgh University Press, 1991.

H. Musurillo, *Acts of the Christian Martyrs: Introduction, Texts and Translations*, Oxford: Clarendon Press, 1972.

C. E. V. Nixon and B. S. Rodgers (eds and trans.), *In Praise of Later Roman Emperors: The Panegyrici Latini. Introduction, Translation and Historical Commentary*, Berkeley: University of California Press, 1994.

A. D. Nock, 'The emperor's divine *comes*', *JRS* 37 (1947), 102–16.

A. F. Norman, *Libanius' Autobiography (Oration 1)*, Oxford: Oxford University Press, 1965.

— *Antioch as a Centre of Hellenic Culture as Observed by Libanius*, TTH 34, Liverpool: Liverpool University Press, 2000.

John North, 'Arnobius and sacrifice', in John Drinkwater and Benet Salway (eds), *Wolf Liebeschuetz Reflected*, *BICS* Supp. 91, London: University of London, 2007, 27–36.

— 'Pagan ritual and monotheism', in S. Mitchell and P. van Nuffelen (eds), *One God: Pagan Monotheism in the Roman Empire*, Cambridge: Cambridge University Press, 2010, 34–52.

Peter Norton, *Episcopal Elections 250–600: Hierarchy and Popular Will in Late Antiquity*, Oxford: Oxford University Press, 2007.

P. van Nuffelen, 'Pagan monotheism as a religious phenomenon', in S. Mitchell and P. van Nuffelen (eds), *One God: Pagan Monotheism in the Roman Empire*, Cambridge: Cambridge University Press, 2010, 16–33.

E. Pagels, *Adam, Eve and the Serpent*, London: Weidenfeld and Nicolson, 1988

E. Papi, 'A new golden age? The northern *praefectura urbi* from Severus to Diocletian', in Simon Swain and Mark Edwards (eds), *Approaching Late Antiquity: The Transformation from Early to Late Empire*, Oxford: Oxford University Press, 2005, 53–81.

F. Paschoud (ed. with Greek text and French trans.), *Zosime, Histoire Nouvelle. Livres I–II*, Paris; Budé, 1971.

Andrew Pearson, *The Construction of the Saxon Shore Forts*, Oxford: Archaeopress, 2003.

R. J. Penella, 'Julian the persecutor in fifth century church historians', *Ancient World* 24 (1990), 31–43.

H. von Petrikovitz, 'Fortifications in the north-western Roman Empire from the third century to the fifth century', *JRS* 61 (1971), 178–218.

P. Pierce, 'The Arch of Constantine: Propaganda and ideology in late Roman art', *Art History* 12 (1989), 387–418.

M. S. Pond Rothman, 'The thematic organisation of the panel reliefs on the Arch of Galerius', *AJArch.* 81 (1997), 427–54.

David S. Potter, *Prophecy and History in the Crisis of the Roman Empire*, Oxford: Oxford University Press, 1998.

— *The Roman Empire at Bay, AD 180–395*, London: Routledge, 2004.

Simon Price, *Rituals and Power: The Roman Imperial Cult in Asia Minor*, Cambridge: Cambridge University Press, 1984.

Claudia Rapp, 'Imperial ideology in the making: Eusebius of Caesarea on Constantine as "bishop"', *JTS* 49 (1998), 685–95.

— *Holy Bishops in Late Antiquity: The Nature of Christian Leadership in an Age of Transition*, Berkeley: University of California Press, 2005.

— 'Old Testament models for emperors in early Byzantium', in Paul Magdalino and Robert Nelson (eds), *The Old Testament in Byzantium*, Washington, DC: Dumbarton Oaks Collection, 2010, 175–98.

R. Rees, 'Images and image: A re-examination of tetrarchic iconography', *Greece and Rome* 40 (1993), 181–200.

— *Diocletian and the Tetrarchy*, Edinburgh: Edinburgh University Press, 2004.

— 'The emperors' new names: Diocletian Jovius and Maximian Herculius', in H. Bowden and L. Rawlings (eds), *Herakles and Hercules: Exploring a Graceo-Roman Divinity*, Swansea: University of Wales Press, 2005, 223–40.

Jan Retsö, *The Arabs in Antiquity: Their History from the Assyrians to the Ummayads*, London: Routledge, 2002.

J. Reynolds and M. H. Crawford, 'The publication of the prices edict: A new inscription from Aezani', *JRS* 65 (1975), 160–3.

— 'The Aezani copy of the prices edict', *ZPE* 26 (1977), 125–51, and 34 (1979), 163–210.

John Rich (ed.), *The City in Late Antiquity*, London: Routledge, 1992.

John Richardson, *The Romans in Spain*, Oxford: Blackwell, 1996.

J. B. Rives, 'The decree of Decius and the religion of empire', *JRS* 89 (1999), 135–54.

Y. Rivière, 'Constantin, le crime et le christianisme: contribution à l'étude des lois et des moeurs de l'antiquité tardive', *Antiquité Tardive* 10 (2002), 327–61.

A. S. Robertson (ed.), *Roman Imperial Coins in the Hunter Coin Cabinet*, Oxford: Oxford University Press, 1982.

Barbara S. Rodgers, 'Divine insinuation in the *Panegyrici Latini*', *Historia* 35 (1986), 69–104.

— 'The metamorphosis of Constantine', *CQ* 39 (1989), 233–46.

Charlotte Roueché, 'Acclamations in the later Roman Empire: New evidence from Aphrodisias', *JRS* 74 (1984), 181–99.

— *Aphrodisias in Late Antiquity: The Late Roman and Byzantine Inscriptions*, *JRS* Monographs 5, London: Society for the Promotion of Roman Studies, 1989, rev. 2004.

— '*Floreat Perge*', in M. M. MacKenzie and Charlotte Roueche (eds), *Images of Authority: Papers Presented to Joyce Reynolds*, Cambridge: Cambridge Philological Society, 1989, 218–21.

J. Rougé, 'L'Abdication de Dioclétien et la proclamation des Césars: degré de fiabilité du récit de Lactance', in M. Christol (ed.), *Institutions, société et vie politique dans l'empire romain au IVe siècle ap. J.-C.*, Collection de l' Ecole Française de Rome 159, Rome: Ecole Française de Rome, 1989, 76–89.

Philip Rousseau, *Pachomius: The Making of a Community in Fourth Century Egypt*, Berkeley: University of California Press, 1985, rev. 1999.

J. Rüpke, *Fasti Sacerdotum*, Stuttgart: Franz Steiner, 2005.

G. Sabbah, 'Présences féminins dans l'histoire d'Ammien Marcellin: les rôles politiques', in J. den Boeft, D. den Hengst and H. C. Teitler (eds), *Cognitio gestorum: The Historiographic Art of Ammianus Marcelllinus*, Amsterdam: N. Jork, 1992, 91–105.

G. E. M. de Ste Croix, 'Aspects of the Great Persecution', *Harvard Theological Review* 47 (1954), 75–113, reprinted in M. Whitby and J. Streeter (eds), *Christian Persecution, Martyrdom and Orthodoxy*, Oxford: Oxford University Press, 2006, 35–68.

Michelle Salzman, *On Roman Time: The Codex-Calendar of 354 and the Rhythms of Urban Life in Late Antiquity*, Berkeley: University of California Press, 1990.

— 'How the west was won: The Christianization of the aristocracy in the west in the years after Constantine', in C. Deroux (ed.), *Studies in Latin Literature and Roman History* 6, Brussels: Latomus, 1992, 451–69.

— 'The Christianization of sacred time and sacred space', in W. V. Harris (ed.), *The Transformations of Urbs Roma in Late Antiquity*, *JRA* Supp. 33, 1999, 123–34.

I. Sandwell, *Religious Identity in Late Antiquity: Greeks, Jews and*

Christians in Antioch, Cambridge: Cambridge University Press, 2007.

Isabella Sandwell and Janet Huskison (eds), *Culture and Society in Late Roman Antioch*, Oxford: Oxbow Books, 2004.

V. Santa Maria Scrinari, *Il Laterano Imperiale I: Dalla aedes Laterani alla Domus Faustae*, Vatican City: Pontificio Istituto di Archaeological Cristiana, 1991.

O. Seeck (ed.), *Notitia Dignitatum*, 1876, repr. Frankfurt: Minerva Press, 1962.

I. Shahid, 'Byzantium and the Arabs during the reign of Constantine: The Namara inscription, an Arabic *Monumentum Ancyranum*', *Byzantinische Forschungen* 26 (2000), 73–124.

T. Shaw, '*Askesis* and the appearance of holiness', *JECS* 6 (1998), 485–99.

N. Shiel, *The Episode of Carausius and Allectus*, Oxford: British Archaeological Reports 40, 1977.

W. G. Sinnigen, *The Officium of the Urban Prefecture during the Later Roman Empire*, Papers of the American Academy at Rome 12, Rome: American Academy in Rome, 1957.

A. J. B. Sirks, 'Reconsidering the Roman colonate', *ZSS RA* 110 (1993), 331–69.

— 'The colonate in Justinian's reign', *JRS* 98 (2008), 120–43.

A. Skinner, 'The early development of the senate at Constantinople', *Byzantine and Modern Greek Studies* 32 (2008), 148–68.

R. R. R. Smith, 'The public image of Licinius I: Portrait sculpture and imperial ideology in the early fourth century', *JRS* 87 (1997), 170–202.

Rowland Smith, *Julian's Gods: Religion and Philosophy in the Thought and Action of Julian the Apostate*, London: Routledge, 1995.

D. Srejovic (ed.), *The Age of Tetrarchs*, Belgrade: Serbian Academy of Sciences and Arts, 1995.

D. Srejovic and C. Vasic, 'Emperor Galerius' buildings in Romuliana', *Antiquité Tardive* 2 (1994), 123–41.

J. Stevenson, *A New Eusebius: Documents Illustrating the History of the Church to AD 337*, 2nd edn, London: SPCK, 1987.

Simon Swain and Mark Edwards (eds), *Approaching Late Antiquity: The Transformation from Early to Late Empire*, Oxford: Oxford University Press, 2005.

Ronald Syme, *Emperors and Biography: Studies in the Historia Augusta*, Oxford: Oxford University Press, 1971.

J. D. Thomas, 'The date of the revolt of L. Domitius Domitianus', *ZPE* 22 (1976), 253–79.

— 'A family dispute from Karanis and the revolt of L. Domitius Domitianus', *ZPE* 24 (1977), 233–40.

M. Tilley (ed. and trans.), *Donatist Martyr Stories: The Church in Conflict in Roman North Africa*, TTH 24, Liverpool: Liverpool University Press, 1996.

R. S. O. Tomlin, 'The army of the late empire', in John Wacher (ed.), *The Roman World*, London: Routledge, 1987, 107–13.

J. Torres, 'Emperor Julian and the veneration of relics', in J-M. Carrié (ed.), *L'Empereur Julien et son temps*, *Antiquité Tardive* 17 (2009), 205–14.

S. Tougher, 'The advocacy of an empress: Julian and Eusebia', *CQ* 48 (1998), 595–9.

— 'In praise of an empress: Julian's speech of thanks to Eusebia', in Mary Whitby (ed.), *The Propaganda of Power: The Role of Panegyric in Late Antiquity*, Leiden: Brill, 1998, 105–23.

— 'Ammianus and the eunuchs', in J. W. Drijvers and D. Hunt (eds), *The Late Roman World and its Historian: Interpreting Ammianus Marcellinus*, London: Routledge, 1999, 64–73.

— *Julian the Apostate*, Edinburgh: Edinburgh University Press, 2007.

Susan Treggiari, 'Concubinae', *PBSR* 49 (1981), 59–81.

— *Roman Marriage: Iusti coniuges from the Time of Cicero to the Time of Ulpian*, Oxford: Oxford University Press, 1991.

W. Turpin, 'Imperial subscriptions and the administration of justice', *JRS* 81 (1991), 101–18.

D. V. Twomey and M. Humphries (eds), *The Great Persecution*, Dublin: Four Courts Press, 2009.

R. van Bremen, *The Limits of Participation*, Amsterdam: J. C. Gieben, 1996.

R. Van Dam, *The Roman Revolution of Constantine*, New York: Cambridge University Press, 2007.

G. Vismara, *La giurisdizione civile dei vescovi*, Milan: Giuffré, 1995.

C. Vogler, *Constance II et l'administation imperiale*, Strasbourg: University of Strasbourg, 1979.

Alaric Watson, *Aurelian and the Third Century*, London: Routledge, 1999.

M. Whitby and J. Streeter (eds), *Christian Persecution, Martyrdom and Orthodoxy*, Oxford: Oxford University Press, 2006.

Michael Whitby and Mary Whitby (eds and trans.), *Chronicon Paschale, AD 284–628*, TTH 7, Liverpool: Liverpool University Press, 1989.

John F. White, *Restorer of the World: The Roman Emperor Aurelian*, Staplehurst: Spellmount, 2005.

C. R. Whittaker, 'Agri deserti', in M. I. Finley (ed.), *Studies in Roman Property*, Cambridge: Cambridge University Press, 1976, 137–65.

Lionel Wickham, *Hilary of Poitiers, Conflicts of Conscience and Law in the Fourth Century Church*, TTH 25, Liverpool: Liverpool University Press, 1997.

E. Wightman, *Roman Trier and the Treveri*, London: Hart-Davis, 1970.

John J. Wilkes, *Diocletian's Palace, Split: Residence of a Retired Roman Emperor*, Sheffield: Department of Ancient History and Classical Archaeology, 1986.

— 'Provinces and frontiers', in CAH^2 12, 212–64.

Kevin W. Wilkinson, 'Palladas and the age of Constantine', *JRS* 99 (2009), 36–60.

Rowan Williams, *Arius: Heresy and Tradition*, London: SCM Press, 2000.

S. Williams, *Diocletian and the Roman Recovery*, London: Batsford, 1985.

P. Zanker, *The Power of Images in the Age of Augustus*, Ann Arbor: University of Michigan Press, 1988.

Index